LEGAL PROTECTION OF THE UNDERWATER CULTURAL HERITAGE:

NATIONAL AND INTERNATIONAL PERSPECTIVES

LEGAL PROTECTION OF THE UNDERWATER CULTURAL HERITAGE:

NATIONAL AND INTERNATIONAL PERSPECTIVES

edited by

Sarah Dromgoole

LLB, PhD (Southampton)
Lecturer in Law
University of Leicester

KLUWER LAW
INTERNATIONAL
THE HAGUE · LONDON · BOSTON

Published by
Kluwer Law International Ltd
Sterling House
66 Wilton Road
London
SW1V 1DE
United Kingdom

Sold and distributed in
the USA and Canada by
Kluwer Law International
675 Massachusetts Avenue
Cambridge
MA 02139
USA

Sold and distributed in all other countries by
Kluwer Law International
Distribution Centre
P.O Box 322
3300 AH Dordrecht
The Netherlands

British Library Cataloguing in Publication Data.
A catalogue for this book is available from the British Library

Printed on acid-free paper

Cover design: James Redmond-Cooper.

The cover drawing is taken from a print of the *Admella*, a small iron-screw steamer, built in Glasgow in 1857 and lost off the Australian coast in 1859 when she hit a reef in rough weather. Her loss was Australia's worst shipping disaster, as the *Admella* went down with 89 of her passengers and crew, as well as a cargo of copper and racehorses. Twenty-two survivors clung to the wreck for seven days and nights before they were rescued. The wreck site was protected under the Australian Historic Shipwecks Act 1976 in 1983. With thanks to Bill Jeffery for providing the print and background information.

Typeset by Emily Beswick and Kuldeep Hair, Institute of Art and Law
Printed and Bound in Great Britain by Antony Rowe Ltd, Reading and Chippenham

ISBN   90-411-9762-1

© Kluwer Law International 1999

Kluwer Law International incorporates the publishing programmes of Graham & Trotman Ltd, Kluwer Law and Taxation Publishers and Martinus Nijhoff Publishers

PREFACE

So much can be learnt through the experiences that others have had in implementing legislation. Yet during my research into the legal protection of the underwater cultural heritage over the last decade, at times I have been frustrated by the difficulty of finding information about the state of law and practice in jurisdictions other than my own. The aim of this work is therefore to provide in one volume a number of different national perspectives on laws for the protection of the underwater cultural heritage, which it is hoped will provide a useful source of comparative material. Of course, a collection of essays on the underwater heritage would not be complete without some treatment of the vast areas of sea beyond national jurisdiction, especially at a time when so much attention is focussed on this zone. The volume therefore concludes with a perspective on the position of wrecks and other remains in international waters in light of the recent UNESCO initiative to draft a convention for their protection.

The contributors have been chosen for their specialist knowledge of a particular jurisdiction and include both lawyers and archaeologists, primarily from an academic or government background. They were asked to provide an exposition of the current law, its history and development; to show how the law functions in practice; and to discuss reform issues. They were also encouraged to illustrate their work with specific examples of situations which have arisen in relation to particular wrecks and other cultural remains. It is my hope that the resulting collection will be of interest not only to lawyers and archaeologists working in the field, but also to legislators, government administrators and others who may be considering revisions to law and practice in respect of the underwater heritage. As far as possible, the work takes account of developments up to 30 June 1998.

I would like to take this opportunity to thank all the contributors for their hard work, and also for their enthusiasm for the project, co-operation and patience, which have made my job as editor a pleasure. Lyndel Prott deserves special thanks for making time, in her hectic schedule, to write the foreword. I am also very grateful to Ruth Redmond-Cooper and her staff at the Institute of Art and Law for their assistance and care in typesetting the collection, and to Kluwer Law International for agreeing to publish the work. Finally, I would like to thank my husband, Michael Pont, for lending me his technical expertise in order to handle the computer files containing contributions, and also for his general advice and support.

Sarah Dromgoole
Leicester
February 1999

CONTENTS

FOREWORD

The legal protection of the underwater cultural heritage is currently a major issue of discussion for those who follow the development of the law of the sea and for those interested in the increasing improvement of law protecting the cultural heritage.

Until the invention of SCUBA diving in the 1940s, and its popularisation as a hobby in the 1950s, relatively little had been recovered from historic shipwrecks. Sponge divers in the Mediterranean recovered some important artefacts from Classical Age wrecks and salvage efforts on some other wrecks soon after they had gone down managed to retrieve certain items of value. But systematic exploration and excavation, as well as large scale treasure-hunting, was imaginable only when these new techniques became available.

The even newer technologies exploited for the exploration of the deep seabed for oil and minerals have made it possible to reach every portion of the sea-floor, even in the deepest areas. This technology is becoming cheaper and more available for other purposes with every year that passes.

Unfortunately, while the great majority of States has taken legal measures to ensure that random ransacking of their important cultural sites on land is suppressed in favour of systematic research, the same is not true of the underwater cultural heritage. First, legislation on land sites long preceded that concerning maritime sites and was well developed before the need for such rules was evident for submarine antiquities. Secondly, complex existing legal systems such as salvage and law of the sea already related to many of the areas, if not where these antiquities lie, then at least where their hunters operate.

For these reasons it is essential to find an appropriate adjustment of existing rules to the need to protect this special category of cultural heritage. As is so often asserted, a shipwreck is a 'closed deposit', a collection of objects, all of which are known to have been in existence at the same time. It can often be dated very accurately, by coins and other objects, and therefore gives land archaeologists a better time frame than they can develop from sites of continuous habitation. Shipwrecks which are partially buried in the sea floor or in very deep water often have very well preserved artefacts or portions of the ship itself – evidence of skills which is no longer available on land sites.

While the Law of the Sea Conventions of 1958 had nothing to say about underwater cultural heritage, some mention of 'archaeological and historical objects' occurred in the United Nations Law of the Sea Convention of 1982. But those provisions, drafted late in the very complex process of dealing with issues such as exploration of minerals on the seabed, freedom of transit, research for natural resources, archipelagic States and reserved fishing areas, got scant attention. Meanwhile, since 1982, the even more rapid evolution of technology and the corresponding rise in the economic exploitation of historic wrecks, with little understanding of or regard to their cultural significance, has grown to alarming proportions.

It is in this context that UNESCO (the United Nations Educational, Scientific and Cultural Organisation), together with DOALOS, the Division of Ocean Affairs and Law of the Sea of the United Nations Office of Legal Affairs, has set in place a procedure which it is hoped will result in a new legal instrument to protect the underwater cultural heritage. While archaeologists applaud this initiative, others are quick to point out the need to co-ordinate this work with the other existing areas of law which are relevant. Without going into the fairly extensive early history of this initiative, it should be noted that the first meeting of governmental experts to examine the draft instrument met from 30 June to 2 July 1998 and that a second meeting on the same topic will take place from 19 to 24 April 1999.

This shows how timely this publication, edited by Sarah Dromgoole, is. There is a great need to have easily accessible information about how different States have regulated this issue at the national level. Thirteen chapters of this book discuss the situation in thirteen States. A fourteenth looks at international legal issues. These essays provide important background to the discussions on how best to preserve the underwater cultural heritage: recovery and museum display of artefacts is one option, study and preservation *in situ* is another, reconstitution of a complete ship in a purpose-built museum is yet another. As on land sites, the worst outcome is the dispersal of an archaeological deposit without provision for its reconstitution for research and, even more dire, the destruction of the site itself without proper recording and conservation.

How this need for protection has been met varies greatly between legal systems: some have amended their salvage legislation to accord special protection to historic wrecks; some have adapted the legislation applying to land sites; other have developed rules on natural parks to create sanctuaries or reservations; and yet others have created new specific legislation on the topic. In other systems, alas, unthinking application of the rules of salvage law to a context for which they were never intended (ships no longer 'in peril of the sea' but embedded in the seabed in a natural equilibrium with the environment) has encouraged treasure hunters by in effect rewarding their commercial approach, causing serious damage to the underwater heritage and the loss of historical knowledge which could have been revealed if an opportunity had been provided for scientific exploration.

This collection of essays should be of considerable assistance in increasing knowledge of the problems and possibilities for protecting this fragile and important resource for cultural history.

Lyndel Prott
Paris
February 1999

LIST OF ABBREVIATIONS

ADU	Archaeological Diving Unit
AIMA	Australian Institute for Maritime Archaeology
ANCODS	Australian and Netherlands Committee on Old Dutch Shipwrecks
ASA	Abandoned Shipwreck Act (USA)
CFT	Comhairle Fo-Thuinn (The Irish Underwater Council)
CNRAS	National Council for Archaeological Research
CRM	Cultural Resource Management
CZMA	Coastal Zone Management Act (USA)
DCMS	Department for Culture, Media and Sport
DETR	Department of the Environment, Transport and the Regions
DOALOS	United Nations Division of Ocean Affairs and Law of the Sea
DPR	Decree of the President of the Republic
DRASSM	Department for Marine and Underwater Archaeological Research
DSR	Deep Sea Research
EEZ	Exclusive Economic Zone
EC	European Community
EEC	European Economic Community
EU	European Union
FAP	Federal Archaeological Program
GCI	Goods of Cultural Interest
ICOMOS	International Council on Monuments and Sites
ILA	International Law Association
INA	Institute of Nautical Archaeology
IUART	The Irish Underwater Archaeological Research Team
KML	Cultural Monuments Act 1987 (Sweden)
MOD	Ministry of Defence
NMI	National Museum of Ireland
NMSA	National Marine Sanctuaries Act (USA)
NOAA	National Oceanic and Atmospheric Administration
RCHME	Royal Commission on the Historical Monuments of England
SMR	Sites and Monuments Record
STAS	Technical Service for Underwater Archaeology of the Ministry for Cultural and Environmental Heritage
UCH	Underwater cultural heritage
UK	United Kingdom
UN	United Nations
UNESCO	United Nations Educational, Scientific and Cultural Organisation
USA	United States of America
US	United States
VOC	Vereenigde Oostindische Compagnie (Dutch East India Company)

NOTES ON CONTRIBUTORS

Thomas Adlercreutz holds a law degree (jur. kand) from Uppsala University (1971). He has served as a judge at several district courts in Sweden, at the Svea Court of Appeals and at the Stockholm Court of Administrative Appeals. He has been a legal adviser at several Swedish ministries and, since 1988, has been legal counsel for the Central Board of National Antiquities, the Swedish government's cultural heritage agency. He had leave from 1994 to 1996 to draft legislation for the government's Cultural Heritage Enquiry (publications *SOU 1995:128* and *SOU 1996:128*). His publications in English include 'The Protection of the Cultural Heritage' in *Swedish National Reports to the XIIIth International Congress of Comparative Law* (1990); *Legal Protection of the Cultural Heritage in the USA* (1991); *Four Issues of Cultural Heritage Law in Six European Countries (France, Germany, Hungary, Italy, Sweden and United Kingdom)* (1993); 'Civil Liability for Costs for Archaeological Investigation Necessitated by Criminal Negligence - A Swedish Supreme Court Case' in *International Journal of Cultural Property* (1997). He is the Swedish correspondent for the same journal and a member of the ICOMOS Committee on Legal, Financial and Administrative Issues. Currently, he is working on a commentary to the Swedish Cultural Monuments Act.

Esther Zarza Álvarez has been a practising lawyer in Madrid since 1991. Since 1992 she has worked in the Spanish law firm Abogados Marítimos y Asociados, which specialises in maritime law. She holds an LLB degree from the University of Madrid School of Law and an LLM on legal aspects of marine affairs from the University of Wales College of Cardiff (UWIST). She is member of the Iberoamerican Institute of Maritime Law and the Spanish Maritime Law Association and has been Lecturer in Maritime Law at the Spanish Maritime Institute.

Janet Blake has been a Leverhulme Research Fellow in the School of Law at the University of Glasgow since 1996, working on a research project in international cultural heritage law. From 1993 to 1994 she worked for the Council of Europe in the Cultural Heritage Division and had specific responsibility for the European Plan for Archaeology, which included a programme relating to the underwater archaeological heritage of Europe. Her PhD, awarded in 1995 by the University of Dundee, was concerned with the international legal protection of underwater archaeological sites and related artefacts and included a case study of Turkey. She is currently working on a revised version of her doctoral thesis for publication and otherwise retains a strong research interest in the international legal protection of the underwater cultural heritage. Her publications on the subject include 'The Protection of Turkey's Underwater Archaeological Heritage - Legislative and Other Approaches' in *International Journal of Cultural Property* (1994) and 'The Protection of the Underwater Cultural Heritage' in *International and Comparative Law Quarterly* (1996). Since 1994, she has been an Expert Consultant to the Council of Europe for various programmes relating to archaeology, including the underwater archaeological heritage.

Caroline M. Blanco (née Zander) is a trial attorney with the US Department of Justice in the Environment and Natural Resources Division, General Litigation Section. Her primary areas of practice include litigation of matters concerning heritage resources law (focussing primarily on historic shipwreck litigation), the Coastal Zone Management Act, the National Environmental Policy Act litigation, public lands law, and oil and gas royalty law. She also serves as her Division representative on several interagency working groups to protect heritage resources, including the subcommittee to develop a treaty to protect the *Titanic*. In addition to her work at the Department of Justice, she serves as a Professorial Lecturer for the Heritage Resources Law course at the American University's Washington College of Law. She is also a frequent lecturer on heritage resources law at Suffolk University School of Law in Boston, Massachusetts. Prior to joining the Department of Justice, she was a litigation associate in the San José, California branch office of the San Francisco-based law firm, McCutcheon, Doyle, Brown & Enersen. She graduated, *cum laude*, in 1989, from the American University's Washington College of Law.

Maria Clelia Ciciriello has been a Full Researcher of International Law at the University of Rome 'Tor Vergata' since 1987 and Chargé de cours of EC Law at the University of Urbino since 1990. Prior to this she was an assistant at the Law Department of the Italian Civil Servant College and a civil servant at the Ministry for Foreign Trade. She has held courses on international and EC law in various public and private institutions and has been a consultant to the Legal Service of the Italian Ministry for Foreign Affairs since 1994. She is the author of a monograph entitled *Le formazioni insulari e la delimitazione degli spazi marini* (Napoli, 1990) and the editor of two collective volumes, *L'impatto ambientale delle attività di esplorazione e sfruttamento dei fondali marini internazionali* (Napoli, 1995) and *La protezione del patrimonio mondiale, culturale e naturale, a venticinque anni dalla Convenzione dell'UNESCO del 1972* (Napoli, 1997).

Sarah Dromgoole has been a Lecturer in Law at the University of Leicester since 1990. She was formerly a Lecturer in Commercial Law at the Centre for Commercial Law Studies, Queen Mary and Westfield College, University of London and, prior to that, a research assistant at the Institute of Maritime Law, University of Southampton. Her PhD, awarded in 1993 by the University of Southampton, was concerned with the legal protection of the United Kingdom's underwater cultural heritage and she maintains a strong research interest in the area of law and the underwater cultural heritage. She has written extensively on this topic, her publications including 'Interests in Wreck' (with N. Gaskell) in N. Palmer, E. McKendrick (eds.), *Interests in Goods* (2nd edn., 1998). She is a member of the Joint Nautical Archaeology Policy Committee, which comprises representatives of a wide variety of bodies with an interest in marine archaeology in the UK and which liaises with UK government departments on law, policy and practice in the field. She is also Assistant Editor of the journal *Art, Antiquity and Law* (published by Kluwer Law International) with special responsibility for contributions on the maritime heritage.

Porter Hoagland is a Research Associate at the Marine Policy Centre of the Woods Hole Oceanographic Institution. He holds Masters degrees in Public Administration (Harvard) and Marine Policy (Delaware) and a Bachelor of Science degree in Biology (Hobart). He is presently a PhD candidate in marine policy at the College of Marine Studies, University of Delaware, where he is researching the economic theory of marine fisheries bycatch. His research focusses on the analysis of the public policy aspects of marine resource management problems and he has a special interest in considering institutional solutions to problems in the management of archaeological resources. With funding from the US National Science Foundation, the US National Sea Grant College Programme, and the Chiang Ching-kuo Foundation for International Scholarly Research in Taiwan, he has served as a principal investigator on several projects examining the management of historic shipwrecks. He is the author of 'Managing the Underwater Cultural Resources of the China Seas: A Comparison of Public Policies in Mainland China and Taiwan' in the *International Journal of Marine and Coastal Law* (1997) and 'The Value of Historic Shipwrecks: Conflicts and Management' with Yoshiaki Kaoru in *Coastal Management* (1994). He serves on the Board of Directors of the Council on Ocean Law, is the Chair of the Marine Resources Division of the Marine Technology Society, and is affiliated with the Centre for Maritime and Underwater Resource Management at Michigan State University.

Bill Jeffery is the Principal Maritime Officer with Heritage South Australia, Department of Environment, Heritage and Aboriginal Affairs, a position he has held since 1981. Prior to this he was employed with the South Australian Museum, recording and documenting aboriginal and historic sites in South Australia. He was a graduate of the first Graduate Diploma in Maritime Archaeology from Curtin University in Western Australia in 1980/1981. As Principal Maritime Officer in South Australia, he is responsible for formulating and implementing an Historic Shipwrecks Program in this state. He was involved with the passage of the (South Australian) *Historic Shipwrecks Act 1981* through the State Parliament. He has written a number of publications on the operation of the legislation and program in South Australia; initiated research into, and conducted archaeological work on, some South Australian shipwrecks; and contributed to the development of the Historic Shipwrecks National Research Plan. As President of the Australian Institute for Maritime Archaeology from 1994-1997, he has been involved in a number of issues in furthering the profession of maritime archaeology and the Historic Shipwrecks Program. He is currently Senior Vice-President. He has implemented, and assisted with, projects in other states and in other countries.

Wojciech Kowalski has been teaching law at the University of Silesia in Katowice, Poland since 1975. His academic interests have been mainly focussed on the areas of intellectual property law and cultural property law and he is now Head of the University's Department of Intellectual and Cultural Property Law. He has published extensively on the subject of cultural property law, both in Poland and abroad. His recent books include *Liquidation of the Effects of World War II in the Area of Culture* (Warsaw, 1994) and *Art Treasures and War* (Leicester, 1998). From 1991 to 1994 he served as the Polish government's Commissioner for Polish Cultural Heritage Abroad. In this capacity he negotiated international agreements and represented Poland in several diplomatic missions. He was also a member of the Council of Europe's Cultural Heritage Committee, as well as a member of various international expert groups. He was one of the founders, in 1997, of the ICOMOS International Committee on Legal, Administrative and Financial Issues and in 1998 he was nominated by the Minister of Culture and Art as a member of the Council for the Protection of Monuments. He is a member of the Editorial Board of *Spoils of War: International Newsletter* and an Assistant Editor of the journal *Art, Antiquity and Law* (published by Kluwer Law International) with special responsibility for contributions on Central and Eastern European issues.

Gwenaëlle Le Gurun has been a Lecturer in Law at the University of Nantes since 1998. She is currently writing a PhD thesis on the legal regime governing the underwater cultural heritage in the Maritime and Oceanic Law Centre at the University of Nantes. Her publications include 'L'épave, bien culturel maritime: une notion à découvrir' (1995) XIII *Annuaire de droit maritime* (Nantes), following her *mémoire* of *Diplôme d'Etudes Approfondies des Sciences juridiques de la mer* of the Faculty of Law and Political Sciences of Nantes in 1994.

Nessa O'Connor is an Assistant Keeper in the Irish Antiquities Division of the National Museum of Ireland. She holds a Master's degree in archaeology from University College Dublin. She has been involved in underwater archaeology on behalf of the National Museum since the mid-1980s as both archaeologist and diver. She has written on this topic for several archaeological and diving publications, and her publications include 'Underwater archaeology' in M. Ryan (ed.), *The Illustrated Archaeology of Ireland* (Dublin, 1991). She was the founding Chairman of the Irish Underwater Archaeological Research Team and has been Honorary Scientific Officer to the Irish Underwater Council. She has also studied law and is a Legal Studies graduate of the Dublin Institute of Technology.

Patrick J. O'Keefe has specialised for the past 22 years in heritage law and management. He is the author of over 100 books, reports and articles on the subject including, as co-author, the five volume (two published) series *Law and the Cultural Heritage*. In 1994 he was elected a Fellow of the Society of Antiquaries of London. He has been Chairman of the International Cultural Heritage Law Committee of the International Law Association since its foundation in 1988, and is also a member of the International Bar Association, ICOM, ICOMOS, Heritage Interpretation International and numerous other bodies. He has initiated or advised on a number of important international instruments (including the Scheme for the Protection of Cultural Heritage Within the Commonwealth and the European Convention on Protection of the Archaeological Heritage (Revised) 1992) and national legislative projects in the heritage field. Now a consultant and author, he previously had a distinguished career as an administrator in the Australian Public Service and then as an academic at the University of Sydney.

Hilton Staniland holds degrees from the University of Natal and the University of Southampton. He is an advocate of the High Court of South Africa as well as the High Court of Lesotho. He is also the Professor of Maritime Law and Director of the Institute of Maritime Law at the University of Natal. He has acted as the Deputy Vice-Chancellor (Planning and Resources) and Legal Adviser to the University. He has a wide range of publications covering matters relating to wreck. He has also drafted the South African Wreck and Salvage Act 94 of 1996, as well as the Wreck and Salvage Bill for Namibia. He is the Chairperson of the Board of Directors of the South African Maritime Safety Authority, which is the responsible authority in South Africa for administering legislation governing wrecks and salvage.

Anastasia Strati has been a Lecturer in Law at the Democritus University of Thrace since 1993. She was formerly a Research Associate at the Hellenic Centre for European Studies and, prior to that, Research Officer at the British Institute of International and Comparative Law. Her specialisms are law of the sea and cultural heritage law. Her publications include the monograph, *The Protection of the Underwater Cultural Heritage: An Emerging Objective of the Contemporary Law of the Sea* (Martinus Nijhoff Publishers, 1995). She is a member of the Cultural Heritage Law Committee of the International Law Association and has participated in the drafting of the International Law Association Draft Convention on the Protection of the Underwater Cultural Heritage (Buenos Aires, 1994).

Ole Varmer is an attorney-advisor presently in the US Department of Commerce, National Oceanic and Atmospheric Administration (NOAA) Office of the General Counsel for International Law. He has been at the Commerce Department since 1987, and for eight years provided counsel on marine environmental and historic preservation law including the National Marine Sanctuaries Act, the Abandoned Shipwreck Act, and related cases against treasure salvors. He has worked on designation of several sanctuaries, and drafted the regulations and policies for the protection and management of the underwater cultural heritage in the Florida Keys Sanctuary. He has represented NOAA's environmental and historic preservation interests in various state, national and international forums. He has written several publications on historic preservation law and the protection and management of the underwater cultural heritage and has lectured on the law pertaining to the underwater cultural heritage at Suffolk Law School in Boston and the American University Law School in Washington, D.C., and on law courses offered by the Department of Justice Office of Legal Education.

EDITOR'S INTRODUCTION

In the broadest of terms the underwater cultural heritage may be said to comprise all traces of human existence to be found underwater. Primarily these 'traces' are composed of shipwrecks dating from prehistoric to modern times. Some of these vessels contain treasures of considerable commercial value including porcelain, gold and silver coins, and bullion; others, are of little commercial but great historical value. Other remains evidencing human existence may also be found underwater, such as submerged ports, harbours and settlements, and a few coastal States have major archaeological sites of this kind. Whatever their type, underwater remains tend to be better preserved than land-based remains and are therefore of particular value for the information they can provide about our past. This volume of essays provides a number of national and international perspectives on the legal protection of this heritage. Generally speaking, the essays concentrate upon the marine zone, since the law governing remains found there tends to be rather different from that governing remains found on land and in inland waters.

Undoubtedly there must have always been some interference with wrecks by treasure seekers and souvenir hunters, but in recent years commercial treasure hunters have become highly active in many parts of the world, and they are now able to make use of the latest underwater technologies to search for, and exploit, wrecks. The challenges that such activities pose to those concerned to protect the underwater heritage have nowhere been better explored than in the USA. Its south-east coast has been renowned for several decades as a centre of treasure-hunting activities and often protracted legal battles have arisen in the US courts over ownership and salvage rights. A recent decision which has particular significance, that of the US Supreme Court in the *Brother Jonathan* case, is discussed by Ole Varmer and Caroline Blanco in their contribution on US law. Courts and legislators in other parts of the world will soon be facing their own challenges, since it is clear that the operations of the treasure salvage industry are becoming increasingly global. Some indication of the impact this development may have is provided by two contributors, Porter Hoagland and Bill Jeffery, in the context of south-east Asian and Australasian waters.

While the most manifest threat to the underwater heritage arises from those that seek to systematically plunder underwater sites, harm may also be caused by many of the other human activities that take place in the marine zone. Pressure on coastal environments throughout the world is increasing from land reclamation schemes, the building of marinas and tourist resorts, oil and gas exploration and exploitation, pipeline and cable-laying, dumping and dredging, fishing, and recreational pursuits such as diving and underwater tourism. In many of the essays in this collection, reference is made to the threat posed by such activities. For example, Janet Blake discusses the particular problems that have arisen in Turkey as a result of the enormous expansion in tourism and Wojciech Kowalski refers to the rapid increase in recreational diving that has taken place in Polish waters as a direct consequence of the relaxation of border controls after the break-up of the Soviet block. While the precise circumstances vary in different countries and regions, the general story remains the same: underwater cultural heritage throughout the world faces all kinds of perils and action must be taken if serious damage and destruction is to be avoided.

General consciousness of the underwater cultural heritage and its potential value from an archaeological, and commercial, point of view appears to have arisen in the late 1950s and 1960s when SCUBA became widely available, and diving became a popular recreational activity. In coastal areas where the waters were particularly inviting, such as in the Mediterranean region, the extent of the destruction of sites which took place at this time was devastating, but it is clear that even in less hospitable waters, such as those of the north-east Atlantic and Baltic Sea, considerable damage also took place. Legal mechanisms to control diving activities had not generally been needed until this time, but suddenly they became urgently required. Some States had general cultural protection laws which – while not designed with the protection of underwater remains in mind – could be applied to the marine environment and provided some level of protection. However, as commented upon by several authors, there have been difficulties in interpreting such legislation, and applying it, in the context of the marine environment. In other States the only applicable legislation was that relating to wreck and salvage, which was designed to encourage the recovery of property from recent maritime casualties and to reunite it with its owners. Such laws were clearly inappropriate for applying to material from historic wrecks. In reaction to the sudden accessibility of the underwater heritage, several countries – including the UK and Australia – introduced special legislation for the protection of underwater sites. However, at a time when marine archaeology lacked respectability even in the archaeological world, it is not surprising that the aims of the legislation were limited and focussed on controlling diving activities on certain wreck sites of particular importance in order simply to regulate excavation operations.

Marine archaeology is now, of course, an established and recognised discipline throughout the world, and marine archaeological remains are generally recognised as being of equal importance to remains on land and as requiring the same standard of legal protection as terrestrial remains. However, exactly how this can be achieved is a question which has no easy answer. For a number of reasons, archaeological remains in the marine environment have different needs from land-based heritage and protective measures have to be designed with this in mind. For example, the interaction of the protective laws with maritime laws has to be taken into account, as has the absence at sea of the equivalent of a landowner or occupier who is able to exercise a strong degree of control over an archaeological site. Esther Zarza Álvarez refers to the fact that the most efficient measures for the protection of Spain's archaeological heritage are those related to the town and country planning system, which are generally unsuitable to the marine environment, and this particular point is echoed in other essays. Where general monuments legislation is used to protect marine remains, there is a danger that the special needs of the underwater heritage may be catered for simply as an after-thought, without sufficient consideration being given to how the measures will work in practice. Some authors have also pointed out that where general legislation is used, there may be inadequate awareness of the underwater heritage amongst those that administer the legislation and consequently it may be afforded a lower priority than its land-based counterpart. On the other hand, separate legislation may not be ideal either. Its provisions may well be drafted without reference to those for land-based remains so that there is no parity or alignment between them and they may be administered by different government departments and agencies. Moreover, such legislation may not carry with it the same level of government funding as land-based heritage legislation. In the late 1980s, quite a number of States introduced new legislation and it is interesting to examine the general structure and approach of these relatively recent measures. For example, while France opted for specific legislation to protect its maritime heritage, Ireland incorporated provisions catering for the underwater heritage into its existing general monuments legislation, and Sweden introduced a new statute which 'seamlessly' integrates protective measures for underwater remains with its provisions for the terrestrial heritage.

The national perspectives in this collection illustrate that there is a clear distinction in approach between States with a common law tradition, such as the UK, USA and Australia, and those with a civil law tradition, such as France, Spain, Greece and Italy. The former tend to pay much more regard to the private interests of owners and salvors, providing for the protection of certain remains of particular importance, and adopting systems allowing for the recovery of material; those with a civil law background tend to favour the public, cultural, interest over private interests, and take a much more protectionist approach, adopting a blanket form of protection aimed at preserving remains *in situ*. This division is reflected in attitudes towards private and public ownership; issuing of permits; application of salvage law and payment of rewards; and enforcement, including severity of penalties and the bringing of prosecutions. There are, of course, exceptions which cannot be so categorised: the approach of South Africa, discussed here by Hilton Staniland, is interesting since its laws have been influenced by both traditions.

The accessibility of shipwrecks and other archaeological sites lying in coastal waters for a period of some four decades has meant that much of this heritage has already been plundered or destroyed. In more recent years, technological advances have made accessible wrecks on the deepest of ocean floors and there are now fears that these wrecks will suffer the same fate unless urgent action is taken. Patrick O'Keefe reviews the current legal position in international waters and discusses the current UNESCO initiative to create an international convention to protect underwater cultural heritage beyond established territorial limits. However, it is clear that some considerable time is likely to elapse before any new multilateral agreement comes into force and, in the meantime, a number of countries are taking unilateral action. Some of this action is based on the two articles relating to the underwater heritage in the 1982 Law of the Sea Convention. Sweden has enacted certain provisions aimed at fulfilling its duties under article 149 in respect of archaeological and historical objects found in the 'Area', as defined in the Convention. A number of other States have extended their jurisdiction to control activities affecting the underwater heritage beyond the generally accepted twelve mile territorial limit and some have based this extension on article 303(2), which allows coastal States to exercise control over a 24-mile contiguous zone. France has already extended its jurisdiction on this basis and Italy is in the process of doing so. Others, including Australia, Ireland, Spain and China, have extended their jurisdiction even further, presumably relying on the possibility that customary international law might afford their actions a legal basis. Other States, especially the UK and US, take a very different attitude, fearing that such extensions of State jurisdiction might result in an unravelling of the Law of the Sea agreement and provide an excuse for extensions of State jurisdiction in respect of other matters. Nonetheless, the US provides the wreck of the *Monitor*, which lies beyond its territorial limit, with some legal protection as a national marine sanctuary and the UK has also adopted measures to protect wreck sites in international waters. These include participation in, and implementation of, bilateral or interstate agreements in relation to specific wrecks.

Be it on the national or international level, attempts are being made to update laws and revise their implementation in order that they may reflect the latest developments in archaeological thought and practice. It is now widely accepted that the underwater cultural heritage must be treated as a non-renewable resource requiring systematic and non-intrusive assessment, appropriate management and protection *in situ* wherever possible. Those concerned to protect the underwater heritage are also recognising that they need to have an appreciation of the significance of laws other than heritage protection laws and wreck and salvage law. The potential impact of national legal rules on good faith acquisition is referred to by Thomas Adlercreutz in his essay on Sweden and Maria Clelia Ciciriello's essay on Italy gives some indication of the importance that EC/EU law is likely to have in relation to the trading of artefacts between Member States, and between Member States and Third Countries. These matters are complex and difficult to grasp by the non-specialist, but they must not be ignored. Lax national controls on the trading of artefacts, or generous rules on good faith acquisition, may encourage plundering of sites and provide salvors with a forum of convenience in which to dispose of material.

Alongside the increasing recognition of the archaeological viewpoint that is taking place, there is also growing recognition of the need to take into account the interests that others have in the underwater heritage, and indeed of the benefits that may arise from so doing. As the UNESCO draft Convention makes clear, the underwater heritage is to be preserved for the benefit of 'humankind'. As several authors point out, there can be little such benefit if only archaeologists are allowed to have access to the heritage and the results of their research remain unpublicised and uninterpreted. If the public is to have the full benefit of the heritage it must be educated to appreciate the archaeological value of shipwrecks and other remains. Public education will also provide benefits for the heritage itself. Several authors comment on the income-generating possibilities that arise from harnessing the public's natural interest in shipwrecks and Anastasia Strati, in her essay on Greece, points out that education of the public may prove more effective in encouraging compliance with legal restrictions than the enactment of draconian enforcement measures. The interests of sportsdivers have been referred to by most authors, who have emphasised the valuable role that they can play in reporting discoveries, policing restrictions, and – if appropriately trained – providing an enthusiastic workforce in archaeological operations. The creation of underwater archaeology parks and site grading systems are methods which have been adopted, or are being considered, to accommodate the interests of amateur divers and Nessa O'Connor discusses the activities of a body that has been set up in Ireland for the purpose of co-ordinating the contribution of sportsdivers to legitimate archaeological work.

A further interest group is, of course, the treasure salvage industry. How far its interests should be legally recognised and protected is an extremely contentious issue. Porter Hoagland, in his essay on China, explains that from an economic point of view the value of an archaeological resource can be optimised by policies which encourage the realisation of the value of both the public and private 'attributes' of the resource, in other words, the public heritage value and the private commercial value. As means of achieving this, he refers to the possibility of, for example, auctioning duplicate artefacts and replicas, and 'fair share' agreements. However one views such arrangements, the careful balancing of all interests involved is undoubtedly one of the keys to successful legislation, at either national or international level.

Considerable attention is now focussed on the subject of the underwater cultural heritage and legal mechanisms for its protection. Many encouraging developments are taking place and general awareness of the importance of the underwater heritage is growing rapidly. At the present time, the question at the forefront of many minds is how to provide legal protection for wrecks in international waters, but a number of States are also in the active process of revising laws for the protection of underwater heritage in their coastal waters. In fact, national and international legislative processes have much to learn from one another. International initiatives can have a positive influence on domestic laws, as illustrated by Gwenaëlle Le Gurun, who refers to the strong influence that Council of Europe Recommendation 848 had on the 1989 French legislation and, equally, there is much that those involved in formulating international law can learn from the experiences of States in implementing domestic legislation. While there are clearly many challenges ahead, the material in this collection leads me to believe that the outlook for the underwater heritage at this juncture, between the twentieth and twenty-first centuries, is promising.

Chapter 1

AUSTRALIA

Bill Jeffery

1. Background to, and Development of, the Law

1.1 Australia's territorial sea

Australia is made up of six states, the Northern Territory and seven external territories.[1] In European terms, prior to 1st January 1901 these states were colonies of Great Britain but after that date they united to form the Commonwealth of Australia (hereafter called Australia) with an Australian Constitution. This is generally referred to as the time of Federation.

In 1973 the Australian government proclaimed the Seas and Submerged Lands Act 1973 which contains two Schedules incorporating the Convention on the Territorial Sea and the Contiguous Zone and the Convention on the Continental Shelf agreed at the United Nations on 29th April 1958. The Act declares Australian sovereignty in the territorial sea (twelve nautical miles), contiguous zone (a further twelve nautical miles out from the territorial sea) and the continental shelf (to a distance of 200 nautical miles from the territorial sea baseline). The low-water mark is the normal baseline for measuring the territorial sea but in some cases where the coastline is deeply indented a line drawn across some bays and joining some islands is used as the baseline. The Schedules, amongst other things, assist in defining the baselines and the nature of the territorial sea, contiguous zone and continental shelf.

The Australian states had held the view for some time that they had sovereignty over three nautical miles of the territorial sea. In 1975 the six states contested the validity of the Seas and Submerged Lands Act 1973 and the outcome on 17th December 1975 was in favour of Australia.[2] This meant that from low-water mark, or from the closing lines of bays or joining islands (baselines), right around Australia the territorial sea, contiguous zone and continental shelf were deemed to be under the jurisdiction of Australia and not the states. In addition, the sea to the landward side of the baselines is referred to as internal waters and Australia has sovereignty in respect of these waters, with the exception of "waters within the limits of the states" which remain the sovereignty of the states. The effect of the Seas and Submerged Lands Act 1973 and its test in the High Court was that Australian legislation is required for the protection of cultural heritage sites in the territorial sea and internal waters. The Australian states require their own legislation for waters within the limits of the state.

Negotiations between the Australian and state governments after the outcome of the Seas and Submerged Lands Case resulted in an offshore constitutional settlement in which jurisdiction and proprietary rights and title were 'returned' to the states in the coastal waters – within the territorial sea and internal waters – adjacent to the states for a distance of three nautical miles.[3] This came about through the proclamation of the Coastal Waters (State Powers) Act 1980 which

---

1   The external territories are Norfolk Island; the Territory of Heard and McDonald Islands; the Australian Antarctic Territory; the Territory of Cocos (Keeling) Islands; the Territory of Christmas Island; the Coral Sea Islands Territory; and the Territory of Ashmore and Cartier Islands. See Fig. 1, p.17.

2   *New South Wales v. The Commonwealth* [1975] 135 C.L.R. 337.

3   *Port MacDonnell Professional Fisherman's Association v. The State of South Australia* [1989] 168 C.L.R. 340.

gave extra-territorial powers to the states as provided by section 51 (xxxviii) of the Australian Constitution. In relation to legislation affecting certain types of underwater cultural heritage sites, namely shipwrecks, the Australian and state governments agreed to continue to apply the Historic Shipwrecks Act 1976, with amendments proclaimed in 1980 that would allow a state to request to cease its operation in that state if it so desired. [4]

There is an exception to this situation. When the colonies were established in the eighteenth and nineteenth centuries certain Imperial Statutes and Letters Patents defined their limits of jurisdiction. In only one case, i.e. the province of South Australia, did jurisdiction extend to include any sea, being "bays and gulfs".[5] The limits of all the other colonies were restricted to land. There are only two gulfs, being Spencer Gulf and Gulf St. Vincent and the Australian and South Australian governments agreed upon four South Australian bays as 'historic bays' under the jurisdiction of this state.[6] This situation makes it necessary for South Australia to proclaim separate state legislation to protect underwater cultural heritage sites located in these waters.[7] In regard to the other states there are waters within the limits of these states and most have their own state legislation to protect underwater cultural heritage sites. In Victoria, Tasmania, New South Wales and Queensland this is through a general heritage act which also covers terrestrial archaeological sites and buildings.[8]

1.2   Types of sites

The types of cultural heritage sites that are located in Australian territorial waters vary from sites related to the first inhabitants to the present day. While only a little work has been done in regard to investigating aboriginal sites underwater the potential is evident, particularly in the now submerged areas – the major sea level rise began about 10,000 years ago – between Australia and New Guinea, and the mainland and the many islands, such as Tasmania and Kangaroo Island,[9] as well as in inland waters.[10] Sites associated with the later discovery, exploitation and settlement of the country include the remains of eighteenth and nineteenth century vessels from the port of Macassar in southern Sulawesi;[11] the remains of seventeenth and eighteenth century European merchant ships and their cargoes, e.g. the Dutch wrecks;[12] seventeenth – nineteenth century whalers;[13] and post European settlement (after 1788) remains such as shipwrecks, jetties and wharfs; through to World War II vessels,[14] and aircraft;[15] and present day vessels and aircraft. The oldest shipwreck known to be located in Australian territorial waters is the *Trial*, an English whaler wrecked off the north-western coast in 1622.[16]

---

4   K. Gurney *Maritime Heritage Legislation – Compliance and the Public Interface* (unpublished).
5   Letters Patent 19 February 1836.
6   Commonwealth of Australia *Gazette* 31 March 1987.
7   See (South Australian) Historic Shipwrecks Act 1981, No. 76 of 1981.
8   Victoria: Heritage Act 1995; Tasmania: Historic Cultural Heritage Act 1995; New South Wales: Heritage Act 1977; Queensland: Heritage Act 1992 and Cultural Record (Landscape Queensland and Queensland Estate) Act 1987.
9   N. Tindale and H.A. Lindsay *Aboriginal Australians* (1963) pp. 13-22.
10   C.E. Dortch, et al. 'Prehistoric human occupation sites submerged in Lake Jasper, south-western Australia' (1990) 14 *The Bulletin of the Australian Institute for Maritime Archaeology* pp. 43-52.
11   C. Coroneos 'The shipwreck universe of the Northern Territory' (1996) 20 *The Bulletin of the Australian Institute for Maritime Archaeology* pp. 11-22.
12   G. Henderson *Unfinished Voyages, Western Australian Shipwrecks 1622-1850* (1980).
13   P. Kostoglou and J. McCarthy *Whaling and Sealing Sites in South Australia* (1991).
14   S. McCarthy 'World War II Shipwrecks and the first Japanese Air Raid on Darwin 19 February 1942' (1992) *Technical Report Series No.1, The Northern Territory Museum of Arts and Sciences.*
15   S. Jung 'Archaeological investigations of the Catalina wreck sites in East Arm, Darwin Harbour' (1996) 20 *The Bulletin of the Australian Institute for Maritime Archaeology* pp. 23-40.
16   J.N. Green *Australia's Oldest Wreck:The loss of the Trial,1622* (1977) BAR Supplementary Series 27.

1.3 Background to, and development of, statute and case law

There are a number of statutes related to the protection of cultural heritage sites located in Australia's territorial waters and internal waters. The Australian Heritage Commission Act 1975 was proclaimed primarily to establish the Australian Heritage Commission and the functions of the Act, amongst other things, are to "identify, conserve, improve and present the national estate". The Act has limited power to "protect the national estate": it only has the power to stop other Commonwealth agencies from interfering with those parts of the national estate that are on the register. The Aboriginal and Torres Strait Islander Heritage Protection Act 1984 was enacted to "preserve and protect places, areas and objects of particular significance to Aboriginals" and is applicable to sites located underwater. The Protection of Movable Cultural Heritage Act 1986 provides controls on the export of objects that are important to Australia for a number of reasons including archaeological, historical, scientific and technological. The Act also provides for the seizure of protected objects imported illegally into Australia from other countries and for the return of the objects to those countries.

At a state level there have been laws in relation to protecting cultural heritage sites in existence for a number of years, such as the Aboriginal and Historic Relics Act 1965 in South Australia, and the Archaeological and Aboriginal Relics Preservation Act 1972 in Victoria. These laws are only applicable to protecting sites within the limits of the state.

The area where most work has been implemented is in regard to shipwreck sites. The United Kingdom's Merchant Shipping Act 1894 was the first legislation applicable to the Australian colonies in regard to shipwrecks. After Federation (1901), a statute based on the Merchant Shipping Act but one more pertinent to Australia, the Navigation Act 1912, was proclaimed. In the High Court case *Robinson v. Western Australian Museum*,[17] the Merchant Shipping Act was considered inapplicable with regard to shipwrecks located off the Australian coastline due to its inconsistencies with the prevailing relationship between the United Kingdom and Australia, and its inconsistencies with the Seas and Submerged Lands Act 1973 and the Navigation Act 1912.

The Navigation Act 1912 does not 'protect' shipwrecks. Instead, among other things, it provides for the orderly salvage and disposition of wreckage from the sea.[18] The Act also provides for the appointment of a receiver of wrecks. If a person finds or takes possession of any wreck they must notify the receiver of wrecks, who is then empowered to seek out the owner of the wreck. If no owner is found within twelve months, the wreck can be sold and the proceeds can be used to pay the salvor. Any unclaimed wreck is vested in the crown, i.e. the Commonwealth of Australia.

The first law specifically designed to protect shipwrecks in Australia was proclaimed in Western Australia in 1964. This statute entitled the Museum Act Amendment Act 1964 was proclaimed on 18th December 1964 to protect shipwrecks located off the Western Australian coast, specifically the remains of four Dutch vessels, the *Vergulde Draeck* (Gilt Dragon) and the *Batavia* which had been discovered in 1963, and the *Zeewijk* and the *Zuytdorp*. This legislation came about because these shipwrecks were being placed under great pressure from treasure hunters, and there was community and political will to protect them. There was considerable debate about material being recovered from the *Vergulde Draeck* which was feeding public and political minds on the preservation of this shipwreck.[19] In 1963 the finders of the *Vergulde Draeck* agreed to assign all their rights in this wreck to the Western Australian Museum.[20]

---

17   *Robinson v. Western Australian Museum* [1977] 138 C.L.R. 283.
18   K. Gurney 'Shipwrecks – Finders, Keepers? Dispelling the Myth' (1995) 3 *Victoria Police Bulletin* pp. 10-11.
19   *Hansard*, Senate 1 December 1976 p. 2334.
20   *Hansard*, House of Representatives 9 December 1976 p. 3638.

The purposes of the Museum Act Amendment Act 1964 included the recovery, preservation and display of any historic wreck vested in the Museum. The Act applied to shipwrecks referred to in a Schedule and to those vessels lost before 1900 – termed 'historic wrecks' – and it vested them in the Western Australian Museum. The shipwrecks referred to in the Schedule were the *Vergulde Draeck, Batavia, Zeewijk, Zuytdorp* and the *Trial*. In addition to the shipwreck sites, the equipment, machinery or other articles belonging to these ships – whether *in situ* or removed from the sites – were protected. Other wrecks considered by the Director of the Museum to be of historical, scientific, archaeological, educational or other special national or local interest could be vested in the Museum.

Other major provisions of the Act were that it was an offence for anyone without the consent of the Museum Board to alter, remove, destroy or in any way deal with an historic wreck. In addition, anyone who held material from an historic wreck referred to in the Schedule and which was removed before the commencement of the Act, was required to notify the Director of the Museum and this material – if considered of historical, scientific, archaeological, educational or other special national or local interest – could not be disposed of without permission. The Director could also give notice to the custodian of material from an historic wreck setting out certain action, such as making the material available to the Museum for a specified time period. Notification of the finding of historic wrecks became obligatory and rewards could be paid for this information.

In 1969 the legislation was amended – and was now re-titled the Museum Act 1969 – to modify some weaknesses. These modifications included ensuring that material that was cargo aboard a ship when wrecked was protected, and it became an offence for a person not being the finder of an historic wreck to remove part of it.[21] The Act was again amended in 1973 (proclaimed 7th December 1973), this time retitled the Maritime Archaeology Act 1973. As the name implies, the 1973 Act encompassed not only historic ship remains but also structures, campsites and fortifications used or occupied by persons from historic ships, and located in water, on land, or both. Power was also provided in this Act to declare areas surrounding sites to be protected zones and the accompanying regulations imposed conditions on what activities and equipment would be allowed in such a zone. The Act also acknowledged an agreement signed by the Australian and Netherlands governments.[22] In all three Acts compensation was not deemed necessary to any person for the action of vesting an historic wreck in the Museum.

On 6th November 1972 the Australian and Netherlands governments signed an agreement to vest the rights to the four Dutch shipwrecks in Australia; which in turn delegated authority to the Western Australian Museum. The Dutch government was heir to the shipwrecks belonging to the Dutch East India Company as this company was nationalised in 1795.[23] A committee was formed which became known as ANCODS (Australian and Netherlands Committee on Old Dutch Shipwrecks) and its role was to safeguard the legal position of the Dutch shipwrecks and to protect the Western Australian Museum's program of recovery and conservation of artefacts. This committee has had the responsibility of ensuring that the artefacts are shared equitably between the state of Western Australia, the Netherlands' and Australian governments. However, the functions of the committee are at present under review. The current thinking is that the collection should not be split up and that the committee should instead be overseeing research on the collection.[24]

---

21 I.M. Crawford 'Maritime Archaeology Legislation in Western Australia' (1977) *Papers from the first Southern Hemisphere Conference on Maritime Archaeology* pp. 30-33.
22 J. Green 'The Management of Maritime Archaeology under Australian Legislation' (1995) 19 *The Bulletin of the Australian Institute for Maritime Archaeology* pp. 33-44. On the agreement, see further below.
23 G. Bolton 'ANCODS – Australian Netherlands Committee on Old Dutch Shipwrecks' (1977) *Papers from the first Southern Hemisphere Conference on Maritime Archaeology* pp. 28-30.
24 Personal communication with J. Green, Western Australian Maritime Museum.

In March 1976, a diver named Alan Robinson contested the validity of the Western Australian legislation. He claimed to have first discovered the *Vergulde Draeck* in 1957, re-discovered it in April 1964, and recovered material, but since December 1964 he had not been permitted to recover material due to the Western Australian legislation. He submitted to the Australian High Court: that relevant provisions of the Western Australian legislation were not valid enactments of the legislature of Western Australia because they purported to have an extra-territorial operation, and lacked a sufficient connection with the state; that these provisions were repugnant to the Merchant Shipping Act 1894 (Imp.) and therefore void; or alternatively that they were inconsistent with the Navigation Act 1912 and with the Seas and Submerged Lands Act 1973 and invalid to the extent of the inconsistency. The six High Court judges were evenly divided on the ruling, but with the Chief Justice's casting vote the ruling went in favour of Robinson on 31st August 1977.[25]

1.4 Development of the Historic Shipwrecks Act 1976

In April 1974 the Australian government commissioned an Inquiry on Museums and National Collections. A committee established to consider the "desirability of establishing an Australian institute to develop, co-ordinate and foster collections of historic, cultural and scientific material of national significance", also touched on the subject of material from historic shipwrecks. In its report the committee acknowledged the importance of material from historic shipwrecks and stated its concern that the present legislative powers and procedures could not protect historic shipwrecks from indiscriminate looting. The Australian government decided on 2nd June 1975 that it should draft legislation to protect historic shipwrecks, although this had not been done by October 1975.[26] A dramatic change of government in November 1975 further delayed the introduction of legislation into the Australian Parliament. The final straw that spurred the introduction of a bill into the Parliament was the impending High Court judgment on the validity of the Western Australian legislation, and the knowledge that the High Court had already ruled in favour of Australia, and not the states, having jurisdiction over the territorial sea. In March 1976, at the same time as the commencement of the *Robinson* case, Australian legislation to protect historic shipwrecks was being drafted, and was first introduced into Parliament on 20th October 1976.[27]

The Historic Shipwrecks Act 1976 received Royal Assent on 15th December 1976 and it immediately came into force in all Australian territories. The short time the Bill was debated in the Australian Parliament – a little less than two months – was indicative of the political will of the government of the day, as well as the opposition parties and the Australian community, for Australia to have adequate legislation to protect its historic shipwrecks. Only minor amendments were made to the Bill in the two houses of the Australian Parliament, and these were made primarily to ensure proper recognition of civil liberties.[28] The only other change was to amend the date of operation of the Act in order to allow for the states to ask for the Act to be proclaimed in their state. The Western Australian legislation and the experience of the Western Australian authorities provided valuable practical background for the Australian government in drafting the new legislation and helped to ensure a quick resolution in Parliament.

---

25 *Robinson v. Western Australian Museum* [1977] 138 C.L.R. 283. In a 1994 Western Australian Parliament Select Committee investigation on Ancient Shipwrecks it was concluded that Graeme Henderson was the primary discoverer of the *Vergulde Draeck* and, although Alan Robinson accompanied him to the site on 14 April 1963, there was no "convincing evidence to support Alan Robinson's reports of a 1957 Discovery": Hon. P. G. Pendal, MLA *Select Committee on Ancient Shipwrecks* (1994).
26 *Hansard*, Senate 1 December 1976 p. 2328.
27 *Hansard*, Senate 20 October 1976 p. 1334.
28 *Hansard*, House of Representatives 7 December 1976 p. 3386.

A good description of the original purpose of the legislation can be seen in the statement made by Senator Withers when he introduced the Bill in the Australian Senate:

> A principal purpose of the Bill is to provide for the continuance on a sound legal basis of the existing high level of co-operation between Commonwealth agencies and such state institutions as the Western Australian Museum. The Bill therefore contains provisions that will allow agreements to be entered into between the Commonwealth and the states relating to implementation and enforcement of the legislation. These include provisions enabling the Minister to delegate his powers for these and other purposes. Such agreements would enable states to continue and expand their efforts to preserve Australia's maritime heritage under secure national legislation. At the same time, the Commonwealth will be able to act in the national interest, when this becomes necessary.[29]

This statement is indicative of how the legislation has been administered over the last 22 years, with the states playing a major role.

At the same time as the Historic Shipwrecks Bill was being debated in the Australian Parliament, amendments to the Navigation Act 1912 were also being debated. Among the amendments to the 1912 Act were some that made certain sections of the Act inapplicable to shipwrecks declared under the Historic Shipwrecks Act. These comprise sections 302-312 which include – amongst other things – a person being able to take possession of a wreck; reporting a wreck to the receiver; the receiver selling a wreck; and the Australian government having claim to any unclaimed wreck.[30] These provisions directly conflict with the way in which the Historic Shipwrecks Act operates so they were made inapplicable to shipwrecks covered by this Act.

2. Outline of Current Law and how it Functions in Practice

2.1 Historic Shipwrecks Act 1976

On the day the Act received Royal Assent, i.e. 15th December 1976, the Act applied only to the Australian territories of the Northern Territory and the seven external territories. For it to apply to the six Australian states, each state needed to request its proclamation and this was done in Western Australia on 3rd September 1977, Queensland on 18th November 1977, New South Wales on 11th April 1979, South Australia on 8th October 1980, Victoria on 11th March 1982 and Tasmania on 23rd February 1982.[31]

The Historic Shipwrecks Act 1976 protects shipwrecks and associated relics in Australian territorial waters. Schedule 2 of the Petroleum (Submerged Lands) Act 1967 defines those waters to which the Historic Shipwrecks Act 1976 applies. Basically it is from the low-water mark, or from the end of jurisdiction of each state of Australia, out to a pre-determined geographical co-ordinate, which is approximately the edge of the continental shelf.

The Historic Shipwrecks Act is different in a number of ways from the only preceding Australian legislation in this field, i.e. the Western Australian legislation. Perhaps the most fundamental differences are that this Act was designed to protect only shipwrecks and associated relics; and the Commonwealth of Australia does not claim ownership of any shipwrecks or relics. However, the Act does provide for vesting of the ownership of a shipwreck and/or relics with the

---

29   *Hansard*, Senate 20 October 1976 pp. 1334-1335.
30   *Hansard*, House of Representatives 18 November 1976 p. 2872.
31   F.J. Kendall *An Assessment of the Effectiveness of Existing Legislative Arrangements for Protecting and Preserving Australia's Underwater Cultural Heritage* (1990) p. 11.

Australian or state governments if it is deemed necessary to protect this material. The Act also allows for the protection of all shipwrecks irrespective of age and six broad criteria were developed to assist in determining which shipwrecks were of historic significance and should be protected.[32] There are also a number of similarities between the Historic Shipwrecks Act 1976 and the Western Australian legislation, such as a provision for the reporting of shipwrecks and a reward provision if the shipwrecks are declared historic and protected under the legislation.

The agreement signed in 1972 by the Australian and Netherlands' governments on the disposition of material from the Dutch East India vessels lost off Western Australia is included as a Schedule to the Historic Shipwrecks Act, together with a Schedule listing the four Dutch shipwrecks. The philosophical principles of this agreement were considered when drawing up the legislation. The agreement notes that it is the collection of material, not individual items, from archaeological sites that is of fundamental importance and while this agreement apportions material between Australia, the Netherlands and Western Australia, it is stated that if required the collection of material, or the collection of rare items, should be capable of being reassembled and made available for scholarly research. This principle that material from shipwrecks should be capable of being reassembled is embodied in the new legislation with several provisions enabling this to occur.[33]

Since its proclamation in 1976, the Historic Shipwrecks Act has been subject to a number of amendments. The major amendments have been: in 1979 with regard to the payment of compensation if acquiring property; in 1980 with regard to the states co-operating with Australia on enacting the legislation in the various states;[34] in 1981 to allow for the protection of shipwrecks straddling Australian territorial waters and waters within the limits of a state; in 1984 to enable the declaration of shipwrecks and relics – located in Australian waters – which have historic or special significance to Papua New Guinea; and in 1985 when a number of amendments were made to allow for blanket declaration.

In its current form the Act protects the 'remains of ships' that are or have been situated in Australian territorial waters and internal waters, but not waters within the limits of a state. This includes shipwrecks that were once located on the seabed, but have been removed and are now located on land. The definition of a ship is a "vessel that is used in navigation by water". The Act also protects relics that were associated with ships. The usual protection practice is to protect a shipwreck and all the relics associated with that shipwreck. Therefore any protected shipwreck and the associated relics, if they have been removed from Australian waters and are now on land, and located in a museum for example, are protected.

There are two ways in which a shipwreck and the associated relics can be protected. The first is through the 'blanket declaration' provision in which all shipwrecks that are at least 75 years old (from the date of wrecking), and all articles associated with those shipwrecks, are automatically protected. The other way, for those shipwrecks that are more modern than 75 years old and their associated relics, is by specific declaration. In both instances the protected shipwrecks and associated relics are then referred to as 'historic shipwrecks' and 'historic relics'. Guidelines for the management of Australia's shipwrecks have been developed[35] and they contain new evaluation criteria which assist in determining the significance of shipwrecks, and in determining whether or not they should be declared as historic shipwrecks under the Act.

A shipwreck that has been declared as an historic shipwreck can be visited and dived on by anyone without a permit. However, without a permit a person cannot interfere with, damage or destroy, dispose of, or remove, an historic shipwreck or associated relics. The exception to this is if a 'protected zone' has been declared around the shipwreck. Under this provision it is possible to declare up to a 200

---

32   P. Ryan 'Legislation on Historic Wreck' (1977) *Papers from the first Southern Hemisphere Conference on Maritime Archaeology* pp. 23-27.
33   *Ibid.*
34   See note 4 above.
35   G. Henderson (ed.) *Guidelines for the Management of Australia's Shipwrecks* (1994).

hectare area around the shipwreck, in which the execution of any activity, including simply entering the zone, may be restricted unless a permit is obtained. The Act provides for permits to be issued for someone to enter a protected zone, to interfere (e.g. implement excavation and recovery activities) with an historic shipwreck, and to dispose of an historic shipwreck and associated relics. A guide to the conditions and the other requirements for a permit to be issued to excavate and remove relics from an historic shipwreck is contained within the document *Historic Shipwrecks – Public Access Guidelines*. The regulations proclaimed to accompany the Act have prescribed the prohibited activities (and penalties) for a protected zone; the prescription of the cards for Inspectors; fees for a copy of the Register; and the prescribed amount for a reward, i.e. the maximum reward of $50,000.

In declaring a shipwreck and the associated relics to be historic, and the establishment of a protected zone, a notice must be placed in the *Government Gazette* (a government fortnightly list of public notices) to make it public knowledge. On many occasions press releases containing information on the declarations are also distributed to the print and electronic media.

The Act also provides for a Register of Historic Shipwrecks, Historic Relics and Protected Zones to be established and for it to be made available to anyone. There are currently 6,176 shipwrecks on the national shipwrecks database of which about 5,000 are protected sites, and there are eleven protected zones declared under the Act. The database is far from complete, particularly for sites in more modern times.[36] The Register of Historic Relics is presently being developed.

The Historic Shipwrecks Act contains provisions making it obligatory for people to report the discovery of shipwrecks. If the newly reported shipwreck is assessed as significant under the evaluation criteria and protected under the Act, then the person reporting the shipwreck may receive a reward up to a prescribed amount, or an award (plaque, replica, medallion). As of 1990 a total of 46 people had received rewards, the largest reward was $30,000 and a total of $55,100 had been paid out.[37] Rewards – from the viewpoint of various state administrators, as well as from that of the communities – have been one of the most contentious issues in the history of the legislation, dating back to the legislation in Western Australia. They were included in the Western Australian legislation to recompense the finders for reporting a site, and to compensate, in a moderate way, for the loss of salvage dues.[38]

Given that the Act provides for the protection of relics that have been removed from shipwrecks (in some cases maybe 100 years prior to a site's declaration) the Act contains powers to assist in locating these historic relics, as well as providing for certain action to be taken in relation to the custody, care and exhibition of the relics. The Act contains a number of penalties for not complying with various provisions and they fall within the following range: $2,000 fine for a person and $10,000 for a corporate body for not complying with a notice from the Minister; $2,000 and/or two years' imprisonment for not complying with conditions contained within a permit; $10,000 and/or five years' imprisonment for a person and up to $50,000 for a corporate body for damaging, interfering with, or disposing of, an historic shipwreck or historic relic without a permit.

Inspectors, in addition to state and Australian police who are automatically inspectors, can be appointed under the Act to enforce compliance with the Act. They are provided with wide-ranging powers including the power of arrest, search and seizure of ships and equipment. The people that are appointed inspectors are generally state or Australian government officers, such as national parks and wildlife staff, fisheries officers, or marine safety compliance officers, who are experienced in the enforcement of comparable legislation. They all receive specific training on the Historic Shipwrecks Act and a handbook has been produced to assist the inspectors in identifying their role.

---

36   L. Edmonds, S. Kenderine, G. Nayton, M. Staniforth *Historic Shipwrecks National Research Plan* (1995).

37   Ryan, *op. cit.*, note 32 at pp. 37-38.

38   Green, *op. cit.*, note 22 at p. 36.

2.2   Administration of the Historic Shipwrecks Act

Both Australian and state government agencies are directly involved in the long-term, and the day-to-day, administration of the legislation.

As the Act is Australian legislation the primary responsibility is with the Australian government and, at the present time, the government minister responsible for the legislation is the Minister for Communications and the Arts. The responsible Australian government agency is the Cultural Property and Institutions Section of the Department of Communications and the Arts, which is located in Canberra. This agency, in association with the seven state and territory agencies, has formulated and directs an Historic Shipwrecks Program for the whole of Australia, of which the Historic Shipwrecks Act 1976 is a fundamental part. Recently a mission statement has been compiled for the program together with three major goals. The mission is "[to] preserve Australia's historic shipwreck heritage and make this cultural resource accessible and of value to present and future generations". The goals of the program are:

> The increased knowledge, use, appreciation and enjoyment of Australia's historic shipwreck heritage;
> world recognised standards of excellence in maritime archaeology, custodianship, wreck-site interpretation, conservation and quality collection practices;
> the continued conservation, protection and preservation of historic shipwrecks, shipwreck sites and associated relics, under the Historic Shipwrecks Act 1976.

As was stated earlier, one of the fundamental purposes of the Act was to provide for a high level of co-operation between Australian and state agencies and to allow agreements to be entered into regarding states implementing and enforcing much of the legislation. This includes provisions enabling the Minister to delegate some of his/her powers. Such agreements and delegations have been implemented in all states and the Northern Territory, and therefore much of the day-to-day administration is handled by the states. The state and territory agencies responsible for the program vary between state government museums and government 'Cultural Resource Management'(CRM) agencies. The state museums responsible for the program are located in Western Australia, the Northern Territory and Queensland, while in the other states, i.e. New South Wales, Victoria, Tasmania and South Australia, the program is conducted through a CRM agency. Although the objectives of the National Historic Shipwrecks program are the same for all agencies, the differing policies and views of these two types of state agencies bring an interesting and stimulating blend into the program. In those states where museums do not formally implement the program, museums are still active in associated activities. Also in Western Australia, South Australia and Queensland, universities are conducting graduate and undergraduate courses and subjects in the field of maritime archaeology.

A convenient way to look at how the legislation and the Historic Shipwrecks Program operate in Australia is to consider some examples, and it was thought appropriate to provide a brief description of how the program operates through the two different types of agency: a CRM agency and a museum in the states of South Australia and Queensland, respectively. The following key objectives provide the unifying thread and each year the states report to the Australian government on their activities according to these objectives:

> to conserve and protect historic shipwreck sites and associated material as a cultural resource;
> to develop a comprehensive register of historic shipwrecks and associated material;
> to obtain the support of an informed public for historic shipwrecks as a cultural resource;
> to promote the protection and preservation of historic shipwrecks and associated material.

It has already been stated that South Australia at the time of European colonisation was given jurisdiction over its bays and gulfs. In terms of protecting shipwrecks in the bays and gulfs this means that South Australian state legislation is required. South Australia therefore has two very similar statutes, the state and the Australian Historic Shipwrecks Acts, to protect all its shipwrecks. The program that is implemented in conjunction with these two statutes is the same. The program is administered by a CRM agency, being Heritage South Australia, Department of Environment, Heritage and Aboriginal Affairs. The program and legislation are implemented using a system of eight regional surveys to identify the total shipwreck resource (between 700 and 800) and those sites that warrant protection under the Acts throughout the whole state. These surveys also identify those sites that warrant further work, such as conservation, excavation and interpretation, which are the next steps after all the surveys have been completed. However, some of this work is implemented soon after the completion of the survey of a particular region so as not to let the initiative and contacts made totally disintegrate. Therefore a number of management, conservation, public education and interpretive projects are continually being implemented. Interested members of the local community play a big role in much of this work and they are the biggest allies in the continued protection of many shipwreck sites, given the remote nature of much of the South Australian and Australian coastline. National parks rangers, fisheries and marine safety compliance officers are authorised as inspectors under the state and Australian statutes and they assist in the important area of public relations and education. The inspectors also monitor illegal activities on certain shipwreck sites.

The Queensland program is conducted by the Queensland Museum, which is part of the Department of the Arts. Queensland also has some waters within the limits of the state that require state legislation – the Queensland Heritage Act 1992 – for the protection of sites. But most of the very long Queensland coastline is under Australian jurisdiction and the Historic Shipwrecks Act 1976. It is estimated that over 1,200 shipwrecks are located along the Queensland coast which is fringed by the Great Barrier Reef for over 2,000 kilometres. The maritime archaeology unit has formulated a program that considers a number of these shipwreck sites within a thematic framework appropriate to the history of the state. This is in contrast to the South Australian program, but indicative of this agency's objectives and the extensive nature of the known shipwreck sites. The themes are: Exploring and Exploiting the South Pacific, The Labour Trade, Immigrants to Queensland, and Maintaining Links with Overseas and Intra-Colonial Ports. Shipwrecks such as the *Pandora* (1791), *Foam* (1893), *Quetta* (1890), *Yongala* (1911) and the Torres Strait Pearling Industry have been selected to represent some of the themes and considerable archaeological excavation, research and collection management has been implemented on the *Pandora* shipwreck and on the others to a lesser extent. An important consideration running throughout all the work in Queensland is the need for public education, and promotion of the need to care for historic shipwrecks. A current priority of the Queensland program is the development of a major exhibition on the *Pandora* shipwreck at the Museum of Tropical Queensland in Townsville, to be developed within the South Pacific theme.[39]

The Australian government supports the Historic Shipwrecks Program with an annual operating budget of about $400,000, which is divided amongst the states and the territories. The states and territories use this money to implement activities which will further the goals of the program and in a manner that is characteristic, *inter alia*, of the states' geography, financial resources, and the number of shipwrecks. For instance, in South Australia the funding from the Australian government is used to employ a maritime archaeologist to implement the regional surveys. In Queensland it is used to pay for a few contracts to initiate a number of projects. However, much of the staffing in the various states is funded through a small state operating budget which is also used to implement a similar program in waters within the limits of the states.

---

39   Personal communication with P. Gesner, Queensland Museum.

A recent initiative by the Commonwealth has been the development of an Historic Shipwrecks National Research Plan which considers and recommends directions for future management of, and research into, Australia's historic shipwrecks.[40]

Another example of the way in which the states and the Australian governments have united to implement parts of the legislation is in the compilation of the Register. The states are very active in compiling their part of the national Register. This information has been collated by the Australian Institute for Maritime Archaeology (AIMA),[41] to form the Australian National Historic Shipwrecks Database.[42] The recently established National Centre of Excellence in Maritime Archaeology at the Western Australian Maritime Museum has assisted in this work.

While the legislation is central to the requirements of the program implemented around Australia, it does not dominate the program. It provides the general direction for the program and the teeth for such things as permits and the conditions that can be imposed on activities in protected zones, as well as for use in the event of some illegality or situation that might threaten a shipwreck site or the associated relics. On some occasions the situations are diffused before they occur through negotiation or peer pressure from within the community. The Australian community of today is much more environment and heritage aware and this extends to the preservation of shipwrecks. The facilities provided by many of the Australian and state governments that assist people to dive on historic shipwrecks, such as the underwater trails, publications and exhibitions, have greatly helped. There are still a few souvenir hunters, but not to the extent of the 1960s and 1970s. Large commercial exploiters of Australian shipwrecks are rare: what commercial exploiters there are are more interested in shipwrecks in the northern Asian waters.[43]

2.3   Site and artefact issues

There have been a few cases around Australia that have found their way into the various Australian/state courts. While it may be appropriate on many occasions to settle issues before taking legal action, it is sometimes a necessary part of the protection process to take legal proceedings. It is often the only way to test the validity and effectiveness of legislation. The following examples are a few of those cases that did proceed. There is an equal number that did not proceed because the prosecutors considered the matter 'trivial', or there was insufficient pressure from the relevant government agency.

In Victoria in the early 1990s two divers were convicted of removing artefacts from the *Loch Ard* (1878) historic shipwreck under the Historic Shipwrecks Act 1976. In 1993 two people were fined on each of ten counts for removing artefacts from the *Karingal* shipwreck under the Navigation Act 1912 and the (Victorian) Crimes Act 1958. Another case was in 1994 in Victoria and involved divers removing artefacts from declared historic shipwrecks in four states. They were fined – although no convictions were recorded – for a number of offences under the Historic Shipwrecks Act.[44]

In South Australia the Historic Shipwrecks Act 1976 was used to seize a brass signal cannon – originating from the *Admella* (1859) – after negotiations broke down to arrange a loan of the cannon for an exhibition. Under the (South Australian) Historic Shipwrecks Act 1981 there have been ten prosecutions and fines for people entering a protected zone without a permit – the latest prosecution involved seizure of their fish catch – which can be a substantial monetary loss.

40   Edmonds et al., *op. cit.*, note 36.
41   W.F. Jeffery 'Australian Institute for Maritime Archaeology' in James P. Delgado (ed.), *British Museum Encyclopaedia of Underwater and Maritime Archaeology* (1997) pp. 46-47.
42   This is accessible through the World Wide Web: URL - http:\\dbase.mm.wa.gov.au\WEBFM\Shipwrecks\ shipsearch.html.
43   See further, ch. 2.
44   Personal communication with Shirley Strachan, Heritage Victoria.

In Queensland, two cases were proved and fines issued for the removal of an artefact on the *Scottish Prince* (1887), and for entering the *Yongala* (1911) protected zone without a permit. The last case was accompanied with a prosecution under the Great Barrier Reef Marine Park Act 1975.[45] In Western Australia a swivel gun from the *Zuytdorp* (1712) was seized and those involved were prosecuted, although no conviction was recorded.[46] As has been highlighted here, there is the possibility of prosecutions under other statutes, such as the Navigation Act, the Crimes Act and the Customs Act, on matters pertaining to shipwrecks.

As a result of the coming into operation in 1993 of the blanket declaration of all shipwrecks older than 75 years (from the date of wrecking), and the requirement of the Historic Shipwrecks Act for people who hold artefacts from these sites to report them within 30 days, a decision was made to extend the 30 day time period for people to come forward. The purpose of this amnesty was to gain details about the artefact and who held it, and not necessarily to acquire it, although if someone wished to transfer custody to the agency then it was generally accepted. An eleven month amnesty was declared on 1st May 1993 and in this time about 25,000 artefacts and a number of new shipwreck sites were reported to the Australian and state governments.[47] As shipwrecks become 75 years old they automatically become protected as historic shipwrecks and the reporting of associated artefacts is therefore an ongoing issue.

A number of issues have arisen from this amnesty. Although the amnesty has finished, people are still coming forward with information about artefacts from protected historic shipwrecks. If people are coming forward in good faith, their information is treated accordingly. However, there are a number of people and commercial interests that appear to be exploiting the system, particularly in regard to the coins recovered from the Dutch shipwrecks. When there are several thousand coins involved, the issue becomes complex and taxing for the very limited resources. While the Act has a number of provisions to allow for the documentation of artefacts, and to allow for the transfer of custody of artefacts, it is not seen as a primary function of the Act to administer a trading system. These provisions were included in the Act to allow for reassembling collections of artefacts for scholarly research and exhibitions for the benefit of the whole community. In situations where there is some doubt about the legality of the custody of the artefacts, then the question is referred to the Australian agency for advice.

3. Reform Issues

3.1 A summary of the issues

The fundamental purpose of the Australian Historic Shipwrecks Act 1976 was to protect the Dutch shipwrecks lying off the Western Australian coast and any other remains of ships assessed to be of historic significance and located in, or removed from, Australian territorial waters. The term 'historic significance' is a generic term used in the Act to include all the criteria applied to evaluate whether a shipwreck should be protected. These current criteria includes historic, technical, social, archaeological, and scientific attributes.[48]

---

45   Personal communication with Peter Gesner, Queensland Museum.
46   Personal communication with Jeremy Green, Western Australian Maritime Museum.
47   Green, *op. cit.*, note 22 at p. 41.
48   Henderson, *op. cit.*, note 35 at pp. 21-27.

Cassidy in his article on the implementation of the blanket declaration provision, which was an amendment made in 1985 and which came into operation in 1993, highlighted the changing nature of the Act.[49] The original purpose of the Act was to protect specifically nominated historic shipwrecks and it was only after all the states approved the proclamation of the blanket declaration provision in 1993 that all shipwrecks older than 75 years became automatically protected. The number of protected historic shipwrecks went from 156 to about 5,000.[50] We therefore have two distinct periods of operation for the Act, from 1976 to 1993, and from 1993 onwards. Apart from the amendments to allow for blanket protection in 1985, all other provisions have remained the same up to the present time.

In the period from 1976 to 1993, the Act handled adequately most situations. The associated program – primarily run on a day-to-day basis by the states – was in various stages of development, depending on the commitment by each state. The program in Western Australia was in full swing and all the other states had, by comparison, smaller resourced programs that were building momentum. The co-ordinating Australian agency developed program strategies and objectives in order that the work around the whole country strived to achieve uniform goals. The community perception of the Act and the program remained sceptical for much of the time and the attitude towards shipwrecks and treasure was still closely related.[51]

However, one of the reasons the Act coped with most situations during this period was because of the relatively small number of sites protected. The other reason was because the Act dealt with these sites within an integrated program. The program encompassed research, site investigation and evaluation, the compilation of a shipwreck register, archaeological excavation, site management, compliance activities, artefact and site conservation, exhibitions, publications and site interpretive work. Many of these activities require the Act to play a significant role in their development, others do not, providing the program with a good blend of legislative and complementary 'community enhancement' activities. However, one of the causes of concern and a major reason for including a blanket declaration provision was the delay in getting newly discovered shipwrecks protected under the Act.[52]

Since 1993, while the program strategies, objectives and activities have remained static, more emphasis has been placed on outcomes for the benefit of the community, as can be seen in the Australian government's mission statement for the program. As a result, the community's perception of the program has developed positively. The focus also shifted from protecting a small number of shipwrecks that contained material of interest to commercial exploiters, to a large number of shipwrecks that were not as appealing to commercial exploitation. Many of the programs in the various states gained valuable assistance from members of the community in locating and managing historic shipwrecks and associated artefacts without using any of the legislative provisions to have sites and artefacts reported.[53]

The amnesty on reporting shipwrecks and artefacts as part of blanket declaration provided some benefits as well as some drawbacks. In order to get artefacts reported, the Australian and state government agencies had to create a favourable atmosphere within the community for people to come forward, and this occurred to a reasonable extent. Undoubtedly there are more artefacts that, through one reason and another, were not reported, of which some are coming to light now and the procedures in handling these situations have been stated in section 2.3. While the reporting and transfer of artefacts is an ongoing issue, the Act should not be greatly amended to simplify the

49   W. Cassidy 'Historic Shipwrecks and Blanket Declaration' (1991) 15 *The Bulletin of the Australian Institute for Maritime Archaeology* pp. 2-3.
50   K. Gurney 'Policing Underwater' (1994) *Police Life* pp. 18-20.
51   F.J. Kendall, *op. cit.*, note 31 at p. 38.
52   *Ibid.* at p. 24.
53   C. Coroneos *Shipwrecks of Encounter Bay and Backstairs Passage* (1997).

problem. It was not a fundamental intention of the Act and it should not be now. There has been discussion between the Australian and state government agencies about introducing a number of fees to shift the burden back onto those in the community that want to transfer custody of artefacts. This may help, but with the additional efficiency that would need to be in place in a fee paying system, it may help to encourage the transfer of more artefacts. It may also drive those underground who do not want to pay. Another approach may be to prohibit the transfer of artefacts altogether. This could be seen to infringe on the civil liberties of those holding artefacts, although this is a moot point, as many of the artefacts would have been obtained prior to the Historic Shipwrecks Act and without the knowledge of the receiver of wrecks, therefore those holding artefacts are not the legal owners, but merely custodians.

There is not a simple solution to the artefacts issue because as Green states "... the problems are partially related to what is happening outside Australia."[54] There have been and continue to be a number of people with high profiles showing off treasure recovered from sites throughout the world and of particular interest to Australia, in the Asian-Pacific region. These Australian groups are actively seeking sponsorship from within Australia to work legally on these shipwreck sites. While there has been some cause for concern in regard to the commercial exploitation of some unprotected Australian shipwrecks in the past, Australian shipwrecks are generally given a wide berth because of their protection under the legislation and the fact that they do not contain the 'treasure' to make commercial exploitation viable on a large scale. The Australian Historic Shipwrecks Program does not allow for the commercial exploitation of Australian shipwrecks. Any 'public' recovery of artefacts has to be implemented under strict public access guidelines[55] and the artefacts must be provided for public use and not for sale. There are, however, some small scale operations of a commercial and illegal nature within Australia that keep some state government agencies occupied.

There may be some solution to the issue of artefacts by reassessing the legislation and making it more applicable to the present day situation. The Act does not reflect the present situation. It is outdated and inadequate. It has served a very useful purpose in initiating programs in all the Australian states and some territories. The last review of the Act was in 1990 and there have not been any amendments to the Act since then. Some of this review's recommendations have been acted upon, particularly in regard to program directions, such as: formulating objectives and guidelines; applying the blanket declaration provision in conjunction with an amnesty; appointing state officials as inspectors; and upgrading the Register. However, the legislative recommendations have not been acted upon, although they do not go far enough for the present situation. Three recommendations that should be considered again and are still relevant are the establishment of a National Historic Shipwrecks Advisory Committee, inclusion of the selection criteria, and a significant increase in funding for the program.[56]

In terms of what could be considered as present day amendments, a useful way to consider this may be to look at how the current program is operating, what it is achieving, and what it is not. One of the great strengths of the Australian Historic Shipwrecks Program is that it is well co-ordinated with the states and there is legislation with some teeth if action is required. Other national heritage programs around Australia have similar systems but not with the same level of co-operation and/or sound legislative back-up. The Australian government is presently looking at rationalising its legislation and commitment to terrestrial and built heritage programs – primarily by a reform of the Australian Heritage Commission Act 1975 – through a National Heritage Strategy.[57]

---

54   Green, *op. cit.*, note 22 at p. 42.
55   See section 2.1 above.
56   Kendall, *op. cit.*, note 31 at pp. 3 and 4.
57   Hon. R. Hill *Reform of Commonwealth Environment Legislation* (1998) pp. 33-36.

The Australian Historic Shipwrecks Program needs to be a step ahead, or at least level with this rationalisation, so that it is not totally consumed. In an ideal world it may be feasible to have one piece of legislation to protect all types of heritage, in all places. But there are many things that are not ideal, different countries have different needs, different states of Australia need to do things slightly differently, and heritage places underwater have different needs to those on land. It would therefore be a set-back to the better management of historic shipwrecks if the Historic Shipwrecks Act were consumed into some national heritage legislation. It would also be a pity if the National Heritage Strategy did not consider how the National Historic Shipwrecks Program could be better co-ordinated with other types of heritage programs.

In what ways could the Historic Shipwrecks Act be amended to better reflect present needs? The National Historic Shipwrecks Program has had its embryonic stage, from 1976 to 1988, at which time the program became a national program and was implemented in each state. From 1988 to the present day, through the blanket declaration regime, a further stage developed where the program took on more issues to do with site and artefact management. The only two maritime archaeological excavations carried out at present, the *Pandora* and *City of Launceston*, both of which have been developing for some years, have carefully considered the management options of the site in formulating the approach to the archaeology, and certainly more than any other maritime archaeological work in Australia in the past.[58] Green in his article on the legislation puts forward the view that heritage management, which examines issues in relation to preservation, can be at odds with archaeological excavation.[59] To put it another way, archaeological excavation without proper management and design could be seen to be the same as treasure hunting or vandalism. Archaeological excavation with the proper design is a tool of heritage management, an important tool that has been considered to be essential to effectively manage the *Pandora* and *City of Launceston* shipwreck sites, for example.[60]

3.2   Specific reforms

The Australian National Historic Shipwrecks Program is now at the stage where site management is the fundamental priority. The Act still concentrates on site discovery, which after 22 years should be well advanced in having a good representative understanding of what sites are where. These provisions should be amended to better reflect the current situation. The Act should not still be concentrating to the extent it does on pursuing information on who has custody of what artefacts, so museums or scholars can carry out research on whole collections. This has rarely been done in 22 years! The Act is centred too much on the archaeological perspective, too much on movable cultural heritage and not enough on the sites, and it is not up with today's thinking on how archaeology is just one of the tools used to effectively manage cultural heritage sites.[61] Nor should the Act be rewarding people with trinkets and silver. As has already been stated, many of the new site discoveries can be done on a co-operative basis with the community, providing rewards of a different kind.

The Act should be assisting the program to implement a better way to manage shipwreck sites and should include appropriate provisions to do this. It should also include amendments to allow for a National Shipwrecks Advisory Committee which should include some prominent individuals and scholars to give the program a higher profile in the community. While the publication, *Guidelines for the management of Australia's shipwrecks,*[62] includes the evaluation criteria, these

---

58   P. Gesner *Pandora: An Archaeological Perspective* (1991).
59   Green, *op. cit.*, note 22 at p. 40.
60   P. Marquis-Kyle and M. Walker *Australia ICOMOS Burra Charter* (1992).
61   *Ibid.*
62   Henderson, *op. cit.*, note 35.

should also be included in the Act so that there is a clear legal statement about why a shipwreck is significant and is managed in a certain way. This should be backed up with sound administration, including the requirement to develop a management plan before any site is subjected to any disturbance or other activity likely to affect it. This requirement is in the current *Guidelines for the management of Australia's shipwrecks*.[63] The Act and its requirements also need to be noted in any other legislation such as planning or development statutes so that any developers are legally bound to consider historic shipwrecks, rather than just left to an administrative process which can be easily overlooked.

The suggested amendments are included in other heritage statutes throughout Australia, together with a provision establishing a heritage fund appropriated by Parliament, which includes the use of money derived from gifts, investments and through program activities such as fees. The establishment of a fund would be a useful consideration for the Historic Shipwrecks Act, which could eventually help to make the program self-sustainable.

The issue of the trading of artefacts should be considered in reforming the legislation, or the administrative arrangements accompanying the Act. However, this particular reform needs to be carefully handled so as not to interfere with the intentions of the Act, i.e. to protect and, what should be a high priority – to manage – for the benefit of all Australians, historic shipwrecks. In the summing up of the debate on the introduction of the legislation in the Australian Senate in 1976, Senator Withers said that "... it [the historic shipwreck heritage] will be part of our tourist attractions in the future."[64] While this is slowly being realised, the Act and the accompanying program should consider ensuring that this is the case.

3.3 International issues

No country lives in a vacuum and they can all be influenced by what happens around them, and by all people. If there was more uniformity in the protection of historic shipwrecks on a global scale, this may have a positive effect on the legislation and programs in all countries. Successful fruition of the UNESCO initiative to create an international convention on the protection of the underwater cultural heritage[65] would be a significant step forward in protecting sites in international waters and would have some effect on the activities of nationals from signatory States. Another development in international law that would have a positive benefit and needs to be pushed forward with greater vigour is the inclusion of shipwrecks on the World Heritage List. In 1993, Henry Cleere said "...[t]he time would seem to be right for a similar study of the underwater heritage" as is happening with cultural landscapes, industrial heritage and twentieth century architecture, which also do not appear on the World Heritage List.[66]

---

63   *Ibid*. at pp. 10-13.
64   *Hansard*, Senate 1 December 1976 p. 2336.
65   See further, ch. 14.
66   H. Cleere 'The underwater heritage and the World Heritage Convention' (1993) 17 *The Bulletin of the Australian Institute for Maritime Archaeology* pp. 25-26.

Figure 1: Australia and its External Territories

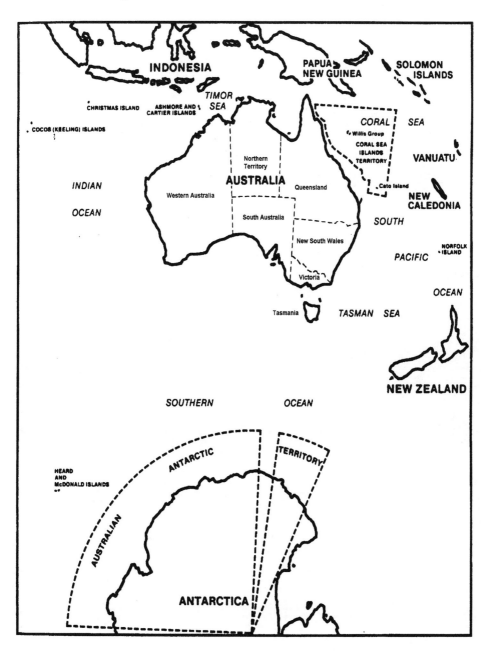

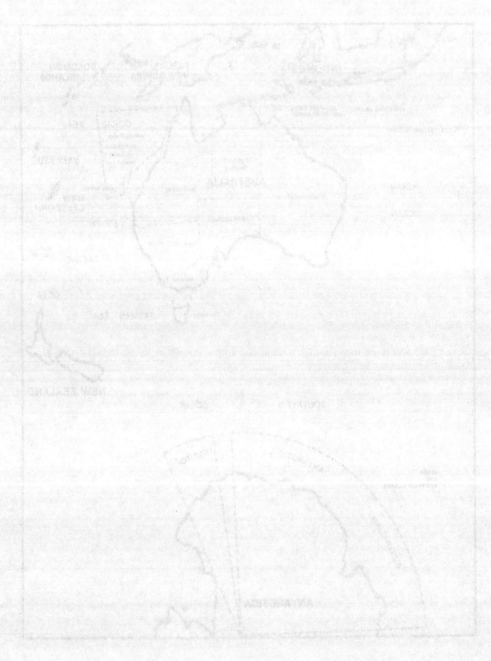

Chapter 2

CHINA

Porter Hoagland*

1.   Introduction

Standing in stark juxtaposition to the deepening currency crisis in Southeast Asia, western interest in Asian history and demand for Asian art and archaeological artefacts is booming. Exhibitions of Chinese art, such as *China: 5,000 Years*, at New York's Guggenheim Museum, have received rave reviews.[1] More than 20,000 advance tickets were sold to the Dayton Art Institute's *Eternal China: Splendors from the First Dynasties*, making it the museum's biggest exhibition to date.[2] Although the currency crisis is expected to dampen demand for art in Asia, Asian consumers of art and archaeological artefacts have emerged with the growing opulence of the Pacific Rim. They have become more sophisticated consumers as well, and Sotheby's auction house expects that consumers from Asia will represent more than a quarter of their business within the next ten years.[3]

International trade in Asian archaeological artefacts is now widespread, occurring through both lawful and illicit (black market) channels. In China, due to restrictions on trade in artefacts, a significant black market trade flourished for years, operating through Hong Kong and other entrepôts.[4] For example, Beijing estimated that, during 1989-90, more than 40,000 tombs were robbed in China.[5] Beginning in 1992, the government of China entered the market itself, selling duplicate artefacts, in part to help curb the smuggling of artefacts.

Like the waters of the Yangtze Delta, the implications of these trends for underwater archaeological resources in China are somewhat muddy. Clearly, as demand for archaeological resources expands, the potential for illicit depredations of underwater resources, such as historic shipwrecks, increases. At the same time, China has recently revamped its policies with respect to underwater cultural relics, and the National Museum of Chinese History and the State Bureau of Cultural Relics seem poised to take advantage of the boom. In January 1998, Zhang Wei, Director of Underwater Archaeology at the National Museum, revealed that Chinese archaeologists have discovered *two thousand* ships dating from the Tang to Qing Dynasties in the coastal areas of southern China.[6] The crown jewel of this discovery is a shipwreck believed to have belonged to

*   I thank Jin Di, James Kraska, Liu Ben An, Bob Nelson, Yang Lin, Ken Vrana, Yu Weichao, Zhang Wei, and Zhao Hongye for helpful discussions and reviews of portions of the work represented in this chapter. Special thanks are due to Jim Broadus and Zhao Hongye for getting me interested in this area and to Lisina and Frank Hoch for encouraging my continued interest. Funding was provided by the Chiang Ching-kuo Foundation for International Scholarly Exchange, the Center for Maritime and Underwater Resource Management at Michigan State University, and the Johnson Endowment of the Marine Policy Center. Woods Hole Oceanographic Institution Contribution No. 9693.

1   For example, see L. Begley 'The Gallery: From Beijing to Broadway' *Wall Street Journal* 19 February 1998.
2   J. Brosse 'Scholars Share Cultures' *Dayton Daily News* 7 March 1998.
3   C. Brown 'What Do You Do After You've Got the Private Plane?' *Forbes* 12 February 1996.
4   S. Mufson 'China Robbed of Its Rich Past' *Washington Post* 13 August 1995; D. Cohn 'Raiding China's Treasure Chest' (1992) 39 *World Press Review* 48.
5   S. Wudunn 'China is Fighting for Its Soul: Its Looted Antiques' *New York Times* 8 December 1992.
6   Anon. 'Wreckages of 2,000 Ancient Sunken Ships Found' *Xinhua News Agency* 22 January 1998.

the fleet led by Admiral Zheng He during the late Ming Dynasty.[7] The enormity of the archaeological resource base is simply staggering.

This chapter has three main parts. The first focusses on the nature of the underwater archaeological resources in China. The published knowledge of the resource is described in general terms, the markets for Chinese archaeological resources are analysed, threats to the resource are identified, and four rationales for public policy in this area are suggested. The second part provides a brief outline of Chinese policy with respect to 'underwater cultural relics', which is the term used in Chinese law to refer to the resource. This outline describes nine distinct policy aspects to the Regulation on the Protection and Administration of Underwater Cultural Relics (1989) of the People's Republic of China. These aspects are:

(1) assertion of resource jurisdiction;
(2) determination of archaeological significance;
(3) encouragement of discovery;
(4) excavation;
(5) diligence;
(6) conservation;
(7) preferential uses of the ocean;
(8) zoning; and
(9) enforcement.

In the third part some specific policy issues of special concern to underwater archaeologists in China are analysed.[8] These issues include the assertion of resource jurisdiction, methods for sharing the proceeds from the recovery of a shipwreck, the sale of duplicate artefacts, and enforcement.

This chapter is not strictly a review of Chinese law in this area. It has been written primarily from a perspective of policy, instead of legal, analysis. The object is to understand the basis for law and to suggest some reforms that might improve the management of underwater archaeological resources. In particular, it is argued that the explicit incorporation of economic incentives into policy has the benefit of improving management. China is used as a timely and relevant example; however, the arguments can certainly be generalised to underwater resource management in other nations.

2.   Nature of the Resource

2.1   The underwater resource

Recent evidence suggests that the China Seas are the birthplace of perhaps the world's most ancient maritime culture. 'Paddleboards' have been discovered at a 7,000 year old Neolithic site of the South Ho-mu-tu Culture, on Hangzhou Bay in Zhejiang Province.[9] Harvard's Professor K.C. Chang has described boatbuilding tools from the Ta-p'en-k'eng Culture (4450-4350 B.C.) in Taiwan, indicating capabilities for constructing canoes for deepsea fishing.[10] Fang has argued that fishermen plied the waters of the East China Sea during the Xia Dynasty (2100-1600 B.C.).[11]

---

7   A very readable account of the voyages of Admiral Zheng can be found in L. Levathes *When China Ruled the Seas: The Treasure Fleet of the Dragon Throne, 1405-1433* (1994).

8   These issues were raised by Professor Yu Weichao, Director of the National Museum of Chinese History, in a discussion with the author at a meeting sponsored by the UCLA Center for Pacific Rim Studies and Institute of Archaeology on *Sunken Treasures: Underwater Archaeology in China* in 1995.

9   B.A. Liu 'Investigation of Yuan Dynasty Shipwreck in Suizhong' in Asahi News, ed., *Artefacts Exhibition of the Southsea of China and the Ancient Ceramic Route* (1993).

10   K.C. Chang *The Archaeology of Ancient China* (4th edn., 1986).

11   S. Fang *Compiled Ancient Annals from Bamboo Ships* (1981).

Friezes of large canoes carrying warriors were etched on bronze drums from the Dong-son Culture (800 B.C. to A.D. 400). Thought to depict funerary 'soul-boats', these drums were buried in locations ranging from southern China out to remote islands of the Indonesian archipelago.[12] Numerous other relics indicating submerged cities and villages, stone roads, and stone anchor hills have also been discovered off the Chinese coasts.[13] Three-legged cooking pots found off the northern coast of China are believed to belong to ancient shipwrecks at least 4,000 years old.[14]

Historic shipwrecks and their cargoes are prime repositories of knowledge about the maritime cultures of the China Seas and their long-standing interconnections through voyages of discovery, searches for natural resources, regional and worldwide trade, and international relations.[15] Through the ages, tens of thousands of ships foundered and sank in the China Seas, succumbing to the forces of nature and warfare. The cultural legacy of many of these lost wrecks, including their stock of potential knowledge, remains entombed beneath the seafloor.

The known underwater cultural resources of the China Seas, located on the map in Figure 1, represent a valuable but grossly incomplete record of the cultural and economic links among the countries of Asia and between Asia and the rest of the world.[16] A sampling of recent finds merely hints at the tremendous store of knowledge still awaiting discovery:

The Bohai Bay Shipwreck (Site C1). Archaeologists at the National Museum of Chinese History in Beijing and China's State Bureau of Cultural Relics currently are studying a thirteenth century shipwreck off the coast of Suizhong in the northwestern portion of Bohai Bay. Several important artefacts, including one that has been designated a 'national treasure' (second class) have been documented and recovered. The porcelain on the shipwreck was produced at the Cizhou Kiln in Ci Xian County, Hebei Province, for coastal or regional trade.

The Changdao Islands Site (Site C3). In 1982, fishermen recovered a three-legged pot, believed to be at least 4,000 years old, from an undisclosed site near the Changdao Islands at the mouth of Bohai Bay. The pot was located in deep water between two islands, indicating that it was probably associated with a shipwreck. The pot resembles other pots found in onshore locations and may be evidence of inhabitation of the islands during this period.[17]

The South Song Dynasty ancient sea battlefield (Site C13). According to historical documents, in 1279 during the Battle of Yamen, the navy of the Yuan Dynasty (A.D. 1271–1368) defeated the navy of the South Song Dynasty (A.D. 1127–1279), ending the South Song rule. Two thousand South Song warships loaded with imperial treasures were sunk during the battle. A stone located on a nearby bank commemorates Lu Xiufu, the Song Prime Minister who plunged from one of the ships to his death, carrying the Emperor on his back. In 1992, Chinese archaeologists and oceanographers recovered a piece of 'shipboard' from the area dating to the period of the sea battle.[18]

The Sinan Ship (Site K1). This Chinese ship, lost during the Yuan Dynasty (A.D. 1323), has been raised and reconstructed in Mokpo, South Korea. Approximately 16,000 ceramic pieces and 28 tons of ancient Chinese coins dating from the Spring and Autumn Period (770–476 B.C.) through the Yuan Dynasty have been recovered and are being conserved. The ship helps to demonstrate

12   P. Bellwood *Man's Conquest of the Pacific* (1979).
13   W. Yu, personal communication, National Museum of Chinese History, Beijing (18 August 1992).
14   W. Yu 'The Four Federated Groups in Early China' (1988) 13-14 *Bulletin of the Museum of Chinese History* 31-40.
15   J.N. Green 'Maritime Archaeology in Southeast and East Asia' (1990) 64 *Antiquity* 347-363.
16   For Fig. 1, see p. 37. The reader can find a complete key to the sites identified in Fig. 1 in Appendix 1. A more detailed description of each site with specific citations to publications is available by contacting the author. A recently published atlas includes a similar map with some additional sites. However, many of the sites in the atlas have no specific published reference to verify their existence. See N. Pickford *The Atlas of Ship Wrecks and Treasure* (1994).
17   Yu, *op. cit.*, note 14.
18   W. Zhang, personal communication, National Museum of Chinese History, Beijing (18 August 1992).

the ocean-going ability of Chinese ships that predate the Ming Ban. These pieces are on display in a special wing of the National Museum of Korea in Seoul.[19]

The Geldermalsen (Site I4). This 240-year-old Dutch East Indiaman shipwreck was discovered in the 1980s on the marine ceramic route in the South China Sea with some 160,000 pieces of delicate ceramics. The wreck and two Chinese junks located near the site were salvaged commercially.[20] Their contents earned roughly $20 million at auction, but much of the shipwreck's archaeological and historical value is believed to have been destroyed in the salvage operation.

The Vung Tau Wreck (Site V1). Discovered in 1989 by a Vietnamese fisherman near Con Dao Island, Vietnam, this wreck was an Asian trading vessel, 110 feet long with 'compartment' construction, which had burned to the waterline on a voyage for Batavia, Java, Indonesia. Some 28,000 pieces of porcelain made within a decade of the reopening of the major kilns at Jingdezhen in the late seventeenth century were recovered and sold, earning $7.2 million (against an estimate of $2.6 million) at a 1992 Christie's auction. Seventy-five percent of the proceeds went to the Vietnamese government.[21]

Many underwater cultural resources containing clues to trading patterns and other cultural linkages are likely to lie beneath the ancient maritime trade routes, but serious study of these resources has only just begun.[22] The major routes include the China-Korea-Japan marine route of the Chunqiu Period (770–476 B.C.); Xu Fu's sea route during the Qin Dynasty (221-206 B.C.), over which he sailed in search of the Holy Islands for the First Emperor; the Marine Silk Route,[23] running from China to Arabia, Africa and Europe, and along which the wrecks of several Chinese junks have already been found; the ancient sea routes of Zheng He's Seven Voyages (A.D. 1405–1433) to Arabia and East Africa; and the trade routes between China, the Philippines and Mexico during the sixteenth and seventeenth centuries. Some of these routes are depicted on the map in Figure 1.

2.2   Threats to the resource

The unique archaeological resources of the China Seas constantly face both real and imminent threats. Commercial salvors have begun to find and exploit shipwrecks and other cultural resources of the China Seas.[24] The State Bureau of Cultural Relics in Beijing reported that, from 1989 to 1992, more than 40 foreign salvage companies sought its consent for salvage rights to shipwrecks in China's offshore waters.[25] Many other foreign treasure hunters are known to be hovering at sea, searching for so-called 'treasure junks' without even attempting to secure the permission of the governments in the region. Significant ancient shipwrecks and submerged historic sites have already been looted and destroyed.[26]

---

19   National Museum of Korea *The Sinan Ship* (1988) and P. Hoffman, K. Choi and Y. Kim 'The Fourteenth Century Shinan Ship—Progress in Conservation' (1991) 20 *International Journal of Nautical Archaeology and Underwater Exploration* 59-64.

20   J.N. Green 'Book Reviews' (1988) 17 *International Journal of Nautical Archaeology and Underwater Exploration* 357-362.

21   Christie's Amsterdam B.V. *The Vung Tau Cargo: Chinese Export Porcelain* (1992).

22   See, for example, H.K. Van Tilburg *The Maritime and Nautical Archaeology of China in Southeast Asia: Song to Early Ming Dynasties (A.D. 960-1435)* (1994). The authoritative maritime history of China is still J. Needham *Science and Civilization in China* (Vol. 4, 1971).

23   The significance of the Marine Silk Route as an international cultural link has been recognised through a ten-year UNESCO project entitled 'Integral Study of the Silk Roads: Road of Dialogue'. See Y. Sun *From Venice to Osaka* (1992).

24   Anon. 'The Treasure Race' *Asiaweek* 6 March 1992.

25   H. Zhao 'Recent Developments in the Legal Protection of Historic Shipwrecks in China' (1992) 23 *Ocean Development and International Law* 305-333.

26   See Green, *op. cit.* note 20.

Scientists, scholars, and government officials from the countries of the region are convinced that important archaeological and historical knowledge is already being lost to illicit plunder. For example, it is said that the *Geldermalsen* was dynamited after only half of its estimated 320,000 articles of delicate chinaware were salvaged, so that the salvor could keep the location of the site unknown.[27] In another location, a Chinese shipwreck of the Song Dynasty is reported to have been looted and then blasted with explosives.[28] In order to protect its marine cultural resources, China in 1989 enacted a Regulation on the Protection and Management of Underwater Cultural Relics. In addition, during the formulation of its eighth Five-Year Plan (1991–1996), the government identified large-scale marine archaeological exploration as one of its priorities.[29]

The nascent capabilities for conservation and management of the underwater cultural resources of the China Seas are jeopardised as well by limited financial resources. As a result, governments face strong temptations to recover relics and auction them off to raise money. Recently, Hanoi (the *Vung Tau* cargo in 1992), Kuala Lumpur (the *Diana* cargo in 1994), and many other governments have succumbed to these temptations.[30] Furthermore, the proliferation of black markets for Chinese cultural relics presents a formidable problem that must be addressed by cultural resource managers.

2.3 The market for Chinese archaeological artefacts

Figure 2 (panels (a) - (c)) indicate some general trends in the international art markets.[31] The indices are calculated from the average value of a representative collection of artworks that have been sold during the relevant period or from subjective estimates made by experts from Christie's auction house. Valuations are conducted every six months, and monthly values are created through a statistical smoothing process.[32] The indices do not represent absolute values but are instead an index of the average sale values of representative works of art. Because of the close linkage between ancient art and archaeology, we can use these indices as a measure of trends in the commercial value of archaeological artefacts in China.

Figure 2(a) depicts the trends in both the international art market as a whole and in the market for Chinese ceramics of all types. Notably there is a large increase in both indices during the late 1980s and early 1990s. This peak is known colloquially as the 'art boom' period.[33] Several hypotheses exist for why the boom took place. Heilbrun explains that the demand for art depends upon the wealth of consumers, the expected return and risk on an art purchase relative to other investments, the liquidity of the asset, and changing tastes and preferences.[34] Passell identifies several factors that may have contributed to the boom including increases in the wealth of art consumers, increased competition among auction houses (leading to discounted brokerage fees

---

27   P. Throckmorton 'The World's Worst Investment: The Economics of Treasure Hunting with Real Life Comparisons' in T. Carrel, ed., *Underwater Archaeology Proceedings from the Society for Historical Archaeology Conference* (1990).

28   Anon. 'News Report on Southeast Asia' (1991) 20 *International Journal of Nautical Archaeology and Underwater Exploration* 256.

29   L. Yang, personal communication, State Bureau of Cultural Relics, Beijing (22 November 1992).

30   The situation faced by the responsible cultural resource managers may be much more complex. The ultimate decision to recover and market underwater archaeological resources may be made at relatively high levels of government. Moreover, the direct benefit – if it exists at all – to underwater cultural management of the sale of artefacts may be attenuated at best.

31   For Fig. 2, see p. 40. The data are from *Art Market Research*, a research firm based in London.

32   B.J.N. Blight 'Christie's Art Market Research Index' mimeo, Art Market Research, London (1995).

33   There was another boom in Chinese ceramics during the early 1980s. The factors contributing to this boom are not well known, but may relate to the growth of the Japanese economy.

34   C.M.G. Heilbrun *The Economics of Art and Culture: An Economic Perspective* (1993).

and large-scale art expositions) and innovative marketing methods (including catalogues, explanations of bidding procedures, and prearranged lines of credit), and minimum price guarantees to sellers.[35] Other more general factors may have included exchange rate fluctuations and economic growth in Japan and Western Europe. It is not clear what contributed to the end of the boom, although an increase in supply of art to the market, caused in part by the removal of tax incentives for donations to museums in the USA, may have played an important role. It is notable in Figure 2(a) that the market in Chinese ceramics outperformed the market taken as a whole, particularly in the recent post-boom period. The growth of Asian-Pacific economies may have contributed substantially to this performance.

Figure 2(b) depicts the market in Chinese export ceramics, including late Ming and Qing ceramics that were manufactured, in part, for the Western European markets. These ceramics include those that have been discovered on historic shipwrecks and sold at auction. The dates of search/discovery and sale of three of these shipwrecks are displayed on the figure. Interestingly, all three sales missed the peak of the art market boom.

Figure 2(c) compares the markets for ceramics from the Han to Yuan dynasties, an extended period from 206 B.C. to A.D.1367, with the market for Ming and Qing ceramics (A.D.1368 to 1910). Clearly the market for the more recent Ming-Qing ceramics has outperformed the older Han-Yuan market. Brown suggests that the latter market, sometimes referred to as 'tomb pottery', is flooded by pieces dug up during highway construction.[36] Further, many Chinese citizens are superstitious about having tomb pottery in their homes, and legal prohibitions on its ownership within China exist. However, Barker reports on the March 1997 sale of Chinese ceramics, including a Han dynasty grey pottery dancing girl, which sold at a price four times the estimate. The sale marked the "widening gap in Han and Tang ceramics between what is very good and what is truly exceptional".[37]

In general, the art market in China is growing strongly. Mu reports that the number of commercial galleries is increasing, now numbering more than 1,000.[38] In 1996, the first insurance policy for classical art works in China was issued by the People's Insurance Company of China to the Guanfu Classical Art Museum. Auction companies have grown up in Beijing and in the coastal provinces, and sales from auctions nationwide topped $60 million in 1995. The main reason apparently is the increase in purchasing power of Chinese consumers who see, as do art consumers in other parts of the world, the value of art as an investment. Brown reports that Sotheby's auction house expects that consumers from Asia will represent from 20-30 percent of their business by 2006.[39]

2.4 Public policy rationales[40]

Underwater cultural resources, such as historic shipwrecks, are a type of archaeological resource. Most archaeological resources have an interesting quality in that they exhibit both 'public' and 'private' attributes.[41] Economic goods or services are 'private' if they are consumptive, meaning that they can be 'used up' or diminished in value when an individual uses or consumes them, and if other individuals can be excluded from consuming them. On the other hand, 'public' goods or services are non-consumptive and non-exclusive.

---

35   P. Passell 'Vincent Van Gogh Meet Adam Smith' *New York Times* 4 February 1990.
36   Brown, *op. cit.*, note 3.
37   G. Barker 'Arts and Books: In the Salesrooms' *The Daily Telegraph London* 29 March 1997.
38   J. Mu 'China-culture: art market witnesses expansion' *Beijing Review* 16 September 1996.
39   Brown, *op. cit.*, note 3.
40   Portions of this section have been published previously in P. Hoagland 'Managing the Underwater Cultural Resources of the China Seas: A Comparison of Public Policies in Mainland China and Taiwan' (1997) 12 *International Journal of Marine and Coastal Law* 265-283.
41   *Cf.* Y. Kaoru and P. Hoagland 'The value of historic shipwrecks: conflicts and management' (1994) 22 *Coastal Management* 195.

Many archaeological resources exhibit some of both characteristics. For example, ancient ceramics salvaged from a shipwreck and auctioned to individual buyers are a good example of an excludable private good. However, if the ceramics are durable, then they are not really used up when they are purchased,[42] and this durability can be considered a 'quasi-public' attribute. Like the understanding that is produced by science, archaeological knowledge is almost a pure public good; once it is supplied, it cannot be used up and it is difficult, if not impossible in some cases, to exclude others from consuming it.[43]

The 'publicness' of an archaeological resource is important because markets, as institutions for allocating resources, often, but not always, result in a less than adequate supply of goods exhibiting public attributes. This phenomenon is especially true for those public goods with the non-excludability characteristic. In the jargon of economics, this 'market failure' can be, and often is, used as a theoretical rationale for collective action to increase the supply of quasi-public goods. A wide array of public policies to achieve this purpose exist, but among the most common are mechanisms to establish property rights in the resource (letters patent, salvage awards *in rem*), government subsidies (bounties on discovery), government regulation (requirements to conduct archaeological studies), government programmes, or combinations of these and other instruments.[44]

A second argument for collective action concerns the potential mutual exclusivity of the realisation of value from either the public or the private attributes. A good example is the removal of an artefact from an archaeological site prior to the careful study of its position relative to the spatial distribution of all artefacts. This can occur through looting, recreational collecting, sanctioned commercial salvage efforts, or just plain bad science. In most cases, however, this kind of artefact removal occurs because of the perceived value of the artefact as a private good in commercial markets. Removal can affect the provenance of both the artefact and the entire archaeological site and the potential for advancements in the field of archaeology, which are both public goods. Although we expect that there should be a premium attached to artefacts with validated provenances, it may quite often be the case that the expected size of the premium in commercial markets is small relative to the commercial value of the incompletely provenanced artefact. More realistically, the costs associated with conducting careful archaeological study to establish a provenance may outweigh the expected size of the resulting premium.

Alternatively, a government might establish a policy to protect an archaeological site from commercial exploitation. There are many examples of actual projects, including several good ones from Asia, in which the public attributes of archaeological sites are given preference to the private ones. One of the best examples is the recovery and conservation of the Sinan shipwreck, artefacts from which are on display in a special gallery of the National Museum of Korea.[45] Such policies involve foregone opportunities for governments to realise the value of artefacts in commercial markets. As we have observed in the recent cases of Hanoi, Kuala Lumpur, Montevideo, and others, some governments are unable to forego these opportunities.

---

42 Without proper conservation or with improper handling, some archaeological resources may deteriorate, and therefore diminish in value. Thus, depending upon how the resource is consumed, it is possible for it to be used up. Durability may depend upon costly investments in maintenance and protection of the resource.

43 Nevertheless there may be costs associated with gaining access to archaeological information through research, for example. These costs may exclude some potential users, rendering archaeological information into an 'impure' public good.

44 *Cf.* R.H. Nelson 'Guiding the ocean search process: applying public land experience to the design of leasing and permitting systems for ocean mining and ocean shipwrecks' (1989) 20 *Ocean Development and International Law* 577.

45 National Museum of Korea 'The Shinan collection: Yuan Chinese artefacts from the seabed' in *National Museum of Korea* (1991) p. 189.

In an ideal world, it may be feasible to optimise the expected net present value from the development of archaeological resources through policies that encourage the realisation of the value of both public and private attributes. For instance, a staged process of careful archaeological study followed by the preservation of some artefacts and the commercial disposition of others may be more efficient, in a strict economic sense, than a choice between the extremes of commercial exploitation and government protection.[46]

Although economists believe that the market in archaeological artefacts functions well according to economic criteria,[47] more general 'distributional' or 'ethical' concerns associated with national interests in cultural property may have an influence on this trade.[48] Therefore, a third argument for collective action involves not economic theory explicitly but, instead, political significance. Clearly, governments have a deep interest in promoting patriotism and national unity, and the promulgation of national symbols is one way of achieving this. Such symbols can take the form of memorials, such as historic landmarks, battlefields, or burial tombs. Historical archaeological resources, in particular, might be used to memorialise past persons, places, or events, or even to provide proof of historical presence and justifiable claims to a dispossessed homeland.

The current excavation of Dr. Sun Yat-sen's flagship, the *Zhongshan*, is a classic illustration of this third argument. As reported by Zhou, the Cultural Bureau of Hubei Province, in co-operation with the PLA Navy and the Yangzi River Salvage Company, is now involved in the excavation and recovery of this shipwreck.[49] The *Zhongshan* lies in the Yangzi near Hankow, one of the three cities of the Wuhan metropolis. The Japanese sank the ship as they advanced on the government of China in 1938.[50]

Dr. Sun is, of course, recognised as the patriot who liberated China from feudalism. Further, before his death in 1925, he arranged an entente between the Guomindang and the Communist Party, which lasted for about four years.[51] Thus, although he led the nationalist movement, the governments of both Mainland China and Taiwan arguably can trace their origins back to Dr. Sun. And Madame Sun Yat-sen, one of the Soong sisters, became an important figure in the Chinese Communist government after the war. In 1938, the Chinese government existed as a coalition, albeit makeshift, between the nationalists and the communists, which sat in Hankow. Thus the symbolism of the *Zhongshan* lies in recognising Dr. Sun as a liberator, as a forefather of modern China, and also in the politically significant notion of a unified Mainland China and Taiwan.

A fourth rationale for collective action is not an argument for it *per se* but rather an observation of the behaviour of nations in international trade. Social scientists have identified two kinds of effects that may operate in the international market for art: the 'endowment' and 'commercialisation' effects.[52] The endowment effect explains a circumstance in which the owner of an artefact has a higher reservation price (the price at which he would be willing to sell the artefact) than the price at which he would be willing to pay for the artefact on the open market if he was not the owner. The endowment effect may be operational at the national level when an artefact

---

46   P. Hoagland 'Deepwater Shipwreck Assessment: Partnerships and Technologies' mimeo, Woods Hole Oceanographic Institution, Woods Hole, Massachusetts (1996).
47   For example, see W.D. Grampp *Pricing the Priceless: Art, Artists, and Economics* (1989).
48   For example, see M. Schneider 'The UNIDROIT Convention on Stolen or Illegally Exported Cultural Objects' mimeo, UNIDROIT, Rome (1995).
49   C. Zhou 'Survey report of the exploration of the *Zhongshan* warship' in H-H. Chou, ed., *Sunken Treasures: Underwater Archaeology in China* (forthcoming).
50   Dr. Sun had passed away much earlier, in 1925. The *Zhongshan* was used by the nationalists in defending Hankow before their withdrawal to Chunking. For a good account of the war with Japan during 1937 to 1941, see J.D. Spence *The Search for Modern China* (1990) ch. 17.
51   J. K. Fairbank *China: A New History* (1992).
52   See B.S. Frey and W.W. Pommerehne *Muses and Markets: Explorations in the Economics of the Arts* (1989). These behaviours have been observed in individuals, but they may operate at the collective level as well.

or a collection is perceived to be a part of the *patrimoine nationale* of a country. The endowment effect acts to restrict trade in artefacts, because a country is less willing to part with an artefact than it would be in the absence of the effect. In China, the endowment effect has been incorporated explicitly into policies that severely restrict foreign ownership of archaeological artefacts.[53]

The commercialisation effect occurs when potential market participants perceive a disutility from the use of the market. At the national level, countries may prefer to prevent trade altogether or to handle trade through bartering or lending arrangements. The commercialisation effect may be manifest in the comments and opinions of specific interest groups, such as archaeologists or others. In contrast to the endowment effect, the commercialisation effect does not seem to drive cultural resource policy in China. Recent auctions of duplicate artefacts and the intense interest of the Chinese government in the auctions of historic shipwreck artefacts by other governments are evidence that the commercialisation effect is not as dominant there as it may be in other parts of the world.

The net effect of the endowment and commercialisation behaviours may be to create an asymmetry in international art trade. National governments prefer to see a well-functioning market when they are interested in buying artefacts; however, they tend to regulate the export of artefacts of national origin.[54] An interesting side-effect of market restrictions are the extensive 'non-market' mechanisms for the international exchange of artefacts, including museum loans (both temporary and permanent) and international exhibitions. In the case of China, two good examples of this type of international trade include the exhibitions in 1998 in the USA of Qin Dynasty terracotta warriors at the Dayton Art Institute and of Chinese art and archaeology at the Guggenheim Museum.

3.   Outline of Chinese Law

In this section, the most salient aspects of the Regulation on the Protection and Administration of Underwater Cultural Relics 1989 of the People's Republic of China are identified. Zhao presents the only published description of the history of the development of public policy in this area in China to date.[55] Readers who are interested in more specifics about the development of the law are referred to that seminal article.

The 1989 Regulation applies specifically to underwater cultural 'relics', supplementing other, more general, policies applying to archaeological resources. A substantial portion of the Regulation is designed to extend control over underwater cultural resources of various classes in different categories of offshore jurisdictions.[56] The Regulation proclaims that underwater cultural resources are owned by the State[57] and encourages individuals to transfer their holdings of antiquities to the State. China does not recognise the legality of private ownership of underwater cultural relics, but does provide moral encouragements or material awards to persons in possession of such relics who donate them to the State. The Regulation requires inter-agency co-ordination at the national level, through a State Co-ordinating Working Group on Underwater Archaeology.

---

53   See L.V. Prott and P.J. O'Keefe *Law and the Cultural Heritage: Volume 3, Movement* (1989).
54   However, Bator suggests that, even in the presence of these behaviours, international trade restrictions may have limited effect. Bator's analysis may be more applicable to privately owned works of art or artefacts, but there are cases of public cultural resources that are moved through black markets: P. Bator 'An Essay on the International Trade in Art' (1982) 34 *Stanford Law Review* 275-384.
55   Zhao, *op. cit.*, note 25.
56   *Ibid.*
57   *Ibid.*

3.1 Assertion of resource jurisdiction

In its definition of underwater cultural relics, China asserts its jurisdiction over, and ownership of, all relics within its internal waters and territorial sea, including those originating from foreign countries. In addition, it asserts jurisdiction over, and ownership of, cultural relics originating from China or from an unidentifiable country that remain "beyond China's territorial sea but within other sea areas under China's jurisdiction according to China's laws". Although the terminology is arcane, "other sea areas under China's jurisdiction" has been interpreted to imply China's contiguous zone, exclusive economic zone (EEZ), and continental shelf.[58] Further, China asserts jurisdiction over relics originating from China but which remain "beyond the territorial sea of a foreign country but within the sea areas under foreign jurisdiction or within an area of the high seas".

Several aspects of these assertions are controversial. In particular, assertion of jurisdiction over relics located in the EEZ or on the continental shelf arguably lies beyond the pale of customary international law. The assertion of jurisdiction over relics of Chinese origin located within another nation's contiguous zone may also be unjustifiable, and the claiming of ownership of relics originating from a foreign country found in China's internal waters and territorial seas may in some cases cause problems. These issues are reviewed in greater detail below.[59]

3.2 Determination of archaeological significance

This aspect refers to the decision that classifies an archaeological resource as 'significant'. Article 38 of the 1989 Regulation states that:

> [t]he grade of an historic site shall be evaluated according to the following aspects:
> (1)   its historic, cultural, artistic, scientific, commemorative, or other scholastic value;
> (2)   its age;
> (3)   its relationship with important historical events or figures;
> (4)   whether it represents the characteristics, technologies, school of an era, or the characteristics of a place;
> (5)   its quantity;
> (6)   how well it is preserved;
> (7)   its size; and
> (8)   the environment in the vicinity of the site.

The Regulation leaves considerable discretion to responsible government agencies and officials in making a determination of significance. As such, it contains neither detailed instructions nor standards and, presumably, the services of professional archaeologists and other experts are to be relied upon. The Regulation does include a 'vintage' criterion, which may simplify decisions: pre-1911 artefacts are to be considered historically significant.

3.3 Encouragement of discovery

The next aspect refers to policies that affect the 'discovery' activity. Such policies are useful for encouraging the supply of 'public' goods, such as archaeological knowledge, which may have a limited market. Policies to encourage discovery can take a number of forms: in the 1989 Regulation, they take the form of discretionary awards given to individuals who report their discoveries. The size of awards or the frequency with which they are bestowed is unknown to the author. Ideally, the size of the award should be related to the commercial value of the artefact. If the

---

58   *Ibid.*
59   See section 4.1 below.

award is too small, then discoverers might be tempted to sell either an artefact or the location of an archaeological site on the black market. The Regulation also provides for 'moral encouragements' to be given to individuals who report a discovery to the authorities. Illicit activities are discouraged with provisions for punishment, including fines and prison terms.

3.4 Excavation

In China, excavation may be conducted for the purposes of scientific research or preservation only. Commercial salvage of underwater cultural relics is prohibited, and nationals who wish to conduct excavations must seek a permit from the State Bureau of Cultural Relics. Non-nationals must apply, through the Bureau, for a special permit from the State Council, and they must co-operate with a government agency in the excavation activity.

3.5 Diligence

In general, the maritime law of salvage incorporates the concept of 'due diligence'. This policy requires that a salvor work continuously and diligently in conducting its salvage. Its purpose is aligned with the main object of salvage law: to return lost goods back into the 'stream of commerce'. If a salvor is not diligent, then another salvor may enter and resume salvage operations. The 1989 Regulation contains no specific diligence provisions, perhaps because it is expected that all excavations will be conducted under the leadership of the State.

3.6 Conservation

Once archaeological resources are excavated, little guidance is given about the conservation of artefacts. Conservation is critical in terms of extracting useful information and in ensuring the durability of the resource. There are many examples of archaeological resources which, once they have been excavated, deteriorate rapidly. Perhaps one of the most shocking examples comes from China itself. Soon after the excavation of the tomb of Emperor Qin began, the paint on the surface of the terracotta warriors and horses quickly faded as it was exposed to the air.

3.7 Preferential uses

The 1989 Regulation contains 'public trust'-type provisions that give preference to pre-existing uses of the marine environment, including military operations, fisheries, marine transportation, communication facilities, and natural resource and environmental protection. Thus it is fairly clear that, relative to these other uses, the conservation of archaeological resources is not of the highest priority in China.

3.8 Zoning

Ocean zoning is clearly a modern method of resource allocation that has received increased use since the 1960s. The concept of zoning is one way to establish a preference for the protection of the archaeological resource because, once established, even the otherwise preferential uses described above cannot take precedence. The 1989 Regulation stands out in terms of its provisions for zoning, or establishing underwater cultural resource 'protection units'. The Regulation intends that such sites be established by either the central or local governments. The latter are expected to be in a better position to administer and enforce the use restrictions in the zone.

3.9 Enforcement

Enforcement is to occur at both national and local levels. Local enforcement is seen as the more pragmatic policy, because resources for national enforcement may be meagre. Local enforcement may also increase the potential for corruption, but there is no direct evidence of this taking place.

4. Policy Issues

4.1 Assertion of offshore jurisdiction

O'Keefe and Nafziger summarise the municipal and domestic law of coastal nations.[60] It is clear that all coastal nations have the right to manage archaeological sites and artefacts within their territorial seas and internal waters. As a result, China's assertion of jurisdiction over underwater cultural relics in these waters is justifiable. China has also claimed ownership of all relics in these waters, including those originating from a foreign country. While it is not unusual for States to claim ownership of such relics which have been – or are presumed to be – abandoned,[61] it is unusual for a State to claim ownership regardless of whether or not relics have been abandoned by the original owner. Problems could certainly arise should China assert ownership over, e.g., a sunken warship, in which case the flag-state might well dispute the claim.[62]

Under the United Nations Convention on the Law of the Sea 1982, article 303(2), a coastal nation may presume that the removal of underwater archaeological resources from the contiguous zone results in the infringement of its territorial customs or fiscal laws.[63] China claimed both a twelve nautical mile territorial sea and a twelve nautical mile contiguous zone in 1992. Therefore, China's claim to jurisdiction over underwater cultural relics of all types may be considered valid in this 24 nautical mile zone.[64]

Beyond the 24 mile contiguous zone, there is no treaty law or accepted customary international law under which a coastal nation may exert jurisdiction over historic shipwrecks. Some commentators have argued that coastal nations may exert such jurisdiction, but the legality of such claims may still be open to dispute. In the specific case of China, Zhao has argued for coastal nation jurisdiction over archaeological resources in the EEZ and on the continental shelf.[65] Regardless of merit, it is worthwhile reviewing Zhao's arguments because they are likely to be put forth by the Chinese government in any future legal dispute that arises over jurisdiction.

---

60   P.J. O'Keefe and J.A.R. Nafziger 'Report on the Draft Convention on the Protection of the Underwater Cultural Heritage (1994) 25 *Ocean Development and International Law* 391-418.
61   See O'Keefe and Nafziger, *op. cit.*, note 60 at p. 395.
62   See S. Dromgoole and N. Gaskell 'Interests in Wreck' in N. Palmer, E. McKendrick (eds.), *Interests in Goods* (2nd edn., 1998) p. 167. For the position of the UK in respect of its military vessels, see Dromgoole and Gaskell, *ibid.*, at pp. 155-156. For the position of the US, see J.A. Roach 'Sunken Warships and Military Aircraft' (1996) 20 *Marine Policy* 351-354. It should be borne in mind that the relevant provision of the 1989 Regulation in general relates to pre-1911 relics, but nonetheless the flag-state may still wish to assert its interest: see Dromgoole and Gaskell, *ibid.*, p. 155 *et seq.*
63   M. Hayashi 'Archaeological and Historical Objects Under the United Nations Convention on the Law of the Sea' (1996) 20 *Marine Policy* 291-297.
64   For an analysis of the art. 303(2) provision, see A. Strati *The Protection of the Underwater Cultural Heritage: An Emerging Objective of the Contemporary Law of the Sea* (1995) pp. 165-170.
65   Zhao, *op. cit.*, note 25.

With respect to the EEZ, Zhao argues,[66] first, that the list of resources over which a nation has jurisdiction is meant to be exemplary instead of comprehensive. Archaeological resources are not mentioned specifically in the text of the 1982 Convention[67] but neither are they explicitly excluded. Secondly, under a combined interpretation of the Convention's EEZ provisions and the article 303(1) provisions relating to archaeological resources, coastal nations have a specific duty under the Convention to protect marine cultural and historical resources in the EEZ. Finally, if archaeological study can be considered to be a type of marine scientific research, then a coastal nation has the right to control access to archaeological resources by regulating marine scientific research.[68]

Notably, under the 1982 Convention, a coastal nation must proclaim an EEZ, and China has not yet done so. [69] One of the issues slowing the issuance of an EEZ proclamation may be the existence of territorial disputes in the South China Sea, particularly in the highly disputed area around the Spratly Island group. In 1996, China conducted an archaeological survey in the Spratlys, in part to buttress territorial claims there.[70] Similarly, the recent announcement of the discovery of 2,000 historic shipwrecks off the southern coast of China was made in part to demonstrate historical occupation and control in the South China Sea.[71] The real issue in the Spratlys, however, is not the presence of archaeological resources but, instead, deposits of oil and natural gas. Further, one can make the argument that the recent announcement is as much an internal tactic designed to draw attention and budgetary resources to the field of underwater archaeology in China as it is to help substantiate territorial claims. In fact, the argument works both ways.

Regardless of the status of China's EEZ claim, it is likely to be the case that any underwater cultural relics located in the EEZ are also located on the continental shelf, which does not require an express proclamation. Zhao argues[72] that a coastal nation can assert jurisdiction over underwater cultural relics on its continental shelf for the following reasons. First, nations have a specific duty under article 303(1) of the 1982 Convention to protect marine cultural and historic resources anywhere 'at sea'. The term 'at sea' is not restricted to any particular area, and so Zhao interprets it as encompassing the continental shelf, among other areas. Secondly, article 81 of the Convention permits coastal nations to regulate drilling for any purpose on the continental shelf. To the extent that exploration or salvage of a historic shipwreck involves drilling, then jurisdiction may be asserted. Thirdly, coastal nations may exert jurisdiction over activities that may potentially damage natural resources. Underwater archaeology or salvage may damage resources to the extent that they are embedded, such as in a coral formation. Finally, jurisdiction over marine scientific research applies to underwater archaeology on the continental shelf as in the case of the EEZ.[73]

Zhao's arguments are strong in the sense that they identify regulatory handles for a coastal nation to control archaeological activities within the EEZ and on the continental shelf. But it may be important to distinguish between regulatory handles and extensions of resource jurisdiction. In particular, it is not clear from an international legal standpoint that commercial treasure salvage activities that involve neither damage to the natural resources of the continental shelf, drilling on the continental shelf, nor archaeology, can be regulated in the EEZ or on the continental shelf solely on the basis of these regulatory handles. Further, treasure salvors are likely to argue, as they have done in the past, that salvage is a means to 'protect' archaeological resources from

---

66   Zhao, *op. cit.*, note 25, pp. 316-317.
67   See art. 56(1).
68   But see Strati, *op. cit.*, note 64, p. 264.
69   As of April 1998, China had not yet declared an EEZ: R. White, personal communication, US Department of State (7 April 1998). China has prepared draft text for EEZ legislation.
70   W. Zhang, personal communication, National Museum of Chinese History (26 June 1997).
71   Anon. 'China Hopes Shipwrecks Will Prove Its Claims to South China Sea' *AAP Newsfeed* 23 January 1998.
72   *Op. cit.*, note 25, p. 319.
73   But see Strati, *op. cit.*, note 64, p. 262.

further degradation in the marine environment and that the salvage exercise complies with the duty to protect archaeological resources.

Notwithstanding the distinction between regulatory handles and extensions of resource jurisdiction, several nations have already begun to extend either management authority or ownership over underwater archaeological resources on their continental shelves.[74] If other coastal nations jump on the bandwagon, then jurisdiction over underwater cultural resources in the EEZ and on the continental shelf may become customary. Alternatively, extended jurisdiction over underwater archaeological resources may become international law more quickly with the adoption of the UNESCO Draft Convention.

4.2   Sharing the proceeds

This particular issue arises most often when historic shipwreck resources are being considered for development by a commercial firm. As antithetical to the ethical norms of academic archaeologists as the notion must be, the sale of recovered artefacts is of practical importance. In China, where underwater archaeology is still a nascent discipline, where government budgets are thin, and whose neighbours Malaysia and Vietnam have been involved recently in deals with commercial salvors, the prospect of working with commercial salvage firms is considered seriously.

There is quite a wide variation in policies concerning the distribution of the proceeds from the sale of artefacts recovered from an historic shipwreck.[75] Figure 3 shows the distribution of gross revenues from the sale of artefacts of some recently discovered historic shipwrecks.[76]

The basic issue concerns the distribution of the 'resource rent' or, generally speaking, the difference between the discounted revenues from the sale of artefacts and the discounted costs of discovering, recovering and marketing artefacts. A resource rent exists because an historic shipwreck is a scarce resource. In theory, a resource rent can exist when a shipwreck is not sold commercially but valued instead for non-market characteristics, such as archaeological knowledge, memorial significance, or for such passive uses as option, vicarious, or bequest uses.[77] In practice, non-market valuation can be costly to conduct, and some purported non-market values, such as 'existence' value, may have more of a religious meaning than an economic one.[78] Further, because no proceeds result from the decision to realise solely the non-market uses of a shipwreck, there is no decision to be made about the distribution of proceeds between the government and the private developer.

Under conditions of relative certainty about the location of a shipwreck and its value upon recovery, it can be expected that the government, as owner, can collect the entire resource rent through an appropriate policy instrument, such as a royalty. (This assumes that a normal profit is included in the costs of development.) However, there may be considerable uncertainty associated with the development of an historic shipwreck resource, including locating the wreck, determining its highest valued use, evaluating the condition of any marketable artefacts, assessing the contribution of archaeological studies to enhancing the value of the shipwreck, etc. Under such conditions, it may make sense for the government to provide additional incentives by turning over a portion of the resource rent to the private developer. Further, if good archaeological work is an

---

74   The following States have made claims: Australia (historic shipwrecks on the continental shelf); Cyprus (continental shelf); Denmark (shipwrecks as obstructions to navigation in a 200 nautical mile 'buoyage zone' and historic shipwrecks in the contiguous zone); France (contiguous zone); Ireland (historic shipwrecks on the continental shelf); Morocco (exclusive economic zone); Norway (continental shelf); the Seychelles (continental shelf); Spain (archaeological resources on the continental shelf).
75   Proceeds might also arise from museum fees or user charges to a marine park.
76   For Fig. 3, see p. 41.
77   See Kaoru and Hoagland, *op. cit.*, note 41.
78   R.H. Nelson 'Does *Existence* Value Exist: Environmental Economics Encroaches on Religion' (1997) 1 *Independent Review* 499-521.

objective of the government, then this kind of incentive can be used by the private developer to cover the costs of providing archaeological data and interpretation.

In the USA, the distribution of the proceeds between a *private* owner of a shipwreck and a *private* salvage firm is determined by principles of admiralty law. Under these principles, if a salvor finds and successfully recovers property in 'marine peril' at sea, such as a shipwreck, then he is entitled to a salvage award for his efforts. In general, such awards cover the cost of recovery plus a premium that acts as an incentive to encourage salvage activity. More specifically, the salvage award depends upon the following 'ingredients':

(1)   The labour expended by the salvors in rendering the salvage service.
(2)   The promptitude, skill, and energy displayed in rendering the service and saving the property.
(3)   The value of the property employed by the salvors in rendering the service, and the danger to which such property was exposed.
(4)   The risk incurred by the salvors in securing the property from the impending peril.
(5)   The value of the property saved.
(6)   The degree of danger from which the property was rescued.[79]
(7)   The degree to which the salvors have worked to protect the historical and archaeological value of the wreck and items salved.[80]

The addition of the seventh ingredient in 1992 is an important change because it provides a specific economic incentive for the conduct of historical and archaeological research. How a court determines the monetary value of the research is an important question left entirely to its discretion.

In the case of historic shipwrecks that have been abandoned by the owner, some jurisdictions claim a 'sovereign prerogative' through which ownership of the cultural property is claimed by the government. This kind of a policy can be seen as 'distributional' in nature, as there is little economic reason why a government necessarily should exert a sovereign prerogative. The government may be acting on the basis of a policy that seeks to create a national 'interest' or 'identity'. Note, however, that if historic shipwrecks are repositories of non-market attributes, if such attributes will be lost through treasure salvage or some other use, and if the lost value is large enough, then there may be clear economic justification for collective action to protect a shipwreck or to regulate its excavation.

Some jurisdictions now have legislation or policies specifying the proportion of the rent that goes to the resource owner, usually the government, and the proportion that goes to a private developer. An example is the 'fair share' agreement negotiated between the Commonwealth of Virginia and Sea Hunt, Inc., a private salvage firm located in New Hampshire.[81] The agreement is part of a permit that allows Sea Hunt to recover artefacts from two small areas off Assateague Island on the Atlantic coast of Virginia. Under the agreement, Sea Hunt receives 75 percent of the gross value of all collected artefacts. Virginia gets to choose whatever artefacts it wants to conserve, and receives 25 percent of the value of the collected artefacts. This policy is similar to that in other US coastal states, including Massachusetts and Florida.

An alternative mechanism for sharing the proceeds involves developing the resource as a tourist attraction. One important example concerns the collection from the seventeenth century Manila galleon *Nuestra Señora de la Concepción*, which was sold to the Japanese developer of a resort complex in Saipan. The collection itself will be on public display, and the developer has

---

79   The first six ingredients were determined in the case of *The Blackwall* (1869) 77 U.S. (10 Wall) 1, 13-14, 19 L.Ed. 870.
80   The seventh ingredient was added in the following case: *Columbus-America Discovery Group* v. *Atlantic Mutual Insurance Company* (1992) 974 F.2d 450 (Fourth Cir.).
81   S. Harper 'Go-ahead Given to Hunt for Booty from Two Spanish Galleons' *The Virginian-Pilot* 26 March 1997.

stated its intention to donate the collection back to the government of the Northern Mariana Islands in 40 years. The government is using its share of the proceeds from the sale of the collection to build a national museum. In China, the *Zhongshan* will be recovered, rehabilitated, and exhibited as a joint project of the national government, the local provincial and city governments, and local real estate developers.

4.3   Sale of duplicate artefacts

In general, duplicate artefacts can be thought of, in economic terms, as nearly perfect substitutes.[82] The important issue with respect to archaeological artefacts is that there be little or no difference in terms of the 'knowledge content' of the duplicates. That is, the data and interpretation possible from duplicates is no different from that obtainable from an 'original' artefact that is kept and maintained in a collection. Several types of benefits can result from the sale of duplicates. First, if the duplicate artefacts are held in storage, and they are not available for public display, then there are only net costs associated with storage. Buyers will realise benefits when the duplicates are sold. Secondly, the sale of duplicates can result in revenues for the government. Thirdly, if the duplicates are close substitutes for artefacts from other sites, then incentives for looting and site destruction are lowered when duplicates are sold. Finally, the same types of effects might be expected for the production of replicates of archaeological artefacts.

Concerns are sometimes raised about the 'creation' of markets through the sanctioned sale of duplicates. Created markets, it is argued, might encourage the entry of artefact suppliers and increase the potential for archaeological site depredations. However, one of the most serious problems for archaeological resources in many jurisdictions is that, when trade in artefacts is prohibited, *underground* markets exist. It may be feasible to regulate the market, in order to ensure that artefacts or sites of national interest are protected. Cohn reports that "more and more these days, Chinese officials are talking about controlling the trade – and the profits".[83]

In the case of Israel, Leventen provides a good example of how a market in duplicates might work.[84] The government could license 'primary dealers' in archaeological artefacts.[85] These dealers would be permitted to bid at auction on duplicate artefacts whose origin from an authorised excavation has been certified by professional archaeologists. The dealers would then be permitted to resell the certified duplicates. The result is a two-tiered market in which the certified artefacts command a premium over uncertified artefacts, thereby reducing incentives for the depredation of archaeological sites.

Leventen suggests, further, that the primary dealers would be allowed to offer artefacts at the government auction. These artefacts could be either certified or uncertified. Dealers would be required to exercise due diligence in the analysis of the origins of uncertified artefacts. If not illicitly obtained, an uncertified artefact could be auctioned as well. If the artefact is obtained from a clandestine excavation, then the primary dealer could act as a go-between in a privileged relationship, much like a doctor-patient or lawyer-client. The dealer would attempt to obtain as much source information as possible, perhaps including the location of the depredated site. The artefact could be sold directly to the government or at auction, providing an incentive for looters to provide archaeological information as well as the artefact through a sanctioned market.

---

82   Interestingly, archaeologists sometimes argue that duplicate artefacts are 'complements' instead of 'substitutes'. In this interpretation, the value of a collection is diminished when individual artefacts are dispersed. However, if a duplicate provides little or no marginal value in terms of archaeological knowledge, or if the knowledge can be extracted from the duplicate before it is dispersed, then its role as a complement is likely to be minor.

83   Cohn, *op. cit.*, note 4.

84   A.C. Leventen 'A Workable Proposal to Regulate Antiquities Trade' (1989) 15 *Biblical Archaeology Review* 44-46.

85   This proposal is analogous to the licensing of primary dealers in government securities markets.

4.4   Enforcement of archaeological sites

This issue arises particularly in cases where an archaeological site has been located, and may be in the process of excavation. As a result of its published location, it may be subject to depredation. The question is one of optimal monitoring and enforcement.

Zhao outlines the relevant provisions of Chinese law.[86] Non-monetary criminal sanctions (imprisonment) are imposed on individuals who illegally traffic in underwater cultural relics, who are involved in the intentional destruction of sites, and who are involved in the illegal exploration and excavation of underwater archaeological sites. Criminal fines may be imposed on those who hide or fail to report on the location of cultural relics or who buy or sell cultural relics without permission. Capital punishment is an option for very serious offences involving the illegal transport of cultural relics abroad. This, of course, is an extreme example of the endowment effect.

In a typology developed by Shavell, this type of law enforcement can be characterised as based upon actual harm, involving non-monetary sanctions, and using public enforcement methods.[87] According to Shavell, in circumstances in which the deterrence of an offence is likely to be weak, such as the case of historic shipwrecks, this type of law enforcement is appropriate and may even be considered optimal from an economic perspective. Deterrence may be weak for the following general reasons:

(1)   the probability of apprehending and convicting offenders is low;
(2)   offenders are likely to be poor, making monetary sanctions ineffective;
(3)   the benefits to an offender from the successful commission of a criminal act are likely to be large relative to his wealth.

Non-monetary sanctions make sense when offenders are poor and the seriousness of the crime to society is perceived to be large (e.g. looting a nation's cultural heritage). Public enforcement makes sense when it is costly to identify and locate offenders.

5.   Conclusions

China has a significant underwater archaeological resource base, the potential of which is only beginning to be realised in the West. Because of an extensive coastline and an expansive ocean jurisdiction, which has not yet been officially delimited, resources for monitoring and protecting this archaeological resource base are critically limited.[88] China's policy response has been to severely restrict exploration and discovery of the resource, limiting such activities mainly to government agencies and the National Museum.

Although academic archaeologists have been known to argue that restrictions on exploration are the best form of protection of the resource, clearly the benefits, both market and non-market, of studying and recovering the resource may remain unrealised for decades to come. Further, there are significant threats to the resource from looting and other depredations on those sites that have been identified and are being worked by the government.

In terms of law and policy, China has positioned itself at the vanguard. This has been achieved through careful analysis of the actions taken by other nations and through some careful thinking about how economic incentives might best be used to encourage individuals to conserve

---

86   Zhao, *op. cit.*, note 25.
87   S. Shavell 'The Optimal Structure of Law Enforcement' (1993) 36 *Journal of Law*.
88   In late June 1998, after this chapter had been completed, China officially proclaimed an exclusive economic zone and continental shelf.

the resource. Notwithstanding these developments, just as it is possible to argue that China's assertions of resource jurisdiction may be too expansive, its policies to manage underwater archaeological resources with economic incentives arguably are insufficient.

For example, the sanctioned sale of duplicates and replicates has several beneficial aspects. First, their sale can produce revenues for the original owner, often the government. Such revenues could, in theory, be employed to conduct a wider range of archaeological studies than are now performed. Secondly, the sale of certified duplicates is likely to reduce the monetary incentive for archaeological site depredation. This effect will reduce the costs of artefact destruction, and of monitoring and enforcement. Further, transactions costs in the market will be reduced to the extent that buyers and sellers will be more certain about the genuineness of the product that is being traded.

With respect to the enforcement of laws pertaining to underwater archaeological resources, several steps might be taken to increase deterrence. First, technological solutions might be applied either to increase the probability of apprehending offenders or to prevent an offence from taking place. For example, a remote surveillance system could be built and deployed at relatively low cost to detect any disturbance of an underwater site.[89] Secondly, monetary incentives (bounties) might be given to individuals to report on the discovery of sites. Because potential offenders are likely to be poor, bounties might be perceived as large relative to their wealth. Incentives might be given to private individuals to report offences as well. This type of incentive has already been incorporated into Chinese policy. Thirdly, removing the black market might reduce the private benefits to offenders. This might be accomplished through the creation of a regulated market in duplicate artefacts.

Given the significant pressures of the international art markets, the clear signals of expanding demand for Chinese art and archaeological artefacts, the historical pattern of black market trade, and inadequate government budgets, reliance solely upon government discovery and excavation of sites is clearly untenable in China. Future underwater archaeology is likely to involve partnerships between Chinese institutions, such as the National Museum, and private or non profit-making salvage firms. Partnerships of this sort have been the *modus operandi* of China in other emerging technology fields, such as offshore oil and gas development. As these partnerships emerge, it will be important for China to harness the power of economic incentives to reap the untapped benefits of archaeological knowledge and cultural heritage embodied in its underwater cultural resource base. The alternative course, perhaps unthinkable, but certainly realistic, is one of lost opportunities, waste and depredation.

---

89   Biasotti presents the specifications of one such system using passive acoustic technology: A. Biasotti 'Remote Surveillance of Underwater Archaeological Sites' (1986) 15 *International Journal of Nautical Archaeology and Underwater Exploration* 185-188.

Figure 1: Underwater Cultural Resources and Historic Trade Routes of the China Seas

For Appendix, see pp.38-39.

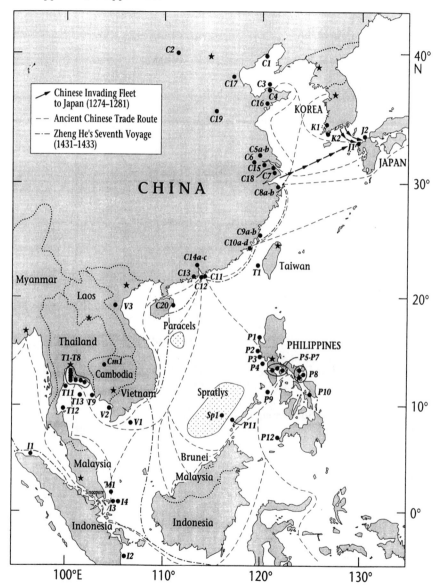

Appendix: Shipwrecks Identified in Figure 1[1]

Cambodia

Cm1   Angkor Thom (1185)

China

C1   Bohai Bay Shipwreck (A.D. 13th century)
C2   Liang-shan Hsien Naval Patrol Boat [Ming Dynasty (A.D. 1377)]
C3   Changdao Islands Site (2000-1000 B.C.)
C4   Peng-Lai Boat [Ming Dynasty (A.D. 1368-1644)]
C5a   Si-Qiao River Boat [Tang Dynasty (A.D. 618-906)]
C5b   Ru-Gao River Boat [Tang Dynasty (A.D. 618-907)]
C6   Nanjing Rudder-Post (A.D. 15th century)
C7   Chuanyang He Boat [Sui-Tang Dynasties (A.D. 581-907)]
C8a   Dongmenkou Wharves (A.D. 6-17th century)
C8b   Ningbo Vessel [Song Dynasty (A.D. 960-1279)]
C9a   Lianjiang Han Canoe [Western Han Dynasty (206-95 B.C.)]
C9b   Baijao Shipwreck [Song-Yuan Dynasty (A.D. 1271-1368)]
C10a Quanzhou Shipwreck [Southern Song Dynasty (A.D. 1277)]
C10b South Song Stone Anchors [South Song Dynasty (A.D. 13th century)]
C10c Fa-Shih Vessel [Song Dynasty (A.D. 960-1279)]
C10d Quanzhou Shipwreck [Southern Song Dynasty (A.D. 1265-79)]
C11   South China Sea Shipwreck [Song-Yuan Dynasty (A.D. 960-1368)]
C12   Window Island Site (A.D. 900)
C13   South Song Dynasty Fleet (A.D. 1279)
C14a Guangzhou Qin-Han Shipyard (200 B.C.-A.D. 100)
C14b Bao Ling Gang Shipwreck [Qing Dynasty (A.D. 1640)]
C14c Dazhou Dragon Boat [Qing Dynasty (A.D. 1640)]
C15   Wujin Shipwreck [Han Dynasty (220 B.C.-A.D. 30)]
C16   Pingdu Shipwreck [Sui Dynasty (A.D. 581-618)]
C17   Yuanmengkou Shipwreck [Song Dynasty (A.D. 960-1279)]
C18   Fengbang Shipwreck [South Song Dynasty (A.D. 1120-1279)]
C19   Nankaihe Shipwrecks
C20   Wenchang Shipwreck

Indonesia

I1   Flor del Mar (1512)
I2   Risdam (1727)
I3   Bintan Wrecks [Song-Yuan Dynasties (A.D. 12-14th centuries)]
I4   Geldermalsen (1752)
I*   Flores Ship Model (A.D. 1st century)

Japan

J1   First Kublai Khan Invasion Fleet (A.D. 1274)
J2   Second Kublai Khan Invasion Fleet (A.D. 1281)

---

1   A more detailed description of each site with specific citations to publications is available from the author.

Korea

K1   Shinan Ship [Yuan Dynasty (A.D. 1323)]
K2   Wando Ship (11th century A.D.)

Malaysia

M1   Palau Aur Wreck (A.D. 1800)

Philippines

P1   Bolineau I and II (undated)
P2   San Antonio [Song Dynasty (1127-1279)]
P3   San Jose (1694)
P4   San Diego (1654)
P5   Puerto Galera (A.D. 16th century)
P6   Nuestra Senora de la Vida (A.D. 18th century)
P7   Marinduque
P8   Manila Galleons
P9   Quiniluban Islands (undated)
P10   Butuan Boats (undated)
P11   Royal Captain Shoal (A.D. 1600-1625)
P12   Griffin (1761)

Spratley Island Group

Sp1   Song Wreck [Song Dynasty (A.D. 13th century)]

Taiwan

T1   Penghu Shipwreck

Thailand

T1   Ko Si Chang Shipwrecks (A.D. 13-17th centuries)
T2   Pattaya (A.D. 16th century)
T3   Ko Khram (A.D. 1520)
T4   Ko Rang Kwien (A.D. 19th century)
T5   Ko Rin [Ming Dynasty (1368-1644)]
T6   Ko Samae San
T7   Samed Ngam (A.D. 1800±150 by ^{14}C)
T8   Rayong
T9   Ko Kradat [Ming Dynasty (Jia Jing) (A.D. 1522-1566)]
T11   Ko Talu (A.D. 19th century)
T12   Ko Samui
T13   Hatcher Wreck 3 (A.D. 16th century)

Vietnam

V1   Vung Tau Shipwreck (A.D. 1690)
V2   Phu Quoc
V3   Dong Son (500 B.C. to A.D. 100)

Figure 2: Trends in the Markets for Archaeological Resources in China

(a) World Art Market Trends

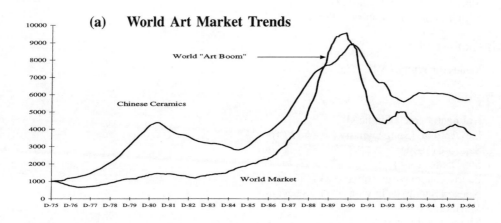

(b) Chinese Export Porcelain Market Trends

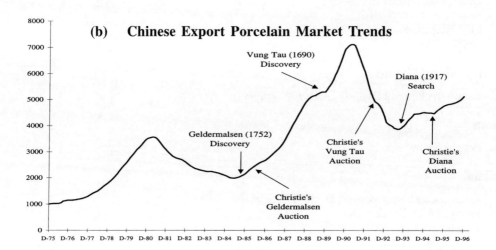

(c) Han-Yuan and Ming-Qing Market Trends

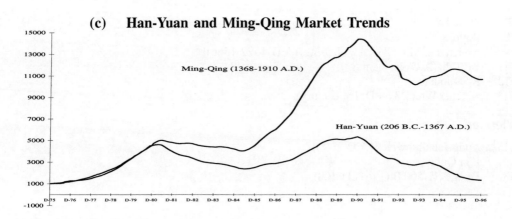

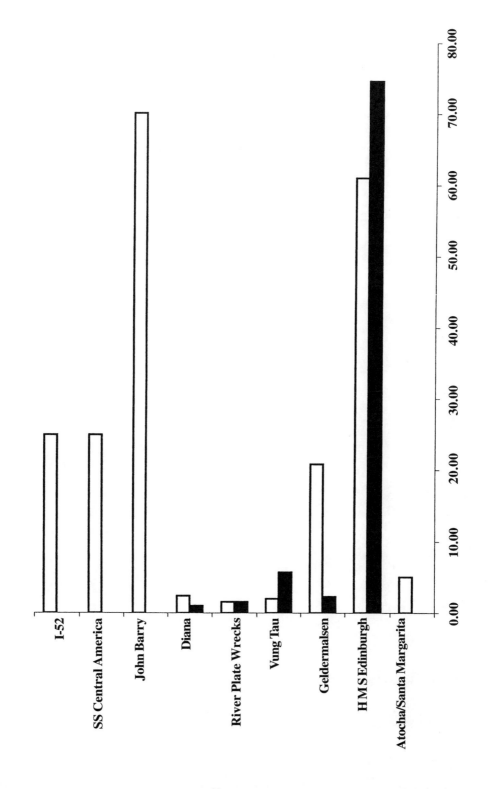

Figure 3: Estimated "In-Place" Value of Some Recently Salvaged Shipwrecks

Chapter 3

FRANCE

Gwenaëlle Le Gurun[*]

Introduction

Marine archaeological activities in France have recently been incorporated into the National Archaeological Programme.[1] They are governed by the following sub-programmes: H7, devoted to the organisation of, primarily maritime, trade; H8, dealing with naval archaeology;[2] and marginally, H6, which relates to the communications network.[3]

The schedule of operations for the years 1990-1994 shows the extent of marine archaeological activities in France, both in terms of quantity and, perhaps more especially, nature. During this five year period, 156 operations, including freshwater archaeological operations, were undertaken under programmes H7 and H8.[4] More significant is the classification of operations by nature. Most marine research activities consist of searches (35 percent) or surveys (39 percent). Excavations represent only 18 percent of all operations, "reducing the real level of marine archaeological research to a more modest scale."[5]

An analysis of activities during this period by geographical area and by period is also interesting. For example, 73.5 percent of operations conducted in connection with programme H7 took place in the Mediterranean Sea. Activities within programme H8 were better balanced geographically, although operations conducted in the Mediterranean Sea were still more numerous (38 percent). An analysis of activities by period shows that the operations within programme H7 were fairly equitably split between ancient (51 percent) and modern and contemporary periods (41 percent), while the Middle Ages were represented by only four operations.[6] In the Atlantic, all the operations concerned modern and contemporary periods, whereas two-thirds of operations conducted in the Mediterranean Sea were in connection with the ancient period. This data illustrates a difference in the historical incidence of shipping, and also of archaeological research, in these two sea areas.[7]

---

*   I am grateful to Mr. Renan Le Mestre, Lecturer in Law at the University of Poitiers, for his patient listening and valuable observations in the writing of this article. I am also indebted to Mrs. Julie Williams and Mr. Michael Williams, both of the University of Wolverhampton, for their comments on this work. Errors remaining are my own.

1   The information provided here about marine archaeological activities in France is based upon data contained in a recent report: Ministère de la Culture *La recherche archéologique en France-Bilan 1990-1994 et programmation du Conseil national de la recherche archéologique* Editions de la Maison des Sciences de l'Homme (Paris, 1997).

2   It should be noted that these two programmes deal only with the archaeology of shipwrecks: Ministère de la Culture, *ibid.* at p. 207.

3   Consequently, programme H6 may encompass submerged port structures.

4   Sometimes, operations mentioned in a programme can also be classified in another so these figures are not totally representative. For more details, see Ministère de la Culture, *op. cit.* note 1 at p. 209.

5   Ministère de la Culture, *op. cit.* note 1. Marine archaeology in France suffers from the fact that it is not directly concerned with rescue archaeology, which is essential for the development of the activity.

6   There was less shipping during the Middle-Ages: men were afraid of the sea and fewer ships meant fewer shipwrecks!: see J.-Y. Blot *L'histoire engloutie ou l'archéologie sous-marine*, Gallimard, Découvertes, No. 266 (Paris, 1995) p. 147.

7   For an analysis of operations in connection with programme H8, see Ministère de la Culture, *op. cit.* note 1 at p. 210.

Finally, a significant feature of marine archaeology in France concerns those running the operations. According to the headings used in the schedule established since 1993 by the Department for Marine and Underwater Archaeological Research, it can be said that 80 percent of operations under programme H7 were conducted by amateurs, and 100 percent of activities in the Atlantic and the overseas '*départements*' were led by amateurs. According to this report, the fact that the majority of operations were conducted by amateurs largely explains the concentration upon search and survey operations, the lack of preventive archaeology, and the small-scale nature of excavations.

The marine cultural heritage is particularly precious and vulnerable. It needs protection, particularly through adequate legislation. However, until recently:

The legislation applicable to the marine cultural heritage [was] comprised of Law No. 61-1262 of 24th November 1961, modified by Law No. 82-990 of 23rd November 1982 relating to the policing of wrecks, and texts adopted for enforcement of Law No. 61-1262, Decree No. 61-1547 of 26th December 1961 fixing the regime for maritime wrecks, modified by Decree No. 78-847 of 3rd August 1978, Decree No. 85-632 of 21st June 1985 and Order of 4th February 1965 relating to wrecks. *It [was] not a question of a body of texts principally concerned with the cultural and archaeological heritage, but a collection of arrangements establishing the law applicable to maritime wrecks, principally to safeguard the property of wrecks, to protect the interests of the finder and the salvors rather than to protect the historic heritage or to favour scientific study. These rules appear inappropriate not only because they consider only a part of the heritage but also because they ignore the demands of conservation.*[8]

Now, however, four legal texts are specifically devoted to the protection of marine cultural heritage in France: Law No. 89-874,[9] Decree No. 91-1226 of 5th December 1991 taken for the application of Law No. 89-874 relating to maritime cultural assets and modifying the Law of 27th September 1941 for the regulation of archaeological excavations,[10] the Order of 4th January 1996 for the creation and organisation of a department of marine and underwater archaeological research[11] and the Order of 8th February 1996 relating to maritime cultural assets.[12] These texts were drawn up in the light of certain developments in the international sphere, notably under the auspices of the Council of Europe, which had some influence on their final form.[13]

---

8 R. Beix *Rapport fait au nom de la commission des affaires culturelles, familiales et sociales sur le projet de loi (no. 535) relatif aux biens culturels maritimes et modifiant la loi du 27 septembre 1941 portant réglementation des fouilles archéologiques*, Assemblée Nationale, No. 616, Seconde session, 1988/1989, Annexe au procès-verbal de la séance du 19 avril 1989, p. 9. Translation in italics: A. Firth 'Recent legislation in France' (1991) 20 *International Journal of Nautical Archaeology* 65-69 at 65.

9 Law No. 89-874 of 1 December relating to maritime cultural assets and modifying the Law of 27 September 1941 for the regulation of archaeological excavations (*Journal officiel de la République française*, 5 December 1989, 15033-15034. Hereafter Law No. 89-874.)

10 *Journal officiel de la République française*, 7 December 1991, pp. 16017-16018. Hereafter Decree No. 91-1226.

11 *Journal officiel de la République française*, 11 January 1996, p. 429.

12 *Journal officiel de la République française*, 20 February 1996, p. 2740.

13 The Council of Europe – through the Roper Report that led to Recommendation No. 848 (1978), and through the Draft Convention on the Protection of the Underwater Cultural Heritage 1985 – had a particular influence upon the French provisions concerning the nature and regime of the property to be protected. The new legal regime differs from that traditionally dealing with maritime wrecks, notably in respect of conservation *in situ* and rewards: on these issues, see Council of Europe, Parliamentary Assembly, Committee on Culture and Education, Report on the Underwater Cultural Heritage (Rapporteur Mr. John Roper), Doc. 4200-E (1978), which caused the Parliamentary Assembly of the Council of Europe to make Recommendation No. 848 (1978) on the Underwater Cultural Heritage. Law No. 89-874 also takes advantage of the United Nations Convention on the Law of the Sea 1982, art. 303 para. 2, by extending French jurisdiction over maritime cultural assets in the contiguous zone. See further, section 1.2.2 below.

This chapter highlights changes made by Law No. 89-874 in order that account be taken of the whole marine cultural heritage (and not just a component of it), and to ensure that the need for conservation of the marine cultural heritage is respected. A new concept is introduced, that of 'bien culturel maritime' or 'maritime cultural asset', the State's ownership is established in most cases, the coastal State's jurisdiction over cultural maritime resources is extended to the contiguous zone, marine archaeological activities are submitted to administrative controls, and the enforcement of the provisions is realised by penal and administrative sanctions.

1. The Concept of a 'Maritime Cultural Asset'

The easiest way to explore this new concept is to examine the first article (isolated from the other provisions) of Law No. 89-874, which starts by giving the following definition:

Maritime cultural assets comprise deposits, wrecks, remains or in general all assets of prehistoric, archaeological or historical interest, which are situated in the *domaine public maritime* or on the seabed in the contiguous zone.

The maritime cultural asset is defined both *ratione materiae* and *ratione loci*.

1.1 The *ratione materiae* of a maritime cultural asset

1.1.1 Real and personal property, components of a maritime cultural asset: the genesis of a new but non-autonomous concept

While a maritime cultural asset is undoubtedly a new concept, it is not an autonomous one in the sense that its underlying features are based on traditional legal concepts. For example, the legal definition of a maritime wreck has not been modified by Law No. 89-874.[14] Furthermore, the bringing into French territory of a chattel that has not been reported constitutes an infringement of customs legislation, as smuggled goods[15] and, in this, the Ministry of the Exchequer's views prevailed over the Ministry of Culture's opinion that maritime cultural assets, as a new concept, are no longer subject to customs regulations.[16] Under article 19 of Decree No. 91-1226, the customs procedure is still applicable to wrecks, despite the fact that they form an important part of maritime cultural assets.

---

14   According to art. 1 of Decree No. 61-1547 of 26 December 1961 fixing the regime for maritime wrecks (*Journal officiel de la République française*, 12 January 1962, 375-376, hereafter Decree No. 61-1547), the definition of maritime wrecks encompasses: floating material, immobilised ships that are abandoned by their crew, their supplies and their contents, abandoned aircraft, small craft, machines, rigging, anchors, chains, abandoned fishing material, remains of ships and aircraft, jettisoned property. After this enumeration, it is added that, generally speaking, all property, maritime cultural assets excepted (by virtue of art. 20-I of Decree No. 91-1226), is a maritime wreck if the owner has lost physical possession and it is situated on the shores belonging to the *domaine public maritime*, or is floating or extracted from the soil of territorial waters, or is floating or extracted property from the soil in the high seas and brought into territorial waters or into the *domaine public maritime*. If this property is voluntarily abandoned or jettisoned in order to breach customs legislation, it is not deemed a maritime wreck according to this decree: see Y. Tassel 'Droit maritime privé' in P.-J. Hesse, J.-P. Beurier, P. Chaumette, Y. Tassel, A.-H. Mesnard, R. Rezenthel *Droits maritimes*, Vol. I *Mer, navires, et marins*, Les Editions Juris-Service (Paris, 1995) pp. 262 to 267.

15   For a recent case on this matter, see Tribunal correctionnel, Nice, 31 May 1994, *Ministère public c/ E.P., A.A., R.J., E.K., J.-P.M., J.-P.O., M.M., G.H., J.-P.V. et Y.G.*, unreported but confirmed at an appellate level, Cour d'appel, Aix-en-Provence, 26 June 1996, *Ministère public c/ E.P., A.A., R.J., E.K., J.-P.M., J.-P.O., M.M., G.H., J.-P.V. et Y.G.*, unreported.

16   Secrétariat général du gouvernement, *Compte rendu de la réunion interministérielle tenue le 20 décembre 1990 sous la présidence de M. Encreve, Conseiller technique au cabinet du Premier ministre*, Paris, 7 January 1991, pp. 2-3.

While not autonomous, the concept of a maritime cultural asset is certainly a new legal expression. Article 1 of Law No. 89-874 begins by specifying three kinds of maritime cultural asset: deposits, wrecks, and remains and artefacts of prehistoric, archaeological or historical interest. As a whole, the marine cultural heritage is comprised of submerged ports and towns, prehistoric sites, shipwrecks and their contents. The new concept[17] extends therefore to both real property[18] and personal property. This represents progress upon the previous legal framework, which encompassed only wrecks and excluded real property. Under the previous legal regime, only the existence of shipwrecks of artistic, historic or archaeological interest was recognised in French law.[19] While it is true that they represent more than 95 percent of the known marine archaeological heritage,[20] by establishing the concept of maritime cultural asset, government and Parliament clearly intended to expand the scope of the assets to be protected.

After listing these specific assets, Law No. 89-874 indicates "or in general all assets of prehistoric, archaeological or historical interest". The need for such a provision is questionable: were the specified categories not sufficiently exhaustive to cover all components of the marine cultural heritage?

The choice of the attributive adjective 'maritime' is also surprising because these cultural assets are located underwater. In a previous draft, the expression 'undersea cultural asset of archaeological, historical or artistic interest' was used.[21] The reason for the replacement of 'undersea' with 'maritime' can be found in the observations made by the Minister of Defence:

> The Bill relates to assets found in the *domaine public maritime*. The *domaine public maritime* is defined by Law No. 63-1178 of 28th November 1963 and encompasses the bed and subsoil of the territorial sea, future accretions and encroachments, and lands that will be artificially removed by the action of the tide. Consequently, the notion of 'undersea asset' seems to be too restrictive in connection with properties cast ashore by the tide.[22]

It could of course be argued that it is too restrictive to use the notion of maritime cultural asset only for vessels found underwater. Ships that are still afloat, like the *Belem*,[23] are – in a non-

---

17   This illustrates how the protection of cultural heritage is accomplished by complex drafting: M. Lacroix *Le principe de Noé ou l'éthique de la sauvegarde*, Flammarion (Paris, 1997) p. 111.

18   For instance see L. Long 'Olbia, structures antiques immergées' in Ministère de la Culture et de la Communication *Bilan scientifique du Département des recherches archéologiques subaquatiques et sous-marines 1996* (Paris, 1997) p. 91. At the archaeological site 'Olbia', the goal is to study submerged structures damaged by the sea. The purpose of this operation is to identify the geographical extent, the date and the function of these remains, situated near the fortified town founded in 330 B.C. by the Greeks from Marseille.

19   See Chapter V "Wrecks having an archaeological, historical or artistic interest" of Decree No. 61-1547. Chapter V is abrogated by art. 20-II of Decree No. 91-1226.

20   R. Lequément 'Les problèmes législatifs concernant la protection du patrimoine archéologique fluvial et maritime' in *Colloque international Estuaire 92* 'Le patrimoine maritime et fluvial' (Nantes, 1992) p. 276. This percentage is unlikely to be modified even if deepwater archaeology leads to the discovery of various, perhaps very well-preserved, sites: see L. Long 'Archéologie en eaux profondes' in *L'archéologie sous les eaux*, Editions Errance-France Culture, Les éclats du passé (Paris, 1994) pp. 9-20.

21   Projet de loi relatif aux biens culturels sous-marins présentant un intérêt archéologique, historique et artistique, 24 September 1985, p. 1, unreported.

22   P. Quilès *Observations sur le projet de loi relatif aux biens culturels sous-marins*, Annexe à la lettre no. 25 février 1986 - 008539, p. 1, unreported.

23   The *Belem*, a three-masted barque, was launched on 16 June 1896 at the famous shipyard of Dubigeon at Chantenay-sur-Loire, near Nantes. Scheduled as an historical building on 27 February 1984, she is now being used as a training ship: see M. Tholon 'L'histoire du *Belem*' in *Colloque international Estuaire 92* 'Le patrimoine maritime et fluvial' (Nantes, 1992) pp. 199-205 and J. Potel 'Patrimoine maritime – Réflexions sur la sauvegarde de bateaux anciens et la construction de répliques' (1997) 446 *La revue maritime* 113-124 at p. 116.

legal sense – maritime cultural assets because they are a component of the maritime cultural heritage. Why should one have to wait for them to sink and thereby attain the status of a wreck before they can be recognised as a maritime cultural asset? In any event:

It is worth noting that the term 'maritime cultural property' arises directly from the draft European Convention [1985]. Many of the innovations in the new law reflect recommendations and discussions arising from the Council of Europe's activities, demonstrating the influence of the initiative despite the lack of conclusion.[24]

This influence is very real. Council of Europe Recommendation 848 (1978) on the Underwater Cultural Heritage provided that: "[i]ndividual, and apparently isolated, underwater objects should be protected to the same extent as wrecks or sites."[25] Law No. 89-874 does not distinguish, as the previous law had done, between isolated objects and sites. The distinction was dangerous for the integrity of the marine cultural heritage. For example, it was a way of legalising and encouraging the looting of such objects.[26] Furthermore, an isolated object is sometimes the single witness of a site: it may be impossible to find the site after the removal of the object. Consequently:

Reference to 'maritime cultural property' has the effect of giving equal protection to isolated finds. Under the 1961 regime isolated finds had to be recovered and were returned to the finder, while complete wrecks of unknown owner [sic] belonged to the State and could not be touched.[27]

1.1.2 The prehistoric, archaeological or historical interest of a maritime cultural asset

The French definition differs in one respect from Council of Europe Recommendation No. 848. It does not use an age criterion, as was proposed by the Recommendation:

Protection should cover all objects that have been beneath the water for more than 100 years, but with the possibility of discretionary exclusion of less important objects (or of less important antiquities) once they have been properly studied and recorded, and the inclusion of historically or artistically significant objects of more recent date.[28]

In the absence of such a criterion, in what circumstances will an asset be designated as a maritime cultural asset?

A recent decision[29] has provided very useful guidance as to the nature of a maritime cultural asset. To the knowledge of the author it is the first time that the courts have had an opportunity to consider the definition. The facts are simple. Without any administrative authorisation, nine divers removed various objects including ammunition and implements from two shipwrecks, the *François Kléber*, a warship, and the *Saracen*, a cargoship, both lost during

---

24   A. Firth 'Archaeology underwater in France' (1992) 7 *International Journal of Estuarine and Coastal Law* 57-67 at pp. 61-62.
25   *Op. cit.* note 13 at Appendix entitled Minimum legal requirements ii, iii.
26   "Actually, the fact that an isolated object is most of the time given to the finder after an expert's report and recording (art. 25 of Decree No. 61-1547) leads to false declarations: several amphorae removed from an unknown site are reported item by item as isolated objects; that is the usual legalised looting. The Directorate of Marine Archaeological Research is aware of this deception but it is very difficult to fight against it": Beix, *op. cit.* note 8 at p. 11.
27   Firth, *op. cit.* note 24 at p. 60.
28   *Op. cit.* note 13, at Appendix entitled Minimum legal requirements ii, iii. In previous versions, the criterion of age (one century) was used but was removed in the final version of the French bill.
29   Tribunal correctionnel, Brest, 25 October 1994, *Ministère public c/. C. S., M. P., T. W., K. C., C. G., M. C., R. D., M. G. et C. H.*, p. 10, unreported.

World War I. In order to decide if Law No. 89-874 applied, the judges had to determine whether the two wrecks could be designated as maritime cultural assets:

> If the accused allege that these ships, because of the time of their sinking, cannot be designated as maritime cultural assets and since the Law of 1st December 1989 does not give any definition of maritime cultural assets or objects, it should be noted that warships sunk during World War I are patently connected with this definition insofar as they appear as remains of a glorious and tragic event of the history of our country, which it is so keen on. The remains of a cargoship sunk at the same time do not come under the provisions of the Law of 1st December 1989 insofar as it is not proved that the ship was of particular interest from the point of view of the technology used or shipbuilding methods.

The drafting used and the general words employed emphasise that this court had to establish for the first time the meaning of a maritime cultural asset. The decision may prove useful in the future, but the greatest care must be taken in analysing this first instance judgment in the absence of a definitive ruling by a higher court.

According to this first instance decision, the *Kléber* is of historical value[30] and therefore is a maritime cultural asset, whereas the *Saracen* – sunk at the same time and in the same terrible circumstances – is not of historical interest and therefore is not a maritime cultural asset. A distinction is clearly made between wrecks of warships and those of cargoships. It is enough that a warship is a witness of, or participant in, a major event of national history to come within the legal definition of a maritime cultural asset; the date of the sinking does not matter. Consequently, this decision might certainly be extended to all warships sunk during World War I and, probably by the same reasoning, to every warship sunk during World War II. The designation of the wrecks of warships as maritime cultural assets is a way of protecting them in the absence of particular legislation devoted to military remains, as exists for example in the UK.[31] In respect of civil shipwrecks, the time of the sinking is not enough to make them worthy of legal designation. The historical background is clearly not taken into account. On the contrary, civil shipwrecks only become worthy of legal protection insofar as they are useful to increase our knowledge of the human past, for instance, where the study of such shipwrecks is helpful to improve knowledge of naval technology or shipbuilding. According to Brichet, the decision has added to the historical criterion another consideration, which consists of the need for a certain quality, not specified in Law No. 89-874.[32] This is that the vessel must improve our knowledge of shipbuilding and the level of technology.

Instead of adding a supplementary requirement for civil wrecks, not provided by Law No. 89-874, it could have been argued that military wrecks are exempted from the check of historical value because this quality is assumed. The court assumed that any military wreck is a maritime cultural asset; its military status is circumstantial evidence so it is not necessary to prove its historical value. The check of historical value is legally required for civil wrecks because they are not subject to this assumption.

Aside from this single case, before Law No. 89-874 it had been judicially recognised that amphorae were of archaeological interest,[33] and this decision has been recently followed.[34]

---

30   Even before Law No. 89-874, judges admitted the historical value of a shipwreck believed to be the *Magnificent* and looted in French territorial waters, which dated from the end of the eighteenth or the beginning of the nineteenth centuries: see Cour d'appel, Rennes, 10 February 1988, *Ministère public c/ W. G. et K. D.*, p. 5, unreported.

31   See further, ch. 12.

32   R. Brichet, *Fouilles archéologiques*, Editions du Juris-Classeur, Administratif, Fascicule 466, November 1996, No. 111, p. 2.

33   Tribunal correctionnel, Bar-le-Duc, 20 May 1981, *Ministère public c/ Isnard et Decheppe*, unreported.

34   Tribunal correctionnel, Draguignan, 15 May 1997, *Ministère public c/ M. M., J.-P.J. et A.J.*, unreported.

Amphorae also constitute maritime cultural assets. Moreover, the marine *Grotte Cosquer* (at 37 mètres depth) is certainly a maritime cultural asset because of its prehistoric interest and its situation in the *domaine public maritime*.[35]

In comparison with the previous legislation, it is interesting to note that material of artistic interest is excluded from the definition of maritime cultural asset.[36]

It is recognised that "archaeology begins yesterday."[37] Consequently, the term 'archaeological interest' can be used to encompass both prehistoric and historical remains.

However, the *ratione materiae* is not sufficient by itself to classify a maritime cultural asset; the geographical situation is also relevant.

1.2   The *ratione loci* of a maritime cultural asset

Law No. 89-874 is applied in the French metropolitan territory, in the four overseas *départements* (Guadeloupe, Guyane, Martinique and Réunion),[38] in the four overseas *territoires* (Polynésie française, Nouvelle-Calédonie, Iles Wallis et Futuna, Terres australes et antarctiques françaises),[39] in the two *collectivités territoriales* (Saint-Pierre-et-Miquelon[40] and Mayotte[41])

---

35 See N. Calderaro, *Droit du littoral*, Le Moniteur, Collection L'actualité juridique (Paris, 1993) No. 326, p. 309; J. Courtin, J. Clottes, 'Grotte Cosquer: le sanctuaire préhistorique sous-marin du Cap Morgiou à Marseille' *Annales 1996 de l'Institut Méditerranéen des Transports Maritimes* (Marseille, 1996) 275-286.

36 See J. Bérard *Rapport fait au nom de la commission des affaires culturelles du Sénat sur le projet de loi adopté par l'Assemblée Nationale, relatif aux biens culturels maritimes et modifiant la loi du 27 septembre 1941 portant réglementation des fouilles archéologiques*, Sénat, No. 467, Seconde session, 1988/1989, Rattaché pour ordre au procès-verbal de la séance du 4 juillet 1989, p. 7. Like a maritime wreck, a wreck of artistic interest comes under the 1961 legislation and surely must be removed from and kept on land. It may be difficult to determine at first glance if the wreck is of artistic or historical interest. Besides, the two interests can overlap! In the latter case, it would be more cautious to comply with the more restrictive legislation (Law No. 89-874). In any event, this exclusion introduces unnecessary complexity in the reading of the law.

37 J.-P. Jacob in Colloque Lyon devoted to the *Protection pénale du patrimoine archéologique*, L'Hermès (Paris, 1992) p. 93.

38 According to the principle of assimilation, every metropolitan regulation, both statutes (*lois*) and regulations (*règlements*), are directly applicable to these overseas *départements*: see R. Chapus *Droit administratif général* Vol. 1, 11th edn., Montchrestien (Paris, 1997) No. 468, p. 296.

39 Initially, it was provided that the State would put forward conventions for protection and study of the maritime archaeological heritage to be concluded with the overseas *territoires*: J. Lang *Projet de loi relatif aux biens culturels maritimes et modifiant la loi du 27 septembre 1941 portant réglementation des fouilles archéologiques*, Assemblée Nationale, No. 535, Enregistré à la Présidence de l'Assemblée Nationale le 25 janvier 1989, p. 5. No such convention has ever been concluded. Finally, art. 23 of Law No. 89-874 has been modified by art. 17 of Law No. 93-1 of 4 January 1993 for various matters relating to the overseas *départements*, the overseas *territoires* and the *collectivités territoriales* of Mayotte and Saint-Pierre-et-Miquelon, *Journal officiel de la République française*, 5 January 1993, p. 203. Under this modified art. 23, Law No. 89-874 is applicable to the overseas *territoires* and the two *collectivités territoriales*, except for section IV (which consists of modifications to the archaeological system on land in order that the penal provisions are now the same for land and marine archaeology). See also Decree No. 96-661 of 22 July 1996 taken for the application of art. 17 of Law No. 93-1 of 4 January 1993 for various matters relating to the overseas *départements*, the overseas *territoires* and the collectivités territoriales of Mayotte and Saint-Pierre-et-Miquelon, *Journal officiel de la République française*, 27 July 1996, p. 11415.

40 Even if it is a *collectivité territoriale* like Mayotte, the principle is that statutes and decrees are immediately applicable to Saint-Pierre-et-Miquelon without any express provision, unlike Mayotte. For instance see Circular of 21 April 1988 relating to the applicability of legislative texts and regulations overseas, with the consultation of overseas local assemblies and the countersignature of ministers in charge of overseas *départements* and *territoires*, *Journal officiel de la République française*, 24 April 1988, p. 5456.

41 Under art. 23 of Law No. 89-874, "the provisions of the present act shall, with the exception of section IV, apply in the [communauté territoriale] of Mayotte." Words in square brackets excepted, translation: Firth, *op. cit.* note 24 at p. 67. Appropriate provisions are brought by Decree No. 96-661 of 22 July 1996, *Journal officiel de la République française*, 27 July 1996, p. 11415.

established under article 72 of the current Constitution (4th October 1958), in the *Ile de Clipperton*[42] and in the *Iles Eparses* (Bassos da India, Glorieuses, Juan de Novo, Tromelin, Europa).[43]

Assets that comply with material conditions will become maritime cultural assets only if they are situated in the *domaine public maritime* or in the contiguous zone.

1.2.1 Maritime cultural assets situated in the 'domaine public maritime'

Law No. 89-874 applies to any maritime cultural assets situated in the *domaine public maritime*. The concept of '*domaine public maritime*' used to mean the "*rivages de la mer*" or foreshores directly assigned to public use. In addition to the foreshores,[44] nowadays according to Law No. 63-1178 of 28th November 1963, the *domaine public maritime* extends to the bed and subsoil of the territorial waters (twelve miles),[45] accretions and encroachments in the future,[46] and any land artificially protected from the action of the sea under a '*concession d'endigage*' (a grant to dam) provided there is no contrary provision in this grant. Lastly, the *domaine public maritime* can be extended by the addition of 'restricted zones' (from 20 to 50 metres in depth) established on private land bordering the *domaine public maritime* without compensation and in which any construction is forbidden.

Salt ponds have also been included in the *domaine public maritime* since a binding decision of the *Cour de cassation* dated 24th June 1842.[47] Conversely, freshwater ponds do not belong to the *domaine public maritime* and Law No. 89-874 does not apply to them.

According to article 37 of Law No. 86-2 of 3rd January 1986 relating to the development, protection and enhancement of the coast,[48] a zone of 50 geometric feet (81.20 metres from the shore) is established in each of the four overseas *départements* and is also incorporated in the *domaine public maritime*.[49]

In all parts of the *domaine public maritime*, Law No. 89-874 is applicable.[50] However, it

---

42   The *Ile de Clipperton* has been incorporated into the *domaine public* of the State by the Order of 18 March 1986 for the classification of *Ile de Clipperton* in the *domaine public* of the State, *Journal officiel de la République française*, 20 March 1986, p. 4745.

43   F. Jaubert, *Note no. 13031 FC/3 à l'attention de Monsieur le Directeur de la Flotte de Commerce* Paris, 24 January 1989, p. 3. Designated as "*bien de la République*" (which refers to no legal category), French laws are directly applied to the *Iles Eparses*. For a marine archaeological operation in the *Iles Eparses*, see M. L'Hour, F. Richez, G. Bousquet 'Découverte d'un East Indianman de l'E.I.C. à Bassas da India, atoll français de l'océan Indien : le *Sussex* (1738)' (1991) X *Cahiers d'archéologie subaquatique*, 177-198.

44   The foreshores have an accurate definition that results from the *Ordonnance sur la marine* by Colbert (1619-1683) dated August 1681 (Livre IV, Titre VII, article 1): "Shall be deemed seashore and foreshore all land between ebb and flow during full and new moons and up to the highest flow of March." According to the spirit of this text, it should be understood that the limits of foreshores are extended up to the highest water mark in the year (which does not necessarily occur in March) in ordinary weather conditions, thus excepting storms and exceptional tides. This interpretation was given for the first time by Conseil d'Etat, Assemblée, 12 October 1973, *Kreitmann*, Recueil Lebon, p. 563. The case follows the previous judicial analysis applied to any foreshores except in the Mediterranean Sea. This case extends the application and the traditional interpretation of the rule of the *Ordonnance* of 1681 to Mediterranean foreshores, to which was previously applied a rule derived from the Institutes of Justinien that foreshores consist of the bed covered by the highest tide of winter.

45   Since Law No. 71-1060 of 24 December 1971 relating to the delimitation of French territorial waters, *Journal officiel de la République française*, 30 December 1971, p. 12899.

46   The previous accretions and encroachments can be incorporated into the *domaine public maritime* if justified in the general interest by a prefectoral order: R. Chapus *Droit administratif général* Vol. 2, 10th edn., Montchrestien (Paris, 1997) No. 469-2°, p. 371.

47   Cass. crim. 24 June 1842, *S.*, 1842, I, 887: see H. Coulombie, J.-P. Redon *Le droit du littoral*, Litec (Paris, 1992) Nos. 377-384, pp. 252-255.

48   *Journal officiel de la République française*, 4 January 1986, pp. 200-206.

49   See A. de Laubadère, J.-C. Venezia, Y. Gaudemet *Traité de droit administratif*, Vol. 2, 10th edn., L.G.D.J. (Paris, 1995) No. 267, pp. 201-203.

50   See C. Lavialle 'La loi du 1er décembre 1989 relative aux biens culturels maritimes' (1991) No. 8 *Juris-Classeur périodique*, Edition G., I, 3489, p. 65.

"does not apply to material floating on the territorial sea, or to archaeology in non-maritime (i.e. inland) waters."[51] Furthermore, unlike the previous law,[52] this law does not provide for material floating on, or extracted from the soil of, the high seas and brought into territorial waters or into the *domaine public maritime.*

Before the Order of 4th January 1996 for the creation and organisation of the Department of Marine and Underwater Archaeological Research (hereafter referred to as DRASSM), it was difficult to determine whether any maritime cultural asset found in the intertidal zone or in freshwater ponds fell within the jurisdiction of the Directorate of Marine Archaeological Research, the forerunner of DRASSM.[53] It was a matter of conflict between land or freshwater archaeological services and marine ones. By a Note, the Minister of Culture decided that where diving methods were used, the Directorate was the competent authority.[54] Since the Order of 4th January 1996, the jurisdiction of DRASSM has been clarified.[55] This Order uses the opportunity of an administrative reorganisation[56] to define the role to be played. Agents of the Department can intervene on all submerged excavation sites and can be called on for freshwater archaeological investigations.[57] DRASSM has a large part to play in the development of the national archaeological record.[58] Article 2 entrusts the Department particularly with implementing Law No. 89-874 and further texts dealing with its enforcement. Under this article, the Department is responsible for any archaeological research using diving in internal waters, in the *domaine public maritime* and in the contiguous zone.

---

51   Firth, *op. cit.* note 8 at p. 65. The *domaine public maritime* encompasses the soil and the subsoil of the territorial sea but not the water of the territorial sea.

52   Art. 1 of Decree No. 61-1547.

53   An Order of 30 September 1966 created the Directorate of Marine Archaeological Research (*Direction des recherches archéologiques sous-marines*), situated at Marseille, whose jurisdiction extended to all French shores in marine archaeology matters (Order of 30 September 1966 relating to responsibilities for marine archaeological research, *Journal officiel de la République française*, 14 October 1966, p. 9056). It was placed under the Directorate of Historical Antiquities (*Direction des antiquités historiques*), the land archaeological division that was also responsible for marine archaeology. The Directorate of Marine Archaeological Research became the Department of Marine Archaeological Research (*Département des recherches archéologiques sous-marines*), part of the Sub-Directorate of Archaeology (*Sous-Direction de l'Archéologie*), part of the Directorate of Heritage (*Direction du Patrimoine*) of the Ministry of Culture, by virtue of the Order of 14 May 1991 modifying the Order of 11 July 1990 for the organisation of the sub-directorates of the Directorate of Heritage, *Journal officiel de la République française*, 17 May 1991, p. 6684. The Order of 4 January 1996 merged the National Centre for Underwater Archaeological Research (*Centre national de recherches archéologiques subaquatiques*, hereafter referred to as CNRAS) (created by Order of 23 January 1980, *Journal officiel de la République française*, 22 February 1980, p. 3394 and having jurisdiction in inland archaeology) and the Department of Marine Archaeological Research into the Department of Marine and Underwater Archaeological Research (*Département des recherches archéologiques subaquatiques et sous-marines*), which is based, surprisingly, in two places: Annecy (Haute-Savoie) and Marseille (Bouches-du-Rhône): see art. 1 of Order of 4 January 1996 for the creation and organisation of a department of marine and underwater archaeological research, *op. cit.* note 11.

54   Directeur du patrimoine, Note of 10 January 1994 entitled 'archéologie et domaine public maritime', published in Ministère de la Culture, *Bilan scientifique du Département des recherches archéologiques sous-marines 1995* (Paris, 1996) p. 85.

55   For instance, the new administrative organisation will act in places like Mediterranean salt water ponds of protohistorical interest where neither the Centre for Underwater Archaeological Research nor the Department of Marine Archaeological Research previously intervened. Legally, they form part of the *domaine public maritime* but archaeologically the excavations of these sites are the concern of inland archaeology in particular: P. Grandjean *Bilan et orientations de la recherche archéologique* in Ministère de la Culture et de la Communication, *op. cit.* note 18.

56   See note 53.

57   Art. 4 of the Order of 4 January 1996 for the creation and organisation of a department of marine and underwater archaeological research, *op. cit.* note 11.

58   Art. 5 of the Order of 4 January 1996 for the creation and organisation of a department of marine and underwater archaeological research, *op. cit.* note 11.

1.2.2   Maritime cultural assets situated in the contiguous zone

Law No. 89-874 has used the opportunity offered by article 303(2) of the United Nations Convention on the Law of the Sea 1982, which provides for archaeological and historical objects found on the bed of the contiguous zone,[59] to extend French jurisdiction to the contiguous zone.

Chapter II of Law No. 89-874, which is devoted to maritime cultural assets situated in the contiguous zone, comprises two articles, 12 and 13.[60] Article 12 provides that:

> Articles 3, 4, 5, 7, 8, and 9 of the present Act shall apply to maritime cultural property situated in a contiguous zone lying between 12 and 24 nautical miles measured from the baselines of the territorial sea, subject to the provisions of delimitation agreements with neighbouring States.[61]

In other words, the provisions of the Act in respect of the obligation to report a discovery and in respect of administrative control of marine archaeological investigations[62] apply in the contiguous zone. However, the provisions about the ownership of an asset (articles 2, 9, 10 and 11)[63] do not. French law therefore complies with existing international law of the sea which excludes a coastal State's right of ownership over marine cultural heritage and only recognises the coastal State's right to control marine archaeological activities so far as such control is designed to combat traffic in cultural artefacts.

The matter of delimitation is not dealt with by Law No. 89-874. The *Section de l'Intérieur* of the *Conseil d'Etat* would have preferred that the bill that became Law No. 89-874 had specified that delimitation would be based upon the principle of equidistance. It should be indicated that no rule of delimitation of contiguous zones is settled in international law.[64] That is the reason why the Foreign Office did not wish that the future Law No. 89-974 mentioned the principle to be used in any delimitation, which would have restrained French possibilities. Consequently, the *Conseil d'Etat*'s recommendation was not followed in the bill.[65]

2.   Rights Relating to a Maritime Cultural Asset

After providing a definition of maritime cultural asset, Law No. 89-874 specifies the different rights related to it. In particular, it deals with the ownership of a maritime cultural asset and the rules to be complied with by the finder or by marine archaeologists.[66]

2.1   Ownership of a maritime cultural asset

Before Law No. 89-874, Chapter V of Decree No. 61-1547 applied only to wrecks of unknown or unascertainable ownership (article 23). Now, State ownership is established as a matter of

---

59   See A. Strati *The protection of the underwater cultural heritage: an emerging objective of the contemporary law of the sea*, Martinus Nijhoff (The Hague, 1995) pp. 158-214.

60   Art. 13 relates to the possibility of a reward granted to the finder: see section 2.2.1 below.

61   Translation: Firth, *op. cit.* note 24 at p. 65.

62   See further section 2.2 below.

63   See further section 2 below.

64   See Strati, *op. cit.* note 59 at pp. 183-184 and also UNESCO Annexe I 'Rapport de la réunion d'experts sur la protection du patrimoine culturel subaquatique' (Paris, 22-24 May 1996) No. 30, p. 6 in 'Rapport du Directeur général sur les actions prises en vue de déterminer l'opportunité d'élaborer un instrument international sur la protection du patrimoine mondial culturel subaquatique' 29 C/22 (Paris, 5 August 1997).

65   Jaubert, *op. cit.* note 43 at p. 2, unreported.

66   The finder is not automatically the person who will be authorised to conduct a marine archaeological activity, which is why there is a distinction here. But, of course, they may be one and the same.

principle, directly, by inheritance, by default or even by public purchase. The case of private ownership[67] is also provided for.

2.1.1 The principle of State ownership

Article 2 of Law No. 89-874 establishes the State's ownership of a maritime cultural asset in two instances where there is no known owner. First, "[m]aritime cultural assets situated in the [*domaine public maritime*] whose owner cannot be located shall be the property of the State."[68] This will be the case for maritime cultural assets of ancient origin where it will be almost impossible to ascertain the original owner. Secondly:

> Assets whose owner has not been located within three years following the date on which their discovery was made public shall be the property of the State. The manner of making such discovery public shall be established by [decree *en Conseil d'Etat*].[69]

Where a private owner has not been identified within three years,[70] by default the State becomes the owner of the maritime cultural asset. An analogy has recently been drawn by the Minister of Culture in response to a deputy's question:

> It should also be emphasised that the provision under which 'maritime cultural assets situated in the *domaine public maritime* whose owner cannot be located shall be the property of the State' is not without precedent: on land one equivalent can be found in article 713 of the Civil Code which provides that 'any abandoned asset belongs to the State'.[71]

These instances apart, the French State is the owner of maritime cultural assets in 80 percent of cases, either because it has always been the owner (in the case of military and other State vessels) or because it has succeeded through inheritance.[72]

The principle of ownership by the French State may conflict with the claims of foreign States. This difficulty recently arose over a French public wreck situated in foreign territorial waters. The USA has now recognised the rights of ownership of the French State in regard to the shipwreck of *La Belle* recently discovered in Matagorda Bay in Texas.[73] Similarly, the French State has recognised the interest of the USA in the *CSS Alabama* discovered near Cherbourg.[74]

2.1.2 Private ownership of a maritime cultural asset

Where a private owner is located within three years following the date of a discovery, the private ownership is respected. That is why, under article 9 of Law No. 89-874, "[w]here the owner

---

67   As the temporal scope of archaeology is extended, it is more likely that a private owner will exist.
68   Words in square brackets excepted, translation: Firth, *op. cit.* note 24 at p. 64.
69   Words in square brackets excepted, translation: Firth, *ibid.*
70   How the discovery shall be made public is detailed by art. 5 of Decree No. 91-1226.
71   Written questions delivered to the presidency of the National Assembly and response of Ministers, *Journal officiel de la République française*, Assemblée Nationale, (Q.), No. 7, Monday 16 February 1998, p. 841.
72   Beix, *op. cit.* note 8 at p. 23.
73   Written questions delivered to the presidency of the National Assembly and response of Ministers, *Journal officiel de la République française*, Assemblée Nationale, (Q.), No. 12, Monday 23 March 1998, p. 1607.
74   See Decree No. 89-914 of 20 December 1989 for the publication of the arrangement between the Government of the Republic of France and the Government of the United States of America on the subject of the wreck of CSS *Alabama*, signed at Paris on 3 October 1989, *Journal officiel de la République française*, 23 December 1989, pp. 15995-15996. On the wreck of the CSS *Alabama*, see also J. Ashley Roach 'France Concedes United States Has Title to CSS *Alabama*' (1991) 85 *American Journal of International Law* 381-383.

of a maritime cultural asset is known, his written consent shall be obtained before any action is taken with respect to the asset."[75] State control for archaeological purposes is clearly distinguished from matters of ownership.

However, by virtue of article 10:

> When the conservation of a maritime cultural asset is jeopardised, the Minister responsible for culture may take, *ex officio*, after notifying the owner if known, such conservation measures as the situation necessitates.[76]

Emergency situations excepted, the decision is taken by the Minister of Culture upon the advice of the National Council for Archaeological Research.[77]

An even greater interference with private ownership is the possibility, exceptionally, of compulsory purchase by the State.

2.1.3 *State ownership after compulsory purchase*

Since the State is already the owner of 80 percent of maritime cultural assets, only about 20 percent of maritime cultural assets[78] can theoretically come within the ownership of the French State after compulsory purchase. This kind of acquisition is provided for by article 11 of Law No. 89-874 and details can be found in article 16 of Decree No. 91-1226.

This measure introduces a very important and remarkable innovation in French public law and is justified on the basis that it is essential for the satisfactory protection of maritime cultural assets.

As is traditional in matters of public purchase, the procedure is split into two parts, an administrative phase and a judicial one.

The administrative phase differs from the traditional procedure of public purchase. Paragraph 2 of article 16 of Decree No. 91-1226 provides that the Minister of Culture should notify the owner of its intention to purchase the maritime cultural asset and of the proposed level of compensation. This notification amounts to the constitution of a 'dossier of expropriation.' As with the traditional 'dossier', the notification includes useful information with regard to the asset, the intention to purchase and the indemnity offered. In the traditional procedure, a preliminary inquiry ('*enquête préalable*') leads to a proclamation of public interest. In respect of maritime cultural assets, there is no preliminary inquiry before the proclamation of public interest: the nature of this kind of material, notably its great vulnerability, the need for a quick reaction and the unquestionable public interest, explains the procedural difference. Moreover, the lack of a preliminary inquiry is compensated for by the obligation imposed upon the Minister of Culture to afford "the owner an opportunity to submit his comments"[79] within three months. Consequently, the aim of a preliminary inquiry to afford the opportunity for an expression of any views related to the project, is achieved. If the owner agrees to the proposal of the Minister of Culture, it proceeds to an ordinary transfer of property. If the owner disagrees,[80] the proclamation of public interest shall be made by decree *en Conseil d'Etat* after the Minister of Culture has applied for the advice of the National Council for Archaeological Research.[81] The proclamation of public interest may always be disputed before the administrative courts. Thus, an archaeological interest has been recognised as constituting a

75   Translation: Firth, *op. cit.* note 24 at p. 65.
76   Translation: Firth *ibid.*
77   Art. 15 of Decree No. 91-1226.
78   Beix, *op. cit.* note 8 at p. 22.
79   Art. 11 of Law No. 89-874. Translation: Firth, *op. cit.* note 24 at p. 65.
80   In any event, the Ministry of Culture can always refuse a proclamation in the public interest: see Conseil d'Etat, 4 June 1954, *Commune de Thérouanne*, Recueil Lebon, p. 339.
81   Art. 16 of Decree No. 91-1226.

public interest: "The drawbacks caused by the expropriation of lands used for agricultural purposes are not excessive compared to the conservation of these gallo-roman remains."[82] The public archaeological interest clearly prevails over private agricultural interests.

The judicial phase of a compulsory purchase of maritime cultural assets also differs from the judicial phase of the traditional form of expropriation in the public interest: the judge having competence to transfer a maritime cultural asset is not a special judge known as 'a judge of expropriation', but instead is an ordinary judge.[83] The preliminary investigation of a judge of expropriation requires that the court and the various parties involved go to the location of the public purchase: in the case of maritime cultural assets such a visit would presuppose that the judge and the parties know how to dive! For this reason an ordinary judge is competent in the case of the purchase of a maritime cultural asset.

As for all compulsory purchases, the compensation allowed is to be fair and paid in advance of property passing. Since no public purchase of a maritime cultural asset has yet taken place,[84] it is difficult to say exactly how the amount of compensation would be assessed. Would the judge take into account the commercial value of the asset,[85] or would the compensation be based upon its scientific value? If the latter, the judge could use the sum awarded to the finder of the maritime cultural asset, which varies according to the scientific importance of the discovery.[86]

In the case of maritime cultural assets, transfer of ownership is ordered by the judge to whom the matter is referred by the minister, and not the prefect as is usual for traditional public purchase. The matter must be laid before the court within three months after the proclamation of public interest, otherwise the proclamation will be null and void.

In conclusion, the procedure for compulsory purchase of a maritime cultural asset does not appear to be very different from the traditional procedure for compulsory purchase: the differences that do exist are easily explained by the nature of the property purchased and illustrate how a procedure can be adapted to suit its objective.

What is significant is that the compulsory purchase of a maritime cultural asset is a legal innovation in that the traditional principle is that only real property can be so purchased. Since 95 percent of maritime cultural assets are chattels, the compulsory purchase provided for by article 11 of Law No. 89-874 is aimed almost exclusively at chattels, whereas the traditional equivalent to compulsory purchase for chattels is requisition. While the compulsory purchase of a maritime cultural asset may theoretically apply to real property, "that circumstance is nevertheless unlikely."[87]

This is only the second time in French law that public purchase has been applied to personal property. Article 45 of Law No. 68-1 of 2nd January 1968 with the aim of enhancing protection for inventive activities and modifying the regime for patent protection provides that:

---

82   Conseil d'Etat, Section, 29 July 1983, *M. Emily et Comité de défense du théâtre gallo-romain de Kergroas-Ploumeventer*, No. 41.354, unreported.

83   This results from the senatorial amendment no. 6 introduced by Bérard, *op. cit.* note 36 at p. 29.

84   The example given by Bérard only illustrates the situation where expropriation might be used. It concerns "a Neapolitan shipwreck dated from the beginning of the eighteenth century where the shipowner's descendants refuse permission for any scientific study of the wreck and its contents and take no interest in its conservation": Bérard, *ibid.* at p. 28. The Ministry of Culture has confirmed that this procedure has never been employed.

85   See for an example of a (very low) award granted for a prehistoric land grotto called Chauvet, after the finder's name: C. Gallus 'L'Etat s'offre la grotte Chauvet au prix de la garrigue' *Le Monde* 16-17 February 1997, p. 7; P. Gaillard 'La grotte Chauvet au prix de la garrigue!' *Ouest-France* 15-16 February 1997, p. 5; S. Cortembert 'La grotte Chauvet (ou la protection des intérêts financiers de l'Etat sous le couvert de celle d'un site paléolithique)' *Les Petites Affiches*, 7 April 1997, No. 42, pp. 11-12.

86   See further, section 2.2.1 below.

87   Bérard, *op. cit.* note 36 at pp. 27-29. All the more so since only 5 percent of maritime cultural assets consist of real property.

"The State may, at any moment, [...] expropriate, wholly or partly, for the sake of the national defence, the inventions, subjects of application for patents or of patents [...]".[88]

The bill relating to marine cultural assets of archaeological, historical and artistic interest dated 8th January 1986 did not provide for the possibility of public purchase. Instead, it was in a 1988 version that one could read for the first time of an exceptional possibility of purchasing a maritime cultural asset: "At last, the interests of research can justify, in exceptional cases, a declaration in the public interest of State acquisition of a maritime cultural asset."[89]

The government was aware of the legal innovation and took care to indicate that expropriation was a last resort. Its main value lies in its existence, not in its use. It forms a deterrent if a private owner's behaviour threatens the integrity of a maritime cultural asset. The willingness of the government to enact such a deterrent is evidence of the State's keenness to play the role of guardian of this part of the cultural heritage.

The drafting of article 11 of Law No. 89-874 is the same as article 11 of the 1988 bill, except for the senatorial amendment mentioned above.[90] This article and the parliamentary debates provide a useful indication of the requirements in respect of the *ratione loci* and the *ratione materiae* of a maritime cultural asset before it may be subject to compulsory purchase.

According to article 11, compulsory purchase may only occur where the maritime cultural asset is situated in the *domaine public maritime*. That means that it is excluded where the asset is removed from the *domaine public maritime*. It is also excluded where the asset is situated in the contiguous zone or removed from it. According to international law of the sèa, coastal States cannot exercise any right of ownership in such a zone. Authorising public purchase in the contiguous zone would therefore be contrary to international law on this matter.

In the absence of a specific instance, it is necessary to resort to parliamentary debates to obtain some indication of the exceptional circumstances in which a maritime cultural asset can be purchased.

On the one hand, it is said that "[...] this measure is justified in the interest of its conservation or in its scientific exploitation."[91] Two alternative conditions seem to be necessary to legitimise the compulsory purchase. In the first case, a maritime cultural asset can be purchased if it is justified in the interests of conservation. This implies that the integrity of the asset must be threatened so as to make compulsory purchase necessary, whatever the scientific interest of the asset. Nevertheless, if the State is so concerned with conservation that it purchases the asset, one may conclude that it is implied that the asset is valuable; consequently the two alternative conditions actually form only one. In the second case, only maritime cultural assets of special interest can be purchased; it is not necessary that they are threatened. Here the scientific interest is sufficient.

On the other hand, in another extract from the parliamentary debates, it is said that only in cases of "exceptional interest"[92] may the State make a purchase.

Of this, two interpretations may be proposed. Perhaps "exceptional interest" means exceptional scientific interest only, covering anything of exceptional archaeological or historical

---

88   Law No. 68-1 of 2 January 1968 with the aim of enhancing protection for inventive activities and modifying the regime for patent protection, *Journal officiel de la République française*, 3 January 1968, p. 18. Before Law No. 68-1, this kind of expropriation was provided for by Decree of 30 October 1935 but had never been used: see R. Plaisant 'La loi du 2 janvier 1968 sur les brevets d'invention et ses textes d'application' (1969) *Dalloz*, Chronique XVI, No. 262, p. 134.

89   Ministère de la culture, de la communication, des grands travaux et du bicentenaire, *Projet de loi relatif aux biens culturels maritimes et modifiant la loi du 27 septembre 1941 portant réglementation des fouilles archéologiques, Exposé des motifs*, NOR : MCCX8800164L/B1/PP, p. 3, unreported.

90   It is this single amendment to art. 11 that shows that the measure has been accepted both by the *Assemblée Nationale* and *Sénat*.

91   Bérard, *op. cit.* note 36 at p. 12.

92   R. Beix, Débats parlementaires-Compte rendu, Assemblée Nationale, Séance du 23 novembre 1989, *Journal officiel de la République française*, p. 5566.

interest. This reminds one of the exceptional scientific interest required for the allocation of a maximum amount of reward to a finder.[93] Taking this interpretation, the proportion of maritime cultural assets which could potentially be purchased would be very low. According to this first interpretation, the private owner's attitude is not taken into account. The second interpretation is even more restrictive: it seems to confirm that the spirit of the text reduces the scope of the material that will fall within the measure in order to minimise the interference with private ownership as much as possible and to legitimise it; that is why this interpretation, being in effect the most restrictive, should be accepted. It adds another condition in connection with the private owner's behaviour: he must put the asset in danger. This analysis is based upon the following parliamentary assertion: the State may purchase a maritime cultural asset "insofar as the owner is known, but in default, and this expropriation is justified by the interest either for conservation or for exploitation."[94] This sentence summarises the two cases where the public purchase of a maritime cultural asset may be possible. Two cumulative conditions should be required: the private owner is in default and an asset of exceptional interest deserves to be protected against him in the public interest.

2.2   Administrative controls from discovery to marine archaeological investigations

Whoever the owner may be, private or public, Law No. 89-874:

sets minimum standards for treatment of material irrespective of ownership, so that archaeological control is consistent, and important finds which have known owners are not lost to archaeological study. This seems to reflect the extension of interest from classical sites, owned by old Romans, to include post-medieval and modern remains. Later sites have proved to be of great importance and require the same degree of management [...].[95]

The obligations imposed on the finder and the individual authorised to conduct any marine archaeological investigation illustrate this.

2.2.1 The obligations of the finder and the possibility of a reward
        Article 3 of Law No. 89-874 describes the conduct to be followed after the discovery[96] of a maritime cultural asset:[97]

Any person discovering a maritime cultural asset shall leave it *in situ* and shall not cause damage to it.
Such person shall, within 48 hours of the discovery or of arrival at the first port, report the asset to the Administrative Authority.[98]

The relevant administrative authority is the Maritime Affairs Administration responsible for the district (*quartier*), or the nearest Maritime Affairs Service of the place of the discovery or the first

---

93   See section 2.2.1 below.
94   J. Bérard, Débats parlementaires, Compte rendu, Sénat, Séance du 19 octobre 1989, *Journal officiel de la République française*, p. 2651. As above, we can speculate whether the second condition is really split into two different situations. They may relate to the same situation.
95   Firth, *op. cit.* note 24 at p. 61.
96   For instance, in 1996 26 sites and 22 isolated objects were reported to the Maritime Affairs Administration. For details, see Ministère de la Culture et de la Communication, *op. cit.* note 18 at p. 132.
97   Generally speaking, all maritime wrecks shall be reported within the same time-limit to the same administrative authority: see art. 2 of Decree No. 61-1547.
98   Translation: Firth, *op. cit.* note 24 at p. 64.

port of arrival.[99] According to article 5, "[w]here an asset is reported more than once, the credit for its discovery shall go to the first person to report it."[100]

The accidental removal of a maritime cultural asset from the *domaine public maritime*[101] or the contiguous zone[102] is also provided for: even in such circumstances, the asset shall be reported to the Maritime Affairs Administration within 48 hours and shall be deposited with it within 48 hours or shall be kept at its disposal. The intention is to make it clear that the finder of an asset discovered by chance as a result of works, or any other public or private activity, is not its owner.

This obligation to report a find is enforced by penal provisions.[103] Under article 14 of Law No. 89-874:

> Any person failing to comply with the reporting obligations provided for in articles 3, paragraph 2, and 4 of the present Act shall be liable to a fine of from 500 francs to 15,000 francs. The same penalties shall apply to any person making a false declaration to the public authority regarding the place and composition of the deposit where the object reported was discovered.[104]

To the knowledge of the author, these provisions have never been applied by themselves since, most of the time, an infringement is not isolated.[105]

> In any event, generally speaking, the maximum fine of 15,000 francs does not seem proportionate compared to penalties provided for more serious infringements (i.e. illegal purchase or clandestine excavations) which only go up to 50,000 francs. It would have been worth harmonising penal provisions as a whole according to the seriousness of damage to the heritage. Indeed, the failure to report is reprehensible, but it is less dangerous for the heritage than is clandestinely discovering and interfering with a site.[106]

Under article 3 of Law No. 89-874, any finder of a maritime cultural asset shall leave it *in situ* and not damage it. This rule breaks with the spirit of salvage in the previous legislation which provided that the material should be removed and put in a safe place (article 2 of Decree No. 61-1547). This was diametrically opposed to the archaeological principle under which the best way to care for a maritime cultural asset is to keep it *in situ*. Moreover the context of a maritime cultural asset is very important for an archaeological study.

Lastly, under article 16 of Law No. 89-874, the finder, like any other person:

> who knowingly sells or buys a maritime cultural asset removed from the [*domaine public maritime*] or from the sea-bed in the contiguous zone in violation of the provisions of articles 3, 4, 7 and 8 of the present Act shall be liable to imprisonment for from one month to two years and to a fine of from 500 francs to 30,000 francs, or to one of these two penalties alone. The amount of the fine may be raised to double the price for which the asset was sold. The authority having jurisdiction may in addition order publication of its decision in the press at the expense of the convicted person, the maximum cost of such publication not to exceed the amount of the fine incurred.[107]

---

99   Art. 1 of Decree No. 91-1226.
100   Translation: Firth, *op. cit.* note 24 at p. 64.
101   Art. 4 of Law No. 89-874.
102   Art. 12 of Law No. 89-874.
103   See also section 2.2.2 below.
104   Translation: Firth, *op. cit.* note 24 at p. 66.
105   In a recent case, three persons were charged with destruction of archaeological remains and non-reporting to the Maritime Affairs Administration. They were given a suspended sentence of six months' imprisonment and fined 40,000 francs: Tribunal correctionnel, Draguignan, 16 May 1997, *Ministère public c/ M.M., G.H., J.-P.J. et A.J.*, p. 7, unreported.
106   C. Rigambert *Le droit de l'archéologie française* Picard (Paris, 1996) p. 117.
107   Words in square brackets excepted, translation: Firth, *op. cit.* note 24 at p. 66.

Provided a finder complies with the obligations laid down, a reward may be granted to him wherever the maritime cultural asset is situated, in the *domaine public maritime*[108] or in the contiguous zone.[109] Nonetheless, the granting of a reward is a possibility, not a right. The Minister of Culture has a discretionary power to allocate a reward to the finder. There are two kinds of reward. The finder can indicate in the application which he wishes; the Minister of Culture will attempt to comply with such a request, but is not obliged to do so.

Two conditions are required in both circumstances: the person must have discovered the maritime cultural asset, and must have reported it.

First, a reward will be awarded to a finder who has properly reported the maritime cultural asset discovered. Either *in specie* or in kind, the value of the reward varies according to the scientific interest of the asset reported, but it must not exceed: 10,000 francs for an asset of great interest, 50,000 francs for an asset of superior interest, and 200,000 francs for an asset of exceptional interest.[110] The amount is determined by the Minister of Culture upon the advice of the National Council for Archaeological Research.[111] If, subsequently, the scientific interest of the discovery is proved to be greater than the first evaluation, the State can increase the amount awarded.

Secondly, the reward can take the form of custody of the asset while property remains with the State. A contract is concluded which provides for the circumstances and conditions of the custody and an indelible mark is used to evidence the State's ownership. This kind of reward would have the advantage of avoiding storage of numerous and similar valueless maritime cultural assets (i.e. amphorae) at DRASSM. Besides, the finder would certainly be delighted to care for it.

About 30 applications are currently being considered by DRASSM and have been submitted for advice to the National Council for Archaeological Research.[112] All the applications concern a reward *in specie*.

---

108   Art. 6 of Law No. 89-874: "Any person discovering and reporting a maritime cultural asset ownership of which is assigned to the State under the provisions of article 2 shall be entitled to a reward of a kind or in amount to be determined by the Administrative Authority." Under art. 6, which refers explicitly to art. 2 in connection with the State's ownership, it is noteworthy to highlight that no reward can be allocated to a finder when the State becomes the owner of the property after a public purchase provided for by art. 11 of Law No. 89-874. Under the previous legislation (art. 25 of Decree No. 61-1547), the salvor could have become the owner of an isolated object. Otherwise if the object was put into a public collection because of its interest, the salvor was entitled to an award. In the case of a wreck that constituted an archaeological site, a 'contract of *concession*' was concluded between the State and the finder, or any other competent person that provided the award. Where the finder did not get a '*concession*', or if the State directly removed the wreck, the finder was entitled to an award under art. 27 of Decree No. 61-1547. Compared to the previous legislation, the term 'reward' replaced the term 'compensation' which was linked to a salvage operation.

109   Art. 13 of Law No. 89-874. Only a reward *in specie* can be granted to the finder.

110   It is interesting to compare these figures with an evaluation from the parliamentary debates. For the instances given, the reward was inferior to the real value. Beix has suggested rewards of 1,000 francs for amphora (real worth about 10,000 francs) and between 20,000 to 50,000 francs for wreck sites: Beix, *op. cit.* note 8 p. 28. It is important that the reward is not too far from the real market value if Law No. 89-874 is to meet its aim: it is a way of deterring looters from selling maritime cultural assets. This may explain why rewards provided in the Order of 8 February 1996 relating to maritime cultural assets (*op. cit.* note 12) are higher and so much closer to the real value.

111   Art. 4 of Decree No. 91-1226 specifies the competent administrative authority and this has not been changed by Decree No. 97-1200.

112   Art. 1 of the Order of 8 February 1996 relating to maritime cultural assets, *op. cit.* note 12. Especially the Commission for Marine Excavation (*Commission des fouilles sous-marines*) of the National Council for Archaeological Research, established by art. 13 of Decree No. 94-423 of 27 May 1994 for the creation of consultative organs in matters of national archaeology, *Journal officiel de la République française*, 29 May 1994, p. 7766. By virtue of art. 1 of Decree No. 94-423, the National Council for Archaeological Research has replaced the Superior Council for Archaeological Research established by art. 1 of Decree No. 64-357 of 23 April 1964 relating to the superior council for archaeological research, *Journal officiel de la République française*, 25 April 1964, p. 3668: see Rigambert, *op. cit.* note 106 at p. 37.

In any event, the practical application of this Order depends upon:

> [t]he existence of enough funds to finance the payment of rewards resulting from reports ... Besides, there are not enough human resources ... to provide a prompt response to all the applications. The take-up implies slow and painstaking work."[113]

Two views exist regarding the level of rewards: DRASSM sees the granting of a reward as an opportunity to thank the finder for his contribution to the marine cultural heritage and therefore considers that the amount of the reward need not *necessarily* be based upon the single scientific value of the discovery; by contrast, the National Council for Archaeological Research adopts a more restrictive approach according to the real scientific value of the find.

2.2.2 Administrative control of marine archaeological investigations

Once a maritime cultural asset has been reported, any marine archaeological activities in respect of it are subject to several administrative controls.

First, because the investigations take place underwater, all persons must comply with professional diving regulations.[114] It was questioned whether these regulations were applicable to amateur archaeologists[115] on the basis that the obligations imposed on professionals were not appropriate to amateurs. The Minister of Culture has replied that a compromise needed to be reached between the interests of safety and the need for more appropriate regulation.[116]

Secondly, any plan to interfere with a maritime cultural asset must obtain several administrative authorisations prior to its implementation:[117]

> No one may engage in surveying using specialised equipment for determining the location of a maritime cultural asset, or carry out excavations or drilling, without obtaining prior administrative authorisation granted in the light of the applicant's qualifications and of the type and methods of the search.
> Any removal of an asset, or of samples from it, shall be subject to the granting of prior administrative authorisation under the same terms.
> The Administrative Authority may also conclude with individuals licensed for the purpose contracts to search for maritime cultural assets, remove them or remove samples therefrom.[118]

---

113 Grandjean, *op. cit.* note 55. (In 1996, for freshwater and saltwater archaeology as a whole, there were 21 employees and four persons were working for the archaeological record: see Ministère de la Culture et de la Communication, *op. cit.* note 18 at p. 133.) According to the Minister of Culture during the adoption of Law No. 89-874, "the amount of a reward would be charged to a budgetary division of the Ministry of Culture's estimates (chapter 43-20 "monumental heritage-subsidies"). From an estimation based upon annual reports of sites and isolated objects, 500,000 francs would be necessary for a fiscal year": Lang, *op. cit.* note 39 at p. 4.

114 Decree No. 90-277 of 28 March 1990 relating to the protection of workers intervening in a hyperbaric environment, *Journal officiel de la République française*, 29 March 1990, pp. 3826-3830; Order of 28 January 1991 defining the form of security for personnel working in a hyperbaric environment, *Journal officiel de la République française*, 2 March 1991, pp. 3020-3025; Order of 15 May 1992 defining the procedures for entering, staying in and leaving, and for the organisation of work in, a hyperbaric environment, *Journal officiel de la République française*, 26 June 1992, pp. 8413-8416.

115 See R. Brichet *Fouilles archéologiques*, Editions du Juris-Classeur, Administratif, Fascicule 466, August 1995, No. 98, p. 16.

116 Two texts have tried to translate this intention: Order of 5 March 1993 modifying and complementing the Order of 28 January 1991 defining the form of security of personnel undertaking underwater operations, *Journal officiel de la République française*, 17 March 1993, p. 4149 and Order of 18 December 1994 modifying the Order of 28 January 1991 defining the form of security for personnel intervening in underwater operations, *Journal officiel de la République française*, 27 December 1994, p. 18435.

117 Law No. 89-874 has simply codified a previous and well-established practice.

118 Art. 7 of Law No. 89-874. Translation: Firth, *op. cit.* note 24 at p. 65. The administrative authority is the Minister of Culture: see Decree No. 97-1200 of 19 December 1997 taken for the application to the minister in charge of culture and of communication of art. 2-1° of Decree No. 97-34 of 15 January 1997 relating to the decentralisation ('*déconcentration*') of individual administrative decisions, *Journal officiel de la République française*, 27 December 1997, pp. 46062 DAI-46065 DAI (hereafter Decree No. 97-1200).

To the knowledge of the author, no such contract[119] has ever been concluded; consequently, any marine archaeological investigations taking place depend only upon several unilateral administrative acts.

Administrative authorisations[120] are only granted to individuals as a result of their competence to lead a marine archaeological investigation. For that reason account is taken of their previous experience, funds, equipment and the goals of the search. Activities must be undertaken under the direction of the authorised person, who is solely responsible for the operations.[121] In 1996, eight out of thirteen authorisations were granted to amateurs.[122] This emphasises the great contribution of amateurs to French marine archaeology: it "appears essentially to be a voluntary archaeology."[123] Co-operation between volunteers and professionals is certainly the best way to fight against looting and increase our knowledge of the past.[124] This behaviour is officially recognised by article 3 of the Order of 4th January 1996. DRASSM gives advice and guidance in respect of any marine archaeological activity, notably information about the treatment of material or any documentary information, and participates, sometimes directly, or by contribution, to the training of archaeological divers.[125]

Where a maritime cultural asset belongs to a private owner, his written consent is required before there is any interference with the asset.[126]

According to article 11 of Decree No. 91-1226, any authorisation may be withdrawn in two cases by Order of the Minister of Culture,[127] upon the binding advice of the National Council for Archaeological Research.[128] The reasons for the withdrawal must be stated. In the first case, withdrawal occurs where conditions imposed for search are seriously or repeatedly breached. The withdrawal constitutes an administrative sanction. The victim of the withdrawal cannot claim any compensation. However he or she is entitled to recover costs in respect of works and installations that shall be used by the State to pursue excavations.[129] In the second case, withdrawal may arise

---

119   Under previous legislation, only two contracts were concluded, relating to the wreck *la Tour Sainte Marie* (Corse) in 1969-1970 and the wreck *Lavezzi 1* (Bouches de Bonifacio) in 1972. In any event, legally, conclusion of such contracts on policy matters may be questioned: see Chapus, *op. cit.* note 38 at No. 666, p. 448 and No. 901, p. 624.

120   Under art. 7 of Decree No. 91-1226, drillings and surveys are authorised by the Minister of Culture for a one month period. Excavations and removal of assets, or of samples of assets, are authorised by the Minister of Culture upon the advice of the National Council for Archaeological Research. The grant of authorisations is in the Minister's hands and is not given to a prefect: see Decree No. 97-1200. Thanks to each authorisation, the State can control different steps of the archaeological investigation. For more details about prior administrative authorisation where specialised equipment is used to find historical, artistic or archaeological objects or monuments, see Law No. 89-900 of 18 December 1989 relating to the use of metal detectors, *Journal officiel de la République française*, 19 December 1989, p. 15739, and Decree No. 91-787 of 19 August 1991 taken for the application of art. 4 *bis* of Law No. 80-532 of 15 July 1980 relating to the protection of public collections against malicious acts and of Law No. 89-900 of 18 December 1989 relating to the use of metal detectors, *Journal officiel de la République française*, 20 August 1991, p. 10959.

121   Art. 8 of Law No. 89-874.

122   Ministère de la Culture et de la Communication, *op. cit.* note 18 p. 51.

123   Grandjean, *op. cit.* note 55.

124   J.-P. Beurier 'Pour un droit international de l'archéologie sous-marine' (1989) 1 *Revue générale de droit international public* 68.

125   Art. 3 of Order of 4 January 1996 for the creation and organisation of a department of marine and underwater archaeological research, *op. cit.* note 11.

126   Art. 9 of Law No. 89-874. According to art. 14 of Decree No. 91-1226, any authorisation is null and void where the private owner withdraws his consent: see 2.1.2 above.

127   This administrative authority has not been transferred by Decree No. 97-1200.

128   "The withdrawal of any authorisation granted is decided by Order of the Ministry of Culture which is compelled to give its reasons and to follow the advice of the Superior Council for Archaeological Research" (which has been replaced by the National Council for Archaeological Research).

129   Art. 13 para. 1 of Decree No. 91-1226.

where the importance of a discovery is so great that the State wishes to proceed directly, or purchases the maritime cultural asset. Within three months, the victim of the withdrawal is entitled to the redemption of expenses directly incurred for any works carried out. He or she can also claim a special compensation: the methods of payment result from an Order taken by the Minister of Culture and the Minister of Exchequer upon the advice of the National Council for Archaeological Research.[130]

Within an unspecified period, the works authorised and undertaken under the control of the Minister of Culture shall be reported, and in particular an inventory of discovered objects shall be drawn up.[131]

Criminal penalties[132] are provided to enforce the principle of prior administrative authorisation. Under article 15 of Law No. 89-874:

> Any person conducting surveying, drilling, sampling or excavations of maritime cultural assets or effecting the removal of such assets or of samples from them in violation of the provisions of articles 3 (paragraph 1), 7 and 8 of the present Act shall be liable to a fine of from 1,000 francs to 50,000 francs.

Nine divers have been charged with unauthorised removal of objects, ammunition and various implements in French territorial waters and each was given a suspended fine of 5,000 francs.[133] It should be noticed that the amount of fine was not high compared to the legal limits. Moreover, it was only a suspended fine. In these matters, where it is very difficult to arrest looters[134] and therefore precedents are not numerous, each case should be exemplary in order to act as a deterrence.

---

130   Art. 13 paras. 2 and 3 of Decree No. 91-1226.
131   Art. 10 of Decree No. 91-1226: see Rigambert, *op. cit.* note 106 at pp. 135-144.
132   Generally speaking, a strengthening of criminal penalties results from Law No. 89-874 relative to penalties provided by art. 32 of Decree No. 61-1547 (*contravention de 4e classe*, first level of criminal offence); art. 32 has been abrogated by art. 20-II of Decree No. 91-1226. As a whole, infringements constitute the second level (*délit*) of seriousness out of three possible levels of criminal offence.
133   Tribunal correctionnel, Brest, 25 October 1994, *Ministère public c/ C.S., M.P., T.W., K.C., C.G., M.C., R.D., M.G. et C.H.*, unreported.
134   The difficult nature of the fight against looting is shown by the long list of persons who can lead investigations: "Violations of the present Act shall be investigated and verified by officers and constables of the criminal investigation department, deputy constables of the criminal investigation department, administrators of maritime affairs, officers in the technical and administrative corps for maritime affairs, customs officials, agents of the Minister responsible for culture specially sworn and commissioned for the purpose under terms established by [Decree *en Conseil d'Etat*], officers and petty officers commanding vessels of the national navy, inspectors of maritime affairs, fishery facility inspection technicians, coast signalmen, representatives of the seamen's registry and in addition, in the ports, port officers and deputy port officers": words in square brackets excepted, translation: Firth, *op. cit.* note 24 at p. 66. This list of persons has been very slightly modified by art. 21 of Law No. 96-151 of 26 February 1996 relating to transport, *Journal officiel de la République française*, 27 February 1996, p. 3098. The terms "inspectors of maritime affairs" and "agents on the board of maritime affairs responsible for aid and supervision" are added; "officers and petty officers commanding vessels of the national navy" are replaced by "the captain, first officers or first officials of vessels of the national navy". Even any approved associations involved in the study and protection of the marine archaeological heritage may prosecute as a plaintiff claiming damages: see art. 5 of Law No. 89-900 and Decree No. 91-787. To date, no such association has applied for the approval required. Lastly, arts. 18 and 19 of Law No. 89-874 respectively deal with the higher probatory value of statements reserved compared to the probatory value of common statements, and competent tribunals to hear any cases involving violations of the provisions of Law No. 89-874. Nevertheless, it should be recognised that the task seems to be impossible: in respect of Mediterranean sites, less than ten percent of 650 sites have ever been visited: see G. Porte 'Trois ans de prison sont requis contre le conservateur du Musée d'Antibes' *Le Monde*, 14 April 1994, p. 13.

Conclusion

With the enactment of Law No. 89-874, France has taken up the challenge to "go into the twenty-first century on more than a slightly modified"[135] regulation. The State has clearly assumed responsibility wholeheartedly for this part of the French cultural heritage. As a whole, based upon co-operation between amateurs and professionals, the legislation is appropriate and well-balanced for the protection of the underwater cultural heritage. It simply needs to be enforced.

---

135   M.V. Williams 'A Legal History of Shipwreck in England' (1996) XV*Annuaire de droit maritime et océanique* Nantes, p. 92.

Chapter 4

GREECE

Anastasia Strati

1. Introduction

Greece, one of the most archaeologically-rich nations in the world, with its 15,021 km coastline and numerous scattered islands, has a particular interest in protecting its underwater heritage. The waters around Greece are full of cultural remains: submerged coastal sites and shipwrecks of all kinds – ancient and modern, prehistoric and historic. The first evidence of seafaring comes from the Mesolithic strata of Francthi Cave in Argolid in the Peloponnese (c. 9,000 B.C.), which contained obsidian tools originating from the island of Melos. The Minoan civilisation was well-known for its trading with Egypt and the eastern Mediterranean, whilst the voyages of the Myceneans throughout the eastern Mediterranean are echoed in the heroic epics of Homer and the tale of the Argonauts. Moving into the historic period of Greece (c. 1,100 B.C.), early writings and archaeological finds show Greek civilisation and colonies spreading throughout the Mediterranean via *penteconters* (oared galleys with fifty rowers), which gave way to the *triremes* of classical Greece. The centuries that followed produced a series of cultures in Greece: Roman, Byzantine, Venetian, Ottoman and others, often in conflict with each other, which left a 'rich tapestry' of archaeological material on the seabed.[1]

Many statues and other 'treasures' of great artistic value were found on the seabed around the coasts of Greece, together with innumerable pieces of pottery, coins, jewels, and instruments in metal or wood. A few examples of such discoveries are the *Poseidon of Kreusis* (Gulf of Corinth,1889), the *Boy of Marathon* (1925), the famous *Poseidon (or Zeus) of Artemision,* the *Jockey Boy* (off Cape Artemision, 1928), the *Venus of Rhodos*, *Augustus* and recently the *'Beauty' of Kalymnos* (1994), a bronze statue of a woman found near the island of Kalymnos. Most of these masterpieces were found accidentally by Greek fishermen and sponge divers and are now displayed in museums around the country.

The first systematic underwater survey was carried out (although unsuccessfully due to technical difficulties) in 1881 off the island of Salamis in an attempt to locate the remains of the famous naval battle of 480 B.C. Another famous early excavation was that of the 'Antikythera Wreck', which was discovered by sponge divers in 1900 and produced remarkable bronze and marble statues, such as the *Youth of Antikythera,* as well as the only truly scientific instrument surviving from classical times, the famous *Astrolabe.* [2]

The invention of the aqualung in 1943 constituted an important landmark in the development of marine archaeology, since it offered archaeologists the opportunity to investigate underwater sites by themselves. After World War II several expeditions were undertaken by Greek or foreign scientists at, for example, the ancient site of Pheia in the Peloponnese, the two ancient harbours of Corinth, Cenchreai and Lechaeum, the Early Bronze Age Settlement of Pavlopetri in the southern Peloponnese, and the ancient harbour of Haliea in the northeastern

---

1   C. Agouridis 'Greece' in J.P. Delgado, ed., *British Museum Encyclopaedia of Underwater and Maritime Archaeology* (1997) pp. 180-183 at p. 180.

2   The expedition, which constituted the first rescue excavation under the authority of the Greek State and was carried out by sponge divers, left one diver dead and two paralysed: Agouridis, *ibid.*, p. 181. See also W. Bascom 'Deep Water Archaeology' (1972) 174 *Science* 261-269 at 262.

Peloponnese. In the 1960s, Peter Thockmorton investigated sites such as Methoni, Porto Logo and Sapienza, whilst the 1970s were years of intensive archaeological activity underwater. One should specifically mention the rescue excavation of a Byzantine wreck near Pelagos Island, necessitated by its looting and the appearance of ceramics plundered from it in foreign museums, and the investigation by Cousteau of Cape Artemision, Navarino Bay and the 'Antikythera Wreck'.[3] During this period two important scientific institutions were established: a private, non profit-making organisation, the Hellenic Institute of Marine Archaeology (1973), and a governmental agency, the Department (Ephoria) of Underwater Antiquities (Ministry of Culture, 1976).

Since the 1980s, the Department of Underwater Antiquities has engaged in many underwater surveys and excavations, occasionally in co-operation with foreign archaeological institutions. Such projects include the investigation of the ancient harbours of Samos, Naxos and Thassos, and the excavations of the Early Bronze Age settlement of *Platygiali* in western Greece, the wreck of Louis XIV's flagship *La Terese* off Crete, and a post-Byzantine wreck off the island of Zakynthos. Special reference should also be made to the excavation of a fifth century B.C. wreck near the island of Allonesos with a capacity of over 100 tonnes and a cargo of three to four thousand *amphorae*.

Similarly, the Hellenic Institute of Marine Archaeology has undertaken three full-scale projects: the excavation of a site at the island of Dokos (which comprises an impressive concentration of pottery sherds, part of the cargo of an Early Helladic II ship, the earliest known wreck, dated c. 2,150-2,200 B.C.); the excavation of a wreck at Point Iria in the Gulf of Argolid, whose pottery assemblage dates to 1,200 B.C. and comes from three different areas, Crete, Cyprus and mainland Greece; and most recently an excavation of a fourth century B.C. shipwreck near the island of Kythera.[4] It has also undertaken numerous small-scale projects, such as the rescue excavation of an Early Roman amphora wreck near the village Limeni in the Peloponnese and the investigation of the shipwreck of *Mentor*, Lord Elgin's ship, which was lost whilst transporting the Parthenon marbles and other antiquities out of the country.

In summary, Greek waters contain rich cultural resources offering unique possibilities for historical studies.[5] However, the growing interest of treasure-seekers, the development of advanced technology and methods of exploring the seabed, and the difficulties of policing the extensive coasts of the country, expose underwater remains to systematic looting. Unless effective measures of protection are taken, deep-water archaeological sites will be subjected to the same fate as many wrecks in shallow water: they will be looted.

2.   Early Developments

Since its independence in 1830,[6] Greece has enacted legislation for the protection of its cultural heritage, including underwater remains. The first legal measures for the protection of

---

3   Agouridis, *op. cit.* note 1.
4   *Ibid.* at pp. 182-183 and 190.
5   According to Bascom, nearly any B.C. wreck will contain new information about the life and times when it sailed, whilst Bass argues that answers to questions in the narrow field of Greek prehistory alone will be startling: see W. Bascom *Deep Water, Ancient Ships: the Treasure Vault of the Mediterranean* (David and Charles, 1976) at p. 7 and G.G. Bass, *Archaeology Under Water: Ancient Peoples and Places* (1966) at p. 165.
6   For the protection of antiquities during the War of Independence (1821-1829), see *inter alia*, A. Kokkou, *The care of antiquities in Greece and the first museums* (1977); V.Ch. Petrakos *Treatise on the Archaeological Legislation* (1982) (in Greek); A.P. Pantos 'Greece and the Greek legislation about antiquities' in *Atti dei Convegni Lincei 93, Convegno Internazionale sul tema: Eredita contestata?*, Roma, 29-30 April 1991 (1992) pp. 59-74; and N. Zias 'Archaeological heritage: the Greek experience' in *Archaeological Heritage: Current Trends in its Legal Protection* Studies 5, Institute of Hellenic Constitutional History and Constitutional Law (P. Sakkoulas Bros. Publishers, 1995) pp. 81-86.

antiquities in the modern Greek State were adopted by Law 10/22 of May 1834 "on scientific and technological collections, on the discovery and preservation of antiquities and their use".[7] According to article 61 of Law 10/22 of May 1834, "all antiquities in Greece, being the creative work of the ancestors of the Greek people, are regarded as national possessions of all Greeks in general". However, the law distinguished between antiquities lying on, or beneath, public land, or on the bottom of the sea, in rivers or public streams, in lakes or marshes, which belonged to the State (article 62), and antiquities lying on private land which were co-owned by the respective landowner and the State (articles 63 and 64). All antiquities were required to be declared to the competent authorities, whilst their export was prohibited. Concerning excavations, there was provision for granting permits since the newly established Greek State did not possess the means to undertake such activities. For the purposes of Law 10/22 of May 1834, "apart from works of sculpture and architecture, blocks of hewn marble or stones of any shape, paintings, mosaics, pottery, weapons, jewellery and other metal or clay objects, precious stones, coins and inscriptions of all kinds are regarded as antiquities" (article 110). However, as specifically stated, "objects of art dating from the earliest times of Christianity or the so-called Middle Ages" were not excluded from its scope (article 111). Finally, the Law 10/22 of May 1834 incorporated important provisions on administrative issues by setting up an archaeological service, responsible for the investigation, supervision and protection of antiquities, as well as providing for the establishment of museums and institutions encompassing a broad range of scientific activities.

The Law 10/22 of May 1834 was replaced 65 years later by Law 2646 of 24th July 1899 'on antiquities'.[8] The most important innovation concerned rights of ownership. Under article 1 of Law 2646 of 1899, "all antiquities, whether movable or immovable, from ancient or subsequent times found in Greece and any national possessions, in rivers, lakes and on the bottom of the sea, and on public, monastic and private land, belong to the State". A more precise and comprehensive definition of antiquities was provided in article 3,[9] whilst the obligation to declare all (now State-owned) antiquities was preserved. Many of the provisions of this Law remain unchanged to this day.

The adoption of the Law of 1899 was followed by the enactment of a number of legislative acts dealing with different aspects of the protection of antiquities, such as Law 491/1914, Law 2447/1920, Legislative Decree of 12/16.6.1926, Law 4823/1930 and, most importantly, Law 5351 of 23rd March 1932 "on amendments and additions to Law 2646 of 1899 on antiquities",[10] which provided, *inter alia,* in article 55 for the codification of all provisions on antiquities in force in Greece. The codification was effected by Presidential Decree of 9/24 August 1932, which codified all relevant applicable provisions into a single legislative act bearing the number 5351/1932 and entitled 'The Antiquities Law', which remains in force to this day.[11]

In conclusion, the first legislative attempts of the modern Greek State (1834-1932) to protect its cultural heritage focussed on the protection of antiquities and displayed a strong commitment to State ownership. However, with the exception of a general reference to antiquities found on the bottom of the sea or in lakes and rivers, in the context of determining rights of ownership, there were no specific rules on the protection of the underwater cultural heritage. Technology had not as yet developed to enable the scientific investigation of underwater sites, whilst jurisdictional limits

---

7   *Official Gazette*   22/1834.
8   *Official Gazette*   A' 158/1899.
9   Article 3 of Law 2646 of 1899 was incorporated into art. 2 of Cod. Law 5351/1932: see section 3.1.1
        below.
10   *Official Gazette* A' 93/1932.
11   *Official Gazette* A' 275, 24.8.1932. For an unofficial English translation, see UNESCO, *The Protection
        of Movable Cultural Property: Collection of Legislative Texts. Greece*, CC-87/WS 5.

at sea had not been definitely settled.[12] It is notable that until the beginning of the twentieth century, Greece had not adopted any legislation concerning maritime zones;[13] hence the reference to antiquities found on the "bottom of the sea" in Law 18/22 of May 1834, which remains unchanged to this day.

3.   The Existing Regime of Protection

As already stated, the current regime of underwater cultural property in Greece is governed by Codifying Law 5351/1932 'on antiquities' (hereafter referred to as Cod. Law 5351/1932). The pattern of national heritage laws varies considerably between States. Greece belongs to that group of States which do not have separate legislation dealing with underwater remains; instead, a general heritage law applies to cultural property found underwater. This general scheme is supplemented by ministerial decisions dealing with specific issues of marine archaeology, such as diving, regulation of aqualung and designation of marine archaeological sites. Also of relevance is legislation dealing with the protection of the marine environment.

The responsibility of Greece to protect its cultural heritage is also mandated by the 1975 Constitution. Article 24 paragraphs (1) and (6) read respectively:

> The protection of the natural and cultural environment constitutes an obligation of the State. The State is bound to adopt special preventive or repressive measures for the preservation of the environment.

> [M]onuments and historic areas and elements shall be under the protection of the State. A law shall provide for measures restrictive of private ownership deemed necessary for the protection thereof, as well as for the manner and the kind of compensation payable to owners.

Finally, one should consider international and regional cultural conventions, which have been ratified by Greece and regulate underwater relics, as well as relevant EC legislation.

---

12   The recognition of the territorial sea as part of the territory of the State was broadly accepted in 1930 at the Hague Conference. Before this, a considerable number of States were claiming separate jurisdictional zones for different purposes and of different widths. In any case, early practice and doctrine were not concerned as much with submerged areas as with the superjacent waters, because of the lack of any significant interest in use of them. See further, G. Marston 'The evolution of the concept of sovereignty over the bed and the subsoil of the territorial sea' (1976/77) 48 *British Yearbook of International Law* 321-332.

13   Thus, the Greek courts were applying, as domestic law, the concepts that prevailed at the time, namely that the breadth of the Greek territorial sea extended to three/four miles, on the basis of the cannon-shot rule: K. Ioannou 'The Greek territorial sea' in Th. Kariotis, ed., *Greece and the Law of the Sea* (Martinus Nijhoff Publishers, 1997) pp. 115-152 at p. 128. The first legislative act dealing with maritime issues was enacted in 1913. More specifically, Law 4141 of 26 March 1913 "on passage and sojourn of merchant vessels along the Greek coasts and on policing of the ports and harbours in time of war" provided in art.1 that, "so far as the application of the present Law is concerned the maritime zone from the coast up to ten nautical miles is considered as Greek sea". This was followed by Law 1165/1918 establishing a 3 km customs zone and, most importantly, by Presidential Decree of 6/18 September 1931, which specified that the territorial waters of Greece for the purposes of aviation and the control thereof have a breadth of ten nautical miles. In 1936, Law 230 of 17 September 1936 fixed the breadth of the territorial sea of Greece to six nautical miles from the coast, "without prejudice to provisions in force, referring to special matters, which fix a larger or a smaller breadth". See also Legislative Decree 187/1973 promulgating the 'Code of Public Maritime Law'.

3.1 Protection under domestic law

Cod. Law 5351/1932 is divided into six chapters dealing with: antiquities in general; import and export of antiquities; archaeological collections; excavations; clandestine excavations; protection of antiquities; sale of 'unneeded' antiquities, and trade in antiquities. In this section only those provisions which are of particular interest to the protection of the underwater cultural heritage will be discussed. Thus, issues such as archaeological collections and trade in, or exchange of, antiquities are not examined.

3.1.1 Definition of the protected cultural property
Under article 1, Cod. Law 5351/1932 applies to:

> all antiquities, whether movable or immovable, from ancient or subsequent times found in Greece and any national possessions, in rivers, lakes and on the bottom of the sea, and on public, monastic and private land.[14]

The term "antiquities" is defined by article 2 as:

> all works, without exception, of architecture, sculpture, graphic art and any art in general, such as all kinds of edifices and architectural monuments, sculptured stones from such monuments, foundations, aqueducts, roads, walls, tombs, hewn stone, statues, bas-reliefs, figurines, inscriptions, paintings, mosaics, pottery, weapons, jewellery, and other works and objects of any kind of material, precious stones and coins. In addition, objects belonging to the early Christian period or medieval Hellenism are not excluded from the scope of this Act.

Consequently, the codification applies to all underwater cultural property, whether movable or immovable, both in salt and fresh water. Despite the absence of any specific reference to shipwrecks or submerged sites, the language of article 2 is broad enough to encompass all categories of underwater cultural property.[15] However, palaeontological finds are excluded from the scope of article 2 since they do not qualify as works of art.[16]

One major disadvantage of the aforementioned definition is the absence of specific time-limits which would clearly identify the items that are protected. For example, article 1 refers to antiquities "from ancient or subsequent times" without further elaborating these notions, whilst in article 2 there is reference to objects belonging to the "early Christian period or medieval Hellenism". In addition, article 52 deals with churches and other artistic monuments and edifices "dating earlier than 1830". What will be the cut-off date for protecting antiquities? The year 1453 (the year of the fall of Constantinople coinciding with the end of medieval Hellenism) or the year 1830 (the year of the creation of the modern Greek State)?[17]

This issue, which is of primary importance since all antiquities in Greece belong to the State,[18] but which is also highly controversial, has been elucidated by jurisprudence. Thus,

---

14   The wording of art. 1 of Cod. Law 5351/1932, which vests title to all antiquities in the State, is identical to that of art. 1 of Law 2646 of 1899: see section 2 above.

15   The language used ("...such as..."), indicates that the list in art. 2 is non-exhaustive.

16   But according to ministerial decision 34593/1108/1983, palaeontological finds are considered as "archaeological objects" under the 1969 European Convention, which is ratified by Greece (see section 3.2 below) and are thus covered by the provision of Cod. Law 5351/32.

17   The year 1830 has been employed as a cut-off date by other legislative acts, such as Law 2674 of 10/18 August 1921 concerning Byzantine and medieval works of art earlier than 1830, *Official Gazette* A' 146/1921 and Law 216 of 29 May 1943. See also Law 1469 of 2 August 1950 "on the protection of a special category of edifices and works of art subsequent to 1830", *Official Gazette* A' 169/1950.

18   See further, section 3.1.2 below.

'antiquities' falling under State ownership are considered to be remains, movable and immovable, dating from very ancient times *until 1453*.[19] Under this approach, cultural property dating from 1454 to 1830 is protected under the terms of article 52 of Cod. Law 5351/1932,[20] as well as under other relevant legislation, such as Law 401/1914 "on the establishment of a Byzantine and Christian Museum"[21] and Law 2674/1921 concerning Byzantine and medieval works of art earlier than 1830.[22] This does not seem, however, to be the prevailing view in the Administration, which is more protective towards cultural property dating from the period 1454-1830.[23] Finally, edifices and works of art subsequent to 1830 are governed by Law 1469/1950.[24]

3.1.2 System of ownership

Greece belongs to that group of States which favour public to private ownership so far as the protection of cultural heritage is concerned. Under article 1 of Cod. Law 5351/1932, *all* antiquities existing in Greece belong to the State. However, despite this all-embracing provision as to title, there has been considerable controversy on this issue, since there is a perceived inconsistency between article 1 and other provisions of the codification, such as article 5 which refers to "compulsory purchase" of antiquities by the State, or articles 6, 20 and 46 which refer to "confiscation", and thus presuppose a right of private ownership. Most of these interpretative problems arise from the fact that the codification included a number of provisions which were incompatible.[25] Nevertheless, despite diverging doctrinal views, jurisprudence has ruled consistently that State ownership under Cod. Law 5351/1932 is absolute and exclusive,[26] the law recognising only a *right of possession* to private individuals, under certain circumstances.[27]

19	See Cases 271/71, 407/72 and 673/73 of the Greek Supreme Court (Arios Pagos) in *Penal Annals* KB' 513, 600 and *Penal Annals* KΑ' 724, respectively.
20	Article 52 prohibits any repair or alteration of churches and other artistic or historic monuments and edifices dating earlier than 1830 without approval by the competent Ministry which, however, must specify the monuments to be covered under this provision. The Legal Council of the State, in its Legal Opinion 953/75, has accepted that the term "monuments" under art. 52 refers both to immovable and movable objects of artistic or historical value.
21	*Official Gazette* A' 347/1914.
22	*Op. cit.* note 17. The provisions of this Law are relevant, although of more limited scope, to those of Cod. Law 5351/1932. However, under Law 2674/1921 cultural property may be subject to private ownership.
23	See further, D. Voudouri, *The Protection of the Cultural Heritage with the Prospect of the Single European Market* (EKEM/Papazisis, 1992) at p. 54 (in Greek). In Dores' view, this controversy concerns only movables. All immovables created before 1830 are protected as antiquities under Cod. Law 5351/1932: E. Dores *The Law on Antiquities* (Sakkoulas, 1985) at pp. 50-51 (in Greek).
24	*Op.cit.* note 17. Law 1469/1950 protects certain categories of cultural property under the condition that they have been designated by the Administration as deserving special protection. Such property is made subject to the provisions of art. 52 of Cod. Law 5351/1932.
25	For example, the codification included provisions of Law 2646 of 1899, which vested title to all antiquities in the State, and Law 5351/1932, which was more flexible and allowed private ownership.
26	The only exception to this rule is provided by art. 4, which stipulates that ownership of icons and old ecclesiastical heirlooms and manuscripts is vested in the monasteries in which they are kept. However, in Roucounas' view, there are three exceptions to the rule of State ownership: (a) in relation to antiquities of very small or no commercial value (art. 5) (see below note 27); (b) in the case of antiquities that have been imported legally (art. 15 *et seq.*); and (c) if they are sold as superfluous antiquities by the State (art. 53): E. Roucounas 'Cultural treasures on the seabed' (1979) 23 *Review of Public and Administrative Law* 10-37 at 25 (in Greek).
27	See, in particular, arts. 5, 12, and 13. The notion of 'possession' under the archaeological law encompasses an obligation to preserve the antiquity under the control of the State and a right - under the conditions and restrictions provided for by the law - to transfer possession to another individual. More specifically, a right of possession is recognised if the person declares within a period of fifteen days the possession, the manner of acquisition and, if possible, the place in which the antiquities were found. If the declared antiquities are of little scientific significance and of very small or no commercial value in the opinion of the Archaeological Council, they shall simply be enumerated and described before being left for the free use of the holder. Compulsory purchase by the State of such antiquities may be effected only if the holder is a dealer (art. 5). Otherwise, the possessor must comply with the instructions of the competent Ephor of Antiquities for their exhibition and preservation (art. 12). Finally, under art. 13, the holder must declare any transfer of the antiquities in his possession to the competent authorities.

3.1.3 Nature of protection

Cod. Law 5351/1932 includes a specific section on the "protection of antiquities". Under article 49, it is an offence to wilfully destroy or damage an antiquity or disfigure or deface the same. Since antiquities belong to the State, the latter has the right and the duty to protect and preserve them (article 2). As already stated,[28] any alteration of any kind whether conservatory in nature or otherwise, may be carried out only with the consent of the competent Ministry[29] upon the recommendation of the Archaeological Council (article 52). Furthermore, under article 50, it is prohibited without approval by the competent Ministry: (1) to dig in order to obtain building materials from ancient ruins of cities or within a distance of 500 metres of any visible ancient monument; (2) to undertake any work near an antiquity which may damage it directly or indirectly; and (3) to undertake any activity whatsoever on ancient buildings and remains or ruins, even if such work causes no damage. The term "work" under article 50 has been interpreted widely so as to include any type of activity, whether permanent or temporary, which may cause damage to an antiquity.

All these provisions, which are rules of public policy and enable the archaeological service to intervene at any time in order to undertake the required measures of protection, apply also to underwater activities and archaeological sites. Thus, the Department of Underwater Antiquities must provide clearance before any type of construction work may begin, such as in respect of harbours, coastal industrial installations, etc.[30]

3.1.4 Reporting of finds

The compulsory reporting of all finds, including those that are purely fortuitous, is a central feature of Greek law. As already stated, under article 5, the possessor of an antiquity must declare it to the nearest competent authorities within fifteen days of the time it came into his possession.[31] The penalty for failure to do so varies according to the length of delay and whether the delay was intentional (article 6).[32]

3.1.5 Rewards

A reward acts as an inducement to the disclosure of finds that otherwise may go unreported. Under article 7, any person working lawfully on State, municipal, communal, monastic or ecclesiastical property, who finds an antiquity and declares it within fifteen days receives one-half of the value as a reward. If no declaration is made within two months he receives no reward.[33] In addition, article 14 provides that anyone indicating to any authority where previously unknown antiquities have been discovered, or showing the location of antiquities and thereby contributing to their discovery, may receive a reward commensurate with the significance of the antiquities and the assistance provided by him. Such reward may not be lower than one-quarter or exceed one-half of the value of the antiquities.

---

28   See above, note 20.
29   Under Cod. Law 5351/1932, the competent Ministry is the Ministry of Education, although today the Ministry of Culture is competent to deal with the protection of antiquities.
30   See further, section 4.2 below.
31   As already pointed out (see note 27), after declaring the antiquity, the holder may keep it or transfer it to another party in accordance with the provisions of the law. In case of transfer, the person to whom the transfer is made is also obliged to declare it to the competent authorities (art. 13).
32   See section 3.1.10 below.
33   Similarly, anyone discovering ancient edifices or other ancient immovable monuments on private property receives a reward according to the value of the antiquity if he declares it within fifteen days (art. 8). Article 8 is of no interest to the protection of underwater cultural heritage, which is found on or under the seabed, i.e. on non-private property.

Consequently, under Greek law private finders are obliged to declare any antiquity found anywhere in the territory of Greece, including the territorial sea,[34] to the competent authorities (archaeological or port authorities or the police), and receive a reward commensurate to the importance of the objects.

3.1.6 Archaeological excavations

Under article 35, excavations may be carried out, under the direction of the competent Ministry, by Greek archaeologists who have served for at least three years as Ephors of Antiquities, or by any other person deemed suitably qualified by the Archaeological Council. A permit is always required for excavation. Greek scientific institutions, and in particular the Archaeological Society in Athens, may also carry out excavations if they are authorised by the Ministry in accordance with the aforementioned provisions (article 36). Foreign archaeological schools based in Greece are permitted to carry out a maximum of three excavations per annum under the supervision of the Ministry (article 37). Individual foreign archaeologists have no right to carry out excavations independently.

Underwater archaeological research, including the removal of shipwrecks and other remains from the seabed, falls within the notion of "excavation" under article 35.[35] So far as underwater excavations are concerned, the competent governmental authority is the Department of Underwater Antiquities, whilst the Hellenic Institute of Marine Archaeology is the only Greek scientific institution which is qualified, in accordance with the terms of article 36, to undertake underwater surveys in co-operation with or under the supervision of the Department of Underwater Antiquities.[36]

3.1.7 Diving

Cod. Law 5351/1932 does not include any specific provisions on diving. This issue has been dealt with by ministerial decisions, which establish the conditions under which underwater activities and in particular recreational diving may be carried out in Greece. As a rule, diving is prohibited; the use of aqualung is permitted only in certain areas of the country. In 1993, however, the Council of State annulled ministerial decision 10033/4.3.1988 "on the codification of decisions concerning sea areas for underwater activities",[37] which prohibited the use of aqualung all over the country with the exception of a limited number of locations specifically mentioned in the decision, after it was challenged by a private divers' association. In the court's view,[38] the decison in question went beyond the scope of Cod. Law 5351/1932, and articles 1 and 50 in particular, which allow prohibition or restriction of works for the protection of antiquities only on an individual case-by-case basis, but do not permit the general prohibition of activities (such as underwater activities with respiratory apparatus) with the intention of protecting antiquities at large. In response, the Minister of Culture issued a new decision in 1994 (26041/1482/14.6.1994) which permits underwater activities in all sea areas referred to in previous ministerial decisions, i.e. sea areas which have already been investigated and do not possess archaeological interest.[39] Since then, more sea areas have been opened for diving. However, in the view of the Administration, the diving issue should be definitely settled by the new archaeological law.[40]

---

34   See further, section 3.1.9 below.
35   This is confirmed by the jurisprudence of the Greek Supreme Court: see, in particular, Case 505/70, *Penal Annals* KA' 137.
36   See further, section 4 below.
37   *Official Gazette* B' 152/1988.
38   Council of State, Case 3094/1993.
39   These were the aforementioned decision 10033/4.3.1988, as well as decisions 30896/1989 (*Official Gazette* B' 542/1989) and 25824/1060/12.5.1993 (*Official Gazette* B' 388/1993).
40   See further, section 6 below.

3.1.8 Designation of marine archaeological sites

Greek law does not provide for the creation of marine archaeological parks. However, archaeological sites have been declared within the national marine park of Northern Sporades,[41] i.e. a marine park designated for the protection of seals around the island of Skopelos. Thus, by a ministerial decision in 1997 the island of Kyra-Panagia and its surrounding sea areas, which contain a significant concentration of antiquities, was declared as an archaeological site of absolute protection, where all construction work is prohibited and diving is not allowed without a permit from the archaeological service.

3.1.9 Import/export of antiquities

Articles 15-18 of Cod. Law 5351/1932 establish a special regime for antiquities, which are imported from abroad. Thus, importation is free, provided that antiquities are declared; otherwise they are considered to be found in Greece. The Law does not specify whether all imported antiquities are deemed to be found in Greece, or only those originating from Greece. According to the prevailing view, which is followed by the Administration, 'Greek' antiquities mean those which originate from Greek territory, even if they do not belong to the Greek civilisation.[42] The export of antiquities imported from abroad in accordance with the aforementioned provisions, is free (article 18).

So far as the export of antiquities found - or deemed to be found - in Greece is concerned, a permit is always required from the competent Ministry, pursuant to a decision of the Archaeological Council.[43] If export is impeded, then the State is obliged to purchase the antiquity if required by the prospective exporter, or it may transfer title to a private collector (article 19). However, according to article 45, the export of finds from excavations is not allowed. Only after complete examination and publication of the results of an excavation may finds which are considered to be superfluous to the requirements of museums be exported, although Law 654/1977 allows antiquities to be exported temporarily for the sole purpose of display in museums abroad. [44]

3.1.10 Sanctions

The Greek archaeological law is reinforced by sanctions, consisting of both fines and imprisonment, for infringement of its provisions relating to, e.g., reporting, excavation and exportation. Thus, if a possessor of an antiquity declares it within two months, but after the expiry of the fifteen-day period, he is subject to a fine. If his default continues beyond this two-month period, the fine increases and the antiquity will be confiscated if he is identified by means other than his own declaration. Where a possessor fails to make the requisite declaration with the purpose of illegally disposing of the antiquity, he is subject to imprisonment for a term of from one to six months (article 6). Similarly, if a person who finds an antiquity on State property does not declare it within two months, he shall be subject to imprisonment for a term of from two weeks to six months (article 7).

So far as illegal excavations are concerned, article 46 provides that any person who carries out an excavation without a permit and notification to the competent authorities, shall be subject to a term of imprisonment of from one month to two years, as well as to a fine. Any items discovered in the course of such an illegal excavation shall be confiscated on behalf of the State. Since the removal of a wreck constitutes excavation, then its illegal removal exposes the offender to the sentences provided for by article 46. In addition, since jurisprudence has accepted that the removal

---

41   See Presidential Decree of 16.5.1992, *Official Gazette* D' 519/1992.

42   Voudouri, *op.cit.* note 23 at p. 67. According to Dores, *op. cit.* note 23 at pp. 116-117, only Greek antiquities dispersed abroad fall within the scope of art. 15. In case of non-declaration of the importation of foreign antiquities, the presumption of State ownership does not apply.

43   It must be noted, however, that since the enactment of Law 654/1977 (*Official Gazette* A' 214/1977), the Archaeological Council is purely a consultative body.

44   *Ibid.*

of antiquities from the seabed without a permit and with no notification to the competent authorities constitutes theft against the State, the relevant provisions of the Penal Code may be applied.[45] Furthermore, under article 49, any person intentionally destroying or damaging antiquities shall be subject to a term of imprisonment of up to two years and a fine and, in particularly grave cases, to a term of up to five years and to a higher fine. Similarly, a person contravening any of the provisions of article 50 concerning the carrying out of activities or construction works near an antiquity[46] shall be subject to imprisonment for a term of from five days to one year and a fine, whilst anyone who proceeds to any repair or alteration of edifices and other historic and ancient monuments without the required permit under article 52, is subject to a fine and imprisonment for a term of up to three months.

3.1.11 Assertion of jurisdiction

As already mentioned, article 1 of Cod. Law 5351/1932 applies to antiquities found "on the bottom of the sea". This phrase is construed to include both the internal and the territorial waters of Greece, over which it exercises territorial sovereignty under international law. Thus, the territorial scope of application of Cod. Law 5351/1932 is confined to a sea-belt of six nautical miles.[47] Underwater remains found beyond the six-mile limit are not protected.

Greece has not asserted jurisdiction over cultural property found in international waters. Nevertheless, Law 468 of 10/12 November 1976 "on prospecting, exploration and exploitation of hydrocarbons and settlement of related matters",[48] empowered Grecce to require licensees of mineral exploration or exploitation projects on its continental shelf to respect its antiquities legislation.[49] Despite the fact that these provisions have not been retained in Law 2289/1995,[50] which specifically abrogated Law 468/1976, Greece could still apply such an obligation to its contractors under article 303(1) of the UN Convention on the Law of the Sea 1982,[51] which establishes the duty to protect archaeological and historical objects found at sea. Such practice, which is followed by a small group of States, such as Denmark, Norway, Israel, Libya, the Netherlands and Thailand, should not be considered as a unilateral extension of coastal heritage legislation over the continental shelf, but rather as the undertaking of protective measures by the coastal State in the exercise of its resource-related rights in this area.[52] Only the licensees of petroleum exploration and exploitation projects are obliged to respect such regulations; other sea users are not affected as they do not operate under the municipal law of the coastal State.

---

45   See Case 505/70, note 35 above.

46   See section 3.1.3 above.

47   See note 9 above. Article 44 of Presidential Decree 941/1977 'on the organisation of the Ministry of Culture and Sciences' (*Official Gazette* A' 320/1977), which deals with the Department of Underwater Antiquities, notably provides that the latter is competent to supervise and carry out excavations of underwater cultural property found on the seabed of the *territorial waters*.

48   *Official Gazette* A' 302/1976.

49   According to art. 16(6): "In carrying out the work of exploration, the contractor must observe the laws and regulations in force, including the regulations referred to in article 39 hereof, relating to archaeological sites and monuments in general, places of historical interest and outstanding natural beauty". In turn, art. 39 stipulated that "Presidential Decrees issued by motion of the Ministry of Industry and Energy shall prescribe regulations for the execution of any and all works and projects for the prospecting, exploration and exploitation of hydrocarbons including *cultural property* and other activities in the exploitation area" (emphasis added).

50   Law 2289/1995 "on prospecting, exploration and exploitation of hydrocarbons and other provisions", *Official Gazette* A' 27/1995.

51   See further, section 3.2 below.

52   A. Strati, *The protection of the underwater cultural heritage: an emerging objective of the contemporary law of the sea* (Martinus Nijhoff, 1995) at p. 261. It must be noted that under current international law, both conventional and customary coastal rights over the continental shelf do not cover underwater cultural property.

3.1.12 Exclusion of the law of salvage

A highly controversial issue relating to the protection of the underwater cultural heritage is the application of salvage/wreck law to shipwrecks of historical significance. Salvage law provides one of the most inappropriate bases for regulating access to, and control of, underwater sites. The protection of the underwater cultural heritage has never been an objective of this ancient maritime law, which evolved to provide compensation for the salvor of maritime property in distress. The salvor works solely for profit, which is reflected in the manner in which salvage operations are conducted. Indeed, good salvage practice may well dictate that a marine archaeological site is destroyed 'piecemeal', or that finds are not recorded. For these reasons, the exclusion of salvage law from the regime governing underwater cultural property has been recommended.[53] Nevertheless, in some jurisdictions salvage law is applicable even to ancient wrecks and there is a need to distinguish the legal framework provided for commercial and archaeological purposes.[54]

So far as Greek law is concerned, this issue is of no particular importance since the antiquities law also applies to wrecks, thus excluding the application of the rules of maritime law. However, there may be some controversy in relation to recent wrecks, i.e. those falling outside the scope of heritage legislation. As already seen, all wrecks found in Greek territorial waters dating earlier than 1453 fall under State ownership and are protected under the terms of Cod. Law 5351/1932, whilst wrecks dating between 1454 and 1830 are still protected but may be subject to private ownership.[55] More recent wrecks, i.e. those subsequent to 1830, may be governed by Law 1469/1950 provided that they are specifically designated as protected property. Otherwise, ordinary maritime law will apply.

In any case, under Greek maritime law ownership of shipwrecks is vested in the State after the passage of a very short period of time. Thus, the State acquires ownership of a sunken wreck, which is found on the seabed with no traces on the superjacent waters, if there is no identifiable owner[56] or the identified owner fails to raise the wreck within three years from the date of the judgment declaring his right of ownership, or if an attempt is made to raise the wreck which is interrupted for three successive years.[57]

3.2   Protection under international law

Under article 28(1) of the Greek Constitution, international treaties which have been 'approved' by formal law, form an integral part of domestic law and prevail over any contrary provision of Greek law. In the context of the protection of its cultural heritage, Greece has ratified a number of cultural Conventions which specifically apply (or are interpreted to apply) to underwater cultural property. These are the following: (a) the Hague Convention for the Protection of Cultural Property in the

---

53   *Ibid* at pp. 45-50. It is therefore important that the International Convention on Salvage 1989 reads in art. 30(1): "[a]ny State may, at the time of signature, ratification, acceptance, approval or accession, reserve the right not to apply the provisions of this Convention... (d) when the property involved is maritime cultural property of prehistoric, archaeological or historical interest and is situated on the seabed". Greece has ratified the Salvage Convention without, however, submitting a reservation under art. 30(1). See Law 2391/1996, *Official Gazette* A' 55/1996. It must be noted, however, that recently admiralty courts have begun to acknowledge the public interest of States in the preservation of historic wrecks off their coasts.

54   See further S. Dromgoole and N. Gaskell 'Interests in Wreck' (1997) 2 *Art Antiquity and Law* 207-231 at 228.

55   See further, section 3.1.1 above.

56   Anyone claiming the wreck must file a petition for the declaration of his rights by the court within six months from the date he is invited to do so, pursuant to art. 201 of the Code of Public Maritime Law, *op. cit.*, note 13.

57   See also art. 41 of Law T4'B of 29.10/7.11 1856 'on wrecks and salvage', *Official Gazette* A' 71/1856.

Event of Armed Conflict 1954,[58] (b) the UNESCO Convention on the Means of Prohibiting and Preventing the Illicit Import, Export and Transfer of Ownership of Cultural Property 1970,[59] (c) the UNESCO Convention concerning the Protection of the World Cultural and Natural Heritage 1972,[60] and (d) the European Convention on the Protection of the Archaeological Heritage 1969.[61] Since all these instruments apply a territorial jurisdictional theory with respect to law-making and enforcement, their application is confined to sites found landward of the outer limit of the territorial sea.

So far as substantive measures of protection are concerned, provision is made for the registration of cultural property, creation of national inventories, delimitation of archaeological sites, application of scientific standards for excavations, prohibition of illegal excavations, prevention of illegal exportation and importation of the protected property, and promotion of co-operation and assistance between States. None of these measures, however, deals with problems which are specifically related to underwater archaeological research, such as conflicts between salvage law and heritage legislation, enforcement at sea of heritage legislation and, most importantly, protection of underwater cultural property found in international waters.[62]

Furthermore, Greece has ratified the Protocol concerning Mediterranean Specially Protected Areas 1982,[63] which provides in article 3(2)b for the establishment of protected areas to preserve "sites of particular importance because of their scientific, aesthetic, historical, archaeological, cultural or educational interest". Within such areas, the parties may regulate the passage of ships, any archaeological activity, and the removal of any object which may be considered as an archaeological object, as well as trade in and export of important "archaeological objects which originate in protected areas and are subject to measures of protection".[64] The territorial scope of application of the 1982 Protocol is confined to the territorial sea.[65]

Greece is also a Contracting Party to the UN Convention on the Law of the Sea 1982,[66] which includes two articles on the protection of the underwater cultural heritage: article 303, which establishes the duty of all States to protect objects of an archaeological and historical nature found in the marine environment and which enables the adoption of 24-mile archaeological zones by coastal States;[67] and article 149, which deals with archaeological and historical objects found on the deep seabed (within

---

58   Law 1114/1981, *Official Gazette* A' 6/1981.

59   Law 1103/1980, *Official Gazette* A' 297/1980.

60   Law 1126/1981, *Official Gazette* A' 32/1981.

61   Law 1127/1981, *Official Gazette* A' 32/1981.

62   See, however, the European Convention on the Protection of the Archaeological Heritage (Revised) 1992, *European Treaty Series (ETS)* No. 143, which expands its territorial scope of application so as to include "any area within the jurisdiction of the parties". According to the Explanatory Report, this area may be co-extensive with the territorial sea, the contiguous zone, the continental shelf, the exclusive economic zone or a cultural protection zone. Greece is a signatory to the Revised Convention. Similarly, the European Convention on Offences relating to Cultural Property 1985, *ETS* No. 119, which has not as yet entered into force, adopts the active and passive personality principle of jurisdiction as bases for prosecution in respect of offences committed outside the territories of contracting States, i.e. on the high seas. Finally, Greece is a signatory to the Unidroit Convention on Stolen or Illegally Exported Cultural Objects 1995, which supplements the 1970 UNESCO Convention.

63   Law 1634/1986, *Official Gazette* A' 104/1986.

64   See art. 7 of the 1982 Protocol.

65   However, its amending Protocol concerning Specially Protected Areas and Biological Diversity in the Mediterranean 1995 (reprinted in (1996) 11 *International Journal of Marine and Coastal Law* 101-112) which is specifically stated to replace - upon its entry into force - the 1982 Protocol, enables the designation of sites even in areas of the high seas (article 9(2)b). Greece is a signatory to the 1995 Protocol.

66   Law 2321/1995, *Official Gazette* A' 136/1995.

67   Article 303(2). For further discussion, see Strati, *op.cit.* note 52 at pp. 165-171.

the 'Area').[68] Under article 149, deep seabed cultural property is to be preserved or disposed of for the benefit of mankind as a whole, while taking into consideration the preferential rights of the State or country of origin, the State of cultural origin or the State of historical and archaeological origin. Article 149 is of no direct interest to Greece, since the deep seabed regime envisaged by the 1982 Convention does not apply to the Mediterranean.[69] Nevertheless, Greece may qualify as the State of origin of an historic wreck or its cargo found on the deep seabed in, say, the Atlantic Ocean.

3.3   Protection under EC law

The European Union has not as yet adopted substantive measures for protecting the underwater cultural heritage[70] or cultural property in general. However, there have been legislative attempts to deal with the issue of circulation of cultural goods within the Community after the abolition of the internal borders and the establishment of the internal market in 1992, as well as the return of illegally removed cultural objects, including underwater remains. More specifically, (EEC) Council Regulation No. 3911/92 of 9th December 1992[71] as amended, deals with the export of cultural goods, and Council Directive 93/7 of 15th March 1993[72] as amended, deals with the return of cultural objects unlawfully removed from the territory of a Member State. Greece has only recently given effect to Directive 93/7.[73]

---

68   It should be noted that the initial inclusion of the archaeological issue on the agenda of the Committee on the Peaceful Uses of the Seabed and the Ocean Floor beyond the Limits of National Jurisdiction ('Seabed Committee'), to which UNCLOS III owes its origins, was proposed by Greece in 1971. During UNCLOS III, Greece along with other Mediterranean countries, proposed the creation of a cultural heritage zone, co-extensive with the continental shelf and/or the exclusive economic zone, where the coastal State would exercise jurisdiction over archaeological and historical objects. When these proposals were not accepted by other delegations, it opted for the compromise formula of art. 303(2), which expands coastal jurisdiction over a 24-mile zone, co-extensive with the contiguous zone. Greece's increased concern for the protection of the underwater cultural heritage is also illustrated by its positive contribution to the negotiations which have taken place under the auspices of the Council of Europe, although unsuccessfully, for the adoption of a European convention on the protection of the underwater cultural heritage. The initiative for the work carried out on the Draft European Convention on the Protection of the Underwater Cultural Heritage 1985 was taken by the Parliamentary Assembly of the Council of Europe, which adopted in 1978 Recommendation 848 on the Protection of the Underwater Cultural Heritage. The Committee of Ministers subsequently decided at its fifth meeting at deputies level (November 1979) to set up an *ad hoc* Committee of Experts on the Underwater Cultural Heritage with terms of reference to draft a European Convention on the Protection of the Underwater Cultural Heritage. The *ad hoc* Committee of Experts finalised the preparation of the Draft Convention and an Explanatory Report in 1985 and submitted them to the Committee of Ministers for approval. No decision was taken to open the Convention for signature due to Turkey's objection to its territorial scope of application: the Draft Convention opted for a provision similar to art. 303(2) of the UN Convention on the Law of the Sea.

69   Under art. 1(1) of the UN Convention on the Law of the Sea, the Area is defined as the seabed and ocean floor beyond the limits of national jurisdiction, i.e. beyond the outer limit of the continental shelf. Since art. 76(1) of the Convention establishes the 200-mile limit as the minimum breadth of the continental shelf and the Mediterranean is less than 400 miles wide throughout its entire length, Part XI of the Convention dealing with the Area is not applicable.

70   Relevant issues were discussed at the European Conference on the Protection of the Underwater Cultural Heritage, Vouliagmeni, 7-8 April 1994, which was organised by Greece during its Third Presidency of the European Union.

71   *Official Journal L* 395 of 31.12.1992 at p. 1.

72   *Official Journal L* 74 of 27.3.1993 at p. 74.

73   See Presidential Decree 133/1998 of 6 May 1998, *Official Gazette* A' 106/1998. For further information on the Regulation and the Directive and, in particular, for a discussion of how they have affected Italian law, see ch. 6.

4. Administrative Issues

4.1 Authorities responsible for protection

The Department of Underwater Antiquities, which was created in 1976 by Law 405/1976,[74] is in charge of exploration, protection *in situ* and recovery of underwater cultural property. In this respect, it exercises control over any activity that may affect underwater remains, such as construction works, industrial installations, aquaculture, illegal fishing, i.e. fishing with dynamite, geophysical and oceanographic research, laying of submarine cables and pipelines, and recreational diving.[75] Conservation of the recovered material and supervision of institutions operating in the field of marine archaeology also fall within the scope of the Department's competence. In exercising its duties, the Department collaborates closely with the Ministries of Merchant Marine and Defence.

The Department consists of three divisions: (a) the Underwater Survey Division, which deals with the planning, technical organisation and carrying out of underwater surveys; (b) the Research and Archives Division, which deals with the classification and listing of underwater remains, and the creation of a national inventory; and (c) the Laboratory Division, which deals with the conservation and display of recovered material.

Archaeological excavations and diving are generally subject to authorisation by the Department of Underwater Antiquities. However, research by foreign archaeological schools in maritime areas under the jurisdiction of Greece requires authorisation by the Interministerial Commission of Scientific Research at the Ministry of Foreign Affairs.[76]

4.2 Private institutions

In Greece, there are several institutions involved in the field of marine archaeology. As already stated, the Hellenic Institute of Marine Archaeology, which was founded in 1973, is the only Greek scientific institution qualified to undertake underwater excavations in Greece. Its aim is to organise and promote marine archaeological research in Greece and to assist the Ministry of Culture with the difficult task of preserving, studying and promoting Greece's maritime heritage. It is notable that between the years 1973 and 1976, i.e. before the creation of the Department of Underwater Antiquities, the Institute acted as official consultant to the Ministry. Finally, one should be aware of the Hellenic Institute for the Preservation of Nautical Tradition, established in 1981; the Aegean Maritime Institute, based on the island of Mykonos; and the Piraeus Hellenic Maritime Museum.[77]

4.3 Management of underwater cultural property in Greece

Management of underwater cultural property in Greece is far from satisfactory. Despite the fact that over one thousand sites had been reported to the Department of Underwater Antiquities

---

74   *Official Gazette* A' 207/1976.
75   Under Presidential Decree 16/1980, *Official Gazette* A' 8/1980, the Director of the Department of Underwater Antiquities may issue permits for underwater activities as well as authorise the undertaking of any kind of construction work in harbours, in accordance with the terms of art. 50 of Cod. Law 5351/1932.
76   E. Roucounas 'Greece and the Law of the Sea' in T. Treves, ed., *The Law of the Sea. The European Union and its Member States* (Martinus Nijhoff Publishers, 1997) pp. 224-260 at p. 249. The Department of Underwater Antiquities is represented in the Interministerial Commission, which is competent to authorise any kind of scientific research in Greek territorial waters and on the continental shelf: see Diplomatic Note No. 6257.1/207/AS of 31 January 1978.
77   Agouridis, *op.cit.* note 1, at p. 182.

by 1997, very few have been thoroughly surveyed, excavated or published. As Agouridis has argued:

> there currently exist no scientific criteria for the assignment of research priorities and efforts, and a long-range plan for Greece's underwater heritage has yet to be formulated. Part of the reason for this is the fact that the Department of Underwater Antiquities must provide clearance before any type of construction work (such as harbours, fish-farms, coastal industrial installations, etc.) may begin. These responsibilities leave little time for purely scientific research, although its personnel and infrastructure have considerable potential scientific contributions to make.[78]

It is interesting to note that the Minister of Culture ordered a stop to any excavations, with the exception of rescue work, for the years 1997 and 1998 so that the Department could concentrate on research already undertaken.

Furthermore, the existing infrastructure of the Department of Underwater Antiquities is inadequate, as there is lack of space and an absence of proper laboratories for the conservation of finds.[79] For this reason, many archaeologists are in favour of a decentralised regime for administering underwater cultural property, effected by the creation of local 'ephorates' in different parts of Greece. Finally, it is important to appreciate the inadequate level of funding, as well as of State interest,[80] currently devoted to marine archaeological research in Greece. This is particularly regrettable given the extraordinary archaeological potential of Greek waters.

5. Conflicting Interests in the Protection of the Underwater Cultural Heritage

The identification of the different interests involved in the preservation of the underwater cultural heritage is essential since the formulation of national cultural policies – which in turn dictate the international legal position of States in cultural matters – is largely determined by those interests. At national level, the main interest groups are the identifiable owners, archaeologists, commercial salvors, hobby-divers, collectors, auctioneers and the State, the latter representing the common interest. Treasures seekers and sport divers naturally favour free access to shipwrecks. The pecuniary interests of salvors are best satisfied by the swift recovery of spectacular objects, while the sport diver's desire for unrestricted access to shipwrecks for recreational purposes, conflicts both with the salvor's interest for exclusive use of the wreck and the archaeologist's concern for ordered collection. Finally, auctioneers and collectors are simply interested in the acquisition of 'sunken treasures', often irrespective of the manner in which they have been acquired and despite the dispersal of unique archaeological collections.[81] The exploitation of submerged cultural resources by private companies and individuals for personal financial benefit is opposed by the preservationist community, since the cultural heritage is a prominent public resource; it reveals shared values and bears witness to the history of a nation. However, in legal systems where there is a strong tradition of private ownership, the State will be more reluctant to intervene

---

78   *Ibid.*
79   There are only three laboratories in Greece which are competent to conserve underwater finds: the laboratory at the Department of Underwater Activities; the laboratory at Niokastro, a castle in Pylos which is intended to serve as a national museum and centre for marine archaeological research; and the laboratory, run by the Hellenic Institute of Marine Archaeology, in the museum in Spetses, for the conservation of finds from the wreck at Dokos.
80   It is noteworthy that, until recently, no marine archaeology course was offered at any Greek university.
81   Strati, *op.cit.* note 52 at p. 19.

and deprive identifiable owners of their title, or to exclude the salvaging of underwater cultural property by the private sector.[82]

In Greece, the situation is less complicated since in the sphere of cultural heritage, the private sector has little sway. Cultural policy in Greece is characterised by State interventionism, coupled with a strong tradition of State ownership of cultural property. This fundamental principle of cultural heritage law is enshrined in the Constitution, which provides in article 18(1) that "the ownership and disposal of ... archaeological sites and treasures shall be regulated by special laws".[83]

Nevertheless, despite the positive measures undertaken by Greece in protecting its underwater cultural heritage, i.e. prohibition of diving, the requirement of a permit for carrying out excavations and underwater research in general, compulsory reporting of finds sanctioned by imprisonment in cases of non-compliance, many sites in shallow water have been plundered. This is primarily due to the inability of Greece to monitor its 15,000 km coastline, as well as to the reluctance of private individuals to comply with the strict rules which offer no real incentive for co-operation.

The effectiveness of any scheme of protection depends to a considerable extent on the co-operation of the public, particularly of interest groups such as underwater explorers and hobby-divers. Since legal action has its limits, educating the public may prove to be more effective than the enactment of draconian measures which cannot be enforced. It is therefore important that positive action is taken, not only in the legislative sphere, but also to ensure that the public is properly educated and the law rigorously enforced. A number of States have recently attempted to incorporate in the legal scheme of protection of cultural heritage the different interests involved so as to achieve a broader agreement on its terms. This approach has been particularly advanced in the United States, where concepts such as 'multiple use' of the cultural heritage, have been developed. Despite the reasonable objections one may have in relation to such practices, it may be advisable to take into account some of these interests, for example by allowing supervised recreational diving in designated marine archaeological parks. In view of this, it is encouraging that the Department of Underwater Antiquities is planning the creation of an underwater archaeological park – the first one to be established in Greece – in Methoni off the coast of the western Peloponnese. The Methoni Centre will, *inter alia,* provide tourists with scuba equipment and glass-bottomed boats.

6. Reform Issues

6.1 Need to amend the heritage legislation

Undoubtedly, the Greek law on the protection of antiquities is archaic and there is a need to update it so as to bring it into line with modern approaches to protection, particularly with regard to underwater cultural property. By 1932, i.e. the year of enactment of the antiquities law, marine

---

82 Despite any objection one may have to vesting title to all antiquities in the State, State ownership of cultural property found underwater is preferable both in terms of the protection afforded to underwater sites and the rights of the State in case of illicit excavation or theft of the recovered items. The vesting of title to all antiquities in the State enables competent authorities to control underwater cultural property without any delay caused by ownership claims. In addition, it provides a 'neat' solution to the problems posed by the difficulty in proving the origins and ownership of ancient shipwreck: L.V. Prott and P.J. O'Keefe 'Final Report on Legal Protection of the Underwater Cultural Heritage' in Council of Europe *The Underwater Cultural Heritage,* Doc. 4200-E, 1978, Appendix II, at p. 68.

83 However, as already pointed out, the situation is less clear in relation to recent wrecks owing to the absence of specific rules governing the complex legal problems involved in their protection. In this context, the issue of immunity of public vessels may also arise.

archaeology had not yet evolved as a separate discipline, whilst the absence of technology made the recovery of artefacts from the seabed far too remote to create any legal and/or jurisdictional problems. Today, the underwater cultural heritage is of sufficient importance to warrant an effective regime of protection. The key issues in its preservation are: the definition of the protected cultural property, rights of ownership, *in situ* protection of remains, regulation of diving, designation of marine archaeological parks and, most importantly, protection of cultural property beyond the traditional territorial sea limit and enforcement of heritage legislation at sea.

6.2   The draft archaeological law

The need to amend the law has been recognised by the Administration since the 1960s, but attempts to achieve this have not been successful. The most recent draft, which is dated 30th April 1998, is still under consideration. For this reason, only those provisions which specifically refer to underwater cultural property will be discussed.

6.2.1   Scope of application

According to article 1(2) of the draft, the cultural heritage of Greece consists of:

> all cultural property, movable and immovable, which bears witness to human existence and the individual and collective creativity of man, wherever it is found within the limits of Greek territory, including the territorial waters and other areas over which Greece exercises jurisdiction in accordance with international law. The term cultural heritage also includes immaterial cultural property.

The draft therefore enables the protection of underwater cultural property found in areas beyond the outer limits of the Greek territorial sea. The terminology used: "other areas over which Greece exercises jurisdiction in accordance with international law", is similar to that employed by the European Convention on the Protection of the Archaeological Heritage (Revised) 1992.[84] As already stated, article 303(2) of the UN Convention on the Law of the Sea, to which Greece is a party, empowers coastal States to establish a 24-mile archaeological zone. The draft allows such an extension of Greece's jurisdiction beyond the six-mile limit of its territorial sea.[85] This is an important development to the previous regime. Finally, one should consider the recent debate in UNESCO for the adoption of an international convention in the field,[86] which would expand coastal State jurisdiction to underwater cultural property found on the continental shelf.

6.2.2   Definition of the protected cultural property

The draft distinguishes between "movable" and "immovable" monuments, as well as between "ancient monuments" or "antiquities" and "recent monuments".

"Ancient monuments" or "antiquities" are considered those which date from prehistoric, ancient or Byzantine times until the year 1453, as well as those elements of the cultural heritage dating from 1454 to 1830 whose protection is necessary because of their historical, artistic or scientific significance (article 2(b)). The notion of ancient monuments also includes palaeontological finds which, as already seen, are excluded from the scope of application of Cod. Law 5351/1932. "Recent monuments" are considered to be those which came into existence after the year 1830 but

---

84   See note 62 above.
85   Such an extension of jurisdiction may be effected by a presidential decree since under art. 2 of Law 2321/ 1995, *op.cit.* note 66, for the application and enforcement in Greece's domestic legal system of any provision of the UN Convention on the Law of the Sea, presidential decrees are issued upon proposition of the Council of Ministers.
86   See ch. 14.

which are not less than 30 years of age and whose protection is necessary because of their historical, artistic or scientific significance (article 2(c)).

In article 6(1), which deals with immovable monuments, a further distinction is drawn *within* the category of recent monuments. Thus, the draft distinguishes between monuments which are more than 100 years old and are designated as monuments because of their architectural, social, ethnological, religious, technical, industrial or in general historical, artistic or scientific significance, and monuments more than 30 years of age but less than 100 years old, which are designated as monuments because of their *exceptional* architectural, social, ethnological, religious, technical, industrial or in general historical, artistic or scientific significance. Both categories must be designated as protected property by a ministerial decision published in the Official Gazette. However, it is specifically stated that all recent monuments which are older than 100 years are under the supervision of the Ministry, even if they are not designated as such. Thus, their demolition or the carrying out of any activity requires a permit issued by the archaeological service (article 6(8)).

A similar distinction is made in relation to movable monuments. Thus, article 18(1) of the draft distinguishes between (a) antiquities dating prior to the year 1453; (b) antiquities dating after the year 1453 which constitute finds from excavations, or which have been removed from immovable monuments, as well as icons and other religious objects used for worship, of this period; (c) antiquities dating after the year 1453, which are designated as monuments because of their social, religious, technical, ethnological or in general historical, artistic or scientific significance; (d) recent cultural objects older than 100 years of age, which are designated as monuments because of their social, religious, technical, ethnological or in general historical, artistic or scientific significance; and (e) recent cultural objects more than 30 years of age but less than 100 years old, which are designated as monuments because of their *exceptional* social, religious, technical, ethnological or in general historical, artistic or scientific significance, with the consent of their creator if they are still in his possession. Cultural objects mentioned in categories (c), (d) and (e) must be designated as monuments by a ministerial decision, published in the Official Gazette.

"Movable" monuments are considered to be ancient or recent monuments which are not immovable (article 2(e)). In turn, "immovable monuments" are those ancient or recent monuments which have been connected to, and remain in, the ground or in caves or on the seabed or on the bottom of lakes and rivers, as well as monuments which are found on the ground or on the seabed and the bottom of lakes and rivers and cannot or should not be removed. The notion of immovable monuments also includes installations, operational equipment, decorative and other elements, which constitute an inseparable part of the monuments, as well as their immediate environment (article 2(d)).

The draft therefore incorporates a very useful definition of cultural heritage, which distinguishes between different categories of cultural property, including underwater remains, requiring different levels of protection. Age is the main criterion for determining the protected cultural property, combined with the archaeological, scientific and cultural significance of particular objects, in the case of protection of recent remains. However, the inclusion in the notion of immovable monuments of "monuments found on the seabed which ... *should not* be removed" is rather unfortunate, since it may also cover shipwrecks, which are by no means immovable.

6.2.3 System of ownership

All immovable ancient monuments dating earlier than the year 1453 belong to the State. Monuments dating after the year 1453 may be subject to private ownership, under the conditions stipulated by the draft (article 7). Movable ancient monuments dating earlier than the year 1453 belong to the State. The right of ownership of movable monuments dating after the year 1453 is exercised under the conditions stipulated by the draft, whilst a right of possession by private individuals of antiquities belonging to the State may be recognised, upon permission by the Minister (article 19).

The draft law is thus more flexible than Cod. Law 5351/1932 since it allows private ownership of antiquities dating after the year 1453 and recent monuments. It has in fact incorporated the approach taken by jurisprudence in interpreting and applying Cod. Law 5351/1932, i.e. that State ownership applies to antiquities dating earlier than 1453. However, this does not preclude the protection of more recent remains. The protection accorded to cultural property is not dictated necessarily by the identity of its owner.

6.2.4 Reporting of finds/rewards

Similarly to Cod. Law 5351/1932, the draft provides for compulsory reporting of finds, both movable and immovable, combined with a system of monetary rewards. Thus, under article 8, every person who discovers or locates an immovable monument must declare it immediately to the nearest archaeological or port authorities, or to the police. The declaration must state the exact place in which the monument was found, as well as all other useful information about it. The person who made the declaration may receive a reward upon decision of the Minister. A reward may also be given to anyone who indicates the location of antiquities. The amount of the reward will be estimated on the basis of the significance of the monument, as well as the contribution of the person who made the declaration to its discovery.

Article 20 of the draft, which deals with the declaration of movable cultural property, establishes similar rules. Every person who finds, or who is in possession of, an antiquity dating earlier than 1453, must declare it to the competent archaeological or port authorities or to the police. If possession of the antiquity passes to the State, then the person who declared it is entitled to a reward commensurate with the significance of the antiquity and the assistance provided by him. Such reward may not exceed half of the value of the antiquity. Finally, anyone who indicates unknown antiquities to the archaeological service, or assists in any way in their discovery, is also entitled to such a reward.

All the provisions relating to compulsory reporting of finds are applicable to the discovery of underwater finds. Both articles mentioned above notably refer to the obligation to report the discovery, or location, of antiquities to the competent archaeological or *port* authorities.

6.2.5 Designation of archaeological and historical sites

The draft introduces the concepts of "archaeological and historical sites". Under article 2(f), "archaeological sites" are defined as areas on land or on the seabed or at the bottom of lakes and rivers which contain, or which it is believed contain, ancient monuments or which have constituted, or it is believed have constituted, from ancient times until the year 1830, groups of monuments, or the site of exceptional historical or mythical events. Similarly, article 2(h) defines "historical sites" as the combined works of man and nature, mostly built after 1830, which are sufficiently distinctive and homogenous to be topographically definable and whose protection is necessary due to their historical, artistic or scientific significance.

According to article 12(1)-(3), archaeological sites are designated pursuant to a decision of the Minister, published in the Official Gazette; a temporary designation of sites is also possible. So far as marine archaeological sites are concerned, article 12(6) provides that a permit is always required for the undertaking of fishing or underwater activities with respiratory equipment within the designated area. These provisions are also applicable to historical sites.[87]

The designation of marine archaeological sites is particularly useful for the *in situ* preservation of underwater cultural property or the protection of sea areas which are believed to contain shipwrecks or other submerged sites. It seems, however, that – at least as presently drafted – the notion of historical sites includes only immovable underwater remains.

---

87   See art. 12(9) of the draft. As drafted, art. 2(h) appears to exclude shipwrecks from its scope since it refers exclusively to immovable monuments.

6.2.6 Diving

With the exception of the aforementioned prohibition of underwater activities on designated archaeological and historical sites, the draft does not address the issue of diving. As already discussed, this issue is rather controversial in Greece especially since the annulment by the Council of State of a ministerial decision prohibiting diving all over Greece.[88] The new archaeological law was expected to deal decisively with this issue. However, at least at this stage of drafting, diving is only prohibited on designated archaeological and historical sites.

6.2.7 Excavations

Under article 31, excavation means the exploration of the ground, the underground, the seabed, the bottom of lakes and rivers by any means, with the purpose of discovering and studying ancient or other monuments. Excavations may be carried out either by the archaeological service or by scientific, research or educational institutions specialised in the field of archaeological research, such as universities, the Archaeological Society and foreign archaeological schools. A permit is always required for the carrying out of excavations. Foreign scientific, research or educational institutions which are based in Greece may carry out a maximum of three excavations per annum. However, foreign institutions which are not based in Greece may carry out a maximum of three excavations, in co-operation with the archaeological service or other institutions based in Greece.

The draft has therefore certainly broadened the number of entities which are qualified to carry out excavations in Greece, whether on land or underwater. Thus, foreign institutions may also carry out excavations, either independently if they are based in Greece or in co-operation with other institutions in Greece. Such provisions, with a prominent international character, are welcomed.

7. Conclusion

The Greek approach to the protection of its underwater cultural heritage has always aimed at the preservation of underwater remains for the public at large, with the exclusion of private interests. In this respect, stringent measures have been adopted in order to prevent any clandestine or unsupervised excavation. Some of these measures, such as the prohibition of diving, are often criticised as being over-protective. However, according to the Administration, the prohibition of the use of aqualung has resulted in the protection of underwater sites around the Greek coast, whilst in other countries bordering the Mediterranean Sea, such as France and Italy, the vast majority of sites in shallow water have been plundered.

A new draft law is under preparation which incorporates new concepts and ideas about the protection and appreciation of the cultural heritage. The draft introduces fundamental changes to the existing regime of protection on controversial issues, such as rights of ownership, the import/export of antiquities, exchanges of cultural property, collections, as well as to administrative matters, such as the structure of the archaeological service.

There are, however, at least at this stage of drafting, only a few references to underwater cultural property. In the view of the author, a general heritage law may provide adequate protection to underwater remains. However, the inclusion of a special section dealing with shipwrecks or the adoption of *ad hoc* rules referring specifically to underwater cultural property would enhance its effectiveness. It is noteworthy that the draft law, similarly to the existing Cod. Law 5351/1932, does not mention anywhere shipwrecks or submerged sites, nor does it address the complex issues involved in the protection of recent wrecks, especially those of sunken warships and other State vessels, or the enforcement of heritage legislation at sea. Furthermore, there is no specific reference

---

88   See section 3.1.7 above.

to the potential threats to the underwater cultural heritage from other activities at sea, such as the exploration and exploitation of natural resources or the laying of submarine cables and pipelines, with the exception of the prohibition of fishing and diving on designated archaeological sites. Although such activities may be covered by the general language used by the draft in relation to industrial plants and other activities affecting monuments, a more specific provision would have accommodated better the needs of underwater sites.

Nevertheless, the draft law constitutes definite progress upon the existing regime.

Chapter 5

IRELAND

Nessa O'Connor

1.   Introduction

The protection of the underwater heritage has become a major issue in Irish archaeology, particularly in the course of the last two decades. During this time, there has been a growing interest in the exploration of underwater sites both at sea and in the inland waterways, at least partly as a consequence of the development and growth of scuba diving as a leisure time activity. This has facilitated much wider access to the thousands of sites which lie in Irish waters, ranging from prehistoric period river crossings through the lake dwellings or crannógs so numerous in the Irish midlands, to prehistoric and later period log boats and shipwrecks of almost every period. These include the two dozen or so west coast wrecks of the Spanish Armada, innumerable seventeenth–nineteenth century wrecks, as well as more recent notable wartime casualties such as the *Leinster*,[1] the *Lusitania*[2] and the *Aud*.[3]

The volume and diversity of sites together with the increase in their exploitation created an unprecedented challenge to the legislature and to the relevant State agencies to introduce the kind of legislation and policies which would help ensure the survival of this very rich underwater heritage.

It has also presented a challenge to the diving community and to its organisations to encourage and become involved in preservationist policy and research-oriented diving on shipwrecks and other archaeological sites.

This background, together with the fortuitous timing of other discoveries and events in the world of archaeology, has resulted in major changes and innovation and much which appears to be of comparative interest regarding recent legislation and case law.

Recent increases in funding from government[4] will also assist in increasing our state of knowledge by allowing more extensive surveying and recording of underwater sites.

1.1   Background

For the greater part of this century, the only legislation in any way relevant to underwater archaeological sites in Ireland – albeit indirectly – was the Merchant Shipping Act 1894.[5] It was largely inappropriate to the protection of archaeological material and sites, being chiefly intended for the protection of contemporary or recent private property.

---

1   City of Dublin Steam Packet Company mail boat torpedoed by a German U-boat near the Kish Lighthouse in Dublin Bay in 1918 with the loss of around 500 lives.

2   Cunard liner on transatlantic voyage from New York to Liverpool torpedoed off the Old Head of Kinsale on 7 May 1915, recently the subject of litigation in the American courts in *Bemis v. Lusitania* [1995] A.M.C. 1665 (ED Va).

3   Ship carrying arms from Germany for the Easter Rising of 1916 which attempted to land at Banna Strand, Co. Kerry. She was scuttled by her own crew near Roche's Point, Co. Cork, after being intercepted by a British destroyer. See further, J. de Courcy *Ireland and the Irish in Maritime History* (Dublin, 1986) p. 326.

4   For example, the funding and establishment of the maritime Sites and Monuments Record (SMR) in early 1997.

5   Part IX, particularly ss. 518-522.

Following independence in 1922, there was a considerable amount of legislative activity that included the passing of the National Monuments Act 1930. However, this statute failed to include any specific protection for underwater sites. The National Monuments (Amendment) Act 1954 did not alter the situation in any significant way.

These Acts did, however, provide for the placing of Preservation Orders[6] on archaeological sites and for restrictions on the export[7] and altering[8] of archaeological objects. These provisions have been used regularly in relation to aquatic sites and to objects from underwater contexts.

However, the fact remained that there was no fundamental restriction placed on anyone who chose to exploit the underwater heritage. This shortcoming became fully apparent only with the advent of the aqualung and the development of detection devices in the 1960s and 1970s. Throughout this period, the provisions of the Merchant Shipping Act 1894 applied but had little effect in protecting or maintaining the integrity of underwater sites. The relevant provisions of the Act provided for the reporting and delivery of salvaged material to the receiver of wreck of a given district; for the posting of notices; the processing of claims of owners; the payment of salvage and the sale of wreck in certain cases. The Act also provided for penalties for offences under these sections. In Ireland the receivers of wreck are almost always customs officers who receive their commissions from the Department of the Marine and are responsible for specific sections of the coastline. Although greatly outdated and not drafted with archaeology in mind, the Merchant Shipping Act and many receivers have had a successful and useful role to play in respect of objects raised from several wrecks of archaeological importance and also in instances of the raising of individual objects such as cannons by salvors, divers or fishermen.[9]

The 1894 Act has been replaced by the Merchant Shipping (Salvage and Wreck) Act 1993 which gives a new role to the receiver of wreck in underwater heritage law, this time in a clearly defined manner in relation to archaeological/historical material and with reference to a role shared with the Director of the National Museum of Ireland.[10]

2.   National Monuments (Amendment) Act 1987: Background

By the early 1980s, it had become apparent that additional controls were necessary in order to enable the State to control the rate and manner of exploitation of underwater archaeological sites. The previous amendment to the principal Act[11] had been passed more than thirty years before. In the interval, a number of new threats, to both dry land sites and artefacts, and to the underwater heritage, had emerged. Cheap metal detectors had become widely available and treasure hunting on archaeological sites had become relatively widespread.[12] Throughout the 1970s and

---

6   Section 8 of the National Monuments Act 1930, as amended by the National Monuments (Amendment) Act 1954, ss. 3 and 4.

7   Section 50 of the National Cultural Institutions Act 1997.

8   Section 25(1) of the National Monuments Act 1930, as amended by the National Monuments (Amendment) Act 1994, s. 20.

9   For example, four cannons from the Armada wrecks at Streedagh, Co. Sligo and a siege cannon from the Armada wreck, *La Trinidad Valencera* raised at Kinnagoe Bay, Co. Donegal.

10   Sections 45 and 49 provide for reporting of wreck in his custody by the receiver to the Director of the National Museum of Ireland (NMI). If any wreck is unclaimed after one year of coming into his possession he (the receiver) is obliged to notify the Director of the NMI who then has a period of 30 days during which he may claim on behalf of the State a wreck which he considers to be of historical, archaeological or artistic importance. Wrecks subject to the provisions of the National Monuments (Amendment) Act 1987, s. 3 are excluded under s. 49(6).

11   The National Monuments (Amendment) Act 1954.

12   For the position on land, see Eamonn P. Kelly 'Protecting Ireland's Archaeological Heritage' (1994) 3 *International Journal of Cultural Property* 213-225.

early 1980s, scuba diving was also becoming increasingly popular and several important underwater archaeological sites had been discovered and material raised, often without proper regard to archaeological method or to the need for the conservation of artefacts. In a treasure hunting context, scuba diving served to extend the scope of the treasure hunter into a new and rewarding medium. The provisions of the Merchant Shipping Act required only that material be reported and deposited once it had been raised. It placed no constraints on the lifting of material and in any case was frequently disregarded. It must also be said that although the importance of some categories of sites was acknowledged, it took a considerable time before underwater archaeology was generally recognised as a legitimate and valuable area of research within archaeology. By the time drafting of a new Act was seriously addressed in the early 1980s, the State authorities were wrestling with the growing problem of damage to monuments as a result of the use of detection devices as well as consequential black marketeering and illegal export of antiquities. The sites which were being targeted included early christian period church sites, lake dwellings (crannógs), ringforts, Spanish Armada wrecks and others dating from the sixteenth century onwards. While many of the archaeological objects were ultimately acquired by the National Museum, the scale of the problem was such that legislative action was essential. The existing penalties for offences under the 1930 Act were also found to be inadequate as a deterrent.[13]

2.1 National Monuments (Amendment) Act 1987: Provisions

The National Monuments Act 1987, which was passed on 22nd July of that year, includes a number of provisions in relation to the protection of underwater remains.

Section 3 provides generally for the protection of sites of historic wrecks. Section 3(1) and 3(2) deal with Underwater Heritage Orders whereby areas on, in or under the seabed may be designated as restricted areas on account of the location or possible location of wrecks or archaeological objects and on account of "the archaeological, historical or artistic importance of the wreck or the object".

The restrictions provided for include the prohibition of any tampering with, damage to, or removal of, a wreck or archaeological object. Diving, survey and salvage operations are also prohibited.

No age limitation was placed on the implementation of these sections and therefore it is possible to place Underwater Heritage Orders on wrecks as recent as the twentieth century.

Section 3(4) places these same restrictions regarding interference and diving operations on the sites of *all* wrecks and objects which are more than 100 years old. However, it also makes provision for the granting of licences under this section.

A licence from the Commissioners of Public Works is necessary not only to raise material from a wreck or archaeological site but also to 'dive only' without altering or disturbing a site in any way. In practice, two types of licence are possible – one to excavate, the other for 'dive only' purposes. The latter are frequently the subject of applications on behalf of diving clubs and individuals on a twelve month renewable basis, often in cases where a given club or group has been in the habit of carrying out regular club dives on sites local to their area. In return they are requested to report on the state of the wreck and the remains which are visible, as a means of augmenting official records. To date only two Underwater Heritage Orders have been made, the first in 1990 on the sites of a number of crannógs at Lough Donogher, Co. Leitrim and the second in January 1995 on the wreck of the *Lusitania* off the Old Head of Kinsale, Co. Cork. In both instances, the Orders were made as a result of possible risk to the sites resulting from diving activity.

---

13   There was a maximum fine of £50 or twelve months' imprisonment for offences under the National Monuments Act 1930 (ss. 24(3) and 25(3)).

Section 3(6) requires that any person who finds a wreck or object of 100 years or more in age must report it within four days either to a member of the *Garda Siochána* or to the Commissioners of Public Works, providing the requisite details of discovery.

Effectively, all wrecks of 100 years old or greater are automatically covered and do not need to be individually named as in the case of Underwater Heritage Orders.

Section 3(10) provides for the claiming of wreck in the custody of receivers of wreck by the Director of the National Museum in cases where no other claimant has established a rightful claim within one year.

The broadly similar provisions of section 49 of the Merchant Shipping (Salvage and Wreck) Act 1993 operate in relation to any wreck not covered by section 3 of the National Monuments (Amendment) Act 1987. In practice, this covers wrecks less than 100 years old which are not protected by Underwater Heritage Orders. This effectively divides the relevant responsibilities between merchant shipping and heritage law.

Section 17 provides for considerable increases in the level of penalty for offences under the Act, i.e. to £1000 on summary conviction and to £50,000 on indictment.

Section 2 places restrictions on the use of detection devices and requires that such be licensed. This section is relevant to the use of underwater detection devices, which are also subject to licensing.

The 1987 Act therefore provided the first comprehensive legal protection for the underwater heritage in Ireland. Its scope is very wide as it allows protection of wrecks and objects of all periods. It has been suggested by one commentator, however, that the geographical area which section 3 of the Act purports to cover may be greater than that permitted under the United Nations Law of the Sea Convention 1982.[14]

3.   National Monuments (Amendment) Act 1994: Background

While the 1987 Act establishes protection for, reporting of, and restrictions on, underwater discoveries, it is the 1994 amendment to the National Monuments Act which addresses the issue of ownership.

The background to the 1994 amendment to the National Monuments Act is to be found in a major case which has changed the face of heritage law in Ireland and has also had a profound effect on many other areas of law as well.

In early 1980, a unique hoard of church metalwork which included a ninth century chalice, an eighth century communal paten and wine strainer was found on a dry land island in the bog at Derrynaflan, Co. Tipperary, in the Irish midlands. It was found as a result of the use of metal detectors in the vicinity of an early church site. The finders, a father and son named Webb, brought their discovery to the National Museum of Ireland and deposited it there pending the determination of its legal ownership. They refused the finders' reward, which they were subsequently offered, and they sought the return of the hoard or its equivalent value.

The subsequent High Court and Supreme Court cases[15] were to serve to determine the ownership not only of this specific hoard but also that of all archaeological objects found in Ireland which had no known owner at the time of their discovery. In the words of John Kelly:

---

14   See Clive Symmons *Ireland and the Law of the Sea* (Dublin, 1993) pp. 69-72. *Cf.* Janet Blake 'The Protection of the Underwater Cultural Heritage' (1996) 45 *International and Comparative Law Quarterly* 819-843. The s. 3 provisions include areas "on, in or under the seabed to which section 2(1) of the Continental Shelf Act 1968 applies." The Irish continental shelf extends for over 500 miles at its furthest known extent.

15   *Webb v. Ireland* [1988] *Irish Reports* 353.

The three judgments pronounced in the Supreme Court, if not a buried treasure, are a sort of open-cast mine of material on the Constitution of the Irish Free State, the Constitution of Ireland, the incidents of sovereignty, the fate of the royal prerogative, the extent of rights of land ownership, the mode of conveyance of chattels … etc. etc.[16]

However, in addition to dealing with all these issues and more, the judgments in *Webb v. Ireland* were to create a unique basis and way forward in heritage law and established the State's right to claim unowned antiquities. The statutory expression of the *Webb* judgment is to be found in the National Monuments (Amendment) Act 1994.

Some understanding of the *Webb* litigation is necessary in order to comprehend the ethos and principles by which the State's role was perceived in that case. For example, Finlay C.J. stated:[17]

> … one of the most important national assets belonging to the people is their heritage and knowledge of its true origins and the buildings and objects which constitute keys to their ancient history. If this be so, then it would appear to me to follow that a necessary ingredient of sovereignty in a modern state and certainly in this State, having regard to the terms of the Constitution, with an emphasis on its historical origins and a constant concern for the common good is and should be an ownership by the State of objects which constitute antiquities of importance which are discovered and which have no known owner. It would appear to me to be inconsistent with the framework of the society sought to be created and sought to be protected by the Constitution that such objects should become the exclusive property of those who by chance may find them.

The need for legislation to give force to the *Webb* decision was referred to in the Supreme Court by Walsh J.:[18] "unless and until legislation is enacted the State must be regarded as owners in the sense of having a better right to possession than anyone else" and, further on:

> It is the duty of this Court to state that pending any such legislation the State is entitled to possession of all such objects unless and until the true successors in title of those who hid them for safe keeping can be ascertained.[19]

Finlay C.J. also addressed the types of archaeological objects which might be claimable by the State:[20]

> It may be thought proper, for instance to provide that all (or specified kinds of) articles or items of archaeological, historical or antiquarian or cultural value or interest should when apparently ownerless on being discovered or brought to light be deemed to vest in the State subject to the claim if established of the true owner. Such a provision might well abolish both any distinctions between objects made of different materials and any request that the objects had been hidden for safe keeping. In ordinary cases it would probably be desirable to have a system of reward so as to encourage finders to deliver up articles or items so found.

---

16   From 'Hidden Treasure and the Constitution' (1988) 10 *Dublin University Law Journal* p. 5, a lecture delivered in Trinity College, Dublin, on 29 January 1988 by the late John Kelly, one-time Professor of Jurisprudence and Roman Law at University College, Dublin, former Attorney General, Minister for Trade, Commerce and Tourism and author of an important work on the Constitution entitled *The Irish Constitution*.
17   [1988] I.R. 353 at 383.
18   [1988] I.R. 353 at 391.
19   [1988] I.R. 353 at 393.
20   [1988] I.R. 353 at 387.

The State's right to claim all categories of archaeological objects was to be borne out in the contents of the subsequent Act.

Finlay C.J. thereby set the scene for legislative reform, as well as for State ownership of the vast majority of recently found archaeological objects.[21]

The relevance of *Webb v. Ireland* to underwater protection relates to the adoption of a similar approach by the trial judge (Barr J.) in the High Court proceedings in *In Re La Lavia, Juliana and Santa Maria de la Vision* (1994)[22] and his reliance on the *Webb* findings.

3.1   National Monuments (Amendment) Act 1994: Provisions

The National Monuments (Amendment) Act 1994, passed on 6th July 1994, establishes in section 2, the State's ownership "of any archaeological object found in the State after the coming into operation of this section where such object has no known owner at the time when it was found."

Sections 4 and 5 deal with the possession of archaeological objects and render illegal the possession of unreported archaeological objects. There is also an obligation to report the purchase, sale, acquisition or disposal of archaeological objects and to provide all requisite details to the Director of the National Museum on a prescribed form. This provides for at least detailed records of material, particularly where State acquisition may not arise immediately or at all.

Also of interest is section 7(b), which deals with the forfeiture of detection devices. This allows a member of the *Garda Siochána* to seize and detain a detection device without warrant if it is in the area of the site of a wreck or archaeological object[23] lying on, in or under the sea bed or on land covered by water "which he reasonably believes is being used in the commission of an offence under the said section."

Section 10 of the Act makes provision for the payment of rewards and sets out a number of criteria to be taken into account by the Director of the National Museum.

In relation to underwater discoveries, section 18 amends section 3 of the 1987 Act in relation to reporting. It provides for the reporting of wrecks and other underwater monuments to the Commissioners of Public Works and for the reporting of objects found in an underwater context to the Director of the National Museum, both within four days of discovery. It also requires that full particulars of the discovery be given to the relevant authority.

4.   *Re La Lavia, Juliana and Santa Maria de la Vision* (1995)

Between the finding of the Derrynaflan hoard in 1980 and the judgment in that case delivered by the Supreme Court in 1988, another discovery was made which was to have a profound effect in legal terms.

In 1985, a group of British divers located the wrecks of three Spanish Armada wrecks at Streedagh, Co. Sligo. The ships were of the Levant squadron of Philip II's ill-fated expedition, namely the *Juliana*, *La Lavia* and the *Santa Maria de la Vision* and all three were lost at Streedagh

---

21   For further analyses of the *Webb* decision, see R. Byrne and W. Binchy (1987) *Annual Review of Irish Law* pp. 104-107; N. Palmer 'Treasure Trove and Title to Discovered Antiquities' (1993) 2 *International Journal of Cultural Property* 275 at pp. 294-297.

22   *Re La Lavia, Juliana and Santa Maria de la Vision* [1996] 1 *Irish Law Reports Monthly* (I.L.R.M.) 194.

23   The term "archaeological object" is defined in the National Monument (Amendment) Act 1994 as:
       any chattel whether in a manufactured or partly manufactured or an unmanufactured state which by reason of the archaeological interest attaching thereto or of its association with any Irish historical event or person has a value substantially greater than its intrinsic (including artistic) value, and the said expression includes ancient human, animal or plant remains.

in September 1588. The divers claimed to be salvors in possession and also sought remuneration for their salvage services and a reward for the discovery of the vessels and/or damages.

However, on the first day of the High Court hearing,[24] in May 1993, it was conceded on behalf of the plaintiffs that the wrecks and all armaments, ordinance, appurtenances and other objects associated therewith on or under the sea bed at Streedagh, or removed therefrom by the group, were the property of the State.

A number of other issues were also to be tried[25] including the matter as to whether the Commissioners of Public Works in Ireland had made a wrongful decision in refusing to grant a licence to the plaintiffs under section 3(5) of the 1987 Act and whether the plaintiffs were entitled to damages under a number of different headings.

At the time of the discovery in 1985, only the relevant provisions of the Merchant Shipping Acts applied together with the National Monuments Acts 1930-1954 which have no specific provisions in relation to underwater sites. The 1987 Act came into force while the Streedagh case was awaiting trial. In the meantime the Commissioners placed a Preservation Order on the wreck sites, under section 8 of the National Monuments Act 1930, as amended by section 3 of the National Monuments (Amendment) Act 1954. The effect of the order was to prevent the group from carrying out any salvage operations at the site of the three wrecks. This order was challenged by the group and ultimately quashed by the High Court on 10th July 1987. An injunction was also granted restraining the State from interfering with the group when it was inspecting the site.

In rem summonses were issued in respect of the three vessels in November 1986 on behalf of the plaintiffs in their perceived capacity as salvors in possession of the wrecks and their contents.

As of July 1987, the group was constrained by the passing of the National Monuments (Amendment) Act 1987 and was therefore obliged to apply for a licence to excavate. This application was refused on the ground that the State did not have adequate conservation facilities to deal with the consequences of such an excavation.

The State did not dispute the plaintiffs' entitlement to a finders' reward, which it considered should be modest in size. In the event that salvage law was found not to apply, the group claimed a right to reward on the basis of the principles of the *Webb v. Ireland* decision.[26]

It is interesting to note that the cases of the *Tubantia*[27] and the *Santa Maria de la Rosa*,[28] relied upon by the plaintiffs, were referred to by Barr J. but regarded as irrelevant as both dealt with disputes between opposing groups of salvors rather than the fundamental issue as to whether salvage law applied to ancient wrecks. Barr J.'s pronouncements on this matter have been of immense importance and have helped to provide a unified code of heritage law in Ireland whereby practically all archaeological remains and artefacts, whether on dry land or at sea can be treated in like manner. With a small number of exceptions, all archaeological objects, including those from a maritime context can now be claimed by the State on the authority of the National Monuments Acts and that of the *Webb* and *Re La Lavia* decisions.

It had been maintained on behalf of the plaintiffs that salvage law applied to derelicts regardless as to how ancient the remains might be. The findings of Barr J. to the contrary are of such importance that it is necessary to quote him here at some length:[29]

---

24   *Re La Lavia, Juliana and Santa Maria de la Vision* [1996] 1 I.L.R.M. 194 at 195.
25   [1996] 1 I.L.R.M. 194 at 195.
26   See section 3 above. Also on the basis of *Pearse v. Bemis & Ors* [1986] 1 Q.B. 384 in which rights were accorded to certain salvors of the *Lusitania*.
27   *The Tubantia* [1924] P. 78, (1924) 18 Ll. L. Rep. 158.
28   Judgment of O'Keeffe P., delivered on 23 May 1969 114 I.L.T.R. 37. See account of the case by Sydney Wignall in 'The "Grey Dove" Affair', appendix 1 in C. Martin *Full Fathom Five: Wrecks of the Spanish Armada* (London, 1975) pp. 233-246.
29   From the transcript of the judgment of Barr J. delivered on 26 July 1994, pp. 92-93.

It seems to me that when so much time has elapsed since the original loss of a vessel that the question of ownership and attendant acolytes such as indemnification, lose their practical significance and merge into history, then the wreck should be regarded as having passed from the commercial realm of maritime salvage law into the domain of archaeological law. I do not see any conflict between admiralty salvage law based on the Merchant Shipping Act 1894 and the foregoing proposition as to the proper law applicable to the finding on the sea bed and recovery of ancient wrecks and/or their contents. The objective of the former is to provide a legal framework for commercial maritime salvage operations. The latter is concerned with the discovery and salvage from the sea of ancient historical remains and artifacts which are part of the national heritage of the nation. .... The common factor is the sea and both are distinct aspects of salvage law which, in my view, dove-tail comfortably. ... It seems to me that there are four fundamental features of an ancient maritime archaeological find in this jurisdiction. First, antiquity; secondly, State ownership; thirdly, lack of commercial market value in practical terms and finally, probable impossibility of tracing the successors in title of the owners and/or indemnifiers at the time of loss.

He goes on to state that none of the three ships lost at Streedagh belonged to Spain in 1588 but had rather been embargoed by Philip II for use in the Armada campaign. It would be virtually impossible to trace the successors in title to the merchants who had originally owned these Sicilian and Ragusan ships. He continues:[30]

... The ownership of the wrecks by the State is special in nature and, as already stated, derives from its function as custodian of the national heritage. It does not have commercial significance as envisaged in admiralty salvage law. I have no doubt that the wrecks of the 'Juliana', 'La Lavia' and 'Santa Maria de la Vision' passed out of the realm of commercial maritime law and into archaeological law long before they were found at Streedagh in 1985.

Barr J. then alluded to recent American case history in which the law of 'finds' is distinguished from maritime salvage law.[31] There are some similarities of rationale in terms of attitude to salvage law and the instances of what must be excluded from it due to the absence of information about an owner or because the owner is deemed to have abandoned his property. However, the 'finds' law situation ceases to compare with Irish law in cases where the American courts decide in favour of the finder. In Irish law, State ownership would apply to archaeological wreck or objects deemed to be outside the realms of merchant shipping law, as *per* Barr J.

Barr J.'s findings as described above are of huge importance and value in the context of Irish underwater heritage law. It is a pioneering judgment, which may well create a suitable blueprint to be followed in other jurisdictions as well.

However, the main thrust of Barr's findings was in favour of the plaintiffs rather than the State. The latter part of the judgment[32] considers whether the Commissioners of Public Works were in error in refusing the plaintiffs a licence to excavate and whether the plaintiffs were entitled to damages arising from the quashing of the Preservation Order under the Act of 1930. He found in the plaintiffs' favour on both of these issues.

He also found that the Commissioners failed in their duty to the public by neither licensing the Streedagh group to carry out a survey nor by arranging for a survey of their own to be carried out.

He found that the Commissioners were obliged both to reconsider and accede to a new licence application from the group or alternatively to have their own survey carried out. In the

30   *Ibid.* at p. 93.
31   Most notably the case of *Columbus-America Discovery Group v. Atlantic Mutual Insurance Co. (The Central America)* 1992 974 F.2d 450. See further, Chapter 13.
32   From the transcript of the judgment of Barr J. delivered on 26 July 1994, p. 99 *et seq.*

latter event, the plaintiffs would be entitled to be informed and consulted and if dissatisfied on any reasonable grounds would then be entitled in equity to a licence to carry out a survey of their own "to enable them to evaluate their claim for reward and to dispute findings by or advice from State experts."

He also found that the nature of the State's negotiations gave rise to legitimate expectation or promissory estoppel on the part of the Streedagh group. He found that a generous award should be paid to the group given the circumstances of discovery and taking into account *inter alia* the conduct of the group, the scholarly research which had been carried out by Mr Birch of the group and also the approach of the Supreme Court in *Webb v. Ireland* with regard to the payment of rewards.

He further held that the group were entitled to damages for the unlawful placing of a Preservation Order at Streedagh on the basis that the officials concerned were aware that the Order was not applicable on the basis of the law invoked, i.e. the application of dry land provisions to a maritime context. However, he found that there was no infringement of property rights under the Constitution, as this would depend on the holding of salvage rights by the group which was clearly not the case.

However, on 29th June 1995 the Supreme Court delivered a decision which overturned the majority of these latter findings while accepting the more general aspects of the judgment relating to Barr J.'s approach to salvage law and its relationship to heritage law.

The judgment of O'Flaherty J. in the Supreme Court addressed only two issues,[33] the first regarding the Commissioners' action in refusing a licence to the plaintiffs and the second as to whether the respondents were entitled in law to a reward for the discovery of the wrecks, as opposed to an award of grace and favour to be given at the discretion of the State. His decision on the first issue was that the licence which had been sought was a licence to excavate, which had been reasonably refused because of the difficulties in providing conservation facilities. Therefore, he stated:

> In holding that the Commissioners had acted unreasonably in not granting a licence to allow a pre-disturbance survey of the sea-bed in the area in question when that was not what was sought, I fear that the learned trial judge slipped into error.

It was agreed however, and approved by O'Flaherty J., that the respondents should re-apply for a licence – to survey only – in order to evaluate the extent and historical importance of the find. This licence was granted forthwith by the Commissioners of Public Works.

On the issue of promissory estoppel, O'Flaherty J. distinguished the present case from that of *Webb*. He stated that, in *Webb v. Ireland*:

> ... the finders of the Derrynaflan treasure trove were held to be entitled to an award based on an unqualified assurance given to one of the plaintiffs by the Director of the National Museum that he would be honourably treated and that that was an integral part of the transaction when the Derrynaflan hoard was deposited in the Museum.[34]

However, in relation to the present case he held that:

> I cannot find anything in the nature of a promise was held out to the respondents at any time by the servants of the State in such a manner as would bind the State ... it is clear that from the outset the respondents claimed to be salvors in possession of the wrecks and they

---

33   [1996] 1 I.L.R.M. 194 at 197.
34   [1996] 1 I.L.R.M. 194 at 199.

maintained that position at the trial in the High Court. Further, they did not recognise any entitlement of the State to the ownership or possession of the wrecks until the start of the case in the High Court. To adopt the position that they were entitled to either ownership or to salvage of the wrecks in question is inconsistent with the concept that they should be regarded as having a legitimate expectation of a reward from the State in the sense described by Finlay C.J. in the *Webb* case as entitling the finders in that case to an award.[35]

However, the judge was happy to adopt the general approach to awards taken by Walsh J. in the *Webb* case, i.e. that the giving of rewards was well founded in cases of finders of treasure trove and that it was in any event a means of safeguarding objects which might be found in the future. He alluded to the fact that the matter of rewards had now been legislated for as suggested by Walsh J., as per section 10 of the National Monuments Amendment Act 1994. It was not, however, applicable to this case which predated the aforementioned legislation.

He continued:

The choice that presents itself to the Court is to declare that there is a legal entitlement to an award, aside from the doctrine of legitimate expectation, in the strict sense, in which case it will be for the High Court Judge to assess what is a fair and just reward in the circumstances; the alternative is that the Court should hold that the matter of a reward is for the State but that its assessment should be reasonable having regard to some – it may be most – of the matters set forth by Barr J. ... the Courts have never taken on themselves an entitlement to declare it a matter of legal entitlement that there should be an obligation on the State to make rewards in circumstances such as the present case. I would hold that the matter of a reward is for the decision of the Commissioners in this case.

The assenting judgment of Denham J.[36] agreed in every respect with the O'Flaherty judgment but emphasised, and made certain new points in relation to, the payment of rewards. She highlighted the fact that the failure of the Royal Prerogative to treasure trove to survive into the Constitution of *Saorstát Eireann* suggested that the reward system, which was part and parcel of it, would not have survived either. The alternative was that the constitutional basis for the State's claim in *Webb* might also envisage an award system. She adopted the statement of Walsh J. already referred to above. She also added that it was not necessary to decide the issue as the Commissioners had already acceded that an award should be paid and that any decision regarding the amount of the reward was postponed pending the results of any licensed survey work at Streedagh. She concluded that the amount was a matter for the Commissioners and must be reasonable in all the circumstances and that it would be judicially reviewable..."in view of the nature of the decision and its place within the public domain."

Thus, the way was opened for antiquities from the sea and archaeological sites at sea to be treated under the same legislation and with the same policy approach as their dry land counterparts. In general, all objects and wrecks are likely to fall within the State's right to claim ownership of archaeological objects. The only exceptions would appear to be in cases where the objects and/or wrecks in question are of sufficiently recent date that a question of ownership or succession in title might arise. In such instances, merchant shipping law can be applied and/or Underwater Heritage Orders made in cases where important wrecks of more recent date may be at risk. In practice, the local receiver of wreck is likely to have an involvement in all cases of wreck or archaeological objects from a marine context because of the terms of the Merchant Shipping (Salvage and Wreck) Act 1993. This may be at formality or reporting level only, when material

---

35   [1996] 1 I.L.R.M. 194 at 199-200.
36   [1996] 1 I.L.R.M. 194 at 201-202.

over 100 years old is concerned, or may involve actual determination of ownership in the case of more recent wrecks or objects. The involvement of the receiver is to be welcomed and has proven very useful in this jurisdiction. The receiver often has the advantage of proximity to the place of discovery, invaluable local information and powers under customs and excise law, which can be drawn upon in difficult situations.

In summary, the effect of case law and new statutory provisions has, in the past decade, totally changed the face of maritime heritage law in Ireland and consequently, the approach to the protection of the underwater heritage.

Discoveries from the inland waterways are an integral part of this aquatic heritage and they are claimable under the terms of the National Monuments Acts 1930-1994 in like manner to discoveries made in any other context.

5.   State Agencies

Responsibility for the protection of the heritage – both dry land and underwater – is essentially divided between the National Museum of Ireland and the National Monuments Branch of the Office of Public Works (now renamed *Dúchas*, The Heritage Service). Both Departments are under the administration of the Department of Arts, Heritage, Gaeltacht and the Islands. In general terms, the National Museum of Ireland is responsible for archaeological objects, while *Dúchas* is responsible for monuments, their respective statutory responsibilities being set down in the National Monuments Acts 1930-1994.

The 1994 Act provides for a reporting system whereby archaeological objects are reportable to the Director of the National Museum of Ireland while wrecks are reportable to the Commissioners of Public Works. *Dúchas* is responsible for the granting of excavation and survey licences under the terms of the Act as well as the placing of Underwater Heritage Orders. It is also responsible for the survey and recording of monuments. This is well established and developed in relation to dry land sites but has recently been extended to include the underwater heritage. A maritime Sites and Monuments Record (SMR) has been established and an archaeological diving unit was set up in 1996 to work on creating and maintaining that record. The Unit is also available to investigate new underwater discoveries on behalf of the State agencies.

The National Museum has statutory responsibility for every archaeological object found in Ireland and claims them on behalf of the State. It is also the State's repository of all archaeological objects and reports of discoveries of new material, which are made under the National Monuments Acts, are investigated by the Museum. It is also responsible for the welfare and conservation of the movable heritage and processes applications for licences to alter and export archaeological objects. This includes overseeing arrangements for the excavation, storage and recording of archaeological material from underwater contexts and the implementation of the law in this regard. It has a consultative role in relation to the granting of excavation licences by the Commissioners of Public Works, which enables the National Museum to ensure that suitable provisions are in place to deal with archaeological objects uncovered in the course of excavation. The Museum has also administered a grant from the National Heritage Council, which enabled a number of archaeology graduates to receive training in scuba diving with a view to involvement in underwater archaeology.

In practice, there is a considerable overlap in the responsibilities of the two organisations. Most matters involving the underwater heritage require input from both and reciprocal consultation takes places very regularly. There has also been joint co-operation in a number of surveys and projects, and in relation to legal proceedings involving joint responsibility.

6.   The Involvement of Sportsdivers

The majority of Irish scuba diving clubs are affiliated to CFT (*Comhairle Fo-Thuinn* – the Irish Underwater Council). In the mid-1980s an underwater archaeology sub-committee was formed to cater for the interests of CFT divers who had an interest in this area of diving.

In 1989, the then membership of the underwater archaeology committee established an organisation known as IUART (the Irish Underwater Archaeological Research Team) made up predominantly of sportsdivers and a small number of professional archaeologists, some representing the relevant State bodies. Its purpose was to provide an opportunity for interested sportsdivers to become involved in legitimate archaeological work; to receive some basic training in underwater archaeology and to organise on a regional basis so as to be available to assist in the survey and recording of any sites or discoveries which might come to light in different parts of the country.

The emphasis was placed on survey rather than excavation because of the conservation implications associated with excavation. Licences to excavate underwater are granted only in exceptional circumstances and when it has been ascertained that all the necessary facilities are in place.

However, licences to dive only and to survey are readily granted to interested divers. In return, they are asked to submit a report on the current state of the sites dived. IUART members have assisted in a wide variety of projects, some assisting the State authorities, others initiated by individual groups within IUART. These have included shipwreck surveys, crannóg surveys, the survey of a medieval period wooden bridge on the River Shannon, the investigation and recording of submerged logboats and river crossings and survey and excavation necessitated by river drainage.

The involvement of the diving community is an important dimension to the preservation of the underwater heritage and to the successful implementation of the law. It is of value from a research and recording point of view but also as a means of gathering information about sites at risk. Divers in different parts of the country – and IUART members in particular – are often instrumental in the referral of reports to the State authorities in relation to new discoveries, or to interference with underwater sites which sometimes requires appropriate legal action.

7.   Towards the Future

The legislation and case law detailed above are, for the most part, very recent. It will therefore take some time before they can be put to the test comprehensively and for their effect to be properly analysed.

However, for the present, the protection of the underwater heritage is well supported in Irish law. Most importantly, it has become an integral part of the legal provisions for the dry land heritage. At administrative level, there is a greater awareness of the underwater heritage and its needs than ever before. Some new financing is becoming available to State agencies in what was previously a poorly funded area.

There is, nonetheless, a need for greater publicity and education in relation to heritage law. A more extensive archive of underwater remains is also required so as to assist the task of preservation. This is now well under way with the setting up of the maritime SMR by *Dúchas*, The Heritage Service, through the survey and archival work of the National Museum and as a result of the many projects initiated by IUART members. Consequently, the availability of an expanded archive and more survey records will assist in the State's task to legally protect the underwater heritage resource.

On paper at least, the outlook appears very positive. However, there are new threats to underwater sites on the horizon, e.g. the damage which could arise from commercial exploitation of the seabed through gravel extraction, dumping, intensive fishing and large-scale harbour works, to name but a few. These potential problems will need to be addressed and probably increasingly so. The existing legal framework appears to be quite comprehensive but undoubtedly there will also be a need for ongoing policy development and perhaps additional statutory provisions, as new challenges and situations arise.

Chapter 6

ITALY

Maria Clelia Ciciriello*

1.   Introduction

The underwater cultural heritage includes both archaeological objects and items of historical or artistic importance that are present in the sea and in river, lake and lagoon waters, in other words the so-called inland waters of a State.

The problems that such a heritage present to any legal regime are undoubtedly quite important. Indeed, on the one hand there is a close interdependence between technological development and the legal system and, on the other, there is a tension between scientific research and the economic exploitation of resources.

The broad meaning of the terms 'protection' and 'enhancement'[1] of the underwater cultural heritage covers a set of closely interrelated activities that are interdependent steps of a single process: research and exploration, recovery and classification of items; the latter step comprises a preliminary organisational phase, analysis and processing of the item by *ad hoc* specialised staff, etc., conservation and so on.

The very notion of protection of the underwater archaeological heritage was to appear rather late in the international arena, and it was only at the Ninth Session of the 1956 UNESCO General Conference, held in New Delhi, that it was first mentioned; for even longer it avoided the issuing of regulations governing the technical and scientific phases of the complex protection operations, leaving it up to domestic systems to regulate both private and public aspects of the matter.[2] Indeed, prior to the 1982 UN Convention on the Law of the Sea, no specific international rules concerning items of archaeological and historical importance found in sea waters were contained in the four Geneva Conventions of 1958, and even the 1982 Convention does not provide a precise definition of the expression 'items of an archaeological nature'.[3]

The international situation as outlined above reflects the attitude of the Italian legal system *vis-à-vis* the protection of underwater archaeological heritage. Indeed, in spite of the

---

*   Special thanks are due to Dr. Claudio Moccheggiani Carpano, Director of the Technical Division for Underwater Archaeology of the Ministry for Cultural and Environmental Heritage, for the valuable information and documents provided. This study was carried out within the framework of the Research Project on Underwater Cultural Heritage submitted by the author to the Italian Research Council (C.N.R.).

1   Editor's note: The concept of 'enhancement' or, in Italian, '*valorizzazione*', literally 'to add value to something', is interesting as it appears to be used as a term of art in Italian law and practice. Presumably, examples of 'enhancement' would include: research work on a particular find, conservation, restoration, and perhaps even the creation around a wreck site of an underwater park providing for controlled public access to the site.

2   See L. Migliorino *Il recupero degli oggetti storici ed archeologici sommersi nel diritto internazionale* (Milano, 1984) p. 27.

3   In the 1982 Convention there are two articles that relate to protection of the underwater cultural heritage: art. 303 which, after stating that States have the general duty of protecting such objects found at sea at any point whatsoever, defines the powers that the coastal State can exercise over such objects as far as the contiguous zone is concerned, hence creating a new principle of an 'archaeological zone'; and article 149 which refers to objects found in the 'Area'. See further, ch. 14.

considerable contribution afforded by submerged finds to the knowledge of the history of ancient art, and in spite of the systematic research carried out in particular in the Mediterranean Sea in recent decades, in Italy underwater archaeology is still considered to be an activity collateral to archaeological research.[4] Suffice it to recall that in its report issued in 1967, the Franceschini Committee - which had been assigned the task of studying the problems relating to the protection and enhancement of the cultural heritage and of suggesting relevant solutions - made no mention whatsoever of the disastrous condition at the time of Italy's underwater archaeological heritage.[5]

Unfortunately, Italy still lacks the much needed specific and comprehensive regulations which are indispensable for putting this matter right. Diving activities need to become subject to legal control, provisions need to be made for the *in situ* protection of sites, and it is necessary to create an archaeological zone off Italy's shores so as to extend its jurisdiction over sea waters up to 24 miles from its coastline and hence effectively protect its underwater heritage from being stolen and illicitly removed.[6]

After examining, *de iure condito,* the current Italian legal regime with regard to the protection of the underwater heritage, various bills pending before Parliament will be considered to evaluate, *de iure condendo*, their suitability for ensuring effective legal protection of this vast heritage which - because of its special nature and location - requires a complex set of measures that will take into account the various and at times conflicting interests that are to be protected.

2.   Legal Regime Governing the Finding and Recovery of Archaeological and Historical Items

As there is no comprehensive body of regulations in this area, the legal regime to be applied to underwater cultural heritage must be constructed by examining the regulations governing cultural heritage in general, which are contained in Act No. 1089 of 1st June 1939 entitled 'Protection of objects of artistic and historical interest',[7] and also in the Code of Navigation and the Civil Code.

Act No. 1089/39 states that its primary objective is to protect the cultural heritage,[8] a task which is to be accomplished through the instruments of conservation and enhancement; these very ideas form the foundations on which the Ministry for Cultural and Environmental Heritage is built. According to the Act, any historical or archaeological item that is found belongs to the

---

4   See W. Johannowsky *Problemi dell'archeologia subacquea in Italia, Bollettino di archeologia subacquea* Year I, Issue Zero, December 1993, p. 7.

5   See Act No. 310 of 26 April 1964: *Enquiry Committee on the protection and enhancement of the historical, archaeological, artistic and landscape heritage. Proceedings and Documents of the Franceschini Committee for the protection of cultural heritage in Italy*, Rome 1967.

6   On this latter point, see further section 7 below, and note Act No. 88 of 30 March 1998, 'Rules on the movement of cultural objects', referred to in section 6 below.

7   Act No. 1089 of 1 June 1939 was published in the Italian *Official Gazette* No. 184 of 8 August 1939. For a thorough and exhaustive examination of the contents of the Act on the preservation of Italy's cultural heritage, consisting of the items and property with regard to which Italy has obligations as provided for in the UNESCO Paris Convention of 1972 on the world's cultural and natural heritage, see P. Simone *'Le incidenze della Convenzione di Parigi del 1972 sulla legislazione italiana'* in M.C. Ciciriello, ed., *La protezione del patrimonio mondiale culturale e naturale a venticinque anni dalla Convenzione dell'Unesco* (Napoli, 1997) p. 359 *et seq.*

8   See art. 12. For an exhaustive study of the goals of the legislation on cultural heritage in Italy, see C. Caturani *'La disciplina giuridica dei beni culturali in Italia: strumenti dinamici di tutela e valorizzazione'* in L. Mezzetti, ed., *I beni culturali* (Padova, 1995) p. 41 *et seq.*

State, but there is no explicit mention of underwater archaeology,[9] an activity which did not exist when the Act was brought into force in 1939. Undoubtedly the scope of the Act must also cover items lying on the seabed of Italian territorial waters, set at twelve miles from the coastline, since there is no limitation to the application of its provisions to this area.

Besides the provisions contained in Act No. 1089/39, there are also articles 510 and 511 of the Navigation Code which cover wrecks at sea,[10] stating that as regards the ownership of the items found, they are to be returned to the owner where the latter claims them; articles 826 and 932 of the Civil Code also regulate this issue.

In seeking to determine which regulation applies, the first problem to be solved is the legal qualification of the item, in other words whether or not it can be defined as a cultural item through the material operations of research, location, discovery or detection, on the basis of which it can be declared that there is a public interest in its protection and enhancement by the State.[11] The definition may refer to the underwater item as a whole or to parts thereof, as happens for instance with navigation instruments of a sunken ship. One such instrument, namely the helm, having lost its original function, could be acknowledged as having an historical and artistic function and hence be defined as a cultural object.

'Cultural heritage' is an expression which appears in the text of one international instrument drawn up during the early 1950s,[12] but in Italian legislation it only appeared much later, in the reports of the Franceschini Committee of 1967.[13] It was given an authoritative definition during the 1970s by scholars,[14] who elaborated an open legal concept, whose content is determined on the basis of relevant technical and scientific elements.

---

9   As is well-known, Italy began scientific underwater research activities in the early 1950s thanks to the commitment of Nino Lamboglia. These activities were totally ignored by national legislative circles. Lamboglia was instrumental in the establishment in 1957 of a private experimental centre on underwater archaeology which later, as a result of an agreement with the Ministry of Education, became a consultative body of the Ministry, with the task of programming and co-ordinating underwater research activities. An exhaustive study of the historical evolution of the organisational structure of the subject can be found in C. Moccheggiani Carpano 'L'archeologia subacquea: una disciplina recente' in *Memorabilia: il futuro della memoria* (Rome, 1987) Vol. I, p. 168 *et seq.*; L. Vlad Borrelli *La situation de l'archéologie sous-marine en Italie* (1995); Programme des Nations Unies pour la Méditerrannée *Protection du patrimoine archéologique sous-marin en Méditerranée, Documents techniques*, V (Marseille, 1995) p. 47 *et seq.*

10 By wreck is meant: "any mobile item, originating as such or mobilised because detached from another item, to be found floating on water or submerged or lying on the seabed, or washed by the waters onto the shore of which the owner has voluntarily or involuntarily lost possession": see Scotti *La rimozione di cose sommerse* (Milano, 1967). According to Querci, the removal of ships, airplanes and submerged materials, as provided for in arts. 72 and 73 of the Navigation Code does not concern the salvage principle: "The assumption maintained in legal commentaries (Scotti, Grigoli) according to which this would be a form of salvage *ex officio*, does not take into account the fact that removing such objects is aimed at eliminating dangers and obstruction to navigation, so as to avoid future damage, rather than being aimed at recovering lost objects in order to obtain an economic profit": see F.A. Querci *Diritto della navigazione* (Padova, 1989) p. 568.

11 See S. Amorosino 'La disciplina italiana sui beni culturali e la tutela del patrimonio archeologico subacqueo' report submitted at the workshop on *La protezione del patrimonio culturale subacqueo nel Mediterraneo*, Anacapri, 1 October 1994.

12 The UNESCO Convention for the Protection of Cultural Property in the Event of Armed Conflict 1954 (the Hague Convention).

13 Cogo makes a systematic and exhaustive study of the process that led the Italian legislator to replace the expression 'items of historical and artistic interest' as in Act No. 1089/39 with 'cultural heritage': see G. Cogo 'Beni culturali ed ambientali tra ordinamento e istituzioni' in L. Mezzetti, ed., *Esigenze umanitarie e pluralità di ordinamenti* (Padova, 1995) p. 27 *et seq.*

14 See M.S. Giannini 'I beni culturali' *(1976) Riv. trim. dir. pubbl.* p. 3 *et seq.*

The aspects to be taken into account in establishing the legal regime applicable to underwater archaeological objects are related, first of all, to questions of title/ownership, secondly to the management of such objects, and thirdly to their circulation. This latter aspect is further complicated by the presence in the Italian system of European Community regulations which have imposed innovations not only in the nomenclature used to define cultural heritage-related operations, in deterrents and in how they are to be applied but - without prejudice to national legislation - they also affect the circulation and display of objects within the Community.

3.   Ownership of Underwater Objects

As concerns cultural finds, legal doctrine espouses a distinction on the basis of which public heritage is classified into two groups according to the subjective or the objective standpoint: the former includes all objects owned by the State, whereas the latter refers to objects, both public and private, of special importance that the State strongly wishes to protect and enhance so that they can be publicly displayed and enjoyed. On the other hand, Act No. 1089/39 distinguishes between objects belonging to the State or to public bodies which are governed by a regime of inalienability, and private property or objects belonging to non profit-making organisations governed by private law and enjoying freedom of movement, albeit conditioned by prevailing public interest[15] in compliance with article 839 of the Civil Code.

Paragraph 1 of article 826 of the Italian Civil Code states that assets belonging to the State which cannot be disposed of include "... objects of historical, archaeological, palethnological, palaeontological and artistic interest, found no matter by whom or how in the subsoil ...". Hence, under this article it is to be deemed that for the Civil Code underwater archaeological objects can be likened to buried objects which - once classified as items of cultural heritage following a technical evaluation by experts of the Administration - come under public ownership, are therefore *subjectively public*, and cannot be disposed of.[16]

Irrespective of the public or private ownership of such objects, the Italian legal system expresses great public interest in the protection of cultural heritage in general, and hence also of underwater heritage, so much so that several recent and important administrative laws[17] contain provisions which preserve access by the community to the cultural heritage. Legal doctrine states that all cultural objects whether they be public or private are *objectively of public interest*.[18] And in Article 9, the Constitution asserts the constitutional importance of the protection of cultural heritage and thus indirectly confirms the importance of enhancing such heritage. Both these functions are attributed to the State and - with regard to privately-owned objects of cultural interest which play a social function which is safeguarded - this justifies the restriction of private

---

15   In this regard, see art. 61 of Act No. 1089/39 which envisages the invalidity of any transaction to alienate privately-owned cultural heritage as a sanction for violating the duty to register the transaction, when the objects involved had been notified as being of "very special importance" through a deed issued by a public authority.

16   See Amorosino, *op. cit.* note 11. According to Frigo, the expression cultural heritage is to be taken in its legal meaning, irrespective of any aesthetic appreciation, as "... the embodiment of individual and collective culture": M. Frigo *La protezione dei beni culturali nel diritto internazionale* (Milano, 1988) p. 133.

17   Suffice it to mention as one of many examples, Act No. 241/1990 on 'Administrative Procedures'.

18   See M.S. Giannini *Diritto pubblico dell'economia* (Bologna, 1993).

ownership rights, which are diminished by a regime of concessions, authorisations, deterrents, and expropriation in the public interest.[19]

Article 932 of the Civil Code adds that " ... in the case of the finding of objects of historical, archaeological, palethnological, palaeontological and artistic interest the provisions of special laws apply". Hence only the 'finders-keepers' principle matters for the Civil Code with regard to the application of the so-called special laws.

On the other hand, Act No. 1089/39 in articles 43-45 considers as "objects found" only those which are the outcome of a search and thus not the result of mere chance discovery, as should be distinguished from the 'finders-keepers' principle which does not distinguish between a find and a discovery.[20] However, Chapter V of Act No. 1089/39, entitled "Regulation of finds and discoveries", sets forth rules concerning both principles. Moreover, whereas for article 48 of Act No. 1089/39 discovery and retrieval may be the outcome of chance, articles 510 et seq. of the Code of Navigation consider 'finds' essentially as the outcome of chance.

From a comparison of the regulatory texts mentioned above it can be inferred that the reference to special laws mentioned in article 932 of the Civil Code is to be taken as referring to Act No. 1089/39 whenever underwater objects of archaeological, historical and artistic interest that have been retrieved have no owner and have been found by chance. However, being special legislation, the provisions of the Navigation Code will apply in cases where such objects are found by chance and are not res nullius.[21] Being designed to protect the primary interest of saving the objects and assets found, the provisions of the Navigation Code do not protect the interest of the finder in being acknowledged as owner of the object found. These provisions only recognise the right of the finder to be reimbursed the expenses incurred and to receive a reward.[22] In the case of an unknown owner, the provisions state that the object must be transferred to the State with loss of ownership rights if it is not claimed before a certain deadline or if the obligations envisaged by the law are not complied with.[23]

Transferring underwater objects of archaeological and historical importance to the State after their salvage confirms that Italian legislators wish to protect the 'function of public enjoyment' attributed to such objects. Indeed, other types of objects that are salvaged have lost their function and thus the legislation in force tends to have them returned to their lawful owners.

---

19   Concerning the legitimacy of the restriction of private ownership rights over cultural items, of significance are certain remarks made by Mazzoni: "Entitlement to ownership rights over a cultural item lies with individuals and the State and with other public bodies. In contrast the power of establishing how it is to be exercised lies with the State, which, consistently with the fundamental constitutional principle with regard to ownership, will determine by law the modes of purchase, enjoyment and limitations so as to guarantee that the ownership of cultural property exercises a social function (art. 41, Constitution)": C.M. Mazzoni 'Aspetti civilistici della tutela dei beni culturali in Italia' (1989) Riv, critica dir. priv. 393 et seq. It is on the basis of this function that the provision of art. 54 of Act No. 1089/39 is justified. Article 54 recognises that the Ministry for Cultural and Environmental Heritage can exercise the power of expropriation of privately owned cultural property when an "important interest" is at stake with regard to the conservation or enhancement of the national cultural heritage.

20   See also R. Albano 'Recupero, ritrovamento di relitti ed occupazione di cose abbandonate in mare' (1954) vol. II Rivista dir. int. nav. 91 et seq.; G. Nasca 'In tema di ritrovamento in mare di relitti e di cose di interesse archeologico' (1963) Giurisprudenza siciliana 379.

21   In the 1963 'Melqart' case, the Tribunal of Sciacca maintained that Act No. 1089/39 was applicable to the recovery of a Phoenician statue by an Italian fishing boat twenty miles off Sicily's coast which, having been hauled on board, was considered as having been recovered on Italian territory and consequently, in accordance with the above Act, was the property of the State: see Tribunale di Sciacca, 9 January 1963, Foro it., 1963, I, p. 1317 et seq.

22   See art. 510, para. 2 and art. 993, para 2.

23   According to art. 522, para. 2 of the Code of Navigation "... objects of artistic, historical, archaeological or ethnographic interest ... shall be transferred to the State".

Even though conceptually the expressions 'underwater archaeological objects' and 'underwater cultural objects' are not equivalent, as the latter category is much broader in scope than the former, the distinction is not relevant with respect to the legal regime governing them because there are two sets of provisions contributing to their classification as State-owned assets, set forth in Act No. 1089/39:[24] the provisions on location (whether underground or underwater), and those on finds and discoveries,[25] without prejudice in any case to the discretionary power of the Administration to transfer the object to a private body by means of an *ad hoc* order,[26] if this is deemed useful.

Finally it must be pointed out that the establishment of an archaeological zone,[27] with the ensuing acquisition by the Italian State of exclusive jurisdiction over the removal of archaeological or historical objects located within 24 miles from the coastline as provided for in article 303, paragraph 2 of the UN Convention on the Law of the Sea to which Italy is a party,[28] would not cause any change in the ownership regime governing the objects removed directly or with the authorisation of a State body, namely the Fine Arts Departments having territorial jurisdiction, nor would there be any change in the rights of the salvor established on the basis of the regulations of private international law. This regime is explicitly saved in paragraph 3 of article 303 of the Convention.[29]

4.   Administrative Organisation of the Management of Underwater Archaeological Objects

As there is no comprehensive and specific legislation on underwater archaeology in Italy, it is necessary to examine the organisational and administrative framework within which this activity, which is extremely specialised and scientifically and technically complex, is being carried out.

In 1986, the Ministry for Cultural and Environmental Heritage, which took over competence for this area from the Ministry of Education in 1974, set up the Technical Service for Underwater Archaeology (STAS) in order to meet the growing need for specialised activities in the protection and enhancement of the underwater archaeological heritage.[30]

This new centralised technical body was assigned a number of tasks, the first of which was emergency action to be taken anywhere throughout the State (except for the Regions of Sicily, Valle d'Aosta and the autonomous Provinces of Trento and Bozen which exercise exclusive competence over this area) upon request by the territorial Fine Arts Offices which had hitherto exercised this role themselves. In carrying out this function STAS is supported by the Carabinieri

---

24   In fact Act No. 1089/39 distinguishes between items belonging to the State or to public bodies, items belonging to private individuals and items belonging to non profit-making organisations governed by private law, providing for a partially different set of rules for each category. Article 23 of the Act is relevant, as is art. 822 of the Civil Code. See T. Alibrandi and P. Ferri *I beni culturali ed ambientali* (Milano, 1995) p. 397 *et seq.*

25   Along these lines, see Amorosino, *op. cit.* note 11.

26   See arts. 46 and 49 of Act No. 1089/39 on this, according to which items found or discovered may be awarded as a prize to the research licence holder or to the finder.

27   See further section 7 below.

28   The Convention was ratified and enacted through Act No. 689 of 2 December 1994, published in *Official Gazette* No. 295, 19 December 1994 (*suppl. ord.* no. 64), which contains the French text and a non-official Italian translation.

29   According to art. 303, para. 3, of the 1982 Convention, "Nothing in this Article affects the rights of identifiable owners, the law of salvage or other rules of admiralty, or laws or practices with respect to cultural exchanges."

30   The STAS was set up by Ministerial Decree of 30 October 1986 within the Central Office for environmental, architectural, archaeological, artistic and historical heritage.

Units for the protection of artistic heritage and by the Diving Units,[31] the *Guardia di Finanza* (naval and diving units), the Fire Brigade and the police. Another task of STAS is the planning and implementation of interregional schemes and projects involving the Fine Arts Offices.[32] These are designed to prevent disturbance and damage to the underwater archaeological heritage through the employment of specialised technical divisions, that are to be set up over the course of time[33] and based near the major underwater archaeological sites, for the management of the many sites which are currently operational.[34] While these centres have been created, they have never entered into operation because it was preferred to enhance the units set up within the various Fine Arts Offices for carrying out these activities.

In spite of its endemic lack of human and material resources, STAS is assigned the additional and third role of being the technical and logistical support centre and co-ordinator of *in situ* operations that come under the competence of the Ministry for Cultural Heritage and of other State bodies. Of special importance is the collaborative effort with the Ministry of the Merchant Navy which began in 1989 and which was aimed at organising the competition for recruiting the military staff of the Harbour Offices to make up the units for the protection of underwater heritage. According to this joint agreement, training is to be provided by the Ministry for Cultural Heritage,[35] whereas the Ministry of the Merchant Navy, which has become the Ministry for Transportation and Navigation,[36] has the task of recognising the permits of underwater operators required for being officially registered.

As concerns the *in situ* protection of underwater cultural heritage (an issue which is closely related to the technical training of the staff that are to provide such protection), a particularly effective instrument to succeed the emergency phase which has characterised the interventions of the Italian Administration for too long a time, would be the establishment of protected marine sites in accordance with the provision of Act No. 394 of 6th December 1991, entitled 'Model Law on

---

31   See Decree by the Minister for Cultural Heritage of 5 March 1992, 'Establishment at the Ministry of a Carabinieri Unit for the protection of artistic heritage', in *Official Gazette* No. 64 of 17 March 1992. Article 1, para. 3 of the Consolidated Text of Provisions for Practising Underwater Archaeology (Seventh Standing Committee of the Chamber of Deputies, Culture, Science and Education, 24 September 1997) without prejudice to the prevention and control activities carried out by the Carabinieri for the protection of artistic heritage, assigns the task of co-ordinating the surveillance activities of marine areas and internal waters of historical, artistic or archaeological interest, carried out by the police and Harbour Offices, by holding periodical duty conferences *ex* art. 14 Act No. 241 of 7 August 1990.

32   Considering that sound management of the underwater cultural heritage requires modern underwater archaeology founded on appropriate methodological and technological content, the projects mentioned in the text are undoubtedly a significant response to the inadequacies of emergency management both from the technical/financial and methodological standpoints.

33   The Technical Units set up thus far are: the Technical Unit for Marine Archaeology at Castello di Baia; the Technical Unit for Fluvial Archaeology set up at the Rome Fine Arts Office; the Technical Unit for Lacustrine Archaeology at Castello di Sirmione, and the Technical Unit for Lagoon Archaeology at the Venice Fine Arts Office. The task of these centres is to elaborate intervention strategies that are best suited to the sites involved.

34   There are hundreds of sites that have been opened in the course of over ten years of activity by STAS, which unfortunately is still understaffed and lacks appropriate resources. In addition, comprehensive legislation regulating underwater archaeological activities, guaranteeing its specificity and the professional suitability of its staff, is still lacking.

35   See Legislative Decree of 12 July 1989, *Disposizioni per la tutela delle aree marine di interesse storico, artistico ed archeologico*, in *Official Gazette* of 28 July 1989, General Series, No. 175, p. 15 *et seq.*

36   See art. 68 of the Code of Navigation, according to which the Maritime Administrations have the authority to set up special registers in which all those exercising any sea-related activity are to enter their names, provided they have the professional requirements and that they undertake to abide by the codes of conduct set forth by the Administrations.

Protected Sites'.[37] This instrument would be conducive to the special management and protection regime which is required by underwater heritage which is also endowed with a naturalistic and environmental value. In pursuance of articles 9 and 32 of the Constitution and in accordance with international agreements,[38] Act No. 394/91 sets forth the fundamental principles for the establishment and management of special sites. The aim of the Act is to ensure and foster, in a co-ordinated manner, conservation activities and enhancement of the natural heritage of the State[39] in areas where the removal of archaeological finds is forbidden.[40] Such sites are monitored by the Harbour Offices.[41]

In pursuance of Act No. 394/91, the creation of underwater archaeological parks would have a number of benefits. First of all, endowed as they would be with specialised facilities for the restoration and conservation of finds, they would ensure adequate *in situ* conservation and so avoid the much deprecated dismembering of contexts associated with the practice of retrieval at all costs; secondly, such parks would combine the needs of conservation and display by creating real open museums, thus attracting attention to the whole of the deposit; thirdly, they would strengthen the effectiveness of monitoring to prevent illicit removal of underwater objects.[42] Underwater archaeological parks would also be the best solution for protecting archaeological sites from threats arising from nearby harbours and coastal areas where industrial plants having infrastructure at sea are located. However, adequate legal protection will be possible only if thorough scientific knowledge can be gathered through a co-ordinated and systematic cataloguing of all the underwater archaeological heritage.

5.   Qualification as 'Underwater Archaeological Operator'

To date there has been no comprehensive legislation regulating and thereby allowing diving activities by the staff of the Ministry for Cultural and Environmental Heritage. However, the issue of the professional qualification of the personnel assigned to search for, excavate and protect underwater objects has been the subject of lengthy debate and of various governmental and parliamentary bills which have so far failed to produce any legislation.

Over the last few years, in commenting on and criticising the various proposals, scientific circles have identified certain features which would have to underlie any future legislation governing underwater archaeological activities. One of the most significant features is the principle of *professional competence*, which demands first of all that archaeologists should take a direct part in any search, excavation and protection activity carried out underwater; secondly, that provided they have the required competence, the personnel of the Ministry for Cultural Heritage should be used in ancillary underwater archaeology-related activities; thirdly, that there should be recruitment

---

37   Published in *Official Gazette* No. 292 of 13 December 1991.
38   In this way the Italian legislator seems to have anticipated the provisions of the European Convention on the Protection of Archaeological Heritage, La Valletta, 16 January 1992. In art. 2 ii) it is stated that each party to the agreement undertakes to protect the archaeological heritage by envisaging " ... la constitution de zones de réserve archéologiques, même sans vestiges apparents en surface ou sous les eaux, pour la conservation de témoignages matériels à étudier par les générations futures".
39   See art. 1 para. 1.
40   See art. 18, Act No. 394 of 6 December 1991, 'Model Law on Protected Areas' (*Official Gazette* No. 292 of 13 December 1991).
41   See art. 28, Act of 31 December 1982, on the defence of the sea (*Official Gazette* No. 16, *suppl. ord.*, of 18 January 1983).
42   Concerning the creation of archaeological parks in Italy, see P.A. Gianfrotta 'Parchi archeologici subacquei (la situazione in Italia)' in G. Vedovato and L. Borrelli Vlad, eds., *La tutela del patrimonio archeologico subacqueo*, Ravello European University Centre for Cultural Heritage (Roma, 1995) p. 57 *et seq.*

of 'archaeological inspectors' specialised in this area; and finally, there should be the establishment of a national committee for underwater archaeology designed to plan investigations and schedule research consistently with the requirements of representation and competence so as to ensure transparency and credibility of the work done by the committee.

Considering that the greatest danger for underwater objects is the damage they may incur through excavation and *in situ*[43] activities carried out by unskilled personnel, the consolidated bill adopted on 24th September 1997 by the Seventh Standing Committee of the Chamber of Deputies for Culture, Science and Education seems to provide for all the above-mentioned needs. Indeed, first of all it adopts the principle of *professional competence* in article 1, paragraph 4, which reads:

> Any search, safeguard and protection activity involving cultural objects ... needs to be carried out under the leadership of archaeologists capable of taking a direct part in the underwater archaeological activities.

In this way underwater search activities are put on a par with search activities carried out on land in terms of complexity and specificity. For these purposes, the Ministry for Cultural and Environmental Heritage is assigned the task, in article 3 paragraph 6, of organising a public competition for recruiting archaeological inspectors specialised in underwater archaeology.[44]

Bearing in mind the foregoing, of special importance is article 3 of the consolidated bill which makes provision for the training of the staff of the Ministry for Cultural and Environmental Heritage assigned to underwater exploration and salvage activities.[45] The function of the new professional profile of 'underwater archaeological operator' is subject to the attainment of a special licence certificate after having completed a theoretical and practical course organised by the Ministry for Transportation and Navigation together with the Ministry for Cultural and Environmental Heritage, the National Civil Protection Service and the Armed Forces.[46] Approval of the law and its subsequent application would finally enable the Fine Arts Offices to take independent and timely action whenever and wherever required, using research methods and restoration techniques that are suited to pursuing the primary goal of conserving and enhancing Italy's underwater archaeological heritage. This would finally put an end to the emergency nature of its interventions to date.

---

43   As is well-known, the *in situ* protection of the underwater archaeological heritage is dealt with by the European Convention on the Protection of the Archaeological Heritage of 16 January 1992, promoted by the Council of Europe, the scope of which includes also archaeological objects found in the ground. It does not provide that signatory States are under an obligation to conserve *in situ* such objects, but that this be done where necessary: see L. Migliorino 'La protezione in situ del patrimonio culturale subacqueo', presentation at the workshop *La protezione del patrimonio culturale subacqueo nel Mediterraneo*, Anacapri, 1 October 1994.

44   Regarding the underwater archaeologist, the establishment of a national register of archaeologists and art historians would be of special importance.

45   The professional profiles of underwater personnel, in particular: underwater technical assistant, specialised underwater operator, archaeologist, and assistant archaeologist, were specified in Decree of the President of the Republic (DPR) No. 1219 of 29 December 1984, in *Official Gazette*, No. 90 of 30 October 1985.

46   As early as 1977, the interim Minister for Cultural and Environmental Heritage, Hon. Pedini, with Circular of 6 August, entitled 'Underwater Archaeological Research', after having confirmed the direct competence of the Ministry in the issuing of excavation permits to third parties, in pursuance of Act No. 1089/39 (arts. 45, 46, 48, and 49) and subsequent amendments, had bestowed upon the Departments for Archaeological Heritage the power to authorise bodies, institutes and private parties to carry out underwater search and salvage activities provided that there are adequate guarantees ensuring professionalism and reliability and, where possible, under the scientific co-ordination and adequate control of the personnel of the Administration, capable of exercising such control, even if not employed directly by the Department having territorial jurisdiction.

6.   Movement of the Underwater Archaeological Heritage

Just as occurs with cultural heritage in general, the underwater cultural heritage may be seriously damaged and jeopardised by recovery/salvage and *in situ* protection measures adopted without appropriate technical and scientific know-how, and also by illicit removal which is a further cause of impoverishment of the cultural heritage.[47] In order to control the latter illicit activity, the movement of such goods should be regulated by provisions designed to protect the integrity of the nation's cultural heritage, especially in the case of certain categories of items that are the expression of the historical and cultural traditions of a people.[48] Since in the Italian legal system there are no specific provisions for underwater heritage, reference needs to be made once again to the regulations governing the movement of cultural heritage in general, which means referring again to Act No. 1089/1939, according to which public intervention in the movement of artistic and historical objects takes one of three forms: controls designed to prevent the movement of objects when this could endanger their preservation and enjoyment; controls aimed at keeping track of the transfers of title and creation of rights over objects; acquisition by the State in order to remove objects from private trade.[49]

Until 1st April 1993, the date of entry into force of EC legislation concerning the movement of cultural property,[50] Italian law differentiated items according to the class to which they belonged, but no differentiation was made with regard to the destination of the items when exported outside the national territory.

Indeed, the heritage indicated in article 1 of Act No. 1089/39,[51] which was subject to conditions of general protection, was accorded full freedom of movement within the national territory, with passage of title not requiring any formality; in addition, the Act envisaged the right of exporting items of such heritage abroad after having been issued with an *ad hoc* permit on

---

47   Concerning the problems of illicit trafficking of underwater cultural heritage, see M. Pedini 'Traffico illecito dei beni archeologici subacquei' in G.Vedovato and L.Vlad Borrelli, eds., *La tutela del patrimonio archeologico subacqueo*, Ravello European University Centre for Cultural Heritage (Roma, 1995) p. 21 *et seq*. To illustrate the scope of the illicit purloining of cultural heritage in Italy, suffice it to mention that in the five-year period 1992-1996, the Carabinieri recovered 131,000 stolen archaeological objects. The so-called 'archaeological war' in the Mediterranean has become topical again after the extensive reporting in the press of the expeditions organised by Robert Ballard, an American researcher, to recover objects from sunken ships, who ploughs the seas on his nuclear submarine No. 1, see *Il Corriere della sera*, 2 August 1997; *L'Unità*, 2 August 1997; *Il Tempo*, 3 August 1997.

48   Concerning the movement of cultural heritage in general, see also A. Lanciotti *La circolazione dei beni culturali nel diritto internazionale e comunitario* (Napoli, 1996); M. Marletta *La restituzione dei beni culturali, Normativa comunitaria e convenzione Unidroit* (Padova, 1987) esp. pp. 39-120.

49   See T. Alibrandi and P. Ferri *I beni culturali ed ambientali* (Milano, 1995) p. 396.

50   The normative texts being referred to consist of two regulations and a directive: (EEC) Regulation No. 3911/92 of the Council of 9 December 1992, relative to the export of cultural heritage; (EEC) Regulation No. 752/93 of the Commission of 30 March 1993, with provisions for the enforcement of (EEC) Regulation No. 3911/92 of the Council of 9 December 1992, relative to the export of cultural heritage; Directive 93/7/EEC of the Council of 15 March 1993, relative to the returning of objects of cultural heritage illicitly transferred abroad from a Member Country.

51   The issuing of a permit for exporting the items mentioned in art. 1 is provided for in the subsequent art. 36 of Act No. 1089/39, as well as in arts. 129 *et seq*. of Regulation No. 363 of 30 January 1913 which enforces Act No. 364 of 20 June 1909, and of Act No. 688 of 23 June 1912, whose enforeability is specifically provided for in art. 7 of Decree Law No. 288 of 5 July 1972 which makes reference both to the fundamental Act and to the regulatory norms other than those expressly amended.

payment of a tax.[52] In this way, the export of cultural heritage was submitted to undifferentiated regulations irrespective of whether the destination was a Member Country of the EC or a Third Country. Moreover, the regulations allowed the competent Offices, namely the Offices for the Exportation of Antiquities and Objects of Art of the Fine Arts Departments, to interpret very broadly, and hence inconsistently, the concept of "damage hindering exportation" expressed in article 35, paragraph 1, of the Act.[53] In this way they were in a position to be able to refuse to issue a licence for any item having some historical or artistic interest in an undifferentiated manner irrespective of its destination, since the regulation does not qualify in any way the damage, if any, that could ensue for the national heritage.[54] In addition, when an export permit is not issued, in accordance with article 39, a right of pre-emption by the State is envisaged, at a price formulated by the Minister for Cultural Heritage, or, if the complainant refuses, at a price set by a board of arbitrators.

In contrast, in the case of heritage objects classified as being under privileged protection because of their special importance,[55] exportation is not allowed outside the boundaries of the State and the State is accorded a right of pre-emption in cases of transfer of title within the national territory.

In this connection one should argue the case as to whether this regime for the movement of cultural heritage established in Italy is consistent with the spirit and the letter of the Treaty of Rome, and secondly, what measures should have been adopted by the Italian State at the time of

---

52   This tax was later declared to be incompatible with the Treaty of Rome by the Court of Justice of the European Communities and hence not applicable whenever the country of destination was a Member Country of the EC. See art. 36 of the Act. In January 1960, the EEC Commission had invited Italy to abolish this tax where Member Countries were involved, setting 1 January 1962, as first peremptory deadline for the transient period, subsequently extended to 31 December 1965. As Italy had not respected the deadline, in its Court ruling of 10 December 1968 for case 7/68 (*Foro it.* 1969, IV, c. 89) and the subsequent Court ruling of 13 July 1972, on case 48/71 (*Foro it.*, 1972, IV, c. 221 with commentary by A. Tizzano *Un non commendevole record dell'Italia membro CEE*), the Court of Justice of the European Communities declared the import tax to be paid by Member Countries on the export of objects of historical and artistic interest incompatible with the Treaty. The Court maintained that the function for which the tax was levied by the Italian government, namely to protect the national heritage, could not be accepted because the exceptions to the fundamental principle of the freedom of movement envisaged in art. 36 are to be interpreted in a restrictive manner. In order to fulfil the duties deriving from the two Court rulings, Italy adopted the Decree Law No. 288 of 5 July 1972, turned into Act No. 487 of 8 August 1972 whereby arts. 35-41 of the Act were modified and the tax on exports to Member Countries of the Community envisaged in art. 37 was abolished. For comments on this aspect, see T. Alibrandi and P. Ferri *I beni culturali ed ambientali* (Milano, 1995) p. 497 *et seq.*
53   See art. 35, para. 1 which states that "It is forbidden to export any of the objects listed in Article 1 of the Act and in DPR No. 1409 of 30 September 1963 from the territory of the Republic whenever this may cause damage to the national cultural heritage because such objects in themselves or in relation to the historical and cultural context to which they belong are of artistic, historical, archaeological, demographic, bibliographic, documental or archival interest, *according to the reasoned opinion of the competent export offices ...*" (author's emphasis).
54   The assessment of the damage may constitute an application of the protection clause contained in art. 36 of the EC Treaty, to the extent to which it is actually aimed at ensuring the protection of national heritage and not at violating the principle of freedom of movement confirmed by the Single Market.
55   All classified objects are listed in an administrative order issued by the Ministry for Cultural Heritage in pursuance of art. 3 of Act No. 1089/39. Article 3 provides "The Minister for Cultural and Environmental Heritage administratively informs private owners, possessors or holders of any title to objects indicated in Article 1 as being particularly important. Being immovables by nature or by competence, the rules in para. 2 of the above-mentioned Article are applied. The list of movable items whose special importance has been notified is held at the Ministry for Cultural and Environmental Heritage and copies have been deposited with the Prefectures. They may be examined by whomsoever may be interested."

entry into force of the secondary Community legislation with a view to harmonising its law with the regime of the Single Market.[56]

With regard to the first query, it is indisputable that the spirit of article 36 of the EC Treaty is to reconcile the principle of the free movement of goods confirmed in articles 30-34 with the imperative need to protect the nation's cultural heritage by applying the protection clause which, given the special nature of cultural heritage, provides a loophole thanks to which imports and exports can be prohibited; and this is justified by the drive to protect the nation's artistic, historical and archaeological heritage, albeit in full respect for important limitations some of which have been confirmed in article 36 itself and others identified by Community caselaw.[57] It must be acknowledged however that, being focussed on controlling movement, the Italian regime was based on general prohibition on exports that could however be overcome on a case-by-case basis by means of permits, which being issued through administrative instruments ended up attributing too great a discretionary power to the competent authorities. And experience has shown that the tendency has not been that of adopting a restrictive interpretation of the exceptions to the principle of freedom as requested by the Court of Justice.[58] This has resulted from the fact that the discretionary assessment as to the possible damage to the national historical and cultural heritage should have been made on the basis of the 'general cultural' guidelines mentioned in article 35, paragraph 2 of Act No. 1089/39, which in most cases have never been made known to the competent Office for the Exportation of Antiquities and Objects of Art.[59] For the above reasons, and in light of article 36, it is just as unjustifiable for the State to purchase the items over which it exercises its right of pre-emption, as envisaged in article 39 of Act No. 1089/39, at a special price and not at their market price.

As concerns the second query, there is no doubt that with the entry into force of the Single Market, and with the enforcement of the Community legislation referred to above, which can be applied to the underwater archaeological heritage as expressly stated in the annex to Regulation No. 3911/92 and to Directive 93/7,[60] it was no longer acceptable that the same export regime was to apply equally to Member Countries and to Third Countries, and hence it was necessary to make a

---

56   On this aspect, see the accurate and exhaustive analysis undertaken by F. Lemme and E. Torri *Relazione sui problemi connessi alla circolazione dei beni culturali in area comunitaria dopo l'integrazione del mercato unico europeo e proposte di modifica della legge 1089/39*. Atti della Giornata di studio, organizzata dal Ministero degli Affari Esteri, *Revisione della normativa sul patrimonio culturale,* Villa Madama, Roma, 5 February 1992.

57   See, e.g., A. Roccella 'Ordinamento comunitario ed esportazione dei beni culturali' (1993) *Dir. com. sc. int.li* 539 *et seq.*, esp, p. 544, who provides an analysis of the residual competences of the State in these matters, in the light of the principle of subsidiarity introduced by the Maastricht Treaty under Article 3B.

58   See Court of Justice, Case 7/68 of 10 December 1968, *Oggetti d'arte, Foro it.*, 1969, IV, c. 89; Case 46/76 of 25 January 1977, *Bauhuis, Racc.* 1977, p. 5; Case 75/81 of 9 June 1982, *Commissione c. Repubblica italiana, Racc.* 1982, pp. 2187 *et seq.* and 2204.

59   If it is true that according to the Court of Justice it is up to each Member State to define its own cultural heritage, the prohibition on the export of items thereof is justified only for objects that are of special importance and therefore can be considered as an expression of the national culture. On the basis of such considerations, the provisions of art. 2 of Act No. 487 of 8 August 1972 on the export of objects of artistic and archival interest, which bestows upon the Ministry for Cultural and Environmental Heritage the power of prohibiting the export of entire categories of cultural items, is not in line with Community Law: see M. Chiti *Beni culturali e mercato unico europeo, Associazione per lo studio e le ricerche parlamentare, Quaderno n. 3* (Milano, 1993) p. 163 *et seq.* On the circulation of cultural heritage within the EC see, *inter alia*, I. Grassi 'La circolazione dei beni culturali nella Comunità Europea' in L. Mezzetti, ed., *I beni culturali* (Padova, 1995), p. 1 *et seq.*

60   See Annex letter A, no. 1, first dash, where "... archaeological finds over a hundred years old coming from submarine excavations and discoveries ..." are among the lists of categories of cultural heritage.

distinction between so-called 'intra-Community delivery' and exports to a Third Country, with all the ensuing regulatory, administrative and organisational problems for the Italian Cultural Heritage Administration.[61]

While awaiting comprehensive reform of Act No. 1089/39, the Ministry for Cultural and Environmental Heritage has issued a circular which gives an interpretation of EC Regulation No. 3911/92[62] on the permanent or temporary export of the cultural heritage listed in the annex, irrespective of ownership. The circular aims at clarifying to the competent Offices the innovative scope of the Community Regulations on the subject, on the incorrect assumption that the regulation of non-Community exports of cultural heritage is a matter which is to be exclusively governed by the Community.[63] Given the direct applicability and supremacy of the EC legislation, it was deemed that the entry into force of the Community rules would, on the one hand, make inoperative the State's right under article 39 of Act No. 1089/39 to purchase any item meant for export (items covered by the scope of application of the Regulation) and, on the other, would abolish the export tax on heritage items envisaged in article 37 of the same Act.[64] Paradoxically therefore, greater protection is afforded to cultural heritage that, being excluded from the classes of items listed in the Regulation because it is less important, goes on being subject to State legislation and hence to the application of the export tax and to the right of purchase by the State.

As concerns the export of archaeological finds to countries other than Community Members, there is still a need for an export permit since Italy has not exercised the right envisaged in article 2, paragraph 2 of the EC Regulation which applies to items of limited archaeological or scientific value.[65]

61　The categories of heritage which come under Community Law are identified on the basis of three criteria: nature of the object, its age, its value, where the range of values set are the outcome of a compromise between the more protectionist States and the more *laissez-faire* States. In this connection we must recall that, in formulating informal remarks on the draft Regulation and draft Directive, and in particular with regard to the definition of national heritage to be protected, the Italian government had pointed out that it did not seem appropriate to follow the criterion of a threshold value according to which an item would be automatically included or excluded from the sphere of cultural heritage, arguing first of all the case that the economic value does not coincide with the cultural value, and secondly emphasising the difficulties in establishing the entity that would have to determine the economic value, and the criteria to be used, given the differences in market valuations in the various countries and the countless opportunities that would arise for arbitrary conduct and for unfair exploitation.

62　(EEC) Regulation No. 3911/92 of the Council of 9 December 1992 (*ECOG* No. A: 3951/1 of 31 December 1992) enacted by the Commission through Regulation No. 752/93 of 30 March 1993 (*ECOG* No. 77/24 of 31 March 1993), was subsequently amended by (EC) Council Regulation No. 2469/96 of 16 December 1996.

63　As already stated previously, art. 36 of the EC Treaty states within certain limitations that its provisions hold without prejudice to national laws of Member Countries in the area of the export of heritage and art. 128 of the Maastricht Treaty applies the principle of subsidiarity to cultural matters. For an in-depth discussion of the evolution of art. 36, see F. Mucci 'La Comunità europea ed i beni culturali mobili: dal Trattato di Roma al Trattato di Maastricht' (1997) LII *La comunità internazionale* p. 89 *et seq.*

64　See A. Lanciotti, *op. cit.* note 48 at p. 116 *et seq.* In this connection it must be pointed out that, as concerns the export of objects covered by the Regulation outside the EC, the permit issued by the Italian authorities holds for the whole of the Community and the object can leave the Community customs territory also through another Member State that will take care of the customs formalities, withholding and informing the Italian authorities of any object unaccompanied by a permit; for objects not included in the scope of application of the Community Regulation and therefore subject to Act No. 1089/39, the permit issued will be valid only in Italy and any object unaccompanied by a permit will be stopped only by the Italian customs.

65　A cultural object falls within the scope of application of Regulation No. 3911/92 if, besides belonging to one of the categories listed in part A of the Annex, which in most cases also entail an age limit, its economic value is equal to or higher than that indicated for that category in part B of the Annex. Besides archaeological finds, the objects for which there is no financial ceiling (category 1) are: elements from the dismembering of monuments (category 2); incunabula and manuscripts (category 8); archives (category 11). See Ministry for Cultural and Environmental Heritage, Circular No. 3615 of 1 April 1993, *Mercato unico europeo esportazione di beni culturali.*

Moreover, in order to execute both Regulation No. 3911/92 and Directive 93/7[66] by introducing measures that make sure that the cultural heritage mentioned therein is returned, on 18th June 1993 the Ministry submitted to Parliament a government bill containing 'Rules on the movement of cultural heritage'. This was approved by the Culture Committee of the Chamber of Deputies on 21st November 1995[67] and, with some amendments, by the Seventh Standing Committee (Public Education, Cultural Heritage, Scientific Research, Entertainment and Sports) of the Senate on 12th February 1997. It was finally passed, as Act No. 88, on 30th March 1998.[68] It must be pointed out that even though the Directive was enacted into Italian law on this day, it will apply retroactively to all illicit exports of cultural items listed in article 1 of the Directive which have occurred after 1st January 1993.[69]

After defining the concept of illicit export consistently with the national legislation in force and with Community Regulation No. 3911/92 and subsequent amendments, Act No. 88/98 sets forth a comprehensive regulation of the subject matter by introducing a clear distinction, as far as customs formalities are concerned, between deliveries to Member Countries, in which case a certificate of free movement is issued which is valid for three years, and exports to Third Countries in which case the permit issued lasts only six months. In assessing whether the free movement permit is to be issued or refused, the Export Offices follow the general guidelines set forth by the National Council for Cultural Heritage.

To make the protective regime effective, the regulation contained in chapter III of Act No. 88/98, which contains the implementation rules for both Community instruments, is of special importance. This is in spite of the different approach it takes to the original text with respect to the provision concerning the authority which is to exercise this right[70] for the establishment of a database of the items of cultural heritage illicitly removed. However, it must be pointed out that even now, after the entry into force of this Act, the effectiveness of such a protective system will depend on the Italian Administration's ability to produce a full catalogue of the national heritage in as short a time as possible. This means cataloguing not only the items under special protection which are not allowed to leave the national territory, but all the privately-owned items which often have intrinsic ties with the fundamental values of Italian culture. Such items can, on the one hand, be the object of transactions and hence be regularly purchased as they do not belong to the inalienable heritage of the State and since private owners have the right of accessing foreign markets, and on the other they will go through the Administration only in cases in which the item is well-known and specifically

---

66   See Council Directive No. 93/7 of 15 March 1993, in ECOG No. L. 74/74 of 27 March 1993 and the subsequent amendment directive No. 96/100 of the European Parliament and Council of 17 February 1997.

67   For the text of the bill, see *Ministero per i beni culturali e ambientali, Notiziario dell'Ufficio Studi*, 1993, p. 24 *et seq.* See also Atto Camera No. 2282 (DDL 12-2282).

68   See XIII Legislatura, Atti Parlamentari, Chamber of Deputies N. 3254-A. For the text of Act No. 88/98, see *Official Gazette* No. 84, 10 April 1998.

69   For the purposes of art. 1 of the Directive the objects classified as cultural heritage are the following: objects defined as objects of the national heritage having artistic, historic or archaeological value, in compliance with national legislation or national administrative procedures, in accordance with art. 36 of the EC Treaty; and which belong to one of the categories listed in the annex, or objects which, though not being included in these categories, are an integral part of public collections entered in the inventory books of museums, archives or conservation stock of a library, and in the inventory books of ecclesiastical institutions.

70   See art. 21 in its original wording.

located.[71] In this connection, in order to facilitate and hasten the process of gaining adequate knowledge of the national heritage, the Regions[72] could be called upon to provide a contribution by requiring them to systematically make catalogues of the items held in the region and then make available such catalogues to the Ministry for Cultural Heritage. This could, to some extent, counter the criticism made against the Covatta Act,[73] considered by many as being over-ambitious in that it prescribes that the whole of the nation's cultural heritage be catalogued. It must be recalled, however, that it was precisely on the basis of the Covatta Act that the Ministry for Cultural and Environmental Heritage started the campaign for making a census of the national heritage, supplemented by the so-called *emergency operation*, undertaken by the competent Offices, on the basis of an *ad hoc* circular which set forth the relative operational provisions.[74] Moreover, it is worth pointing out that for Regions' cultural objects, or those objects under their monitoring, or in respect of which Regions have been transferred the functions concerned, the competent Export

---

71   See the observations made by S. Amorosino *Note per la riforma dell'Amministrazione dei beni culturali, in Sistemi ambientali e discipline amministrative* (Padova, 1990) as well as *Note sulla tutela delle opere d'arte tra principlio comunitario di libera circolazione e disciplina amministrative nazionale di beni a circolazione controllata*, Proceedings of the Conference on 'Libera circolazione e tutela delle opere d'arte nell'Europea del '93', Bologna, 25-26 January 1991. Amorosino feels that it is rightly urgent and necessary '[o]n the one hand to catalogue and systematically arrange the knowledge about known artistic heritage, on the other to survey the existing heritage that is not "officially" known to the public powers'. The suggestion is, for the latter aspect, to begin '... with the works and authors for whom there is documentation and hence some critical and scientific "recognition"; the scientific cataloguing operations, carried out by means of computer technology, are to be attributed the function and effectiveness of legal recognition (what they are, where they are, who produced them)'. A first important instrument in this direction is Act No. 84 of 19 April 1990 (so-called Covatta Act) which is not believed to be suitable because it supports the idea of a cataloguing operation which is too vast in that it is meant to include all public and private works. See, on this, F. Micheli 'Nota in materia di esportazione delle opere d'arte', proceedings of the workshop organised by the Ministry for Foreign Affairs, *Review of the Italian legislation on cultural heritage*, Villa Madama, Roma, 5 February 1992.
72   Concerning the distribution of powers between State and Regions in cultural heritage export matters, the Italian Constitutional Court issued Decision No. 278 of 23 May 1991, which cancelled the Decree of the Minister of Foreign Trade of 30 October 1990 containing a list of the products requiring authorisation to be exported or put in transit, which states that: "It is not up to the Offices for the Exportation of Antiquities and Objects of Art that report to the Ministry for Cultural and Environmental Heritage which are based in some Fine Arts Departments, to issue permits and authorisations for permanent or temporary export of objects that are of historical, archaeological, paleontological or artistic interest, including codices, manuscripts, incunabula, prints, books, engravings, and objects of numismatic interest belonging to the Region or to other bodies, even if lying outside its territory, over which it exercises control or that are of local interest". For an exhaustive discussion of the breakdown of competences between State and Region in cultural heritage matters, see F. Piergigli 'I beni culturali nell'ordinamento delle Regioni e delle Autonomie locali' in L. Mezzetti, ed., *I beni culturali* (Padova, 1995) p. 79 *et seq.*
73   See note 69.
74   The circular referred to here of 1 August 1992, after recalling Acts No. 160/1988, No. 84/1990 and No. 145/1992, provided that the Central Cataloguing and Documentation Institute that has the task of setting up and managing the general catalogue of cultural heritage of archaeological, historical, artistic and architectural interest *ex* art. 13 of DPR 805/1975, was to be assisted by the Fine Arts Departments whose task would be that of taking stock of their documentation and that of other bodies so as to provide in as short a time as possible a clear catalogue of the national heritage, albeit restricted to essential data, hence offering a comprehensive view of the state of protection of this heritage throughout the territory. In order to co-ordinate the work of the operative units a working group has been set up at the Central Office for Environmental, Architectural, Archaeological, Artistic and Historic Heritage of the Ministry for Cultural and Environmental Heritage, with the task of controlling the status and progress of the cataloguing, precataloguing and inventory activities at each Fine Arts Department and of monitoring respect for deterrents.

Office has to consult the Region before issuing a certificate of free movement, within thirty days from the date the certificate has been requested, in accordance with article 18, paragraph 3, of Act No. 88/98.

Again, to prevent the illicit trade, trafficking and holding of cultural heritage items, on 11th February 1997, the Senate (Seventh Standing Committee, Public Education, Cultural Heritage, Scientific Research, Entertainment and Sport) approved a government bill[75] which, amongst other things, specifically deals with movable property of archaeological interest and sets forth the criteria according to which the possessors or holders under whatever title of such heritage may ask to become owners thereof, subject to the rights of third parties, through a measure supported by proper reasoning issued by the competent Fine Arts Department.[76]

7.   Establishment of a Marine Archaeological Area

Before completing this overview of Italian legislation on the underwater cultural heritage, a last reference needs to be made to the creation of a marine archaeological area off the Italian coast and to the problems related to it, given the current non-existence of the maritime contiguous zone.[77] Indeed, as Italy has failed to extend its contiguous zone to 24 miles, the contiguous zone is encompassed within the twelve miles of Italy's territorial waters,[78] and not 24 miles as suggested in article 33 of the 1982 Convention. Article 1, paragraph 1 of the Consolidated Text adopted by the Seventh Standing Committee (Culture, Science and Education) of the Chamber of Deputies at its session of 24th September 1997,[79] extends the scope of application of Act No. 1089/39 to a marine area covering twelve miles from the external boundary of the territorial sea, or to a zone delimited by the median line in cases where this zone overlaps with an identical zone or the territorial waters of another State, pending an agreement with that State.[80]

---

75 See XIII Legislatura, Atti Parlamentari, Chamber of Deputies, N. 3216, forwarded by the President of the Senate on 14 February 1997.
76 According to art. 3 para. 4 of the bill being examined "Within 180 days from the deadline (filing the report and request for acquiring ownership) pursuant to para. 1, the Fine Arts Departments shall either accept or reject, with a measure supported by proper reasoning, the acquisition of ownership of the objects. If the application is accepted, the objects are catalogued as being privately owned and rules are set forth for appropriate conservation. If the Fine Arts Department recognises that the objects are of exceptional historical and artistic interest and that it is invariably imperative for them to be part of State heritage, it will reject the application, informing the committee for archaeological heritage of the National Council for Cultural and Environmental Heritage, setting forth at the same time the provisions for their appropriate conservation under the responsibility of the possessor or holder who is appointed caretaker/custodian".
77 This is established at twelve miles by art. 33 of Act No. 1424 of 25 September 1940.
78 With DPR No. 960 of 16 December 1977, "Corrective rules as supplement to the consolidated text of the legislative provisions on customs matters approved by DPR No. 43 of 23 January 1973 (OG No. 1, 2 January 1978), the zone of customs supervision was made to coincide with the territorial sea extended out to twelve miles through Act No. 359 of 24 August 1974 (OG No. 218, 21 August 1974).
79 See further, note 31.
80 Upon the initiative of the government a bill had been presented (Ministry for Cultural and Environmental Heritage, Fisichella), in which art. 1 extended the application of Act No. 1089/39 to all marine areas adjacent to the territorial sea and overlying the Italian continental shelf (see Atto Camera N. 1812, of 21 December 1994). This provision was removed as a result of doctrinal criticisms, because it was deemed to be in conflict with the provisions of art. 33 of the 1982 Convention which, for matters concerning underwater cultural heritage, extends the jurisdiction of the coastal State to 24 miles. See U. Leanza and I. Caracciolo, 'Le incidenze della Convenzione di Montego Bay del 1982 sulla legislazione italiana in materia di spazi marini' (1995) L *La Comunità internazionale* nn.3-4, p. 469 *et seq.*, esp. pp. 493-497. Though art. 2 of the consolidated text of the bill does not extend the archaeological zone out to the marine areas coinciding with the continental shelf, it does impose on the holders of research permits or firms holding a concession for exploiting natural resources in accordance with Act No. 613 of 21 July 1967 the duty to have respect for objects of historical or archaeological interest located in the zone covered by the permits and/or concessions, and an obligation not to remove them.

It can be inferred from articles 303 and 33 of the 1982 Convention that the marine zone out to 24 miles, corresponding to the contiguous zone, is used by the Convention to bestow upon the coastal State power to control the unauthorised removal of archaeological and historical objects from the State's territory and sea. Hence the coastal State is given law enforcement powers not only for matters related to customs, tax, health and immigration, but also new powers to control violations against the laws and regulations concerning the illicit trade in archaeological and historical objects of the said coastal State, allegedly perpetrated on its territory or in its territorial waters. Such powers are quite different from those of a functional nature exercised in the traditional contiguous zone. The bestowing upon a coastal State of jurisdiction to prevent the unauthorised removal of archaeological property from the zone, so as to reduce illicit trafficking of such property and hence reduce infringement of the customs laws of the State, creates an indissoluble bond between contiguous zone and archaeological zone, so much so that the latter may be established only after the former has been established, in order to effectively pursue the aims for which it is meant.[81] The practice of various States seems to confirm this assumption. Indeed, among the few European and/or Mediterranean States that have established a 24 mile contiguous zone[82] and that have adopted domestic legislation to protect their underwater archaeological heritage, France, for example, with Act No. 89-874 of 1st December 1989, has authorised the search for underwater cultural heritage within the 24 mile zone off its shores and has provided that the chance discovery of any such property be reported to the French authorities.[83]

Taking the above into account, it is therefore appropriate for Italy to re-establish the contiguous zone before the adoption of the Consolidated Text of 24th September 1997, so as to facilitate the exercise of the new functional powers concerning the protection of underwater archaeological heritage in a more appropriate manner than is possible at present where customs supervision covers only a marine area of twelve miles.[84] On the other hand, Italy seems to have already shown its intention in this direction since the government report accompanying the bill authorising the ratification of the 1982 Convention mentions the possibility of establishing a contiguous zone of 24 miles within which the Italian State can exercise its competences *vis-à-vis* the protection of the underwater archaeological heritage.

---

81   See *contra* N. Ronzitti 'Stato costiero, archeologica sottomarina e tutela del patrimonio storico sommerso' (1984) *Il diritto marittimo* 16; T. Treves 'Stato costiero e archeologia sottomarina' (1993) No. 3 *Riv. dir. int.* 797 *et seq.* It is worth pointing out that the assumption in the text is supported by article 2, para. 2 of the Draft Convention of the Council of Europe on the Protection of the Underwater Cultural Heritage 1985, which expressly subordinates the establishment of an archaeological zone to the proclamation of a contiguous zone.

82   Reference is made here to Bulgaria, Egypt, France, Spain, Tunisia; whereas Syria claims a contiguous zone of only six miles beyond the external boundary of the territorial sea fixed at 35 nautical miles: see U.N., 'Status of the Convention and Table of Claims to Maritime Zones Worldwide' *Law of the Sea Bulletin* N°. 30, New York, 1996. In this connection it must be recalled that, through Act No. 86-35 of 9 May 1986, in *Journal officiel de la République tunisienne*, 13-16 May 1986, Tunisia claims protection over the archaeological heritage located "dans toute étendue acquatique, y compris les eaux intérieures, la mer territorial et la zone contigue d'une étendue de 24 mille des lignes de base à partir desquelle est mesurée la largeur de la mer territoriale".

83   See the text in *Journal Officiel*, 5 December 1989. See also, ch. 3. For a comment on doctrine, see M.L. Pecoraro 'Reflections on the French Law N° 89-874 of 1 December 1989, on Maritime Cultural Heritage Containing Modification in the Law of September 27, 1941, on Archaeological Excavations, and of the Decree of the Italian Ministry of the Merchant Navy of July 12, 1989, Containing Provisions to Protect Maritime Areas of Historical and Archaeological Interest' *University of Rome II, Department of Public Law, Yearbook 1989* (Rome, 1990) p. 569 *et seq.*; L. Escande 'Aspects législatifs de la tutelle du patrimoine archéologique subacquatique en France' in G. Vedovato and L. Vlad Borrelli, eds., *La tutela del patrimonio archeologico subacqueo*, Ravello European University Centre for Cultural Heritage (Roma, 1995) p. 29 *et seq.*

84   See note 77 above.

Even though the establishment of the archaeological zone is a principle which concerns the protection of resources, even if *sui generis*, and thereby concerns each coastal State involved, the provision contained in the Consolidated Text adopted by the Seventh Standing Committee of the Chamber of Deputies concerning the delimitation of the zone appears to be most appropriate. Indeed, in this case, unlike the traditional contiguous zone which had a purely functional role, the need undoubtedly arises to clearly determine the actual area over which the Italian State has competence and can thus exercise its power of issuing authorisation for the removal of objects of archaeological and historical importance from the seabed and hence be able to control illicit trade activities. In particular, being able to delimit the zone is most important when the distance between opposite or adjacent coasts does not make it possible to apply the principle of maximum extension envisaged by international law.[85] Since the power of authorising the removal of objects of archaeological and historical interest from the marine area is attributed exclusively to the coastal State, the exercise of such authority could never occur in competition with any other State over the same marine area, as is admissible for the exercise of functional powers of control attributed to a coastal State over the traditional contiguous zone.

---

85   The principle of an archaeological zone as such does not seem to have raised much interest either in the practice of States nor in doctrine. Among the authors that have dealt with this issue, see T. Treves *La Convenzione delle Nazioni Unite sul diritto del mare del 10 dicembre 1982* (Milano, 1983) p. 21 *et seq.*; L. Migliorino *Il recupero degli oggetti storici, op. cit.* note 2, p. 190; N. Ronzitti 'Stato costiero, archeologica sottomarina e tutela del patrimonio storico sommerso' (1984) *Il Diritto Marittimo* p. 3 *et seq.*; E. Roucounas 'Sub-Marine Archaeological Research: Some Legal Aspects' in U. Leanza, ed., *Il regime giuridico internazionale del Mare Mediterraneo* (Milano, 1987) p. 309 *et seq;* U. Leanza 'Zona contigua e zona archeologica nell'ordinamento intenazionale e nell'ordinamento interno' in *Nuovi Saggi di diritto del mare* (Torino, 1988) p. 43 *et seq.*; M.L. Pecoraro 'Il regime giuridico della ricerca acheological marina nell'ambito della CEE' in U. Leanza and L. Sico, eds., *Zona economica esclusiva e Mare Mediterraneo* (Napoli, 1988) p. 137 *et seq.*; S. Karaggiannis 'Une nouvelle zone de juridiction: la zone archéologique maritime' (1990) *Collection espaces et ressources maritimes* No. 4, p. 2 *et seq;* M.C. Ciciriello *Le formazioni insulari e la delimitazione degli spazi marini* (Napoli, 1990) p. 166 *et seq.*; U. Leanza *Il nuovo diritto del mare e la sua applicazione al Mediterraneo* (Torino, 1993) p. 253 *et seq.*; T. Treves 'Stato costiero ed archeologia sottomarina' (1993) *Riv. dir. int.* No. 3, p. 698 *et seq.*; T. Treves 'La protezione del patrimonio culturale subacqueo nella Convenzione di Montego Bay del 1982 sul diritto del mare; in particolare il nuovo istituto della zona archeologica', report submitted to the seminar on *La protezione del patrimonio culturale subacqueo nel Mediterraneo* Anacapri, 1 October 1994; T. Treves *Il diritto del mare e l'Italia* (Milano, 1995) p. 61; M. Hayashi 'Archaeological and Historical Objects under the United Nations Convention on the Law of the Sea' (1996) 20 *Marine Policy* 291 *et seq.*; E.D. Brown 'Protection of the Underwater Cultural Heritage. Draft Principles and Guidelines for Implementation of Article 303 of the United Nations Convention on the Law of the Sea, 1982' (1996) 20 Marine Policy 325 *et seq.*; J. Blake 'The Protection of the Underwater Cultural Heritage' (1996) 45 *International and Comparative Law Quarterly* 819 *et seq.*

Chapter 7

POLAND

Wojciech Kowalski

1. Historical Development of Underwater Archaeology in Poland

Poland is a medium-sized country, endowed with a well-developed system of rivers running from the south to the north of the territory, where a 500 km strip of coastline constitutes its natural border. It is thanks to Poland's central-European location and wide access to the Baltic Sea, that Polish inland[1] and coastal waters were used in the past as trade routes of importance to the whole continent, with ports and barter centres built at the crossings of the routes. Poland's numerous lakes provided most convenient conditions, especially in prehistoric times, for the foundation of human settlements and the country's advantageous geographical location was, at the same time, a major cause of wars and the ensuing movements of armies in almost all possible directions.

Having such dramatic history, these inland and coastal waters were recognised as fields of archaeological exploration long before now and considered as potential sources of cultural heritage objects, deposited there in the course of the long-lasting development of European civilisation and as a result of Poland's active contribution to this process.

Such potential has been borne out by numerous objects recovered from lakes and rivers on different occasions. Many years ago, the collections of Polish museums were enriched with several important heritage objects, including: the only copy of a stone statute of the pagan deity Swiatowid dating back to the ninth century, which was found in the Zbrucz river in 1848; a very well-preserved Dutch gun carriage from the seventeenth century extracted from the Vistula in Warsaw in 1913; one of the very few Neolithic cups preserved in a complete form and belonging to the so-called 'Funnel Beaker' culture, found in the Warta river in Poznan in the 1930s.[2]

All these finds, and many others, were recovered by chance in the course of hydro-technical or other engineering works. Accidental as they were, these finds aroused human imagination and mobilised people to undertake planned searches for other heritage objects hidden in the waters, especially in the vicinity of former crossings, bridges and settlements. Such exploration in the nineteenth century of the Mazurian Lakes discovered, among other antiquities, numerous sections

---

1   The term 'inland waters' has been used here to mean lakes, rivers, etc., and the term 'internal waters' should be understood as meaning estuaries, bays, harbours and similar waters which are located landward of the baselines from which the territorial sea is measured. It should also be noted that there are no tides on Poland's coastline.

2   Swiatowid's statue is undoubtedly one of the most precious heritage objects ever found in Poland. The statue is a 257 cm high stone obelisk weighing almost half a ton, engraved with human shapes of mainly male features and four faces turned to the four directions. Most probably it represents a Slavic deity from pre-Christian times and is the only known depiction of this pagan god. At present the statue is kept in the Archaeological Museum in Cracow. The gun carriage extracted from the Vistula and kept in the Polish Military Museum in Warsaw had been brought over to Poland at the time of the Polish-Swedish Wars. The sepulchral funnel cup goes back to Neolithic times: 3,500-2,000 B.C. For further examples of finds in inland waters, see Z. Bukowski *Stan i perspektywy archeologicznych badañ podwodnych w jeziorach i rzekach Polski* [The Current State of, and Perspectives on, Underwater Research in Poland's Lakes and Rivers] (1978) 23 *Archeologia Polski* 53 *et seq.*

of wooden piles embedded in the bottom of the lake, constituting the remains of 'platforms' on which prehistoric palafitte settlements were constructed at some distance from the waterside.[3]

Systematic underwater archaeological explorations were commenced by Z. Rajewski, who in 1936-1938, conducted a complex and wide-scale investigation into one of the lakes in Central Poland, following the discovery of a fortified settlement in Biskupin, which had been founded about 550 B.C. on the island of that lake. In order to determine the original range of the Biskupin settlement, part of which is still underwater, to examine the underwater wooden structures and, possibly, to find movable objects belonging to the settlement, scuba divers from the Polish naval service were employed, and professional diving equipment was used.[4] Rajewski's examination is considered to mark the beginning of a fully scientific approach to the archaeological investigation of Poland's inland waters.

On the other hand, archaeological exploration of coastal waters, particularly of internal and territorial waters, was initiated after World War II. At first, the area of investigation entailed the vicinity of Wolin island situated not far from the Baltic Sea shore; the next stage encompassed Szczecin Bay at the Odra estuary on the Polish-German border. In 1952, apart from personal diving equipment, caissons were used to penetrate the areas of the former early medieval port.[5] Among the heritage objects discovered at that time were multiple remains of early medieval ships, thanks to which it was possible to classify the types of construction that had been used in the period A.D. seventh-twelfth centuries.[6] These discoveries resulted in Polish-German co-operation in experimental underwater archaeology. Following the discovery of a wreck in the Eckenforder Bucht, a ninth century Slavic ship was reconstructed; it was then taken on a sea voyage to obtain relevant navigational data and to confirm structural and technological characteristics.[7]

Equally important, but even more spectacular, were the discoveries brought about in the investigation of the eastern part of the Polish coast undertaken several years later, in particular in the area of Gdansk Bay, housing one of the biggest medieval ports of the Baltic Sea and a very important trade centre. The most famous discoveries included shipwrecks and their cargoes, such as the wreck of a medieval merchant vessel, together with its cargo of five tons of copper from Hungarian mines, Swedish iron ore and over 100 barrels of pitch, birch tar, wood ash and wax, found in 1969 during engineering works on the construction of the Northern Port in Gdansk. Such cargo was extracted from the shipwreck in the course of archaeological works conducted by

3   The nineteenth century exploration was undertaken by German explorers: see E. Balduhn 'Bericht über die Pfahlbauten bei Werder im Kr. Lötzen' (1867) 4 *Altpreussische Monatsschrift*; J. Berghaus 'Noch einmal die Pfahlbauten von Lübtow' (1880) 30 *Baltische Studien. Alte Folgen*; J. Heydeck 'Der Pfahlbau im Kownatken-See' (1888) 13 *Sitzungsberichte der Altertumsgesellschaft Prussia*.

4   Z. Rajewski *Sprawozdanie z organizacji badan w latach 1936 i 1937. Grod praslowianski w Biskupinie* [Report on the organisation of the investigation in 1936 and 1937. Pre-Slavic fortified settlement in Biskupin] (Poznan, 1938) pp. 6-7.

5   W. Filipowiak 'Port sredniowiecznego Wolina' [Medieval port of Wolin] (1956) 2 *Materialy Zachodnio-Pomorskie*; R. Wolagiewicz 'Badania podwodne Muzeum Pomorza Zachodniego na Zalewie Szczecinskim w 1961 r.' [Underwater exploration of the West-Pomeranian Maritime Museum in Szczecin Bay in 1961] (1961) 7 *Materialy Zachodnio-Pomorskie*.

6   See, *inter alia*, P. Smolarek 'Inwentaryzacja zrodel do dziejow techniki szkutniczej Slowian pomorskich' [Inventory of the sources to the history of Pomeranian Slavic shipbuilding] (1955) 1 *Materialy Zachodnio-Pomorskie*; R. Rudolph 'Die Notwendigkeit weiterer Forschungen über die Kleinboote am Oderhaff' (1962) 8 *Materialy Zachodnio-Pomorskie*.

7   A replica of the ship was made in co-operation with the National Museum in Szczecin and the Archaeological Laboratory at the Institute of Archaeology and Ethnology of the Polish Academy of Sciences in Wolin at the order of Siftung Oldenburger Wall for a local museum in Oldenburg. For more details, see K.W. Struve 'Ein slavisches Schiffwrack aus der Eckernförder Bucht' (1980) 37 *Offa* p. 160 *et seq.*

the Central Maritime Museum in Gdansk in the 1970s.[8] Another shipwreck examined by the same museum was *Solen*, a Swedish warship which had sunk on 28th November 1627 in the Polish-Swedish sea battle near Oliwa. Again, the archaeological investigation was successful, recovering, among other objects, fifteen cannons of Swedish, Polish and Russian origin, multiple items of military equipment and a human scull.[9] The research results advanced considerably the development of the underwater archaeological department of the Central Maritime Museum in Gdansk, which was then able to acquire a research vessel, thanks to which further systematic investigation of shipwrecks in the waters close to the central part of the Baltic shore was possible.[10] More recent discoveries include those arising from the 1995 investigation of the shipwreck of *General Carleton of Withby* from 1777. The vessel was indisputably identified when the ship's bell with the ship's name inscribed on it was found. Other items brought out of the wreck included items of sailors' equipment and considerable cargo, including a shipment of German-made shoe buckles.[11] Other shipwrecks of less historical importance to be found in the waters of the Baltic Sea include the remains of ships from more recent times, especially from the period of World War II, for example, the wreck of *Wilhelm Gustloff*, a German ship located at a distance of 21 miles from the shore in Rozewie. The ship sank in 1944, together with refugees from German East Prussia and cadets of the submarine school based there, who had been evacuated in the escape from the approaching Red Army. There are some grounds to believe that the ship could have carried the famous 'amber chamber' that the Nazis had removed from Russia to Königsberg, the capital of East Prussia.[12]

To conclude this outline of the development of underwater archaeology in Poland, it should

---

8   This shipwreck, referred to as the 'Copper Wreck', is what remained of a hulk vessel. On the grounds of results obtained using the radiocarbon method (C 14), the ship is considered to have been built at the end of fourteenth century (the most probable date is A.D. 1392). The ship sank in the third decade of the following century, most probably in 1424. See J. Litwin 'The Copper Wreck, The Wreck of a Medieval Ship Raised by the Central Maritime Museum in Gdansk, Poland' (1980) 9 *International Journal of Nautical Archaeology and Underwater Exploration* 217 *et seq.*; A. Kola, G. Wilke 'The Drawing up of a Height Plan of the Late-Medieval Wreck, the 'Copper Ship' (W-5) from Gdansk Bay and its Utilisation in Exploratory Work' (1983) 9 *Acta Universitatis Nicolai Copernici. Archaeologia. Underwater Archaeology* 66.

9   According to a protocol made after the battle by the Swedish Commission for Royal Ships, *Solen* sank "after the boarding of the 'Solen' from the Polish ship 'Wodnik', when the Poles got the upper hand, the skipper of the Swedish vessel, seeing the hopeless situation, ran to the powder compartment with a burning torch and blew the ship up". The results of the archaeological investigation of *Solen* have fully confirmed this version of the sinking. For more details of the results, see P. Smolarek 'The Genesis, Present State and Prospects of Polish Underwater Archaeological Investigations in the Baltic Sea' (1983) 9 *Acta Universitatis Nicolai Copernici. Archaeologia. Underwater Archaeology* 25 *et seq.*

10   For information on the exploration works, see P. Smolarek 'Underwater Archaeological Investigations in the Gdansk Bay' (1979) 6 *Yearbook of the International Association of Transport Museums* and, by the same author, 'The Underwater Investigations of the Polish Maritime Museum in Gdansk from 1982 to 1985' (1991) 15 *Acta Universitatis Nicolai Copernici. Archaeologia. Underwater Archaeology*.

11   Further information on this ship was obtained from the archives of Lloyd's of London. Thus, it has been established that the ship's port of origin was Liverpool and, apart from full information on the ship's owner, it was even possible to obtain a list of crew members and the route of the voyage. I would like to take this opportunity to express my thanks to Mrs Iwona Pomian, Head of the Underwater Archaeological Department of the Central Maritime Museum in Gdansk, for her assistance in gathering information on the ship.

12   *Wilhelm Gustloff* was the third biggest ship (213 m long) of the German passenger fleet at that time. Not only did several thousand people die in the catastrophe, but also all the possessions they had taken were lost. The property of the German institutions based in Königsberg must have been loaded on the ship as well. That is why the shipwreck has been examined on numerous occasions by research crews, starting with the Russian expedition immediately after the end of World War II, which was followed by many others in subsequent years, including Polish and English expeditions. Because of its special importance to Germany, the ship was also the subject of a publicity campaign in the early 1990s and presented in the mass media as a good exploration opportunity for amateurs pursuing 'underwater tourism'.

be emphasised that the discoveries made in the course of underwater explorations were accompanied by scientific research and reflection. This is manifested in the documentation of the investigations and the scientific approach taken to the research results. There are now three research institutes that are absolute leaders in underwater archaeology in Poland: the Central Maritime Museum in Gdansk and the National Museum in Szczecin as far as marine archaeology is concerned, and Nicolas Copernicus University in Torun, which specialises in the exploration of inland waters.[13] A Polish archaeologist, in his account of the achievements of underwater archaeology in Italy, France, Austria, Switzerland and the USA in the early post-war period, expressed a certain vision which, it may be said, has become true:

> Thus archaeology has gained yet another source of knowledge about the societies of the past. It is only a question of time before underwater explorations are conducted on a wide scale, and then, archaeologists in Poland will also have an opportunity to contribute with no less spectacular discoveries.[14]

On the basis of professional publications on underwater archaeology and interviews undertaken with representatives of the above-mentioned museums, the basic categories of underwater cultural heritage objects in Polish coastal and inland waters can be identified as follows:

> all types of shipwrecks located in the sea, comprising the remains of ships built in the period from the seventh to the twentieth centuries, and minor ships and boats (log-boats, 'dugouts', frame construction boats, clinker boats) in inland waters, in one case dating back to at least Roman times;
> coastal structures, crossing structures and objects of coastal archaeology of various historical origins, starting with Neolithic times;
> single objects coming from ships or their parts, such as anchors, remains of cargo, etc., and other objects which have accidentally fallen into water from the adjacent land, dating back to different times of history, from Neolithic times onwards.

2.   Threats to Poland's Underwater Cultural Heritage

It is impossible to exactly assess the number of objects that exist underwater, especially with regard to inland waters. Nevertheless, according to various sources on coastal waters, the

---

13   The addresses of these institutes are: 1) Central Maritime Museum in Gdansk, Underwater Archaeology Department, Szeroka 67/68, 80-835 Gdansk; 2) National Museum, Maritime Department, Staromlynska 27, 70-561 Szczecin; 3) Nicolas Copernicus University, Institute of Archaeology and Ethnography, Underwater Archaeology Division, Podmurna 9/11, 87-100 Torun. For information concerning their research activity, see P. Smolarek 'The Underwater Investigations of the Polish Maritime Museum in Gdansk from 1982 to 1985', op. cit. note 10; W. Filipowiak 'Dzial morski Muzeum Narodowego w Szczecinie i morskie dziedzictwo kulturowe' [Maritime Department of the National Museum in Szczecin and Nautical Cultural Heritage] in Muzealnictwo morskie i rzeczne [Nautical and River Museology] (Warszawa, 1995); A. Kola, G. Wilke 'Torunski osrodek archeologii podwodnej - potrzeby i perspektywy badawcze' [The Torun Centre of Underwater Archaeology - its Needs and Research Perspectives] (1980) 6 Acta Universitatis Nicolai Copernici. Archaeologia. The Torun research centre also runs regular honours courses in underwater archaeology for university students. For example, in the academic year 1991/92, five students were granted M.A. with Honours in underwater archaeology: see J. Olczak 'Absolwenci Studium Archeologii Uniwerytetu Mikolaja Kopernika w latach 1991-1992' [Graduates of Archaeological Studies at Nicolas Copernicus University in 1991-1992] (1995) 25 Acta Universitatis Nicolai Copernici. Archaeologia 96 et seq.
14   Z. Bukowski 'Archeologia podwodna' [Underwater Archaeology] (1956) 3 Dawna Kultura 174.

number of 4,000 objects of potential historical interest can presently be given.[15] Part of these resources has already been listed in two types of register. The first one, kept in the three local maritime offices, encompasses navigational obstacles of all kinds, which may also include underwater objects of historical interest. At present, the register has 200 entries. The second register lists only those shipwrecks that are considered as cultural heritage, but its scope is limited to the eastern part of the Baltic Sea. The register is kept in the Central Maritime Museum in Gdansk and, as at February 1998, there were already 32 detected shipwrecks dating from the fifteenth to the twentieth centuries.

Although further possibilities for exploring inland and coastal waters to discover other cultural heritage objects look very promising, there are certain dangers involved, particularly in relation to two factors. Immediately after World War II, and especially in the 1970s, the main threat to underwater cultural heritage was extensive construction works undertaken to liquidate war damages, and later continued in accordance with the guidelines of ambitious investment projects for the economy. Thus, many shipwrecks were destroyed in the course of engineering works, often with no awareness of the damage inflicted. The then political system had other priorities, such as absolute accomplishment of the investment plans and, under the circumstances, there was no place for consideration of the underwater cultural heritage. Such was the case with the construction of the Northern Port in Gdansk, mentioned above, and the engineering works performed at the estuary of the Stopnica river, in the course of which two lighters of historical importance were blown up with dynamite, as they had impeded water access to a newly founded production company.[16] Although such danger has now been considerably reduced, thanks to the recognition of this problem by the Ministry of Transport and the Sea Economy, another increasingly important threat over the last few years is the activity of amateur scuba divers hunting for underwater treasures. The flourishing of this activity is a direct consequence of the relaxing of control of the coastal border zone after the 1989 political break-through,[17] and easier access to modern diving equipment. Following the fashion which has spread through other countries, especially in the Mediterranean, Poland also witnesses the popularity of amateur scuba diving. This phenomenon may have positive aspects, provided that the scuba diving clubs co-operate with professional archaeologists as, for example, is the case with the underwater works conducted in the research institute in Torun.[18] Such amateur sources have also provided the information on several shipwrecks listed in the register kept in the Central Maritime Museum. Unfortunately, there have also been many reported cases of the great and irreparable damage that uncoordinated amateur explorations inflict on the underwater cultural heritage. One of the best publicly known cases involves the removal of copper from the 'Copper Wreck', mentioned above, and its sale to

---

15   This is a very general estimate of known objects given by Pomian on the basis of information gathered from all possible sources, for example archives, data on navigational obstacles received from maritime offices, museum underwater inspections, etc. See report of discussion which took place during the archaeological conference held in Wilkasy, on 21-22 April 1994, in *Archeologia podwodna jezior nizu polskiego* [Underwater Archaeology of Poland's Lakes] (Torun, 1995) p. 208.

16   W. Filipowiak 'Ochrona zabytkow archeologiczno-morskich: Stan i potrzeby' [Protection of the nautical heritage: present state and needs] *Materialy III Konferencji Muzealnictwa Morskiego i Rzecznego* [Materials for III Maritime and Inland Underwater Museology Conference] (Szczecin, 1996) p. 9 *et seq.*

17   Up to 1989, free diving in the Baltic Sea was practically impossible, or at least subjected to the very strict supervision of the border protection forces. Undoubtedly, thanks to such rigid control, many shipwrecks were saved from amateur interference and destruction. As far as the Baltic Sea coastline of former East Germany is concerned, some German authors have recently expressed their satisfaction with similar effects of strict border control: see H. Schlichtherle 'Die Kommission für Unterwasserarchäologie in Verband der Landesarchäologen in der Bundesrepublik Deutschland und Gründung des Arbeitskreises Unterwasserarchäologie' (1996) 1 *Archäologisches Nachrichtenblatt* 94 *et seq.*

18   For information on the co-operation and its results, see A. Kola, G. Wilke *Archeologia podwodna* [Underwater archaeology] (Torun, 1985) p. 225 *et seq.*

scrap shops as raw material, which archaeologists managed to recognise and which finally led them to this ship. In another case, an unusually large supply of Staffordshire pottery in the antique shops and flea markets of the Gdansk area led to the discovery of an eighteenth century shipwreck lying in Baltic Sea waters near the town of Sopot.[19] Amateur explorations will be difficult to eliminate or control, but their detrimental effects may be reduced by an effective legal framework. Legal measures are also required to control other associated threats, such as engineering rectification works, the deepening of navigation channels and waterfront construction works. What, then, is the presently binding legislation protecting the underwater cultural heritage?

3.   Historical Development of the Law

As far as the historical evolution of today's regulations is concerned, the former laws governing the eastern and southern part of the Baltic coast were not very different from the laws and customs adopted at that time in other parts of Europe. The sea has always 'fed' the inhabitants of the coastal area, and the latter have always fought with their sovereigns for the commonly recognised title to the property washed ashore. According to some legends, unverified but quoted from time to time, the inhabitants of the Baltic Sea coastal region followed the habits of the wreckers from Dorset in England, who had been notorious for 'going straight from church to light their beacon fires' to lure ships to dangerous places.[20] For example, some authors claim that the inhabitants of Jastarnia, a village on the Hel peninsula, lighted a special beacon; whereas their neighbours from the town of Hel used to say an old prayer for 'the blessed shore', which meant that – besides the natural gifts of the sea such as *'fruti di mari'* – they hoped to find objects washed ashore from wrecked ships. Similarly, the little coastal town of Leba was featured in a legend, thanks to a story about six local fishermen who would plunder wrecked ships.[21] The long struggle of the ports of the Baltic Sea with *'ius naufragii'* – the right of third parties to claim the property of shipwrecked persons – proves the extent of losses that the shipping trade suffered under this common custom.[22] Therefore, more and more towns made efforts to be excluded from this customary law principle.[23] As early as 1293, the inhabitants of Elblag obtained the right to such exclusion,[24] and in 1407 the same privilege was granted to Szczecin.[25] Finally, *ius naufragii* was proclaimed as 'unjust and cruel' and completely abolished in respect of all shipwrecked persons and their possessions in the Baltic coastline area in 1454, on behalf of King Casimir

---

19   The threats resulting from such amateur explorations have been discussed by many authors, for example, W. Filipowiak, *op. cit.*, note 16 at   p. 5 *et seq.*
20   F.C. Hamil *Wreck of the Sea in Medieval England* (Ann Arbor, 1937) p. 1 *et seq.*
21   To find information about lighting a special beacon called 'bliza', see A. Swierkosz *Z wybrzeza polskiego. Brzegiem miedzymorza* [From the Polish Coast. Along the Coastline] (1916) p. 64. The last known confirmation of the habit of saying a prayer for 'the blessed shore' is to be found in the letters exchanged between Gdansk and Hel in 1524: see S. Matysik: *Prawo morskie Gdanska* [The Maritime Law of Gdansk] (Warszawa, 1958) pp. 174-175. The legend about the six plundering fishermen is quoted by T. Karpowicz in *Legendy pomorskie* [Pomeranian Legends] (Szczecin, 1948) p. 187 *et seq.*
22   For detailed analysis of *ius naufragii* and the history of its abolition, see S. Matysik *Prawo nadbrzezne. Ius naufragii. Studium z historii prawa morskiego* [The Coastal Law. Ius naufragii. A study of the history of maritime law] (Torun, 1950) (the abstract is available in English).
23   For more detailed analysis of this practice, see S. Braekhus 'Salvage of Wrecks and Wreckage: Legal Issues Arising from the Runde Find' (1976) *Scandinavian Studies in Law* 43 *et seq.*
24   Perlbach *Pommerellisches Urkundenbuch* (Danzig, 1882) Nr 504.
25   *Hansisches Urkundenbuch, herausgegeben von Verein für hansiche Geschichte.* Halle-Lepzig, 1873-1939, Vol. V, Nr 792.

Jagiellonian and his successors to the Polish crown.[26] It is one of the next Polish kings who gave irrefutable arguments in favour of this decision in his letter to the town authorities in Lübeck:

> If no human power is capable of reverting the misfortune of a ship being wrecked, it is a true wickedness to take profits from it. If the sea storm has not managed to deprive the shipwrecked person of all his possessions, why should we be more cruel than the winds and the seas? Neither we nor our predecessors, have ever regarded shipwrecked persons as more than those, whose unhappiness deserves our protection. Thus we have commanded that the shipwrecked persons be returned their possessions, should be left free, as we think that in their misfortune they are not our foes and bring no harm upon us.[27]

Studies completed by Matysik revealed that in Poland the ban upon the plunder of shipwrecked persons had been observed, at least formally, since the sixteenth century. In the reign of Stephen Bathory, the author of the above-quoted letter, there were several reported ship disasters after which the shipwrecked property was returned to its rightful owners with no difficulty whatsoever, and in 1598 King Sigismund III decreed a judicial decision in favour of a claim advanced by the shipwrecked against the town authorities of Riga. Nevertheless, the next Polish kings had to strengthen the observance of the ban by granting small rewards for assistance given to shipwrecked persons. This is certified by one of the provisions of the Warsaw Constitution proclaimed by the Polish Parliament in the reign of the last Polish king, which stipulated that:

> No one should dare to exercise the inhumane law of capturing property washed ashore, but if any one provided any assistance to those in such peril, they should be contented with a proper reward for their efforts.[28]

The said Constitution was proclaimed in 1775, several years before the partition of Poland. In the next period of history, Poland disappeared from the map and the former Polish coastal territory was subordinated to Prussian, and later, to German laws, which were still binding long after Poland regained its independence after World War I. It was only after the preparation and adoption of a modern maritime code on 1st December 1961, that the evolution of Polish 'coastal laws' was completed.

4.   Current Legal Framework

It is clearly noticeable that the process of formation of the legal rules regulating rights to property recovered from the sea constitutes only a part of the much broader issue of the protection of underwater cultural property. Our discussion has so far been limited to this part, because in the past only this aspect was recognised. The protection of underwater cultural heritage, treated as an

---

26 Nevertheless, the King reserved to himself the right to these possessions that were not the subject of claims advanced by the owners or their respective heirs. Later it was King Stephen Bathory who relinquished this right in favour of the town of Gdansk: see Matysik, *op. cit.* note 22 at p. 163 *et seq.*

27 Stephen Bathory's letter to Lübeck dated 1580, quoted after Z. Gloger 'Prawa nadbrzezne o rozbitkach i korsarzach' [The coastal laws on shipwrecked persons and pirates] in *Encyklopedia staropolska ilustrowana* [Old Polish Illustrated Encyclopaedia] Vol. IV (Warszawa, 1903) p. 113.

28 Matysik, *op. cit.* note 22 at pp. 168 and 169. In his later study on the laws of Gdansk the author admits that in the Gdansk area some of the old coastal laws were still maintained in the form of wilful confiscation of a third of the property brought out of shipwrecks. According to the author, the fact that the town of Gdansk owned many estates on the lands in which this custom had been observed for ages, explains its lingering in successive years: see Matysik, *op. cit.* note 21 at p. 180.

integral part of cultural heritage, is a completely modern legal concept. Unlike in some other countries, in Poland this issue has not been regulated by one separate act, but instead is far more complex. In order that it may be considered fully, it is necessary to outline three areas of law that converge in this area: the Maritime Code and other regulations of maritime law; some provisions of the Civil Code; and last, but not least, the law on the protection of cultural property.

The most universal stipulations are to be found in the Civil Code,[29] regulating the issue of property found in three different types of circumstances, with different procedures provided for each type. Pursuant to article 183, paragraph 1, if lost property (in the most general meaning of these words) is found, it is the finder's obligation to notify the person entitled to regain it and, consequently, to return it to its rightful owner. If the owner's identity is unknown, the finder is obliged to notify the relevant State agency and, upon the agency's possible request, to hand it over for custody. Pursuant to article 187, if the entitled person does not collect the lost property within one year from the date of notice, or within two years from the date the property has been found, the finder has the right to keep it. An entirely different procedure is applied if money, marketable securities, valuables and property of scientific or artistic value is found. Pursuant to article 184, paragraph 1, of the Civil Code, such property must be handed over for custody to the relevant State agency. If the property in question is not collected by the person entitled to it within one year from the date of the notice to regain it, or within two years from the date it has been found, pursuant to article 187 it becomes State property. In both instances mentioned above, the finder has the right to a reward, constituting ten percent of the property's value, provided that he has fulfilled his obligations (article 187). The third type of circumstances in which property is found refers to the old Roman legal institution of 'treasure'. According to article 189, the following solution has been adopted in Polish law:

> If property of considerable artistic or scientific value is discovered under circumstances which make the search for its entitled owner unavailing, it is the finder's obligation to hand it over to the relevant State agency. The State assumes the ownership title to the property and the finder is entitled to an appropriate reward.

The second area of law regulating the issue of finds is maritime law. Pursuant to the Maritime Code,[30] Chapter IV entitled 'Property recovered from the sea', special procedures are to be observed if such property is found in the sea and brought ashore. Furthermore, the Maritime Code also governs ownership entitlement in three types of circumstances which, in comparison with the above-mentioned instances reflected in the Civil Code, have a naturally different character. Thus, the regulations refer particularly to property which had sunk in territory governed by Polish law, property found outside of this territory but later brought within it, and property found on the surface of the sea or washed upon the shore.

The first case is regulated by article 246 of the Maritime Code. Pursuant to paragraph 1, the owners of property, including a ship, its cargo or any other object, lost in Polish internal or territorial waters should notify the relevant maritime office about their intention to recover the property in question within one year from the day the property sank, specifying the period at the end of which the recovery is to be completed. If necessary, the maritime office is entitled to demand a change to the term of such recovery within three months from receipt of the notice, or, in its own capacity, to set the term for completion of the recovery no shorter than one year from delivery of notification of the decision concerning this term. According to paragraph 2 of this regulation, failure to undertake the recovery within the specified term, or to complete it within

---

29   The Polish Civil Code dated 23 April 1964: *Journal of Laws*, 1964, No. 16, entry 93.
30   The Maritime Code issued on 1 December 1961: *Journal of Laws*, 1961, No. 58, item 318 as amended.

one year from this term, will entail the forfeiture of the property in question to the benefit of the State. A different variant of this procedure is provided for in the next two articles, pursuant to which some special circumstances are to be considered. For example, if the property has sunk in a fortified area, or in any other area of importance to the national defence, or if the property in question has a military character, an additional permission of the relevant military authorities is required to recover it. If such permission is denied, the owner of the property has the right to apply to the maritime office for the recovery of the property in question at the owner's expense. If the property constitutes an obstacle to navigation or hinders coastal traffic, the maritime office may undertake its recovery, notifying the rightful owner about the time of the delivery of the property, provided that the latter shall refund the costs of the works. If the owner fails to collect the recovered property, or does not pay the costs of the works, the maritime office may decide to sell the property and, after deducting the cost of all recovery works, deposit the received amount at the court, which will award it later to the proper owner.

Cases of property sunk on the high seas are regulated by articles 249-253 of the Maritime Code. According to the first provision, the relevant maritime office should be instantly notified about the recovery of someone else's property lost at sea and its consequent removal to Polish internal or territorial waters, with the exact specification of the time, place and circumstances of such recovery. As far as possible, the owner of the property should also be notified about the fact of recovery and the property should be secured until it is handed over to its rightful owner. Pursuant to article 250, the person recovering someone else's property is entitled to a refund of his expenses and to a reward, which is calculated in accordance with the principles of the sea rescue and salvage service.[31] If the owner of the recovered property fails to appear within fourteen days from the date of the notice, or if the owner has not been identified, the person that has recovered the property in question is obliged to hand it over to the maritime office, or to the relevant military authorities in the case of property having a military character. Further procedures are undertaken by the maritime office, on the basis of special regulations concerning the search for owners and the securing of property recovered from the sea.[32] If the efforts to find the owner under these regulations are unsuccessful, and the rightful owner does not appear within six months from the date of the notice issued by the maritime office, the latter may decide to sell the recovered property, in which case the proceeds must be deposited at the court, after the costs of the recovery and the reward are deducted.

The third case provided for in article 254 of the Maritime Code refers to property found on the surface of the sea or found upon the shore. In both instances, proceedings must be initiated to find the owner of the property, following the same procedures as those described above. Furthermore, the regulation stipulates that the finder of someone else's property which 'floats on the surface of the sea', or any persons that have contributed to the rescue of such property, are entitled to a reward in accordance with the regulations concerning the rewards granted in the sea rescue and salvage service. Similarly, the person that 'has found and secured someone else's property washed upon the shore' is also entitled to a reward, but this time it is determined as no higher than 30 percent of the value of the property found. Claims to a finder's reward are accepted only if the claimants advance them no later than the date the property in question is handed over.

In a discussion on property found at sea, there is yet another aspect that should not be ignored. According to a relatively new law on Polish territorial waters,[33] the width of Polish

---

31 The reward and the cost of works are to be paid by the owner.
32 Two regulations particularly apply in this case: 1) Regulation issued by the Minister of Shipping on 31 August 1962, concerning the means of identifying the owner of property recovered from the sea: *Journal of Laws*, 1962, No. 55, item 279; 2) Regulation issued by the Minister of Justice on 29 April 1963 concerning the means of proceeding with property recovered from the sea: *Journal of Laws*, 1963, No. 34, item 198.
33 Law dated 21 March 1991 concerning the sea territory of the Republic of Poland and sea administration: *Journal of Laws*, 1991, No. 32, item 131.

territorial waters is now twelve nautical miles (22,224 m) measured from the sea shore or from the external baseline of the internal sea waters. Due to the limited size of the Baltic Sea and the shape of the shoreline, the determination of Poland's exclusive economic zone has been handed over to the authority of international agreements. Nonetheless, it should be mentioned that under article 17 of the above law, as far as this zone is concerned, Poland has reserved the right of 'sovereignty' over "scientific exploration of the sea" and "protection and preservation of the sea environment". The conditions of such exploration are laid down in the subsequent provisions of the law.

The last area of law which should be examined in our discussion of Poland's underwater cultural heritage refers directly to finds and discovered antiquities regulated under the Law on the Protection of Cultural Property and Museums.[34] This law is a general legal act adopted to protect cultural heritage located throughout the country's territory. Pursuant to article 21, all works and activities in respect of cultural heritage objects, as well as archaeological and excavation works, are allowed only after permission is obtained from a regional inspector of monuments. The obligation to obtain such permission relates to any and all planned works to be conducted on State property. However, in accordance with article 23, to conduct archaeological investigations on land which is not State property, a prior "agreement with its owner or user" is required. If the owner refuses to agree, administrative coercion may be applied, including the expropriation of the estate; at the same time, the owner is entitled to compensation for damage inflicted in the course of securing archaeological research sites and in subsequent works.[35] Separate provisions regulate the procedures to be followed in the case of accidental finds or discovered antiquities, providing for two types of circumstances. The first instance involves finds or discovered antiquities recovered accidentally in the course of "construction or digging works". Pursuant to article 22, the persons conducting the construction or digging works are obliged to immediately notify the relevant local administrative agency and inspector for historical monuments, at the same time "securing the discovered object and terminating all works that may damage or destroy it" until the inspector issues a decision concerning the said object. The inspector's decision should be issued within three days; in the absence of a decision in the appointed time, the works may be continued. The second instance refers to absolutely accidental finds or discoveries made mostly by private persons in circumstances not indicating that such event may occur. Pursuant to article 24(3), the finder of "an archaeological object" or "discovered antiquity" is obliged to follow the same procedures as those described above in the case of construction or digging works, with one small difference: "the finder is entitled to a reward granted by the State" provided that he has fulfilled his obligations. To supplement the above procedures, by virtue of article 24(1), finds and discovered antiquities are explicitly regarded as State property.

It should also be mentioned at this point, that the Law on the Protection of Cultural Property and Museums is administered by the State Service for the Protection of Monuments. Broadly speaking, it consists of two administrative levels supervised by the Minister of Culture and Arts. On the lower level there are regional inspectors, who are authorised to issue all decisions aimed at the protection of cultural properties located on a territory of their competence. These decisions are controlled by the higher level, namely the Principal Inspector of Monuments.[36]

---

34   Law on the Protection of Cultural Property and Museums, as amended, dated 15 February 1962: *Journal of Laws*, 1962, No. 10, item 48.

35   The coercion as well as the ensuing compensation due to the owner or user of the estate are administered pursuant to the Law on Land Management and Expropriation of Real Estate dated 21 April 1985: *Journal of Laws*, 1989, No. 14, item 74 as amended.

36   For more details on the State Service for the Protection of Cultural Property, see the Law on the Protection of Cultural Property and Museums, in particular Chapter III entitled 'Authorities responsible for the protection of cultural property and supervision of museums'.

The three areas of the law outlined above regulate any and all possible finds and discovered antiquities, also including all underwater objects deposited in inland as well as sea waters. The character of objects found or discoveries made, as well as the type of waters, shall resolve the application of relevant laws and regulations. At first, it should be determined if the object in question has any cultural heritage value and if it should be classified as an underwater cultural heritage object. The second legal determinant is the type of water concerned, with particular focus on the classification of the waters into: inland, Polish sea waters, sea waters outside the Polish territory. The starting point for any further discussion on the legal status of underwater cultural heritage is the determination of its objective scope. Because the notion of 'cultural heritage' is hardly used in Polish law, it should be assumed that cultural heritage is comprised of all 'cultural property'. Article 2 of the Law on the Protection of Cultural Property and Museums defines cultural property as: "any movable or immovable property, old or modern, important to the national heritage, history or culture because of its historical, scientific or artistic value". In the provisions of article 5, exemplary cultural property objects are enumerated, but shipwrecks or other underwater objects are not mentioned *expresis verbis*. Nevertheless, this does not mean that underwater heritage is not regarded as cultural property. The enumeration of cultural objects is only exemplary and, similarly to the definition of cultural property as such, it denotes a broad and general category of "other movable or immovable objects that should be preserved because of their scientific, artistic or cultural value" (article 5, point 12). In view of this, all underwater objects may unquestionably be assumed to be cultural property, provided that they are important to history, science or art. It is essential to indicate here, that the above definition does not regard the age of the object as a criterion for assessing its cultural value. Consequently, ships sunk even in recent years also constitute cultural property, provided that for some reason they are of historical value. On these grounds, the first completely Polish-made ship built after World War II has been classified as cultural heritage, as well as *Blyskawica*, the Polish destroyer renowned for its participation in the battles and escorts of the same war.[37] All such objects are, *ex lege*, legally protected even if they have not been listed in the register of monuments or inventories kept in museums. Pursuant to article 4(3), it is enough to state their "evident historical character".[38]

Once the objective scope of underwater cultural heritage has been determined, its legal status may be analysed. The analysis will be presented in the following order: ownership, scientific (archaeological) research and recovery works, *in situ* protection of underwater objects.

4.1 Legal status of objects found in inland waters

As far as inland waters are concerned, the present legal status of underwater objects does not raise difficulties in interpretation. Underwater objects deposited in inland waters are regulated by the Law on the Protection of Cultural Property, which is treated as *lex specialis* in relation to the general provisions of the Civil Code, abrogating the application of the latter.[39] Irrespective of the ownership title to the waters, which – in the case of ponds or lakes in Poland – may constitute private property, pursuant to article 24 of this law, all finds and discovered antiquities are State

---

37   The first Polish-made ship after World War II, *Soldek*, was launched in 1952; it now has its own museum in Gdansk. *Blyskawica* has its own museum in Gdynia.

38   Similar conclusions have been drawn by Matysik, after his analysis of the applicable laws: S. Matysik 'Legal Problems of Recovery of Historical Treasures from the Sea-bed' in M. Frankowska, ed., *Scientific and Technological Revolution and the Laws of the Sea* (Wroclaw-Warsaw-Cracow-Gdansk, 1972) p. 143. On the other hand, a contrasting opinion has been expressed by archaeologist W. Filipowiak, *op. cit.* note 16 at p. 9.

39   As the present author has attempted to indicate, this is not always in the best interests of the archaeological heritage: see W. Kowalski 'Title to Finds and Discovered Antiquities under Polish Law' (1996) 1 *Art Antiquity and Law* 141 *et seq.*

property. It does not make any difference if they have been found on land or in inland waters. The lack of difference also concerns the formal conditions for conducting archaeological research works or any other repair, construction or demolition works. There are no formal obstacles to listing the underwater immovable objects in the register of monuments. They are subject to the same legal protection as structures located in, or on the surface of, the ground.

4.2 Legal status of objects found in Polish internal and territorial waters

The status of underwater heritage deposited in Polish internal and territorial waters is far more complex. Just as in the case of inland waters, the Civil Code provisions regulating finds deposited in these waters are subject to the legal exclusion. But, unlike the above-mentioned instances of objects found in inland waters or on land, there are two separate sets of apparently competitive regulations that are applicable to coastal waters: the Maritime Code regulations, and the law on the protection of cultural heritage. It should be emphasised that there are no formal grounds to abrogate the application of the latter in respect of sea waters within Polish territory. First of all, the law on the protection of cultural heritage as such does not provide any basis for such abrogation, referring, in principle, to the whole Polish territory. Secondly, the legal principle of *lex specialis derogat legis generalis* does not abrogate this law, because maritime law is not concerned with the issue of cultural heritage at all. It is assumed that maritime law is mainly, if not exclusively, focussed on property which sank 'relatively not long ago',[40] with the objective to return it to its rightful owner. Thus, if a given find or discovered antiquity, such as a shipwreck, complies with at least one of the prerequisites that make it possible for it to qualify as cultural property, apart from the maritime law, the law on the protection of cultural heritage should be applied concurrently, in accordance with the given circumstances. Failure to identify the owner of the discovered property would imply the abrogation of maritime law regulations in this particular case.

The adoption of the principle dividing the 'competence' of the discussed laws is still consistent with the general principles governing them. According to the doctrine of maritime law, ownership is perpetual;[41] thus, shipwrecks are not regarded as *res nullius*. After all, they have been lost against their owners' will with no intention whatsoever of abandoning their property. As long as there is any chance of establishing their identity, the maritime law makes it possible to summon the owners to collect their lost property. On the other hand, the law on the protection of cultural heritage does not seek to nationalise cultural heritage. Although it considers finds and discovered antiquities as State property, yet their 'archaeological nature' is not determined by age but by the circumstances in which they have been found or discovered, assuming that it is not possible to identify the owners or their respective heirs.[42]

In practice, the owner of any property, including objects of historical, scientific or artistic interest, which has sunk in Polish internal or territorial waters, has a legal opportunity to have it restored pursuant to article 246 *et seq.* of the maritime law. If he does not fulfil the conditions specified there, he shall lose his ownership title in favour of the State. By virtue of the law, all objects encountered in Polish internal or territorial waters are State property, provided that they are archaeological finds or discovered antiquities as defined above. The procedures involved in the investigation or recovery of cultural heritage objects are subject to compliance with the conditions specified for all works pertaining to monuments of the past and laid down in the Law on the Protection of Cultural Property. Likewise, similar protection should be extended to all objects that are to remain on the sea-bed. Consequently, such objects may, or – one should say – must, be listed in the general register of monuments covering the whole Polish territory.

---

40   This is, at least, in accordance with the conclusions drawn by Matysik, *op. cit.*, note 38, at p. 144.
41   S. Matysik *Prawo morskie* [Maritime Law] (Wroclaw-Warszawa-Krakow-Gdansk, 1975) p. 97.
42   For a discussion of the notion of 'archaeological' object as understood by the Polish law on the protection of cultural heritage, see W. Kowalski, *op. cit.*, note 39 at p. 144 *et seq.*

4.3 Legal status of objects recovered from the high seas and brought into Polish territory

The legal status of cultural objects recovered from the high seas and brought into Poland is much more difficult to resolve. The regulations pertaining to such cases involve, first of all, the general stipulations of article 249 *et seq.* of the maritime law discussed above. They require a search for the rightful owner of the recovered property, and it is only when the said owner cannot be found that the property in question may be sold. The United Nations Convention on the Law of the Sea 1982 is of little help in such cases. Although this issue is mentioned in two articles, there are no explicit resolutions. Certain laws of the State may be inferred only from article 303 of this Convention, pursuant to which the strip of water adjacent to the territorial waters has the same status as the latter. Unfortunately, Poland has not determined this strip, so the stipulation is irrelevant anyway, unless an assumption is made that the provisions concerning this strip are to apply to a part of the economic zone which comprises the area of twelve miles from the baseline of the territorial waters.[43] Another stipulation in article 149 of the Convention may only provide grounds for a general interpretative clause for countries to whose territory the cultural property recovered from the high seas was removed.[44] In view of the relevant maritime law regulations, as well as article 149 of the Convention, what should be done in the case of shipwrecks, cargo or other cultural heritage objects recovered from the high seas and brought within Polish territory? The first step, in accordance with general principle, should involve a search for the rightful owner. If his identity is not established, the finds cannot be declared as State property, as is possible in the case of objects found in territorial waters.[45] The regulations of the Law on the Protection of Cultural Property do not apply to lands or waters outside Polish territory, unless an assumption is made that, pursuant to the directive contained in article 303 of the 1982 Convention, they apply to the area of 24 miles from the coastal shore, as in the case of the adjacent water strip. Although article 253 of Polish maritime law stipulates the possibility of selling the property in question, it does not state an option of nationalising it, because the proposed solutions result from some technical problems involved in dealing with the said property, not leading to expropriation. After all, the money obtained from the sale of this property is to be deposited at the court, where it is to be kept for the rightful owner. Under such legal circumstances, the only workable solution to resolve the fate of cultural property recovered from external waters and brought within Polish territory is the sale of the objects in question. But, pursuant to article 149 of the 1982 Convention, as far as the sale of such cultural property is concerned, some preferences, for example preemption, should be given to the country of its origin.

---

43   The practical importance of this new, as it is called in legal literature, 'archaeological zone' ('la zone archéologique') created by art. 303 is not yet clear. See, for example, the Hague lecture of T. Treves, who said that "L'influence de cette regle sur la pratique n'est pas encore claire": T. Treves 'Codification et pratique dans le droit de la mer' *Recueil des Cours* 1990, IV. 223 (Dordrecht–Boston–London, 1991) p. 140.

44   According to this article: "All objects of an archaeological and historical nature found in the Area shall be preserved or disposed of for the benefit of mankind as a whole, particular regard being paid to the preferential rights of the State or country of origin, or the State of cultural origin or the State of historical and archaeological origin".

45   For the same reason, it is impossible to regard such finds as state property by declaring them to be 'treasures' pursuant to art. 189 of the Civil Code. The doctrine explicitly rejects the possibility of applying the civil law to such cases: see Matysik, *op. cit.* note 38 at p. 148.

5.   Conclusions

To conclude this analysis of the protection of underwater cultural heritage under Polish law, the practical implementation of the regulations discussed above, and further prospects for introducing changes and amendments proposed by the archaeological lobby, will now be considered. Generally speaking, apart from in inland waters, the regulations are not observed.[46] This must be partly due to the novelty of the issue itself, and partly to practical difficulties in exercising the regulations in sea conditions. Also, another reason for the inefficiency of the law is the widely accepted opinion that the Law on the Protection of Cultural Property does not apply to territorial waters, even though they are part of Polish territory. Sometimes such attitudes result from the fact that underwater cultural property has not been listed clearly enough in the relevant legal acts.

To improve the situation, some proposals have been made to amend the law and to introduce special regulations. The first proposal refers particularly to internal waters but, apart from the obligation to list already identified underwater objects in the records kept by water management agencies, it does not recognise the need for major changes.[47] As far as coastal waters are concerned, a proposal has been made to introduce an entirely new law regulating the issue of marine cultural heritage as a whole.[48] Based on the 1989 French model of such a law,[49] the Polish version, among other changes, would establish an official register of marine archaeological sites, exactly specify the finder's and the State's obligations in the case of discovery of new underwater sites, indicate the relevant decision-making agencies, and introduce appropriate penal sanctions.

If this proposal is to be assessed, first of all it should be stated that the suggestions generally do not go far beyond the presently binding regulations, boiling down to the introduction of some modifications only. Under these circumstances, there is no need to establish a special law for underwater cultural heritage of the sea only, because such law would consist only of an amended version of the existing regulations. On the other hand, an attempt to amend the law on the protection of cultural heritage should receive full support, because the amendments would 'reinforce' the issues regulated by this law. Such is the current direction of the proposed changes, although some of the proposals raise serious doubts. For example, a proposal to appoint a Conservator of Nautical Heritage for the whole Polish coastal area.[50] Such position seems absolutely redundant and impractical, because the protection of this type of cultural heritage should be the responsibility of regional inspectors, or their deputies who may specialise in marine archaeology. Such functions could also be bestowed upon the larger museums.

---

46   An attempt to improve the situation was made in 1992 when the Ministry of Transport and Shipping issued a circular obliging the maritime agencies to co-operate with the Central Maritime Museum in Gdansk in the investigation of shipwrecks. This attempt has been criticised and deemed unsuccessful, as it is unworkable in practice: see Filipowiak, *op. cit.* note 16 at p. 9.

47   J. Niegowski, G. Sztandarski 'Ochrona archeologicznych stanowisk podwodnych w wodach srodladowych Polski. Aktualny stan prawny oraz postulowane zmiany' [Protection of underwater archaeological sites in Polish inland waters. Actual legal status and postulated changes] in *Archeologia podwodna jezior nizu polskiego* [Underwater archaeology of the Polish lakes] (Torun, 1995) p. 200 *et seq.*

48   I. Seweryn 'Tezy do proponowanej ustawy dotyczacej ochrony podwodnych dobr kultury(stanowiska archeologiczne' [Theses on the proposed law on the protection of underwater cultural heritage (archaeological sites)] in *Muzealnictwo morskie i rzeczne* [Marine and River Museology] (Warsaw, 1995) p. 37 *et seq.*

49   See further, note 48 and ch. 3.

50   The most outspoken commentator on the proposal is W. Filipowiak: see, *op. cit.* note 16 at p. 9 *et seq.*

Chapter 8

SOUTH AFRICA

Hilton Staniland

1.   Background

South Africa has a rich historical and cultural heritage of shipwrecks (hereafter referred to as 'wrecks') of national – and even some international – significance that lie off, or on, the long South African coast.[1]

The Phoenicians, it is fabled, may have rounded the Cape of Good Hope (the 'Cape') as early as 600 B.C.; and, if so, unrecorded shipwrecks may have occurred since that time.[2]

The first recorded Western power to discover the spice route to the East via the Cape was, of course, Portugal. And in 1505 the first recorded shipwreck occurred off the coast of South Africa, when a Portuguese sailing vessel loaded with pepper ran aground west of Mossel Bay.[3]

The English East India Company and the Dutch East India Company received their charters in 1601 and 1602 respectively. This ensured that, after the demise of the Portuguese trading monopoly, Dutch and English ships traded to the East via the Cape. In 1652 a permanent Dutch presence was established at the Cape under Jan van Riebeeck; while in 1795 a British task force defeated the Dutch at the Cape and, except for a short period, the Cape remained in British hands. So it is not surprising that Dutch and English ships also came to be wrecked off the South African coast.

During World War II the Cape again assumed international importance, and as many as 133 merchant ships were sunk in that period off the South African coast;[4] but by far the greatest number of shipwrecks on the South African coast occurred during the nineteenth century, most of them being British ships. The twentieth century, on the other hand, has seen a dramatic decline in the number of shipwrecks due to improved safety standards and increased aids to navigation.

2.   Some Famous Shipwrecks

Many of the shipwrecks occurred in circumstances of great drama and heroism. The wrecks of the *Grosvenor* and the *Birkenhead* are two of the more famous losses.[5]

The *Grosvenor*, an English East-Indiaman, went suddenly aground on the Pondoland coast of South Africa on 4th August 1782. In the chaos that ensued, it was a case of every man for

---

1   As to shipwrecks on the South African coast, see generally: A.C. Addison *The Story of the Birkenhead* (1902); D. Bevan *Drums of the Birkenhead* (1972); J.L. Burman *Great Shipwrecks off the Coast of Southern Africa* (1967) and *Strange Shipwrecks of the Southern Seas* (1968); G. Carter *A Narrative of the Loss of the Grosvenor East-Indiaman* (1791); P.R. Kirby *A Source Book on the Wreck of the Grosvenor East-Indiaman* (1953) and A. R. Willcox *Shipwreck and Survival on the South-East Coast of Africa* (1984).
2   M. Turner *Shipwrecks and Salvage in South Africa 1505 to the Present* (1988) p. 11.
3   *Ibid.*
4   *Ibid.*
5   *Ibid.* at p. 71.

himself. The survivors who reached the shore set out to walk to the nearest Dutch settlement, but they were harassed and attacked by the indigenous inhabitants and wild animals, and the women and children slowed down the progress of the other survivors. So, Captain Coxon and the women and children stayed behind – most of them never to be seen again – while the rest of the men arrived safely at the Cape.

The wreck of the *Birkenhead,* on the other hand, is a tale of heroism. The *Birkenhead,* which was an iron paddle steamer under the command of Captain Robert Salmond, steamed from Ireland with a complement of 23 officers and 469 men to aid Lieutenant-General Sir Harry Smith in the Eight Frontier War being waged in South Africa. After reaching the Cape, the *Birkenhead* left Simon's Town on 25th February 1852 for East London. While steaming across False Bay she ran onto a rock. The men were commanded to stand in ranks, while the women and children were rowed away from the wreck. Even when Captain Salmond ordered the men to save themselves by swimming for the boats, the soldiers stood firm not wishing to endanger the lives of those already in the boats. When the *Birkenhead* broke up, many men were either drowned or attacked by Great White sharks in the open sea. Of the 638 persons on board only 193 were saved, but among these was every woman and child. To this day a reference in South Africa to the '*Birkenhead* drill' is taken to mean a reference to the heroic principle of women and children first.

3.   Disputes Concerning Shipwrecks

Disputes concerning shipwrecks may, for example, relate to the right to salvage and the ownership of property salved. Such disputes become particularly fierce when a shipwreck is thought to contain valuable property. The cargoes carried aboard the ships that were wrecked around South Africa have varied widely; but of course those ships said to carry valuable cargo, especially specie, have attracted the greatest interest of salvors.

Both the *Grosvenor* and the *Birkenhead* were said to have been carrying gold. No gold has been reported as being found on the *Grosvenor* despite numerous attempts to salve the ship. With regard to the *Birkenhead*, disputes arose which involved the British and South African governments as well as private salvors. But the parties negotiated a commendable agreement as follows:

> The wreck of the Birkenhead shall, as a military grave, continue to be treated at all stages with respect. In particular, the South African Government shall seek to ensure that the salvors treat reverently and refrain from disturbing or bringing to the surface any human remains which may be discovered at the site of the wreck or in its vicinity. British military historians shall have temporary access for research purposes to salvaged artefacts designated for South African museums.
>
> The South African Government shall as far as possible ensure that representative examples of salvaged artefacts identifiable with a particular British regiment or institution are offered without charge to that regiment (or its successor) or to such institution.
>
> The British Government shall not enter into any salvage contract in respect of the Birkenhead and shall not object to the South African Government maintaining its existing salvage arrangements in regard to the wreck under the applicable South African legislation.
>
> If any gold coin (apart from the coins considered to have been in private ownership) were to be recovered, such coin (after deduction of the share due to the salvors in accordance with the existing salvage arrangements) would be shared equally between our two Governments.

In order to facilitate the implementation of these arrangements, consultations shall be held as necessary between representatives of our two Governments, the salvors and other South African institutions concerned.

This settlement is without prejudice to the respective legal positions of our two Governments.[6]

Few disputes arising out of the salvaging of shipwrecks are so amicably resolved. Recourse will mostly have to be made to the law, which is set out below.

4.   Jurisdiction Over Wrecks

Section 1(1) of the Admiralty Jurisdiction Regulation Act 105 of 1983 defines the maritime claims over which the Admiralty Court has jurisdiction.[7] Although no explicit mention is made in section 1(1) to a maritime claim relating to, or arising out of, a wreck such a claim may, it is submitted, be defined as a maritime claim where it is brought in the nature of a claim for salvage,[8] or as a claim for ownership[9] or possession of a ship,[10] which surely includes a wreck. Alternatively, a claim relating to, or arising out of, a wreck may be defined as 'any other matter which by virtue of its nature or subject matter is a marine or maritime matter'.[11]

5.   Laws to be Applied to Wrecks

The law which has to be applied by the Admiralty Court is governed by section 6 of the 1983 Act.[12] In order to determine the application of section 6 it is necessary to establish whether the Colonial Court of Admiralty, the predecessor to the Admiralty Court, had jurisdiction to hear and determine any claim relating to wreck. It is submitted that such a claim may, depending upon the facts, have been brought under the jurisdiction of the Colonial Court of Admiralty to decide a claim for salvage,[13] or a claim relating to ownership and possession of a ship.[14] Because the

6   Government Gazette no. 12117 of 6 October 1989, notice no. 2150.
7   As to admiralty jurisdiction over a wreck, see: See H. Staniland 'Admiralty Jurisdiction over Wrecks' (1991) 108 *South African Law Journal* 594. The Act does not expressly exclude maritime claims from the ordinary jurisdiction of the Supreme Court [now the High Court]. But, if a maritime claim is instituted in a Provincial or Local Division (including a Circuit Local Division) exercising its ordinary civil jurisdiction, the question will ordinarily arise whether the claim is a maritime claim or not. The question may be raised by one or other of the parties or by the Court *mero motu*. Once the Court decides that it is a maritime claim, s. 7(2) requires that the matter "shall be proceeded with in a Court competent to exercise its admiralty jurisdiction". To this extent, and subject to the discretion of a Court to decline to exercise its admiralty jurisdiction in terms of s. 7(1)(a), the intention underlying s. 7(2) is undoubtedly that maritime claims are to be heard by the Court exercising admiralty jurisdiction and by no other Court. But the peremptory provisions of s. 7(2) become applicable only once the Court decides that the claim is a maritime claim. It is the decision which has the effect of depriving that Court of its ordinary civil jurisdiction to hear the matter: *per* Scott J.A. in *The Wave Dancer Nel v. Toron Screen Corporation (Pty) Ltd* 1996 (4) SA 1167 (A) at 1176G-1177A.
8   Admiralty Jurisdiction Regulation Act 1983 s. 1(1)(k).
9   Admiralty Jurisdiction Regulation Act 1983 s. 1(1)(a).
10   Admiralty Jurisdiction Regulation Act 1983 s. 1(1)(b).
11   Admiralty Jurisdiction Regulation Act 1983 s. 1(1)(ee).
12   As to the genesis and meaning of s. 6, see H. Staniland 'The Implementation of the Admiralty Jurisdiction Regulation Act in South Africa' [1985] 4 *Lloyd's Maritime and Commercial Law Quarterly* 462.
13   English Admiralty Court Act 1840 s. 6.
14   English Admiralty Court Act 1840 s. 4; English Admiralty Court Act 1860 s. 8.

Colonial Court of Admiralty thus had jurisdiction over such claims, it follows in terms of section 6(1) of the 1983 Act that the English law as of 1st November 1983 (including statute and precedent) is applicable in the South African Admiralty Court.

However, in terms of section 6(2) of the 1983 Act, English law is not applicable where there is a South African statute that governs the matter. There are such statutes and they are considered below. The manner in which matters relating to wreck are governed by the statutes depends upon the circumstances in each case. In some instances, more than one act may govern the situation: it may, for example, be necessary for a person intending to salvage a wreck to obtain the co-operation of different government departments. Where the statutes are silent then, of course, the common law applies.

The manner in which these laws interrelate is not always clear. Legislative attention should, it is submitted, be directed especially at the interrelationship between the statutes. At the time of writing there would appear to be no reported decisions in respect of the statutory provisions that are considered below.

6. Customs and Excise Act 91 of 1996

In section 112 of the Customs and Excise Act 91 of 1996, wreck is defined as follows:

(1) For the purposes of this section 'wreck' includes:
  (a) flotsam, jetsam and lagan;
  (b) any portion of a ship lost, abandoned or stranded or of the cargo, stores or equipment thereof or any other article thereon; and
  (c) any portion of an aircraft which has been wrecked or abandoned or of the cargo, stores or equipment thereof or any other article thereon.

The definition makes no reference to the age of the wreck or to whether the wreck must be of historical or cultural significance. In terms of the plain and ordinary meaning of the language of the provision it is therefore reasonably clear that all wrecks of whatever description fall to be governed by the Act.

Under section 64C(1) of the Act no person shall search a wreck or search for a wreck unless he is licensed with the Commissioner for the South African Revenue Service (the 'Commissioner') to do so and has furnished such security as the Commissioner may require. The Commissioner may, by virtue of section 64C(2), prescribe the circumstances under which and the conditions on which such a licence may be issued to any person, but no such licence shall give the holder thereof the exclusive right to search, or to search for, any particular wreck. Section 60 provides that the person shall not be issued with the licence unless the prescribed licence fee has been paid. Furthermore, the Commissioner may, subject to an appeal to the Minister of Finance, refuse any application for a new licence or refuse any application for a renewal of any licence or cancel or suspend for a specified period any licence if the applicant or the holder of the licence has contravened or failed to comply with the provisions of this Act; or has been convicted of an offence under the Act, or has been convicted of an offence involving dishonesty.

In terms of section 112(2) of the Act, any person who has in his possession any such wreck:

shall without delay give notice thereof to the nearest Controller [of Customs and Excise] and shall (unless he is the owner of such wreck or the duly authorized agent of the owner) if required, forthwith deliver that wreck or permit it to be delivered to the said Controller, and unless it is necessary for the preservation or safe-keeping thereof, no person shall without the permission of the said Controller remove or alter in quantity or quality any such wreck.

In terms of this provision, it would thus appear that any person who has any wreck in his possession, whether or not he is the owner of the wreck, must notify the Controller of the wreck.[15]

Once any wreck is found in, or brought into, the Republic it may, at any time after it has come under the control of the Controller, be disposed of by him under section 43, but is otherwise subject to the provisions of the Act.

Under section 43 the Controller is, *inter alia*, empowered to sell any goods, which clearly includes any wreck, and to apply the proceeds thereof to the discharge of any duty and other specified expenses which may have encumbered the wreck. After the payment of all such expenses, no payment of the surplus proceeds in respect of the wreck may be made to the owner of the wreck unless the application for such payment is supported by proof of ownership of the wreck and is received by the Commissioner within two years from the date of sale of the wreck.

7. National Monuments Act 28 of 1969

The National Monuments Act 28 of 1969 provides for the preservation and protection of the historical and cultural heritage of the country. By virtue of section 2, a National Monuments Council (a body corporate capable of suing and being sued, hereafter referred to as the 'Council') is established for the purposes of performing all such acts as are necessary to give effect to its objective. And, in section 2A, the objective of the Council is expressed to be the co-ordination of all activities in connection with monuments and cultural treasures so that they will be retained as tokens of the past and may serve as an inspiration for the future.

'Monuments' and 'cultural treasures' are wide generic terms that can, by means of declaration under the Act, be made to apply to virtually any immovable or movable property. Such property may include a wreck. More particularly, the Act adopts the definition of wreck in section 112(1) of the Customs and Excise Act 91 of 1964, as set out above.

The Council may, in respect of any wreck in South Africa which is 50 years old or older or which the Council upon reasonable grounds believes to be 50 years old or older, perform or carry out any power, function or duty assigned to it or imposed upon it in terms of the 1969 Act.[16] The manner in which a wreck is to be treated depends upon whether or not the wreck has been declared to be a national monument.

7.1 Declaration of wreck to be a national monument

The Council may declare any wreck which is 50 years old or older to be a national monument; and, in order to make such a declaration, the Council may require any person whom the Council is satisfied possesses information relating to the wreck to furnish the Council with such information.[17] The first official publication of the provisional declaration of wrecks as national monuments in terms of section 5(1)(c) of the Act was made on 23rd March 1984 in respect of 23 wrecks, including the wreck of the *Birkenhead*. All the wrecks lie within the territorial waters of South Africa.[18]

Any abandoned wreck which has been declared, or is about to be declared, a national monument, may in such manner and subject to such conditions, including the payment of compensation (if any), as may be determined by the Secretary for Customs and Excise, be placed at the disposal of the Council or other cultural institution.[19]

---

15   For a case in which a licence was issued in terms of the 1964 Act, see *Underwater Construction & Salvage Co. Ltd v. Bell* 1968 (4) S.A. (C) 190.
16   National Monuments Act 1969 s. 10A.
17   National Monuments Act 1969 s. 10A(3).
18   Government Gazette no. 9134 of 23 March 1984, notice no. 537.
19   National Monuments Act 1969 s. 10A(4).

Having declared a wreck to be a national monument, it follows that the national monument enjoys the protection set out in section 12, which provides, *inter alia*, that:

> (2) No person shall ... destroy, damage, excavate, alter, remove from its original site or export from the Republic any monument except under the authority of and in accordance with a permit issued under this section.

In terms of section 5 the Council has wide powers which include the right to preserve, repair, restore, purchase, sell or hypothecate and generally to exercise control over any property declared to be a national monument.

7.2 Wreck not declared to be a national monument

Even if the wreck has not been declared to be a national monument, it still enjoys the protection provided by section 12 of the 1969 Act. Thus, section 12(2B) states that:

> No person shall destroy, damage, alter or export from the Republic ... any wreck or portion of wreck, or any object derived from wreck, known or generally accepted to have been in South African territorial waters longer than 50 years except under the authority of and in accordance with a permit issued under this section.

Such a permit may be issued free of charge by, and in the discretion of, the Council. The permit may be issued at such time or within such period and subject to such terms, conditions and restrictions as may be imposed by the Council; but subject always to the directions of the Minister of Education.[20] Furthermore, section 12(2C) specifies the powers conferred by, and particulars of, such a permit as follows:

(a)   No person shall disturb or remove any wreck which is 50 years old or older, except by virtue of a permit issued by the Council on such conditions as it may deem fit and by virtue of a licence issued by the Commissioner of Customs and Excise.
(b)   A permit referred to in paragraph (a) may only be issued to a person providing written proof of affiliation with a museum approved by the Council.
(c)   (i) A permit referred to in paragraph (a) may only be issued by the Council after it has by notice in the Gazette afforded the opportunity for the submission of representations to it on the issuing of such permit and after representations received thereon have been considered by it.
(ii) The location of wreck shall not be disclosed in the notice referred to in subparagraph (i).
(d)   Any person to whom the Council issues a permit referred to in paragraph (a), shall thereby acquire no other right to wreck than the right granted to him by such permit.
(e)   (i) The Council shall not issue a permit referred to in paragraph (a) with regard to wreck in a security area or nature conservation area, or in an area adjacent to a security area or nature conservation area, without obtaining the prior approval of the department controlling such security area or nature conservation area.
(ii) The department concerned may grant its approval subject to certain conditions, which shall be binding on all parties concerned.
(f)   All material recovered from wreck or a wreck site shall be placed in the custody of the museum referred to in paragraph (b), and the museum, in consultation with the Council and

---

20   National Monuments Act 1969 s. 12(4)(c).

the holder of the permit, shall decide on the disposal thereof: provided that in the case of a dispute among the parties referred to in this paragraph the said museum shall refer the matter to arbitration.

By virtue of section 18(g) the Council may, with the approval of the Minister of Education, make by-laws regarding the keeping of proper records during work on wreck, the submission of reports on such work and the application of suitable conservation measures on material recovered from the wreck.

7.3 Offences in respect of a national monument or wreck

Any person who contravenes or fails to comply with any provision of section 12(2), and any person who disturbs or removes a wreck without a permit referred to in section 12(2C)(a), shall be guilty of an offence. On conviction in a magistrate's court such a person shall be liable to a fine or imprisonment not exceeding two years or to both such fine and such imprisonment.[21]

8. Legal Succession to the South African Transport Services Act 9 of 1989

When a wreck is within the area owned by the Company established in terms of section 2 of the Legal Succession to the South African Transport Services Act 9 of 1989, the Company is entitled by virtue of section 10 of schedule 1 to the Act to:

raise, remove or destroy any sunken, stranded or abandoned ship or wreck within the area owned by the Company, to recover from the person liable in terms of this paragraph all costs incurred in such raising, removal or destruction and in lighting, buoying, marking or detaining the ship or wreck and, on non-payment after written demand of such costs or any part thereof, to sell such ship or wreck and out of the proceeds of the sale defray such unpaid costs, rendering the surplus, if any, to the person entitled thereto and recovering any unpaid balance from the owner of such ship or wreck or from the person who was the owner of the ship at the time it was sunk, stranded or abandoned.

It would appear that the rights of the Company over the wreck may be exercised by the Company regardless of the historical or cultural significance of the wreck.

9. Wreck and Salvage Act 94 of 1996

A wreck which is less than 50 years old is governed by the Wreck and Salvage Act 94 of 1996, which came into operation on 1st February 1997. The Act, which is not retrospective in operation,[22] does not refer to national monuments or to cultural treasures. Furthermore, given the intense concern in South Africa to preserve the historical and cultural heritage of the country, the 1996 Act is expressly stated not to derogate from the operation of the National Monuments Act 1969.[23]

However, that does not mean that the 1996 Act is of no relevance to a wreck of historical or cultural significance: even a wreck of less than 50 years old may be of such significance. In any

21   National Monuments Act 1969 s. 16(j).
22   National Monuments Act 1969 s. 2(3).
23   National Monuments Act 1969 s. 23.

event, the 1996 Act has immediate application to a wreck that would most probably in the fullness of time have acquired historical and cultural significance. Any wreck entirely disposed of in terms of the 1996 Act will, of course, no longer fall to be governed by the 1969 Act.

The South African Safety Authority, a separate legal entity established by the South African Maritime Safety Authority Act 5 of 1998, administers the 1996 Act, while the Minister of Transport is empowered to order, or to perform, certain acts in terms of that statute. In practice, however, the Minister will usually only act on a recommendation made by the South African Maritime Safety Authority.

Wrecks are more widely defined in the 1996 Act than in the 1969 Act. In section 1(xii) of the 1996 Act it is stated that:

> wreck includes any flotsam, jetsam, lagan or derelict, any portion of a ship or aircraft lost, abandoned, stranded or in distress, any portion of the cargo, stores or equipment of any such ship or aircraft and any portion of the personal property on board such ship or aircraft when it was lost, abandoned, stranded or in distress.

In order to determine fully the meaning of a wreck it is, of course, necessary to establish the meaning of a ship. Section 1(x) states that a ship means:

> any vessel used or capable of being used on any waters, and includes any hovercraft, power boat, yacht, fishing boat, submarine vessel, barge, crane barge, crane, dock, oil or other rig, mooring installation or similar installation, whether floating or fixed to the sea-bed and whether self-propelled or not.

The 1996 Act provides that the Minister may appoint suitably qualified persons to be salvage officers at ports or other places in the Republic in respect of any defined area.[24] The powers, duties and functions of salvage officers appointed under the Act are as prescribed;[25] but no regulation has, as yet, been promulgated to prescribe these matters. The Act itself does, however, expressly empower a salvage officer to suppress plunder or disorder at the scene of a wreck,[26] and to conduct an investigation into the wreck.[27] Any person acting for a salvage officer must comply with the provisions of section 112(2) of the Customs and Excise Act 1964, as set out above.

The Minister of Transport is empowered to direct the owner or master of a ship that has been wrecked to be raised, removed, or destroyed or dealt with in such a manner as may be deemed fit.[28] In order to defray any expenses that the Minister may have incurred in the exercise of such powers, he or she may cause any goods to be removed from the wreck and detained until payment is made.[29] (It does not appear that this provision impliedly gives rise to a maritime lien over the wreck in favour of the Minister.)[30] Alternatively, the Minister may sell any wreck and apply the proceeds of the sale towards the defrayal of any expenses incurred in connection with the exercise of his or her power to have the wreck raised, removed, destroyed or otherwise dealt with.[31]

---

24 Wreck and Salvage Act 1996 s. 8(1).
25 Wreck and Salvage Act 1996 s. 8(3).
26 Wreck and Salvage Act 1996 s. 13.
27 Wreck and Salvage Act 1996 s. 11.
28 Wreck and Salvage Act 1996 s. 18(2).
29 Wreck and Salvage Act 1996 s. 18(4) and s. 18(5)(b).
30 In terms of s. 6 of the Admiralty Jurisdiction Regulation Act 1983, the English law of maritime liens is applicable in South Africa: *The Fidias* 1986(1) SA 714 (D). For commentary on this decision, see H. Staniland 'The Admiralty Jurisdiction Regulation Act and the Claim of a Saudi Arabian Necessaries Man' (1986) 103 *South African Law Journal* 350.
31 Wreck and Salvage Act 1996 s. 18(5)(a).

10. Ownership of Wreck

An owner can always vindicate his property wherever it may be found. In *Salvage Association of London v. S.A. Salvage Syndicate Ltd*[32] cargo was abandoned by its owners to the underwriters who made no attempt to raise the cargo from the wreck for seven years. De Villiers C.J. held that the underwriters had not abandoned the property:

> a person cannot be held to have abandoned his property unless his intention so to abandon it is clearly proved ... A person whose property has gone down in a shipwreck cannot be presumed to have abandoned it because for some years he has taken no steps to raise it. He may hope that in the meanwhile some appliances may be discovered by which the recovery of his property might be facilitated. Anyhow, in my opinion clear proof of abandonment must be given, and in the present case there is not in my opinion, such clear proof of abandonment. But the respondents are in possession of the field, they are working at this wreck, and they are entitled to recover the cargo except as against the true owner.[33]

It is, however, clear that the longer the period of time during which the owner has not taken steps to recover his property, the easier it may be to rebut the presumption that the property has not been abandoned.

An abandoned wreck – *res derelicta* – becomes a *res nullius* and ownership in the thing may pass to another. For ownership to pass, it is a prerequisite that there be an intention to abandon the wreck by the original owner. Such intention is not presumed unless clearly proved, especially where the wreck has value. The burden of proof rests upon the claimant.[34] The owner may limit the abandonment of ownership rights to the underwriter.

Ownership of a *res nullius* occurs, for instance, where there is a seizure of the thing with the intention of acquiring ownership viz. *occupatio*. In *Underwater Construction and Salvage Co. (Pty) Ltd v. Bell*[35] both the plaintiff and the defendant had been issued with licences to search for wreck in terms of the Customs and Excise Act 1964. The plaintiff had blasted four propeller blades, with a view to acquiring ownership, from an admittedly abandoned wreck. The plaintiff took two of the propeller blades ashore. The plaintiff left the other propeller blades lying at a marked spot in the sea next to the wreck with the intention of removing the two propeller blades some time later. But the defendant removed the propeller blades. The plaintiff sued for the delivery of these blades. Banks J. held that:

> While on the one hand it is not sufficient if there is a mere 'seeing' of the thing claimed, ownership is acquired as soon as there is a seizure with the intention of becoming owner. Ownership, once acquired, cannot be lost by a failure to remain in physical possession ... the fact that they (the two propeller blades) were not hoisted onto the ship does not mean that they had not been seized. There was a seizure - a taking into possession - as soon as they were forced apart from the wreck, and this having been done with the intention of acquiring ownership rendered plaintiff owner thereof.[36]

---

32   (1906) 23 SC 169.
33   *Ibid.* at p. 171.
34   *Salvage Association of London v. S.A. Salvage Syndicate Ltd.* (1906) 23 SC 169 at p. 171.
35   1968 (4) SA 190 (C).
36   *Ibid.* at p. 192.

Ownership of a *res nullius* may also pass to the State. In *Johnson and Irvin v. Mayton*[37] Bale C.J. held that:

> There appears to be considerable authority under Roman Dutch law that flotsam and jetsam unclaimed or not lawfully claimed, belong to the Crown or to some person who derives the right of flotsam and jetsam from the Crown. It seems to me that until some person has shown a lawful title it is the duty of the Government to hold the property, by virtue of eminent domain, against a person who may not be able to make out his claim to it. This is a right inherent in the Crown by virtue of its prerogative.

11. Conclusion

South African law governing wrecks of historical and cultural significance is, in general, reasonably well-developed. But the relationship between the various acts has not been sufficiently clarified. The removal or even destruction of a wreck in the interests of safe navigation and the protection of human life must surely enjoy the highest priority. On the other hand, the preservation of a wreck of great historical and cultural significance deserves the highest protection that circumstances permit. The precise ranking of these priorities should be expressly enshrined in the legislation. Finally, legislative attention could also be directed to the assumption that only a wreck of 50 years old or older is deserving of special legislative protection.

---

37   (1908) 29 NLR 696 at p. 699. See also *Salvage Association of London v. S.A. Salvage Syndicate Ltd.* (1906) 23 SC 169 at p. 171, where operations conducted on a wreck were held to be justifiable "except as against the Crown and as against the true owners."

Chapter 9

SPAIN

Esther Zarza Álvarez

1.   Introduction

Recent developments in technology have enabled the discovery and recovery of many long-lost treasures submerged at sea. Some of these treasures, recently located and recovered, are Spanish ships such as the *Girona*, the *Santa Maria de la Rosa*, the *Santa Margarita* and the *Nuestra Senora de Atocha*. The publicity given to these cases has focussed attention upon the right of the Spanish State to claim and recover ancient relics deemed to form part of its historical and cultural heritage.

Spain has in fact been quite reserved about stating a claim to ancient wrecks and items of Spanish origin found off the coasts of foreign states; indeed the Spanish government until now has not asserted ownership over any of the long-lost treasure galleons that have been located. The reasons for this attitude are complex and should be analysed taking into account the implications of the national laws of those countries in which relevant procedures have been brought, particularly their laws concerning abandonment, finds and/or salvage, as well as international law. As a preliminary remark, it should be noted that this apparent lack of interest on the part of the Spanish government does not accord with the high level of control and protection of the historical heritage provided by Spanish legislation.

This chapter will discuss current developments in Spanish national law concerning protection of the underwater cultural heritage within the boundaries of Spanish jurisdiction. The particular issue of the property rights of Spain, as the state of origin, over underwater historical, or culturally valuable, objects located in other jurisdictions will not be discussed, nor will issues relating to ownership and salvage except in so far as they pertain to, or are in some way connected with, the above.

It should be noted that under Spanish national law there is no specific regulation dealing with the underwater cultural heritage as separated and distinguished from the cultural or historical heritage as a whole. Therefore, reference must be made to the national legislation protecting the cultural heritage generally, with special attention to the rules concerning archaeological patrimony as far as these provisions are applicable to items of archaeological or historical significance located underwater.

2.   The Meaning of Cultural Heritage under Spanish Law: the Archaeological Patrimony

Nowadays, several adjectives are used to accompany the word 'heritage'. In Spain, expressions such as 'cultural heritage', 'historical heritage' or even 'artistic heritage' are often used in newspapers and even in political circles. All these expressions refer to the same wide concept, inclusive of all those historical items and remains which are part of the national heritage and in respect of which there is substantial public interest in their protection.

Internationally, the expression 'cultural heritage', which has been used since the middle of this century in international regulations, is now tending to be defined in a broad sense to include 'all traces of human existence'. In Spain, use of the adjective 'cultural' to broadly define the national legacy is on the increase, having been incorporated into legislative instruments in recent years.

Traditionally, however, Spanish law has referred to the national 'historical heritage'. History appears to be the significant element. Use of the adjective 'historical' in Spanish national legislation is motivated by the social desire to emphasise the 'preservation' element, directly associated with history. The Spanish historical heritage is defined in the 1985 Law on the Spanish Historical Heritage (the 13/85 Act). Article 1 provides that:

> The Spanish historical heritage is comprised of those objects, either movable or immovable, having an artistic, historical, paleontological, archaeological, ethnographic, scientific or technical interest.

As a consequence of the implementation of the 13/85 Act, some of the Spanish Autonomous Regions (*Comunidades Autónomas*) have enacted regional statutes concerning their own cultural heritage.[1] Most of these instruments refer to the 'cultural heritage' instead of using the term 'historical heritage' as used in the national legislation, which could give rise to some confusion. However, it is quite clear that the term 'cultural' is extensive enough to cover the historical element.

This chapter will use the term 'historical heritage' in the broad sense in which it is used in the 13/85 Act, in other words as including any object or site of an artistic, historical, paleontological, archaeological, ethnographic, scientific or technical value.

2.1 Archaeological patrimony

The archaeological patrimony, as defined by the 13/85 Act, forms part of the historical heritage (article 1(1)).

A definition of 'archaeological patrimony' is provided by article 40(1) of the Act, which states:

> In accordance with the provision of article 1 [defining the Spanish historical heritage], *movable or immovable property of an historical nature and capable of being studied with an archaeological methodology* belongs to the Spanish historical heritage, whether removed or not, either on the ground, in the subsoil, *in territorial waters or on the continental shelf* (emphasis added).

The regional instruments later enacted by some of the Spanish Autonomous Regions to protect their own cultural heritage have followed this definition of archaeological patrimony.

In order to apply the archaeological methodology criterion used in the Spanish legislation, it is necessary to answer a scientific question. Archaeology is a science with its own methodology, dealing with the study of historical remains. The directive of modern archaeology is that its scope of application is not limited to 'relics' in a strict sense but extends to any human remains which can be used to reconstruct traces of human existence. It is interesting to note that the 13/85 Act does not provide any chronological criteria to determine the historical significance of assets forming part of the historical heritage;[2] nor do the legislative instruments subsequently enacted by some of the Autonomous Regions.

---

1   The Andalucian, Vasc Country, Catalonian, Galician and Valencian act on 'cultural' heritage.
2   The statutory instruments governing the matter prior to 1985, and the draft Historical Patrimony Act of 1981, referred to items of more than 100 years of age as those which should be covered by the protective legislation.

Another important provision dealing with the archaeological patrimony is found in article 44(1) of the 13/85 Act, which provides:

> All objects and material remains falling within the definition of the Spanish archaeological patrimony and which have been discovered either as a consequence of excavations, land removals or any other work whatsoever, or by chance, are deemed to be *public property*. The finder must report the discovery to the appropriate authorities within the following fifteen days, or immediately in the case of findings by chance. Article 351 of the Civil Code (containing the general principles of the law of finds) will, in no case, be applicable (emphasis added).

This provision is contained within Section V of the 13/85 Act, which deals with archaeological property,[3] leading to the conclusion that one of the characteristics which distinguishes the archaeological patrimony from other items of an historical nature is its treatment as goods of public dominion.

Public property is defined as being outside the scope of private commercial transactions, an exclusion which is motivated by a desire to satisfy the public interest in goods of an historical significance. This public interest is, in important respects, incompatible with the assertion of rights of private ownership. The immediate consequence is that, in order to control trade in such objects, the Spanish State asserts sovereign jurisdiction and title to objects of an archaeological interest. Consequently such property is inalienable and unmarketable.

The exclusion of the general principles of the law of finds and salvage from the archaeological patrimony will be discussed in section 3, but at this stage the concept of archaeological patrimony should be considered in light of the above considerations. The legislation does not make clear the boundaries between items of an archaeological interest and other historically valuable goods also contemplated by the law, the expression 'public property' not being enough to define them. It can be said, however, that when dealing with archaeological patrimony, and therefore with public property, reference is being made in general to buried or hidden items of an historical or cultural significance which, by any means, have been discovered. Although this approach may be deemed as archaeologically unscientific to the extent that it ignores an archaeological interest in those objects or sites which have always been visible, it is wide enough for present purposes, enabling the conclusion to be reached that those items of an historical or cultural nature found underwater may be properly deemed to be archaeological patrimony. Indeed, underwater sites where items of an historical nature are located are considered as sites of archaeological significance. The management of these sites would require the application of archaeological methodology (through survey and excavation techniques) and, therefore, as far as an historical, artistic or cultural significance may be determined, those sites or properties located either in Spanish inland waters, territorial waters or on the continental shelf, will fall within the definition of archaeological patrimony set out in article 40 of the 13/85 Act.

---

3   Following art. 44(1) are provisions requiring an express authorisation from the competent authority to carry out archaeological activities and compelling the delivery of items so obtained to a public museum: art. 42, paras. 1 and 2.

3. Protection of the Archaeological Patrimony: National and Regional Legislation

The 13/85 Act regulates the protection and preservation of all objects of an archaeological and historical value located within Spanish territory .

It should be noted, however, that this matter has also come under the control of the Spanish regional governments (Autonomous Regions). Since the transfer of competence in questions of historical heritage to the Autonomous Regions between the years 1979 and 1983, each has drawn up and published rules and regulations with varying scopes to deal with archaeological activities in their territory. Some Autonomous Regions have also published their own laws on the historical or cultural heritage, making use of their legislative competence. Only five have been published until now (Cataluña, Andalucia, Galicia, the Vasc Country and Valencia), although some other projects are at the discussion phase. A number of innovations have been introduced in these laws, mainly as a consequence of experience over the years, aimed at perfecting and facilitating the legal protection of the historical heritage. Although generally speaking these texts are similar to the 13/85 Act, they all complement it, introducing innovations for protection: some general, relating to the protection of all cultural goods, and others specifically relating to the archaeological heritage, particularly that which is presumed to exist. Another interesting improvement relates to the assessment of environmental impact, a question that in 1985 had not yet been addressed in Spain, but which the majority of the Autonomous Regions that have their own legislation are now taking into account.

The special requirements and procedures for carrying out archaeological activities to search for, and recover, objects of an historical value will be dealt with in section 5 below, using the Andalusian government regulations as an example. However, at this stage the general measures provided by the national 13/85 Act for the protection of the archaeological patrimony will be outlined.

The 13/85 Act provides various measures for protecting Spain's historical heritage. The Act includes protective measures relating to those assets of historical/archaeological interest which are neither recorded nor inventoried; these measures, leading to the preservation and disposal of these assets, include the creation of management plans and the imposition of some restrictions on exportation.[4] Special protective measures are provided for those goods which have been registered with the Public Inventory of Movable Goods (inventoried assets). However, the highest level of protection applies to those assets in respect of which a declaration as Goods of Cultural Interest (GCI) has been made which, in the case of sites, implies a declaration of those sites as 'archaeological zones'. Article 15(5) of the 13/85 Act defines 'archaeological zones' as:

> those places where movable or immovable property of an historical nature, capable of being studied with archaeological methodology, whether removed or not, either on the ground, in the subsoil, in territorial waters or on the continental shelf, *is located* (emphasis added).

Generally speaking, the instruments providing for the highest level of protection are primarily a number of measures based on town and country planning regulations, aimed at documenting the remains before their destruction, or at preserving them *in situ*. It follows that, in principle, the measures providing for the highest level of protection are not easily applicable to the underwater cultural patrimony. Nevertheless, those measures which are most interesting, and which could be put into practice following declaration of an underwater site as an 'archaeological zone', will be highlighted.

---

4   The export of goods that are more than 100 years old will require an express authorisation.

Mere declaration of assets as GCI will cause municipal licences for building sites, construction or demolition work to be suspended. The declaration dossier will include a description of the asset, of the environment affected by the declaration, and of the elements that form part of it (article 11(2)). The environment is considered as part of the GCI and cannot be separated from it save in cases of *force majeure,* or when a social interest applies (article 18). Article 27 of the 13/85 Act also considers as GCI the movable property located in an 'archaeological zone', provided the declaration acknowledges it to be an essential part of its history.

After being declared, the asset must be registered at the GCI Registry managed by the Ministry of Culture (article 12) and the local authority where it is found must draw up a 'special protection plan' for the affected area, or another instrument of the kind envisaged in town planning legislation that is used to provide protection, and this scheme must be approved by the Ministry of Culture (article 20). Any work or intervention must follow this scheme and, in the case of archaeological zones, it must be authorised by the Ministry of Culture, which may require the undertaking of survey work or preliminary excavations (article 22(1)).

There are measures that are common to all GCI, whether movable or immovable property. For example, the competent governmental authority may suspend any demolition or other kind of work or action affecting a declared property when it considers this to be appropriate (article 37(1)). As far as preservation treatment is concerned, this is governed by the provisions set out for inventoried assets, but in the case of GCI a specific authorisation is required (article 39(1)).

Aside from this special protection scheme, the possibility of efficiently protecting the 'unknown' archaeological heritage is also of great interest. The content of article 43 of the 13/85 Act, which allows the competent authority to order survey or excavation work on any public or private land where there is presumed to be the presence of archaeological sites or remains, has provided a starting point for implementing new and detailed provisions in the regulations of the Autonomous Regions which allow such an idea to be put into practice. In this context, some of the laws enacted by the Autonomous Regions have established a wider protection scheme than that provided by the 13/85 Act, by enacting special provisions for the protection of those places where the existence of cultural heritage is not necessarily confirmed (as in archaeological zones) but is merely presumed. This is the case with the 'archaeological easement zones' of Andalucia and the 'archaeological protection spaces' of Cataluña.

Even prior to 1985, Spanish legislation bestowed upon the competent authority power to order that archaeological surveying or excavation be carried out on any public or private land. In 1985, however, the expression 'presumed' appeared for the first time, which is related to the development in recent decades of a very special type of archaeological management: preventive management, based essentially on progress achieved in surveying techniques that allows it to be presumed that there are remains in places where excavations have not yet taken place.

Paragraphs 1 and 2 of article 41 define 'archaeological activities' (including archaeological surveying and excavation) as those works, with or without land removals, on the ground, in the subsoil, or underwater, aimed at discovering, investigating or studying any kind of historical or palaeontological remains, as well as the geological aspects relating to them.

In accordance with article 42, any archaeological work or activity (surveying and/or excavating) requires the prior authorisation of the competent authority. This authority will take appropriate measures to control and supervise the authorised works, ensuring that they are conducted in accordance with conditions and requirements relating to their suitability and to the scientific interest of the project. Article 42 also provides that the beneficiary of the authorisation shall be obliged to deliver items found to the appropriate body or museum, as designated by the competent authority. The Act further expressly provides that persons to whom an authorisation to carry out archaeological research or other activities is granted will not be entitled to any award or compensation whatsoever. Finally, article 42 provides that any archaeological project carried out without the necessary authorisation having been granted, or otherwise infringing these provisions, will be considered an unlawful act.

The 13/85 Act also contains rules governing archaeological remains which are discovered by chance, or in the course of any work. Article 41(3) defines chance finds as being:

> discoveries of objects and material remains which, possessing the values that characterise Spain's historical heritage, have occurred by chance or as a consequence of some kind of land removal, demolition or other sort of works.

As stated earlier, article 44(1) provides that:

> All objects and material remains falling within the definition of the Spanish archaeological patrimony and which have been discovered either as a consequence of excavations, land removals or any other work whatsoever, or by chance, are deemed to be public property. The finder must report the discovery to the appropriate authorities within the following fifteen days, or immediately in the case of findings by chance. Article 351 of the Civil Code (containing the general principles of the law of finds) will, in no case, be applicable.

Accordingly, the discoverer must report such finds immediately to the competent authority and in no event will article 351 of the Civil Code, which states the general principles of the law of finds, be applicable. This latter reads:

> hidden treasure belongs to the owner of the land where it is found. When however the discovery is made on someone else's property, or on State property, or by chance, half the find will be awarded to the discoverer.

This reference to the Civil Code leads us to consider the term 'treasure', which has a long tradition in Spanish law. The importance accorded to private property throughout almost the entire history of the Spanish State resulted in the 13/85 Act, while trying to adapt itself to a modern approach to cultural goods, including a provision establishing the right of both the finder and the owner(s) of the land where the discovery takes place to a monetary reward. This reward comprises the value attributed to the find in a legal appraisal shared equally between them (article 44(3)).

The right to a reward therefore applies to discoveries produced as a consequence of non-archaeological excavations, land removals, or works of any kind, or by chance. This means that, to be entitled to a reward, it must be proved that there was no intention to discover remains: if there was such an intention, such activity would qualify as archaeological surveying or excavation, lawful or unlawful, depending on whether or not it was authorised in accordance with article 42.

In any case the 13/85 Act sets out a number of conditions that must be fulfilled before a finder can exercise his right to the stipulated reward. Not only must the discovery be reported immediately (article 44(1)), but also:

> after the discovery has been reported and until the objects are handed over to the competent authority, the rules on a legal deposit will apply to the finder, unless the objects are given to a public museum (article 44(2)).

Failure to comply with these two points, apart from resulting in forfeiture of the right to a reward (article 44(4)), converts the discovery process into an illegal activity, penalised by law. A clause is also added whereby there is no right to the reward when what is discovered comprises a fixture of property registered as GCI (article 44(5)).

Practice over the years has made it quite clear just how difficult it is to prove that most discoveries were found by chance.

4.   Underwater Archaeological Patrimony

As mentioned in section 1, under Spanish law there are no specific provisions for the protection of the underwater cultural heritage distinguishable from those applicable to the cultural heritage generally.

Some maritime law regulations include provisions dealing with underwater finds. For example, the Law on Salvage, Assistance, Findings, and Removals at Sea, dated 24th December 1962, contains rules about ownership and salvage rights, although it explicitly excludes those objects which are outside private traffic by virtue of the law and which are regulated by special legislation (as is the case with heritage property). Similarly, the Law on Ports and Merchant Marine dated 24th November 1992, provides that the Maritime Administration (which is under the control of the Ministry of Transportation) has no competence to deal with marine finds or removals in so far as they relate to items of an historical, archaeological or cultural interest, being, in such a case, within the competence of the Ministry of Culture.

It follows that when dealing with the underwater cultural heritage reference must necessarily be made to the legislation on the general cultural heritage and, in particular, to the 1985 Law on the Spanish Historical Heritage (the 13/85 Act).

The 13/85 Act expressly includes inland waters, the territorial sea and the continental shelf as areas in which archaeological items can be found. This was the first Spanish legislation on the historical heritage to refer specifically to submarine areas as zones where archaeological goods could be located. However, the Act does not incorporate specific provisions on the protection of the underwater cultural heritage as distinguished from any other heritage property, nor do the regional statutes.

The 13/85 Act refers to three maritime zones: inland waters; the territorial sea, extending up to twelve nautical miles from the baseline; and the seabed and subsoil of the submarine areas that extend beyond the baselines from which the territorial sea is measured to the outer edge of the continental margin up to a distance of 200 miles, in other words, the zone over which Spain exercises its sovereign rights for the purpose of exploring and exploiting its natural resources.

At present Spanish sovereignty extends to the territories of the seventeen Autonomous Regions inclusive of their inland and territorial waters, as well as to the inland and territorial waters of the two isolated Spanish territories in Africa: Ceuta and Melilla. The complexity of the underwater patrimony, in respect to its location and protection, has given rise to certain problems and disputes regarding competence between the Spanish central government and the regional governments. The matter was, however, definitively resolved in 1989 when an appeal by the Andalusian regional government against an authorisation for underwater surveying off the Andalucian coast granted by the Ministry of Culture, was upheld. Since this decision, the matter falls conclusively under the control of the different Spanish regional governments (for the Autonomous Regions).

To be able to access the underwater heritage, careful and closely regulated diving techniques are required. Both the management of, and activities undertaken in relation to, the underwater archaeological heritage require specialised methodology and technology, and an administrative procedure appropriate for the medium in which it is found. In addition, as has already been mentioned, the most efficient measures for the protection of the archaeological heritage in Spanish legislation are those that are connected with the town and country planning system, measures that are generally unsuitable for use underwater. For example, the ability to establish archaeological zones is of little use in relation to the underwater heritage. There are no criteria for defining an archaeological zone underwater and planning provisions, which have proved to be the most efficient means of protecting archaeological zones on land, are not applicable to submerged areas.

Various proposals have been suggested to resolve these problems:

(1)   The promotion of underwater archaeological inventories and incorporation of their data in cartography in order that underwater sites may be taken into consideration and protected by the public works and defence authorities.

(2)   The incorporation of a requirement for a management plan in the procedure for the declaration of an underwater archaeological zone, which would include a number of specific measures aimed at investigating, preserving and promoting the site, and also establishment of a requirement that authorisation be obtained for shipping, berthing or mooring of boats, fishing with any tackle, and diving.

(3)   The establishment of a designation similar to the archaeological easement zones of Andalucía and the archaeological protection spaces of Cataluña, in other words, the designation of areas where there is presumed to be underwater heritage. Such areas should be recorded in the inventory and defined and marked in the cartography. A favourable report should be required before any work or activity is allowed within them.

To be able to put all this into practice, it is essential that there be co-ordination between the public works authorities, the marine authorities (*Capitanias Maritimas*) and the police (*Guardia Civil del Mar*) who should be aware of the location and extent of the inventoried underwater heritage, and there should also be some linkage with the procedures for maintaining environment protection standards in order to take advantage of these mechanisms for the management of the underwater heritage.

Furthermore, measures for the protection of the underwater heritage should include setting up specialised institutions, with suitable technical equipment and personnel trained in the management of the underwater heritage, specially dedicated to preparing and maintaining inventories and to perfecting underwater research techniques.

5.   Control and Supervision of Archaeological Activities: the Andalusian Government Regulations as a Case Study

Any archaeological work or activity requires prior authorisation from the competent governmental authority. All Spanish Autonomous Regions have enacted their own regulations on archaeological works, the application of which necessarily assumes that the regional government is to control and supervise all activities associated with those works.

It would be beyond the remit of this chapter to analyse all the instruments concerning archaeological activities that exist in the Spanish Autonomous Regions. However, reference will be made to one of these instruments, that of the Andalucian regional government, as an example of the procedures and requirements involved in carrying out archaeological activities in Spain.

As previously indicated, the Andalusian government has adopted its own regulations on this particular matter. Following enactment of the national Law on the Spanish Historical Heritage (the 13/85 Act), the regional government of Andalucía implemented its own legislation relating to the Andalusian historical patrimony (1/1991 Act, dated 3rd January 1991), and additional legislation to complement the Act has also been recently enacted (Royal Decree 19/95 dated 7th February 1995 on Regulations for the Protection of the Andalusian Historic Patrimony). Furthermore, archaeological activities within the Andalusian Region are governed by Decree 321/1993, which establishes an administrative procedure to control and supervise archaeological excavations and any other activity leading to the search for, and recovery of, historically valuable objects.

Pursuant to article 1 of Decree 321/93, the prior authorisation of the Andalusian Council of Culture is required for the performance of archaeological activities (expressly including underwater survey or excavations). To this end, persons who wish to apply for authorisation to undertake an archaeological project must comply with a number of conditions and legal requirements.

5.1 Qualification standards for applicants

In accordance with article 2, the following persons can apply for an authorisation to carry out archaeological activities:

(1)   Spanish or foreign persons having a university degree and providing satisfactory evidence of academic training, either in archaeology or in palaeontology. (If the degree is obtained from a foreign university, it should have been recognised by the Spanish authorities).

(2)   Exceptionally, Spanish or foreign persons providing evidence of technical capability and previous experience in similar activities, even though they do not have the university degree stipulated in paragraph 1 above).

(3)   Spanish or foreign teams having among their members persons meeting the professional qualification standards provided for in sub-paragraph 1 above.

(4)   Spanish universities and museums of Andalucía.

(5)   The Spanish Institutes of Archaeology.

(6)   Public authorities or institutions having personnel qualified as provided by paragraphs 1, 2 and 3 above.

Further, pursuant to article 2, the director of the project must be an archaeologist and, in case of marine or underwater activities, both the director and at least half of the staff must provide satisfactory evidence of professional qualification and experience in diving.

Finally, article 2, paragraph 4, establishes that the applications presented by foreign persons or foreign institutions must be submitted together with a supporting report issued by any of those Spanish persons or bodies which are entitled to apply for the authorisations pursuant to article 1 above. Therefore, provided that all the requirements contained in article 2, paragraphs 1, 2 and 3, are fulfilled, there is no need to create a Spanish entity in order to apply for authorisation to carry out a project.

5.2 Applications

In order to proceed with search and recovery operations, two different types of authorisation may be requested and obtained from the appropriate Andalusian authorities.[5]

The usual procedure is to request from the local authorities approval for a general programme to undertake comprehensive archaeological activities in the area for a maximum period of six years. Exceptionally applicants may apply for a one-off authorisation to carry out specific search and recovery operations in the area, with a particular and determined objective. In the latter case, the national General Directorate of Goods of Cultural Interest will grant the permit, provided that there are scientific reasons to justify the project.

The documentation required to complete the appropriate application is as follows:

(1)   A proposal containing details of the specific archaeological operation and plan of work.

(2)   A memorandum of the goals the project will attempt to achieve.

(3)   A detailed explanation of the different phases to be undertaken.

(4)   A report attaching the appropriate charts and any other relevant documentation specifying details about location, presumed age of the remains, etc.

(5)   Authorisation from the owner of the land where the works will be carried out.

(6)   A description of the location, specifying the area covered by the plan of work and a report on the protection and preservation measures to be taken.

---

5   It is worth noting that subsidies can be formally requested from the Andalusian government.

The application must also include personal data relating to the applicant; names, curriculum vitae and academic background of the director, vice-director and other members of the team; as well as any other information or details that may be requested by the competent authority from time-to-time.

Applications must be submitted to the appropriate local representative of the Andalusian Council of Culture.

In the subsequent fifteen days, the Andalusian Council of Culture will file the application with the General Directorate of Goods of Cultural Interest, attaching a technical report issued by an archaeologist from the Andalusian government[6] on the feasibility of the project.

This report will be followed by a scientific report issued by the Andalusian Commission of Archaeology.[7] The General Directorate of Goods of Cultural Interest, upon examination of both reports and taking into account the needs of protection and preservation of the Andalusian historical patrimony, will issue a final resolution granting or denying the authorisation. The resolution should be issued within a period of two months from the date of submission of the application.

The authorisation shall be effective until the 31st day of October of the year following that in which it was granted.

Once the authorisation is granted, the applicant must take out insurance covering the professional legal liability which may arise as a consequence of its activities, as well as an insurance covering accidents in respect of all members of staff participating in the work. Non-fulfilment of this duty will lead to the revocation of the authorisation (article 11).

The works must be conducted under the control and management of the archaeological director of the project, who shall be held personally liable and responsible for any damage arising out of the conduct of the operations.

5.3   Control and supervision of operations

All the incidents and circumstances arising in the course of the operation must be noted in a daily record-book by the director of the project. This record-book must be registered with the General Directorate of Goods of Cultural Interest and presented before the Andalusian Council of Culture upon completion of the works.

Further, the General Directorate of Goods of Cultural Interest shall appoint one or several inspectors to take control of, and supervise, the approved works.

The functions of the appointed inspector(s) during the course of the works will be the following:

(1)   to supervise the operations so that they are conducted in compliance with the terms and conditions of the approved plan of work and in accordance with the applicable regulations;

(2)   to take control of any items that are discovered so that they are properly recorded and listed in the appropriate record-books;

(3)   to communicate all relevant information about the development of the work to the local authority;

(4)   to recommend and request from the local authority the revocation of the authorisation in cases where it is considered that the work is not being conducted in compliance with the approved terms and/or that the applicable registration is not being complied with.

The director of the project, acting on behalf of the team, shall submit to the local authority a scientific report showing the results of the work and any other information as may be required from time-to-time by the local authority.

---

6   Each local government has its own archaeologist.
7   One of the consultative bodies of the Andalusian Council of Culture.

Upon conclusion of the works a receipt, signed by both the director of the project and the inspector(s), shall be drawn up. The receipt should refer to the conformity of the activities as performed to the previously approved plan of work, and to the adoption of appropriate measures and practices for the conservation and protection of the archaeological remains.

Once the archaeological work is completed, an inventory, listing all objects found and attaching graphical documentation, shall be prepared and signed by both the director of the project and the archaeological inspector(s).

Afterwards, any items found must be delivered to the appropriate museum or other institution, as designated by the local authority when granting the authorisation. For this purpose a delivery agreement shall be executed, acknowledged and signed by the director of the project, the archaeological inspector and the director of the particular museum or other institution. The inventory referred to above shall also be attached to the delivery agreement.

The holder of the licence may request from the General Directorate of Goods of Cultural Interest authorisation to retain any or all the items found in its custody for a maximum period of two years. In such a case the director shall be personally liable for any damage or loss to the objects whilst they are in his custody and until they are finally deposited with the appropriate museum or other institution.

Finally, Decree 321/93 provides that the General Directorate of Culture, taking into account the importance and historical significance of the discovery, may divulge the results of the scientific research always provided that it does not interfere with the preferential rights of the discoverers in their scientific research.

Chapter 10

SWEDEN

Thomas Adlercreutz

1. Background

Whereas statutory measures for the general protection of Sweden's cultural heritage were adopted comparatively early, provisions concerning wrecks have been in existence for merely thirty years. The tardiness of the legislation with regard to underwater remains may seem particularly surprising in light of the spectacular salvage in 1961 – and subsequent careful restoration – of the seventeenth century man-of-war *Vasa*, now on view in some of its original splendour in Stockholm's most visited museum. It is also surprising when one reflects upon the fact that the brackish waters of the Baltic Sea, in which most of Sweden's territorial sea is to be found, provide excellent physical conditions for the natural preservation of wooden wreckage, of which large measures have been deposited over the years by bad weather and naval action.

1.1 The early history

As of the sixteenth century, records show that the kings of Sweden have entertained an interest in ancient remains. In 1599 royal instructions were issued for a fact-finding tour around the land in order to document stones with runic inscriptions.[1] This mission was followed by others, and in a memorandum of 1630 the scope of the inventorising was widened to comprise many elements of what we today think of as entities of the cultural heritage. The first instrument of legal protection of ancient remains dates from 1666. A royal decree of that year, dedicated to the "immortal glory of the realm", prohibited carelessness with and destruction of ancient "monuments" and "antiquities".[2] The decree furthermore ordered repair and conservation of damaged remains. There is no mention of remains situated underwater.

In this latter respect, however, account should also be taken of the early rules pertaining to the right to finds. In Sweden – unlike in Denmark – there probably never was an unconditional royal prerogative right to treasure trove, i.e. finds of gold and silver.[3] The first nationwide Swedish code – issued in 1350 and 1357 – laid down the provision that rare finds on land or shore accrued by two-thirds to the king and one-third the finder.[4] Finds from sea- or lake-bed, however, were to be divided equally between king and finder, no doubt as a reflection of the greater trouble involved in making finds under difficult conditions.[5] One of the provincial codes,[6] the earliest written edition approximately simultaneous with the national code, had the same provisions for finds from sea- and lake-bed, but also an interesting exception for wrecks. For unclear reasons wrecks – unlike

---

1   Torsten Fogelqvist *'Svensk kulturminnesvård. Ett trehundraårsminne'* (2nd edn., 1930) p. 14.
2   The decree seems to have excepted land bestowed of old on the nobility.
3   It should be noted that the Scandinavian countries have had somewhat different concepts of treasure trove to those of the common law of England, Wales and Northern Ireland.
4   Magnus Erikssons allmänna landslag, Tjuvamålsbalken XXXI, and Stadslag, Tjuvamålsbalken XI.
5   Bengt Thordeman 'Skattfyndsregalet i Sverige och Danmark' (1945) 2–3 *Fornvännen* 190.
6   Östgötalagen, Byggningabalken XXXVII.

155

other finds from the seabed – would fall by two-thirds to the king, and the remaining third to the finder, i.e. the same apportionment as the national code stipulated for rare finds on land or shore.[7]

It would be futile to look for efforts to preserve the cultural heritage in these early provisions. In the medieval statutes it is difficult to find even a royal intention of glorifying the realm, such as the one quoted from the decree of 1666. In that vein, however, was conceived another royal decree, of 1684, in which references were made to the old rules of apportionment of finds in the national code. This decree introduced an element of protection. Finders were prohibited from dispersing, melting, or in any other way transmuting, rare finds. All finds were to be delivered to the crown, which would then reimburse the finder for his share.[8] From the seventeenth century onwards, valuable finds would thus not simply be disposed of for profit, but kept in the Royal Treasury and later in the museums.

The fact that finders received just one-third, or at best half the value of the find probably served as a deterrent to the dutiful reporting of finds. The rules on finder's award were changed in the new national code of 1734. Finds from lake or sea – and other buried hoards – were now to be divided equally between landowner and finder, but if it was treasure trove, then the finder would still have to deliver to the crown but would be reimbursed to the *full* value *plus* an increment of one-eighth.[9]

A royal decree of 1827 amalgamated the older rules for protection of ancient remains and for delivery of finds for redemption by the crown. The latter were expanded in scope: "Anyone, who finds old coins, or older works of gold, silver, copper, metal, stone and wood, or other pieces of art, either in the soil or in water..." had to deliver the find and – if not allowed to keep it – was entitled to compensation for the value plus one-eighth. A new decree issued in 1867 retained in different wording the gist of the earlier provisions, but an amendment in 1873 withdrew items of metal (thus also bronze), stone and wood from the duty to report and deliver. There was still no mention of wrecks, to which only general provisions under maritime law would be applicable.

1.2   Development of present rules

Parliament had not been involved in the issuing of the earlier rules on ancient remains, but various demands for reform in the 1920s and 1930s led to the adoption in 1942 of an Act on Ancient Monuments.[10] This statute brought about a strengthening of the crown's position with regard to finds. Ownerless objects, found on or in connection with a protected ancient monument, were proclaimed to be crown property. As wrecks still were not considered for inclusion in the categories of protected remains, this provision meant little for objects pertaining to sunken ships. With regard to finds in general the old rules were retained in essence as concerns finds of gold, silver and copper, but the provisions were edited differently. An age requirement was introduced. All ownerless objects more than one hundred years of age, and found in places other than on protected ancient remains, were to accrue to the finder, but he was under a duty to report the find for redemption by the crown if the object in question consisted wholly or partly of gold, silver or copper, or was found adjacent to such an object. Mention of a finding place "in the soil or in water" was omitted. This omission, however, could not have been intended to lead to any change of the earlier scope of application. An important change was that a finder's reward could be given, in addition to the lawful compensation by 112.5 (100 + 1/8) percent for redeemed finds.

---

7   Thordeman, *op. cit.* note 5 p. 191.

8   *Ibid*. p. 194; I.A. Hedenvind 'Fornfynd och hembudsplikt' in *Ad patriam illustrandam* (1946) p. 376.

9   The introduction of the landowner on the receiving end – replacing the king – was probably an influence of Roman law, but a similar order had been practised in the Middle Ages both in Iceland and in Gotland, where there was no king or the king was weak: Thordeman, *op. cit.* note 5 p. 197.

10   Proposition (Government Bill) 1942:8, Svensk författningssamling 1942:350.

In the 1940s and 1950s skin-divers became active in larger numbers and protection against undue exploration of, and the causing of damage to, wrecks and other underwater remains became an object of increasing concern. The *Vasa* story made politicians and the general public aware of the hidden heritage values. A memorandum published in 1965 by the Ministry of Justice[11] as a result of initiatives from the Central Board of National Antiquities and the National Maritime Museum, set out that the existing rules were less than satisfactory in providing protection for shipwrecks and other cultural objects from lake- or sea-bed. Under obvious influence of rules already adopted in Denmark and Norway the solution proposed was an extension of the crown prerogative right to cover wrecks, finds from wrecks and other finds made in Swedish waters provided that the object could be presumed to have been lost more than 150 years ago and that it seemed apparent that a private owner could no longer be found. A solution disfavoured was one recently adopted in Finland, where the Act on Ancient Monuments of 1951 had been amended in 1963 to include shipwrecks among the categories of monuments protected from physical interference directly by law. Such a solution – which does not involve the question of ownership, but is an expression of State powers under public law – could have been recommended for Sweden as well. The Finnish Monuments Act had, in fact, been modelled on the corresponding Swedish legislation and it used the same public law concepts.

It was in fact the Finnish solution that was adopted in the Government Bill[12] amending the Act on Ancient Monuments. Shipwrecks became protected in the same way as ancient monuments already were, i.e. wrecks – as other categories of remains enumerated in the Act – were not to be physically interfered with unless permission had been given by the Central Board of National Antiquities, the government agency responsible for the monitoring of the Act. This would apply regardless of ownership. The State claimed a prerogative right only to *salvaged* ownerless wrecks. The age requirement was determined thus that one hundred years could be presumed to have elapsed since the wreckage. The Central Board of National Antiquities became authorised to conduct investigations and to salvage wrecks, as well as to take other measures for care and protection. With regard to ownerless movable objects pertaining to wrecks, the general provisions of the Act on Ancient Monuments would become applicable, i.e. such items accrued automatically to the crown as did finds from protected remains. Underwater finds unrelated to a wreck were to be treated as were finds on land.[13] The proposed amendments were approved by Parliament and gained legal force as of 1st January 1967.[14]

In 1987 a report was published by the Ministry for Education[15] with a proposal for the amalgamation of various statutes and regulations into one statute concerning monuments of an archaeological nature (the above-mentioned Act on Ancient Monuments), historic buildings, ecclesiastical buildings and their inventory, and export of older cultural movables. This proposal resulted in the adoption of the current provisions for the underwater heritage in the Cultural Monuments (etc.) Act.

2.   Current Law

Before going into a detailed account, the reader should note, first, that the Swedish Constitution has no provisions regarding government obligations to preserve or protect the cultural

---

11   Ju 1965:13.
12   Proposition (Government Bill) 1967:19.
13   *Ibid.* p. 24.
14   Svensk författningssamling 1967:77.
15   Government Memorandum DsU 1987:9.

heritage. Thus there are few constitutional aspects that need to be considered here.[16] The civil law environment, in which the current Cultural Monuments Act (hereinafter referred to under its Swedish acronym KML) is set will, however, be described. Secondly, issues regarding the underwater heritage are not always solvable only by recourse to domestic legislation. Questions regarding the heritage in international waters have in recent years been subject to regulation – embryonic to some minds – by international law,[17] a fact which has also affected Swedish internal legislation. These rules will be given special consideration. Thirdly, it should be pointed out that protection under the KML in principle is the same for monuments and finds underwater as on dry land. There are many maritime vestiges which are now to be found well ashore.

2.1　Monument law

The KML[18] gained legal force on 1st January 1989. Preparatory works are to be found in the Government Bill and Parliament's Committee Report:[19] preparatory comments play a considerable part in the construction of Swedish statutory provisions. The Act is divided into six chapters, out of which the second, on ancient monuments and finds, is of interest here.

2.1.1 Ancient monuments

Under the KML archaeological remains are protected directly by law, i.e. no administrative decision will normally be issued in order to identify what is protected. The scope of protection is laid out in Chapter 2, section 1:

> Permanent ancient monuments are protected under this Act. Permanent ancient monuments are the following [remains] of human activity in past ages, having resulted from use in previous times and having been permanently abandoned: ... 7. routes and *bridges, harbour facilities, beacons*, road markings, *navigation marks* and similar transport arrangements, as well as boundary markings and labyrinths, 8. *wrecked ships*, if at least one hundred years have presumably elapsed since the ship was wrecked ... (italics added).

In section 2[20] it is further stated: "An ancient monument includes a large enough area of ground or area on the seabed to preserve the remains and to afford them adequate scope with regard to their nature and significance". This protected area is normally not delimited in advance, but may be so by an order of the County Administration, the State agency responsible at the regional level for managing the KML.

Section 6 defines the word 'protection': "It is prohibited, without permission under this Chapter, to displace, remove, excavate, cover or, by building development, planting or in any other way, to alter or damage an ancient monument".

Section 7 gives the State agencies, i.e. the Central Board of National Antiquities and the County Administration access to ancient monuments in order to take measures for their care.

16　The Constitution, in fact, embodies a minor problem with regard to the possibility of issuing detailed regulations regarding ancient monuments, but that problem will be dealt with in section 3 below.
17　On the position in international waters, see further, ch. 14.
18　Svensk författningssamling 1989:950. The translation used here is one unofficially prepared in 1997 by the Central Board of National Antiquities. There is no authenticated English version.
19　Proposition (Government Bill) 1987/88:104, Kulturutskottets betänkande (Report by Committee on Cultural Affairs) 1987/88:21.
20　Hereafter the Chapter number of the KML will be mentioned only if other than 2.

These powers are, of course, essential for the upkeep of monuments on land, but of less practical significance underwater.

Section 8 empowers the Central Board of National Antiquities and the County Administration to "examine ancient monuments, salvage a shipwreck being an ancient monument and investigate a place where archaeological finds have been discovered". It further provides that "[i]f a shipwreck constituting an ancient monument and having no owner is salvaged, it shall accrue to the State."

Section 9 further empowers the County Administration to:

> issue regulations for the protection of an ancient monument. ... Regulations may also be issued for an area, which under section 2 does not belong to the ancient monument, provided that this does not significantly impede current use of the land. ... The ... County Administration may issue a protection order for a place where archaeological finds have been discovered, if this can be done without causing any significant inconvenience. A protection order may apply until the place has been investigated as provided in section 8. ... Regulations and protection orders may carry contingent fines.

All development projects should be preceded by investigation as to the existence of ancient monuments which might be affected, and, if this be the case, consultation with the County Administration. If an ancient monument is discovered in the course of works, these are to be immediately suspended (section 9).

Under section 12 all interference with ancient monuments is subject to permission by the County Administration. Such permission may not be granted unless the monument causes a hindrance or inconvenience out of all reasonable proportion to its significance, but:

> [i]n the case of the owner of a shipwreck or of an archaeological find belonging to a shipwreck, permission may be granted unless there are special reasons to the contrary. ... If any person other than the owner of the land or water area or the owner of the shipwreck applies for permission the application is to be refused if the owner objects to the measure and if there are no particular reasons why the application should be allowed.

In granting permission the County Administration may make reasonable stipulations for special investigations to record the ancient monument, to conserve archaeological finds or special measures to preserve the monument (section 13). The costs of such measures are to be borne by the developer, unless certain special criteria are met, one of which being that the monument was previously unknown (section 14).

> Any person refused permission under section 12 with reference to an ancient monument which, when discovered, was completely unknown and without visible sign above ground, is entitled to reasonable compensation out of public funds if the ancient monument causes him substantial hindrance or inconvenience ... (section 15).

The provisions outlined so far pertain to ancient monuments, *inter alia* shipwrecks. It should be noted at this point that elements that in some countries would be considered underwater cultural heritage, e.g. underwater geomorphical or palaeontological remains, are not protected under the KML. Such remains may be protected specially by decisions on nature reserves under the Nature Conservation Act,[21] but that Act will not be dealt with here. The discussion here will continue with the current provisions for *movables* related to the underwater cultural heritage.

---

21   Svensk författningssamling 1964:822.

2.1.2 Archaeological finds

The definition of 'archaeological finds' is to be found in section 3: "objects which have no owner when found and which 1. are discovered in or near an ancient monument and are connected with it, or 2. are found in other circumstances and are presumably at least one hundred years old."

Archaeological finds under 1. accrue to the State. Other archaeological finds accrue to the finder. He or she is, however, duty-bound to invite the State to redeem the find if it "contains objects partly or wholly of gold, silver, copper, bronze or any other copper alloy, or if the find consists of two or more objects which were presumably deposited together" (section 4).

Anybody who discovers archaeological finds which either accrue to the State or must be offered for redemption, has to report to the County Administration or certain other authorities. Finds belonging to shipwrecks can be reported to the Coastguard Service. Upon request the finder must surrender the object in return for a receipt and state where, when and how the find was discovered (section 5).

Decisions to redeem archaeological finds are taken by the Central Board of National Antiquities. Payment shall be assessed at an amount which is reasonable with regard to the nature of the find. For precious metals, payment must be no less than the value of the metal by weight, augmented by one-eighth. In addition a special finder's reward may be paid (section 16).[22]

The Central Board of National Antiquities may transfer archaeological finds to museums, which undertake to care for the objects in the future. This also applies specifically to shipwrecks (section 17). If the museum is a non-State entity, then ownership is also considered as being transferred.[23]

2.1.3 Common provisions

Of importance to the protection of both ancient monuments and archaeological finds are the following provisions.

There is a general ban on the use of metal detectors in Sweden, not just on archaeological sites but everywhere, unless provisions exempting certain usages by the authorities apply, or an individual permission issued by the County Administration has been given (sections 18-20).

Sections 21 and 21(a) impose penalties of fines or imprisonment for deliberate and negligent offences against the protective rules for ancient monuments and archaeological finds. In aggravated cases with intent, imprisonment for up to four years may be imposed.

Under section 22 measures of enforcement can be imposed upon offenders against the protective provisions in order to rectify unauthorised infringements. Section 22(a) makes it possible to forfeit archaeological finds which do not already accrue to the State, the value or proceeds of such finds, and metal detectors and other equipment used in offences, or the value of such equipment.

Section 23 empowers the County Administration to issue provisions to apply pending final determination of the matter.

Sections 24 and 25 have procedural rules on appeal and judicial review of decisions. Depending on the matter, the government, an administrative court of law or a real property court of law is competent to try appeals or undertake judicial review.

2.2 Related civil law

Under Swedish civil law finds in general are treated somewhat differently depending on whether made on land or in water. In both cases wilfully discarded objects (*res derelicta*) become ownerless, and free for anyone to take possession of (provided the object will be legally held, unlike e.g. some weapons or drugs). Objects which have been lost inadvertently or by accident do not lose their owners; ownership is not considered to be time limited. Such objects, if found on land, have to be reported by the finder to the police under provisions of the Act on Finds.[24] If no

---

22   The sum of redemption is for tax purposes considered to be a capital gain, but the special reward is tax-exempt.
23   Government Memorandum DsU 1987:9 p. 135.
24   Svensk författningssamling 1938:121.

owner appears within certain time limits, then the objects accrue to the finder, provided he pays police procedural costs. Under the Act Concerning Certain Finds from the Waters[25] the same principles also apply to objects found in lakes, rivers, canals, harbours, bays and inlets and other water areas between islands, bordering on the territorial sea.[26] Finds which have to be reported include deserted vessels, shipwrecks, tools and goods from vessels, regardless of whether they have been taken from the bed, or the shore, or found floating. One difference from finds on land is that the police have to put on public notice reported finds from the waters. Finds claimed are returned to the owner subject to payment of costs for publication, care of the object and salvor's reward. Finds not claimed become property of the salvor upon payment of police costs.[27]

Neither the Act on Finds, nor the Act Concerning Certain Finds from the Waters are applicable to ancient finds under the KML. Somewhat paradoxically, this might mean that an ancient find becomes property of the finder more quickly than if the time limit requirements of the first two mentioned Acts had to be met.

Another aspect of civil law that should be considered with respect to finds is the provisions of the Act on Acquisition of Movable Objects in Good Faith.[28] Whereas ownership in principle does not become void when an object has been lost, the opposite occurs if an object has been *transferred* by an unlawful holder to a person who acquires *bona fide*. Title passes regardless of whether the object had originally been stolen or lost, or whether the transferor for other reasons had no right to pass it on. By good faith is meant that the acquisitor in all probability ought not to have realised that the unlawful transferor lacked title, taking into account what kind of property was offered, the circumstances under which it was offered and other circumstances. The former owner, however, has a right to reclaim the object within three months of when he came to know, or ought to have known, from whom to recover, on condition he reimburses the acquisitor his costs.[29]

Archaeological finds are *not* exempted from this legislation.

2.3 Provisions relating to international law

As of 1979 the breadth of Sweden's territorial sea is twelve nautical miles.

Under the 1958 Geneva Convention on the Continental Shelf, Sweden has entered into bilateral agreements with other States regarding borderlines of the shelf, and has adopted national legislation[30] for the application of the Convention and bilateral agreements. This legislation allows for State control of mineral and other non-living natural resources as well as living resources on the seabed or subsoil thereof. Although no attempt has been made to invoke the Swedish legislation for protection of the cultural heritage – and consequently such attempt has not foundered either – it is safe to assume that such traces of humankind which are considered as part of the cultural, rather than the natural heritage, are not covered.[31]

---

25 Svensk författningssamling 1918:163.
26 The definition given here coincides for practical purposes with the definition of internal waters in the Act on Sweden's Territorial Sea, Svensk författningssamling 1966:374.
27 The salvor may acquire exclusive salvage rights under the Act on Exclusive Rights of Salvage, Svensk författningssamling 1984:983.
28 Svensk författningssamling 1986:796.
29 Sections 3 and 4 of the above-mentioned Act.
30 Continental Shelf Act, Svensk författningssamling 1966:314, and Continental Shelf Regulation, Svensk författningssamling 1966:315.
31 Unlike the situation in e.g. Australia, Ireland, Jamaica, Portugal and Spain: Patrick J. O'Keefe, 'Protection of the underwater cultural heritage: developments at UNESCO' (1996) 25 *International Journal of Nautical Archaeology* 171.

In 1992 an Act on Sweden's economic zone was adopted.[32] The State authority upheld under this Act does not stretch as far as giving ground for measures to protect specifically the cultural heritage. Other related acts regarding pollution from ships and the dumping of environmentally hazardous waste[33] do, of course, contribute to better conditions for the preservation of underwater cultural vestiges.

Sweden ratified the United Nations Convention on the Law of the Sea 1982 in 1996. Of interest here are the parts of the Convention which apply to the Area, particularly article 149. The concept of the Area goes back to a UN General Assembly Resolution of 1970,[34] which declared the seabed and the subsoil thereof beyond national jurisdiction to be "the common heritage of mankind". Article 149 obliges the State parties to preserve and dispose of all objects of an archaeological and historical nature found in the Area with particular regard to preferential rights of States or countries of origin. Although the Area is far from Sweden, certain provisions have been added to the KML in order to implement Sweden's duties under article 149. Section 4 has been amended to stipulate that archaeological finds and wrecks discovered in the Area and salvaged by Swedish vessels or taken to Sweden accrue to the State, if at least one hundred years can be presumed to have elapsed since the ship was wrecked.[35] Furthermore, section 17 has been supplemented with a paragraph to the effect that the Central Board of National Antiquities under section 4 may assign rights to wrecks to museums undertaking their care for the future.

As Sweden still has not proclaimed a contiguous zone, no provisions for the implementation of article 303 of the Convention with its provisions on control of objects of an archaeological and historical nature have yet been proposed.

3. Observations on Scope and Application

3.1 Two schools of thought

From a comparative perspective, laws for protection of the cultural heritage can be seen to oscillate between two basic conceptions. One is State or public claims to property rights in monuments, fixed or movable. The heritage is seen as a kind of *domain*, to which private possessors may have more or less extensive rights, but a controlling power rests with an ultimate owner: the monarch, the republic, or nowadays the State through its representation by government or a government agency. Laws dominated by this view may find it consequential to control also the transfer of cultural property. The other approach, which seems to be the more modern one, is that the State – in which much authority has been vested under principles of democratic government – has a duty to control the use of property in the interest of the common good.[36] It need not claim property rights to do so: democracy permits restrictions to be imposed in *public law* on owners and those who derive their rights from owners. With either basic view may also be consistent a delegation of State powers to local levels of government. In a federal society the origin of power may, instead, be seen at the regional level. In practice, of course, there may not be dramatic differences between the two conceptions.

In Sweden, as we have seen above, both the public law and the domain concepts are being used. Restrictions are imposed on ancient monuments *in situ*, among them old shipwrecks, but

---

32   Svensk författningssamling 1992:1140.
33   Svensk författningssamling 1980:424, 1971:1154.
34   Resolution 2749/XXV.
35   The provisions that wrecks and finds should have no owner still apply.
36   This approach is very evident in paragraph 14 of the German Federal Constitution.

ownership is not claimed by the State, even if there is no other owner, as may often be the case with wrecks, but very rarely with monuments on *terra firma*.[37] When it comes to archaeological finds of a movable nature, then for historical reasons the crown prerogative rights are still exerted.[38] The State claims ownership to anything that derives from a protected ancient monument, regardless of the fact that the State does not own the monument, and the State also claims a right of redemption, comparable to forced pre-emption, to many other finds, which under civil law normally would accrue to the finder. (It may be noted that landowners, under Swedish law, have a self-evident right only to fixtures to real property, and very limited rights to ownerless movables found on or in their real property).

3.2   The importance of age and ownership

Swedish law poses two important questions when a new underwater discovery is being made or when someone wants to investigate or salvage vestiges already known. If it is a wreck, the first question would be: since how long? If the wreck is younger than one hundred years the Act Concerning Certain Finds from the Waters is applicable. The find will have to be publicly announced, and the further issues of salvage would depend on whether an owner appears. So this would lead to the second question: is there an owner?

If more than one hundred years have elapsed since a vessel was wrecked, the KLM alone applies. With regard to the wreck itself the question of ownership becomes, if not unimportant, at least of limited significance. Under section 12 there is a presumption that an owner of a wreck, or of an archaeological find belonging to it, should be given permission to salvage or take other measures which may disturb the remains, unless there are special reasons against doing so. This is a position more favourable to owners of wrecks than to other owners of ancient monuments, but it is not an unconditional green light to take any measures. It is difficult to predict how strong the owner's position is in practice, as – to the knowledge of the author – no cases have arisen falling under this provision.

The reason for this would seem to be that there are seldom any known owners of wrecks that are more than a hundred years old. When commercial interests in salvaging hull and cargo have ceased, then ownership is rarely claimed. Even if that should happen, ownership may still be presumed to have been abandoned earlier through dereliction. Although modern techniques of salvage may sometimes revive a commercial interest in wrecks that are more than a hundred years old, claims to ownership of wrecks so far do not seem to have occurred in Swedish waters. The few claims to ownership of movables that have been made all seem to have been settled amicably. And even when ownership in itself seems indisputable, as for instance with wrecks of Danish man-of-wars capsized in Swedish waters, the Kingdom of Denmark has refrained from making any claims and has – informally – rather pointed to the Swedish authorities as responsible for further investigation. Thus there is little to report in respect of case law.[39]

However, it would still seem likely that claims could one day convincingly be made by legal successors of a shipowner, cargo-owner, or by descendants of passengers whose belongings can be traced. If the claim is to the wreck the question of ownership will be relevant for the County

---

37   Section 8, giving the State ownership, applies only after salvage.

38   This applies to archaeological finds only; other movable heritage items may be under export restrictions without any State claims to ownership.

39   At sea, that is. In 1937 a sumptuous treasure (the so-called Lohe treasure) was found hidden below the floor of a Stockholm Old Town basement. It was claimed by the estates of various descendants of the one time owners of the property – not necessarily the same as the owner of the treasure – at the probable time of hiding. The Supreme Court upheld the lower courts' adjudication that sufficient evidence had not been brought to support the claims, *Nytt Juridiskt Arkiv*, 1940 p. 413.

Administration in trying an application for salvage or investigation of the wreck under section 12, as mentioned above. The County Administration's primary duty would not be to solve the civil law questions involved, particularly not if there are several conflicting claims. It would still need to take a position on ownership, if it considers it detrimental to heritage interests to grant the application, because if it finds that the application is being made by an owner it would also have to find special reasons for refusing it.

If the application is refused, the applicant may appeal, to the government. The government's decision is without appeal, but the claimant can bring proceedings under the Act on Judicial Review of Certain Administrative Decisions,[40] an Act which allows the Supreme Administrative Court to quosh decisions taken by administrative authorities and found to violate provisions of law. This, so far, has not happened to any decision taken under the KML by the government.

If the claims are for archaeological finds from a wreck, section 16 makes it a task for the Central Board of Antiquities to determine whether there is substantiating evidence. If the Central Board does not accept the claims, an appeal could be filed with the Administrative Court of Stockholm County, and from there to the two higher echelons of the administrative judicature.

As mentioned in section 2.2 above, archaeological finds are not exempted from the Act on Acquisition of Movable Objects in Good Faith. One implication of this is that a find which – when found on a protected ancient monument – accrues to the State, may be hard for the State to recover if the finder has turned it over to someone who received it in good faith. Whether the acquisitor would pass the good faith test is, of course, a question in itself, but if so, then the State will have to negotiate a settlement if it wants the object secured. Many finds from shipwrecks in Swedish waters are pieces of china of a kind normally bought and sold, so the prospects of making a *bona fide* acquisition stick are in some circumstances not slim.

At the time of writing, an interesting case is under police investigation. Two bronze cannons, cast in Denmark, but believed to have been mounted in a Swedish ship belonging to the king and sunk in the 1520s in Swedish waters, have recently been found in private, clandestine possession in a Swedish city. About six years ago, the cannons had been offered for sale, but their whereabouts could not then be ascertained, nor the identity of the offeror. It now seems that the possessors, while denying having taken the cannons from a shipwreck, have admitted to hiding them, which could be a crime in itself. But before the fate of the cannons can be decided several other questions may need to be answered.

Given that the cannons have indeed been taken from a wreck that is more than one century old, the most basic question seems to be: where was the wreck located? If found within the limits of Swedish territorial jurisdiction, the time of discovery and/or salvage is critical, as statutes of limitation could bar prosecution.

If beyond penal action, the civil law question would have to start by establishing who has title. Theoretically, the present possessors could claim acquisition in good faith from a salvor or a go-between, a fact which – if established – would erase all previous claims questions. The likelihood that the courts would find such a statement proven seems slim: sixteenth century bronze cannons are not traded without strict due diligence requirements. But if the present possessors have not acquired in good faith, who then is the owner? Presuming that the cannons were, indeed, from the king's ship, ownership would in all likelihood not be deemed to have ceased, and the cannons would be the property of the State. This would apply regardless of the ownership provisions of the KML. However, if it can be established only that the cannons were found on or near a wreck of uncertain identity, then section 4 of the KML would be instrumental in affording ownership to the same party: the State of Sweden.

---

40   Svensk författningssamling 1988:205.

If indictment is not time-barred, the crucial fact would again be to establish that the cannons were found in or near a wreck within Swedish jurisdiction. Finders/salvors would be liable to punishment, and the present possessors perhaps as accessories. The question of title would be important in the sense that if it is established that the cannons are already State property, they need not be declared forfeit in the penal procedure.

State claims, however, would be more problematic if it cannot be proven that the cannons had indeed a connection to a wreck when found. The time of the discovery would then again be crucial. Archaeological objects of bronze have been redeemable only as of 1st January 1989, so if found before then the cannons would be the finder's property.[41]

If the cannons – contrary to what is now believed – were found outside Swedish territory, the salvage probably has not been in violation of any Swedish penal provisions, even considering that the goods and the salvors are now under Swedish authority.[42] It would be primarily a question for private international law whether there was a right of salvage under the jurisdiction – if any – where the cannons were found. It does not, however, seem hopeless for the Swedish State to claim ownership, provided it can be established that the cannons did indeed belong to a Swedish ship of State.[43]

3.3 The collection and dissemination of knowledge

Before going into the subject of knowledge in detail, it should be stressed that the KML does not apply just to maritime vestiges found underwater. It also protects wrecks and related items found on *terra firma*. Rivers may have changed course, old harbours may have been filled in, landslides may have covered up what was once afloat. But in the case of Sweden, one need also take into consideration the tectonic process still at work of land emerging out of the sea after the last Ice Age. Since Neolithic times, about one-fifth of the present surface of the country has risen from underwater. Where the vessels of yesterday found a resting place, or one time harbour installations crumbled, may today be a building site in which archaeologists in the course of routine investigation find maritime debris of scientific importance.

To some extent, it is also the other way around. In the southernmost part of Sweden and in the Danish straits, the sea has submerged remains of Neolithic settlements.

The Central Board of Antiquities keeps a register of ancient monuments and archaeological finds. As to items of the underwater heritage it concentrates on those found on land. The most comprehensive record of the underwater heritage is kept at the National Maritime Museum in Stockholm. This record is the result of both archival and underwater research. It contains published notices and other excerpts from the press on maritime losses from the eighteenth century onwards. It also contains excerpts dating back to 1745 from the reports of the diving companies which operated as State authorised monopolies until 1831, when their reports also ceased. Further there are excerpts from maritime inquiries. Mainly it has files on almost every known wreck, not just in the Swedish territorial sea, lakes and rivers, but also in adjacent waters. When the territorial seabed was thoroughly scanned in the 1980s and 1990s in search of suspected foreign submarine activities,

---

41   The earlier provisions for redemption of old objects of *inter alia* bronze had been abolished in 1873: see section 1.1 above.

42   In this case it is not possible for the cannons to have been found in the Area after 1 July 1996. Consequently, section 4 of the KML, which as of that date is applicable to objects from the Area brought into Sweden or onto a Swedish ship, could not be invoked.

43   This supposition appears not to be contradicted by a seemingly rather opposite verdict by the Swedish Supreme Court, which rejected claims made by the State of Sweden for restitution to the Federal Republic of Germany of marine research equipment, belonging to the Republic, but held as security by two fishermen for damage caused to their trawl. The Supreme Court did not support the Swedish State's position that it could exercise immunity *ex parte* the Federal Republic. *Nytt Juridiskt Arkiv* 1965 p. 145.

knowledge of wrecks also grew considerably. The collected knowledge on each wreck varies a great deal, of course. Some entries can be classified as qualified guesswork. As to knowledge of the most famous wreck of them all, the *Vasa*, it is assembled in a museum of its own.

The records of the National Maritime Museum are in the process of being made accessible in a database. In time, this will provide for more easy dissemination of the information they contain. This is vital, of course, not just to scholars and researchers, but also to the County Administrations responsible for the monitoring of heritage values and for trying permissions to investigate and salvage wrecks and related items.

3.4   A legal flaw

As related above under section 2.1.1, section 9 of the KML empowers the County Administrations to issue regulations for the protection of ancient monuments and their protective zones, etc. This provision has often been used to prohibit diving and anchoring in waters where there are wrecks of heritage importance in need of extra protection. However, the constitutional validity of this empowerment has been questioned.

Under Swedish constitutional doctrine the issuing of rules directed to the public at large, not just to a particular person or landowner, is under Parliament's legislative prerogative. The Swedish Constitution, Chapter 8, section 7 of the Instrument of Government, allows Parliament to delegate legislative powers to the government in certain specified subject areas. Heritage protection is not mentioned. Furthermore, if government intends to subdelegate legislative powers to other official bodies, it needs Parliament's consent (Chapter 8, section 11). It seems then that the Swedish Parliament, when enacting the KML, violated the Constitution on two counts. First, the Constitution does not at all permit delegation of legislative powers in matters of protection of the cultural heritage. Secondly, delegation may not be done by Parliament directly to any body but the government.

It took a long while after the enactment of the KML for this situation to even be recognised.[44] Now, however, it does seem probable that constitutional and legislative amendments will be submitted to Parliament in order to rectify the situation.

In the meantime, the fate of the many regulations so far issued remains uncertain. The question whether they should be disregarded as unconstitutional has not yet been tried by any court of law. Even if a court were to overturn a regulation issued under the KML, it would mean only that the specific regulations do not apply, but would not leave wrecks and other ancient monuments without protection.[45] Some regulations restricting diving and anchoring may not be affected at all, i.e. regulations issued under legal provisions for restriction of maritime traffic, where the constitutional requirements for the delegation of legislative powers have been properly adhered to.

3.5   Legal developments

Apart from repairing the constitutional flaw just described, there is no national legislative work currently being undertaken that would concern the underwater heritage. Three issues have been under debate, but so far have led to no official proposal.

First, when Parliament decided to ratify the United Nations Convention on the Law of the Sea, the government declared that it would later return with proposals for establishment of a contiguous zone.[46] This has not yet happened, but preparations have been made for the widened

---

44   Sveriges Offentliga Utredningar (SOU 1996:128), p. 285, and Thomas Adlercreutz 'Någrafrågor om normgivningsmakten i ett utredningsbetänkande' *Förvaltningsrättslig tidskrift* (1997) p. 7.
45   Chapter 11, section 14 of the Instrument of Government.
46   Proposition (Government Bill) 1995/96:140 p. 158.

responsibility towards the underwater heritage that such a step would entail under articles 33 and 303 of the Convention.

The second issue is the one of an age limit and heritage values. Wrecks are the only category of ancient monuments dependent for protection on a fixed age requirement. True, few if any items belonging to other categories are younger than one hundred years. There are many who think, however, that wrecks are special in the sense that they command a special interest regardless of age. One might cite the *Titanic* as an example. The question, however, seems moot.

The third issue is whether there should be unrestricted access to information. The records of both the Central Board of Antiquities and the National Maritime Museum are publicly available under constitutional freedom of information provisions, and there are no provisions for secrecy even for sensitive information. True, there are such provisions for the protection of endangered species, and a strong case could be made for similar rules pertaining to vulnerable parts of the cultural heritage, but this issue too seems moot. To argue restrictions in freedom of information principles is hard in a country where such principles have been enacted since 1766 and have had constitutional standing since 1810. They too are part of Sweden's heritage.

Chapter 11

TURKEY

Janet Blake

1. Introduction

1.1 Turkey's underwater archaeological heritage

There are a large number of archaeological sites of great importance lying on the seabed within Turkish territorial waters covering a wide range of periods and peoples as do those on land, with known sites from the Bronze Age and classical Greek, Phoenician, Roman, Byzantine, early Islamic and Ottoman periods. Pulak and Rogers[1] describe the range of ancient vessels to be found in Turkish waters as follows:

> [t]housands of years of maritime history lie hidden beneath the waves of the Turkish coast. Bronze Age merchantmen, Byzantine dromons, and Venetian and Ottoman galleys are among the hundreds of vessel types that plied the waters around Turkey in the past.

As well as the wrecks of ancient trading vessels, warships and other types of vessel, there are also other kinds of underwater remains to be found, including the remains of the sunken city of Kekova, the ancient harbour works at Çesme and the semi-submerged city of Cnidos near Datça (celebrated in ancient times for its statue of Aphrodite by the Greek master). Turkey has played a major role in the development of marine archaeology with the pioneering work of George Bass in the 1960s which now continues through the work of the Institute of Nautical Archaeology (INA), which has established a permanent centre at Bodrum on the west coast of Turkey. Trained and experienced in archaeological field techniques on land and having learnt to dive in order to excavate underwater, Bass has applied archaeological field methods to underwater sites. Underwater archaeological techniques have subsequently been developed and improved but such a step was vital in the development of marine archaeology as a discipline within the broader discipline of archaeology. An early excavation conducted by Bass in Turkey was of a Byzantine shipwreck at Yassiada (near Bodrum) between 1961 and 1964 with the University Museum of Philadelphia.[2] One of the primary purposes of this excavation was to continue developing techniques for underwater excavation work and the team was mostly made up of archaeology students and other specialists who had learnt to dive.

The Yassiada wreck, which was found lying on a slope of 32 to 38 metres below sea level, was dated to A.D. seventh century by the discovery of four gold coins from the time of Heraclius. Amongst artefacts found in the first season were six iron anchors, a cargo of amphorae and a complete set of tableware, copper and terracotta cooking pots, a set of inscribed weights and eight lamps. Another early excavation by Bass's team in Turkey was that of an early Bronze Age shipwreck at Cap Gelidonya (near Bodrum),[3] started in 1961 with a team from the University of

---

1   C.M. Pulak and E. Rogers '1993-1994 Turkish Shipwreck Surveys' (1994) 21 *Institute of Nautical Archaeology Quarterly* 17.

2   G. Bass 'A Byzantine Shipwreck: Underwater Excavations at Yassiada, Turkey' (1962) 66 *American Journal of Archaeology* 194.

3   See e.g. G.F. Bass 'The Cape Gelidonya Wreck: a Preliminary Report' (1961) 65 *American Journal of Archaeology* 267.

Pennsylvania, following its original discovery in 1959 during a survey of the Carian and Lydian coasts. This was a good illustration of the great potential of marine archaeology to add to and even completely revolutionise theories developed from land archaeology. It was found to have been carrying copper ingots shown to be of Cypriot copper which have led scholars of Bronze Age trade to reassess their understanding of trade routes in the East Mediterranean, contributing new evidence about the ancient economy. It was as the result of lead-isotope analysis of the copper ingots conducted in 1990 (about twenty years after they were excavated) that this could be concluded. This supported Bass's view that "[i]t's what happens after the diving is over, not field technique, that turns archaeology into good archaeology", involving a continued commitment to the site (often over a lifetime) and to the conservation, preservation and study of the finds.

Another wreck excavated by Bass in Turkey (now with the INA) between 1977 and 1979, was an A.D. eleventh century Islamic shipwreck at Serçe Limani.[4] During the excavation one tonne of glassware was found in the form of over a million sherds, some of which was identified as a cargo of scrap glass for recycling. Over three hundred glass vessels were reconstructed from the sherds between 1980 and 1995, the reconstructions including many previously unknown vessel shapes. Between 1983 and 1994, the INA team excavated another Bronze Age wreck at Uluburun off Kaş in southwest Turkey.[5] This wreck also offered up copper ingots which reinforce the theories on the Bronze Age economy developed from the Cap Gelidonya finds. Surveying the provinces of Izmir, Aydin and Muğla (an area running from Foca to Bodrum) in 1993, the INA located six 'exciting' wrecks, of which five were found at Kızılburun (southeast of Çesme) including an A.D. tenth century Byzantine wreck carrying marble architectural elements thought to be evidence of some level of pre-fabrication in the construction of Byzantine churches at this period.[6] Seventeen miles to the northwest, a cargo of millstones (dated around A.D. tenth to twelfth centuries) was located which "will be of substantial significance in so far as it will provide new information concerning the millstone trade"[7] in the Middle Ages. A Turkish team from Middle East Technical University is currently excavating a Russian flagship which sank in Çesme harbour during the 1770 campaign.[8]

1.2   Threats to Turkey's archaeological heritage

A major and relatively new potential threat to Turkey's marine archaeological sites, especially those near the coastline, is posed by the activities of recreational divers who may disturb a site and even remove artefacts from it. The growing dependence of the Turkish economy on the tourist industry as a hard currency earner[9] and the threat to marine sites that increased tourist activities represent is an important factor here. Many ancient wrecks situated off the Turkish coast are of trading vessels which generally sailed close to land in ancient times and so are often found in waters shallow enough to be reached by recreational divers. For example, the Bronze

---

4   T.O. Alpözen 'Maritime Trade in Anatolia: the Evidence of Wrecks' in *Palmet I* (Sadberk Hanım Müzesi, Istanbul, 1997) pp. 111-133.

5   See e.g. G.F. Bass 'A Bronze Age Shipwreck at Uluburun (Kaş): 1984 Campaign' (1986) 90 *American Journal of Archaeology* 269; C.M. Pulak and R.H. Siegfried 'Excavation at Uluburun: the Final Campaign' (1994) 21 *INA Quarterly* 8.

6   Pulak and Rogers, *op.cit.* note 1.

7   *Ibid.*

8   See M. Özturk 'An Underwater Survey for Historic Wrecks of the 1770 Ottoman-Russian Battle for Çesme Bay, İzmir, Turkey' in *Thirteenth International Excavation, Survey and Archaeometry Symposium*, Ministry of Culture and Tourism, 23-27 May 1993, Çanakkale, Turkey.

9   'Turkey: the most rapidly developing country in world tourism' 8 *Newspot* (Turkish government newsletter) 10 March 1995 gives, for example, the information that tourist numbers to Turkey between 1994 and 1995 increased by 50 percent.

Age site of Uluburun is located approximately one hour from the major tourist resort of Kaş on the southwest coast of Turkey. The number of marine excavations in Turkey is small compared with those annually on land, reflecting the fact that marine archaeology is enormously costly, involving expensive technology. This makes it difficult to identify marine sites, which contributes to their vulnerability to interference from recreational divers and treasure-hunters. The question of financing marine excavations is thus a major consideration and it is significant that most marine archaeological work in Turkish waters is carried out by foreign teams. The commercial exploitation of archaeology through illegal excavation and the subsequent illegal export of antiquities from Turkey is already a huge problem where land sites are concerned,[10] and threatens to become an equal danger to marine sites with increased diving activity off Turkey.

There are also other threats to marine sites in Turkish territorial waters which are of a more 'indirect' nature and tend to be common to many Mediterranean countries. The Directorate of Antiquities already faces the problems posed to the preservation of archaeological remains on land by the construction industry and its experience shows that these can come from both public and private sector construction activities. There is no system of planning laws such as those for land sites, and the main protection afforded to underwater sites is through a system of designation.[11] This is inadequate to deal with the potentially large number of ancient harbour works, shallow water wrecks and submerged settlements which could be destroyed by coastline construction of marinas, ports, harbours and tourist developments. Construction activities which can pose a danger to marine archaeological sites are many and various: the construction of quays, moles, barrages and marinas which can all trigger off changes in the erosion and sedimentation patterns along a coastline, thus affecting any archaeological sites found in the area; pipe- or cable-laying (for gas, oil, telecommunications, etc.); dredging of silted estuaries or for mining operations; drilling operations for oil and other minerals; and some fishing methods. There is much fishing close to the Turkish coastline and it is not uncommon for fishermen to snag their nets on amphorae from ancient wreck sites, which is often the way in which they are first discovered.[12] Most of these threats are relevant to the Turkish situation, particularly with the building of new marinas, sewage facilities and other constructions related to the tourist industry and military establishment. The only way to minimise the potential damage which such activities can do to marine archaeological sites is through planning laws which require construction companies (and those involved in other commercial activities on the seabed) to conduct surveys of the area in which they are working and to inform the relevant authorities of any materials of archaeological value located in the area. This would, in part, be an extension to coastal waters of the existing planning rules for land-based construction activities.

Another indirect threat to Turkey's marine archaeological sites is that from marine pollution, a threat also faced by other Mediterranean and Black Sea States.[13] The main causes of this problem are sewage and industrial effluents, and the great expansion of tourist facilities along the west and south coasts of Turkey (where many archaeological sites are located) has obviously made the problem of sewage pollution much more acute in recent years. This is especially true since existing sewage treatment facilities are often not equipped to deal with the suddenly increased demands from new hotels and other facilities, resulting in a lot of raw sewage being discharged into the

---

10   See J. Blake 'Export Embargoes and the International Antiquities Market – the Turkish Experience' (1997) 2 *Art Antiquity and Law* 233.
11   See section 2.3 below.
12   The wreck at Uluburun was initially discovered by a sponge diver and, in 1993, the INA searched for a late Hellenistic wreck known to be located at Foca that had been carrying bronze statues, parts of which had been snagged in trawler nets some years previously.
13   See e.g. United Nations Environment Programme 'A Cleaner Mediterranean' (1991) 21 *Environmental Policy and Law* 203 and H. Somsen 'The Regionalization of EC Pollution Law: the Example of the Mediterranean Sea' (1991) 6 *International Journal of Estuarine and Coastal Law* 229.

sea, often quite close to the shore. Another source of marine pollution off Turkey is the heavy traffic of shipping in the Sea of Marmara and the Bosphoros which provide passage from the Black Sea to the Mediterranean. This, the busiest shipping lane in the world, is particularly heavily used by large tankers and occasionally there are spillages.

Until recently the importation into Turkey, and the use, of scuba-diving equipment was strictly controlled, with any diving equipment which was imported into Turkey without a special licence being immobilised while inside the country. Diving in most Turkish waters except the Black Sea and Sea of Marmara (including the Mediterranean coast) was forbidden except with a recognised diving club. Although the initial purpose of these controls had been military security,[14] they allowed the authorities to monitor the activities of divers in Turkish waters. Although it is not desirable to have such a strict level of control, it did provide a useful infrastructure for controlling the activities of divers near wreck sites. In the Sea of Marmara and Black Sea where diving has never been so tightly restricted (and which are within easy reach of Istanbul, Turkey's wealthiest and most populous city), there has been much disturbance of ancient wrecks,[15] illustrating the potential level of threat to sites off the west and southwest coast which, up until recently, have been relatively unscathed.[16] It is now possible to bring scuba equipment into Turkey if it is declared at customs on entry and to dive freely in the coastal waters from Alanya (on the south coast) to the Syrian border, for example, without encountering any restricted areas. The fate of wreck sites in the Sea of Marmara and Black Sea serves as a reminder of the urgent need to design a workable system of protection of archaeological remains in the hitherto better protected Mediterranean coastal areas off Turkey.

2.   The Legislative Framework in Turkey

2.1   Development of the Turkish antiquities legislation

The first Ottoman museum was established in the Church of St. Irene in Istanbul in 1846, followed by the establishment of the Imperial Museum in the same building which conducted the first archaeological excavations by an Ottoman team in the late 1860s. The Historic Monuments Act was passed in 1874, the first piece of legislation to deal specifically with antiquities and which was concerned particularly with archaeological activities. Amongst its provisions, it stated that excavation finds should be shared amongst the excavation team, the owner of the land and the State, granting the best third of all finds to the State. It also placed all foreign excavation teams under the control and supervision of the Ministry of Education. A second version of the antiquities laws passed in 1884 made some major changes to the law, providing for State ownership of all antiquities and the establishment of the Department of Antiquities to administer the antiquities legislation. The third version of the antiquities laws in 1906 added further provisions including: central organisation for museums and the Department of Antiquities; State ownership of all movable and immovable cultural property; a prohibition against damaging monuments; the institution of a

---

14   These were introduced at the time of the landings of Turkish troops on Cyprus during the crisis of 1974.

15   Of eleven ancient wrecks discovered since 1992 by Dr N. Gunsenin of Boğaziçi University (Istanbul) around the Marmara islands, amphorae had been removed from every one; and in their 1994 survey season, the INA located a looted wreck site from A.D. first century at Papaz Adası near the ancient city of Didyma.

16   The assertion that "[w]ithin the Turkish territorial sea, all known historic wrecks have been plundered..." in *International Law Association Cairo Conference (1992) 'Report and Draft Convention for Consideration at the 1992 Conference'* (Rapporteur: J.A.R. Nafziger) at p. 3 is probably based on the situation in the Black Sea and Sea of Marmara areas.

permit system for research and excavations; and a blanket prohibition of the export or removal overseas of any antiquities.[17]

The establishment of the Turkish Republic in 1923 led to increased interest in the archaeology of ancient Turkey with more than 3,500 ancient and historic monuments inventoried between 1933 and 1935. The first modern antiquities law of the Turkish Republic was passed in 1973 to replace the 1906 law,[18] and included new definitions and concepts such as: the division of cultural property into movables and immovables for the purposes of the legislation; the idea that sites of whatever kind (urban, rural or natural) should be treated as a whole: a concept vital to preserving the integrity of a site; and the importance of a national inventory of the cultural and natural heritage as a form of protection.

2.2   The 1983 Antiquities Law No. 2683 and related regulations

The 1973 law, as the Ottoman legislation, was designed with land sites in mind and did not refer to underwater archaeological remains. The current Law Protecting the Cultural and Natural Heritage (No. 2683)[19] passed in 1983 extended the scope of the antiquities legislation to cover for the first time underwater archaeological sites and other remains, while retaining most of the provisions and philosophy of the 1973 law. It is interesting to note that this development in Turkish law occurred at the time of the Council of Europe's 1985 Draft Convention on the Underwater Cultural Heritage[20] which had urged Member States to include protective measures in national legislation. The Turkish law as regards the protection of the underwater archaeological heritage is a dual-purpose one in which protection of the underwater archaeological heritage is incorporated into pre-existing antiquities legislation. This leads to a certain lack of clarity as to the extent to which some of the provisions can be applied to underwater sites since some are clearly designed for land sites even though they could be usefully applied to coastal zones as well. A special system of designation for underwater sites to be protected[21] is also provided for by the 1983 law, which raises the question of how far the other general provisions of the antiquities legislation should apply where sites have not been designated.

Part I (articles 1-5) deals with general questions such as the aim and content of the law and the definition of terms. The definition of what is included in the term 'cultural property' for the purposes of the law is given in article 3(a)(1) as: "[A]ll movable and immovable property above or under ground or underwater that belongs to the prehistoric and historic periods and relates to science, culture, religion and the fine arts". Although a definition of 'sites' is given in article 3(a)(2), it relates mostly to those sites which constitute towns or remains of towns of which few examples are to be found underwater. 'Preservation', as defined in article 3(a)(4), includes "operations for the preservation of" immovable cultural and natural property and movable cultural property: this is sufficiently wide-ranging to cover various actions necessary for the preservation of marine archaeological remains, such as post-excavation conservation of fragile materials, or the covering over of a site after its discovery to prevent illicit interference. Article 6 lists 60

---

17   S.J. Shaw and E.K. Shaw *History of the Ottoman Empire and Modern Turkey* Vol.2 (Cambridge University Press, 1977); E. Madran *The Restoration and Preservation of the Historic Monuments of Turkey (From the Ottoman Empire to the Republic of Turkey)* (unpublished).

18   Law No. 1710 of 25 April 1973.

19   Law for the Protection of Cultural and Natural Property No. 2683, 21 July 1983; published in *Resmi Gazete* (Official Journal) of 22 July 1983 at 18 113.

20   Draft European Convention on the Protection of the Underwater Cultural Heritage (1985); an earlier version of the draft text was published in Council of Europe Doc. DIR/JUR (84)5; the final version, which was never officially adopted as a text, is published in Doc.CAHAQ (85)5 [restricted] which is not to be distributed or published outside the Council of Europe.

21   See section 2.3 below.

examples of the immovable cultural property to be protected by the law, of which only about four can be related to marine archaeological remains: "excavation sites ... shipyards, ports ...[and] remains of old monuments and walls". This illustrates the point that the law is not primarily designed to protect underwater sites, rather they appear to be tacked on to a law written with land sites in mind. Article 23 defines the movable cultural (and natural) property covered by this law as:

(a) All kinds of cultural and natural property that belong to geological, prehistoric or historic periods, and have documentary significance in terms of geology, anthropology, prehistory, protohistory, archaeology, art history and ethnography or that reflect the social, cultural, technical and scientific characteristics and achievements of their periods and that are rare.

This would include artefactual finds from underwater sites as well as shipwrecks themselves. Article 5 grants ownership to the State of all cultural property located in the territory of the State, whether already excavated or not. This provision is important for attempts by the Turkish authorities to seek the restitution of stolen cultural artefacts through litigation in foreign courts and would be relevant where artefacts, such as amphorae or ancient anchors, have been recovered illegally from an underwater site in Turkish territorial waters and subsequently removed from the country.

The provisions of Part II (articles 6-22) concern measures to protect the immovable cultural and natural heritage which could include submerged settlements and harbourworks, for example. Article 7 establishes methods of listing and registration, now understood to be a fundamental tool of protection. The designation of 'conservation areas' by local authorities set out in article 8: "to ensure their conservation within context" would be of value in protecting underwater sites, especially those near the coast. However, the wording of the provisions in Part II and the existence of a special regime for the designation of underwater archaeological sites in article 35 suggests that Part II is not intended to be applied to marine sites. This is unfortunate since some of its measures could provide important protection to coastal sites. Article 9, for example, prohibits any intervention on these sites, including the construction of installations, a provision which could be useful in prohibiting coastal seabed constructions such as harbourworks and marinas. Articles 13 to 22 constitute a very detailed scheme for control of construction and other interventions in conservation areas on land, and this can be contrasted with the much lower level of protection from construction activities afforded to marine sites. This is a possible area in which the legislation could be modified or developed in order to control coastal and seabed construction activities which might affect archaeological remains.

Part III (articles 23-34) deals with the protection of movable cultural and natural property, including measures relating to the establishment, administration and supervision of museums (article 26) and museum acquisition policy. These provisions apply equally to artefacts recovered from underwater sites as to those from land sites (article 23) and therefore – although wrecks themselves are not explicitly referred to by Law No. 2683 – any artefacts recovered from them would be covered by these provisions. Article 24(a) provides that movable cultural and natural property to be preserved and which is State property (under article 5) is to be kept by the State in museums. Article 25 deals with the listing and registration of movables "according to scientific principles" and their acquisition by State museums where necessary. Several articles in Part III relate to control of trade in cultural artefacts within Turkey as well as the export of such artefacts from Turkey (articles 27, 28 and 30).[22] Article 32 prohibits the smuggling out of Turkey of any cultural property covered by this law, stating that "movable cultural and natural property that has to be preserved inside the country cannot be removed from its borders", including any movables from underwater sites. The temporary removal of such artefacts for the purpose of exhibitions

---

22   Regulation No. 18 278 regulating the trade in movable cultural property and commercial premises, published in *Resmi Gazete* (Official Journal) 11 January 1984 at 18 278.

and loans is allowable under this law and is governed by a strict set of regulations. Article 25 also contains a reference to guns and other equipment relating to Turkey's military history (to be evaluated by the office of the Commander-in-Chief of the Turkish Army), which would apply to cannons and other military equipment found on wrecks from the Ottoman period onwards.[23] Military wrecks are the responsibility of military (naval) museums which come under the authority of the Commander-in-Chief of the Army. This is a potential source of problems because the military authorities cannot be expected to follow all developments in policy and methodology relating to protection of archaeological sites and the post-excavation conservation of organic materials raised from underwater sites. It also creates a hiatus in the protection regime provided by the Directorate of Antiquities.

Part IV (articles 35 to 50) governs the conduct of research, trial digs, excavations and treasure-hunting in Turkey and establishes a permit system to regulate those activities. The granting of excavation, survey and research permits is the sole remit of the Ministry of Culture and is strictly controlled and applies to archaeological activities conducted underwater as well as those on land. Article 35(3), which provides for the designation of underwater sites, is the sole provision relating specifically to the underwater archaeological heritage and creates a special regime for underwater sites.[24] The system governing the issuing of permits for research, survey and excavation is established by article 37 and includes regulations concerning their non-transferability (article 38), their validity for one year (article 40) and the grounds upon which they may be annulled (article 39). Article 43 requires the publication of the results of any archaeological work conducted under permit, stating that the renewal of the permit is dependent on: the presentation of a yearly end-of-season report; the publication of a scientific report within two years; and the publication of a final report within five years of completing the research project (generally an excavation). This is extremely important in view of the essentially destructive nature of excavation. There are also provisions which deal with financial and administrative aspects of archaeological projects which are of particular value where underwater archaeology is concerned in view of the cost of equipment and post-excavation conservation. The excavation director is required to ensure any necessary conservation of artefacts recovered during excavation and to make "environmental arrangements" for sites, which suggests the preservation of a site's context post-excavation. "Treasure-hunting" permits may be granted to individuals wishing to search areas where there are no designated immovables or registered archaeological sites if accompanied by a Ministry of Culture official (article 50). Currently, this provision applies only on land, but it could in future be used to control treasure-hunting by recreational divers in marine areas where it is known that few archaeological remains exist.

Part V of Law No. 2683 deals with the administration of the provisions of this law and involves the establishment of a Superior Council and several Regional Councils answerable to it. The Superior Council is made up of: the Directors General of Antiquities and Tourism; two officials from the Ministry of Culture; two other Directors General; and academics from relevant disciplines. This Council meets monthly and its duties include: designating the principles to be adopted in the conservation of the cultural heritage; overseeing the registration of cultural property to be conserved; "scientifically to guide any intervention on immovable cultural and natural property" (article 51); and advising the Ministry of Culture on the implementation and evaluation of principles adopted. The Regional Councils, made up of local officials and academics, are established to ensure that the principles set out by the Superior Council are implemented at local level. Anyone who discovers a site which is to be protected under this legislation must report the find to the nearest State museum, to the local police or other local official. These reports are then

---

23   For example, a series of A.D. eighteenth century Ottoman military wrecks found in Çesme harbour by Middle East Technical University; see note 8.

24   For details of the regime, see section 2.3 below.

investigated by experts from the Directorate of Antiquities and/or the local museum in order to evaluate the significance of the find and the need for protection. In the case of underwater finds, experts from the Underwater Archaeology Museum at Bodrum are usually called upon to examine the site and advise the Directorate as to its importance and whether it should be designated. Rewards for the reporting of finds are provided for by article 64 (Part VI).

As well as establishing a system of rewards for reporting finds, Part VI also sets out the penalties for breaking, or acting against, the terms of Law No. 2683. Article 68 provides for a five to ten year term of imprisonment for contravening article 32, which prohibits smuggling of movable cultural and natural property to be retained within the borders of Turkey, as well as for a fixed fine, the seizure of the artefact(s) involved and the seizure of any equipment employed in the action. With inflation in Turkey running at over 80 per cent, it is vital that imprisonment is an element of the sanctions imposed for serious infringements of the Law since fixed fines rapidly lose their effectiveness. The seizure of any equipment employed in the act is a powerful sanction against the looting of underwater sites given the huge cost of equipment – including the vessel itself – necessary for underwater excavation work. Article 74 provides for a two to five year prison term plus a fine for conducting illegal trial digs or excavations, while those involved in illicit treasure-hunting may face imprisonment for one to five years. Interestingly, the above punishments are to be doubled where those involved have been entrusted with the protection of the property concerned, or the offence was committed for the purposes of smuggling the property out of Turkey.

2.3 The designation of underwater protection zones

A central feature of the regime protecting underwater archaeological sites to be protected under Law No. 2683 is the designation of sites, with the prohibition of any diving in these areas. The special rules relating to designated zones provide the sole direct form of protection to underwater sites although, as has been seen, other provisions of the Law can be applicable to protecting underwater sites, the conduct of archaeological activities underwater and the treatment of any artefacts recovered. The designation of protection zones is provided for by article 35(3) of the Law, which states:

> Underwater regions of cultural and natural heritage which are in need of protection shall be identified by the Ministry of Culture in co-operation with concerned bodies and institutions and shall be published by the Council of Ministers. Diving as a sport is forbidden in these areas. Survey (arastırma) and excavation can be carried out under permit [in these zones].

Designation is enacted by the 1988 Presidential Decree *Relating to the identification of the underwater cultural heritage and the designation, using map co-ordinates, of zones in which diving activities are prohibited.*[25] Under this Decree, the areas in which diving is to be prohibited are identified by the Ministry of Culture with advice from the Underwater Archaeology Museum at Bodrum. The map co-ordinates for these protected areas are publicised and maps showing these zones are published in order to: "protect the underwater cultural and natural heritage and associated artefacts". Following this Decree, diving activities have been prohibited in 21 designated areas since 26th August 1988. These areas include: the area around Sedef Island (in the Sea of Marmara); Kumkale Burnu and Baba Burnu (near Çanakkale); and areas around Dalaman, Fetihye

---

25   Presidential Decree No. 89/14 235 of 5 June 1989 published in *Resmi Gazete* (Official Journal) 19 August 1989 at 20 257.

and Marmaris (three of Turkey's most popular tourist resorts on the southwest coast).[26] One of the designated areas which will be best known to tourists is that surrounding the ancient sunken city of Kekova which lies about one and a half hours by tourist boat from the resort of Kaş on Turkey's south coast. The trip to Kekova from Kaş is a popular tourist activity and tourists are reminded that they are forbidden from diving or even swimming in the designated area. The use of designated zones to protect the underwater archaeological heritage is of only limited value and can be problematic when the number of sites meriting designation or some degree of protection is too great.[27] The increase in recreational diving means that archaeological sites situated in Turkish coastal waters are now in much greater danger of interference and possible destruction and new approaches to protection will need to be considered.

3.   Conclusions

The 1983 antiquities legislation suffers from a difficulty common to 'dual-purpose' laws originally designed to protect land sites but which have been extended in scope to cover underwater sites. Although interference with underwater archaeological sites is technically controlled by this law, most of its measures appear to have been designed for sites and monuments on land, such as the rules dealing with planning controls in 'conservation zones'. The permit system for controlling archaeological activities is comprehensive and covers archaeological sites underwater, but is much more difficult to police and enforce than on land. Furthermore, the existence of a special regime for the designation of underwater sites under article 35(3) renders the position of those underwater sites which have not been designated unclear. UK experience suggests that site designation is of limited value[28] and the fact that only 21 sites have been designated in Turkey since 1988 supports this view. There are, however, aspects of the legislation which are currently applied only on land which could be of great use in protecting marine archaeological sites and there is room for a creative approach to be taken within the existing legislative framework. This could provide for a much more effective protection regime for the underwater archaeological heritage.

3.1   The problem with commercial salvage

Experience from various regions of the world and different national legislation has shown that ancient and historic wrecks are vulnerable to commercial salvage operations under traditional salvage rules unless they are specifically excluded. Although the definition of cultural property in Law No. 2683 can include such wrecks, it fails to provide any specific definition of ancient or historic wrecks which are to be excluded from commercial salvage rules. This is compounded by the fact that the thrust of the law is strongly biased towards sites on land: only four out of 60 types of site listed in article 6 relate to underwater sites and it is notable that the definition given for sites does not refer at all to shipwrecks. One must *infer* their protection which, given their vulnerability to commercial salvage, is not sufficient. Thus there is no blanket protection for a

---

26   The full list of designated zones reads: Sedir Island; Büyükcekmece; Kapidağ Peninsula; Maramara Island; the Dardanelles; Gökçeada; Müsellim Strait; Çandarli Bay; Izmir Bay; Cap Karaburun; Güllük Bay; Gökova (Aegean Sea side); Datça Peninsula; Bozburun; Marmaris Bay; Dalyan Beach; Cap Akça; Fethiye; Belceğiz; Yediburunlar; Kalkan; Kaş; Finike; Side; Manavgat (Mediterranean Sea side). New designated areas are planned for the Black Sea and eastern part of Turkey's Mediterranean coast.

27   There could be as many as 10,000 ancient and historic wrecks lying in Turkish territorial waters.

28   'All at sea and undefended' (1994) *News* (Council of British Archaeology Newsletter) 6; see further S. Dromgoole 'Protection of Historic Wreck: the UK Approach, Part I - the Present Legal Framework' (1989) 4 *International Journal of Estuarine and Coastal Law* 26 at p. 51.

specific class of archaeological or historic wreck sites granting them automatic exclusion from wreck and salvage laws and they must be designated as protected sites under article 35(3) and the 1988 Decree to be properly protected from disturbance and damage. This is in contrast to the situation under the legislation of such countries as Finland, Norway and Sweden under which wrecks which are over 100 years old are automatically protected.[29] Wrecks relating to Turkish military history (from the Ottoman period onwards) are under the control of the Navy and the position of these military wrecks in terms of salvage rules is even less clear. The vast majority of Ottoman wrecks fall into this category, such as a series of Ottoman naval wrecks from the Battle of Çesme during the Russo-Turkish war discovered in Çesme harbour in 1992.[30] This renders military wrecks even more vulnerable to salvage than other wrecks which are under the control of the Ministry of Culture, particularly since it creates a further confusing detail in a situation which is already lacking in clarity. The latter, if identified as being of historical or archaeological significance, are more likely to be listed as designated sites and researched in a scientific manner since they fall within the administrative structures designed to achieve this end.

3.2 Tourism and 'archaeological diving parks'

The increase in the number of recreational divers in Turkish waters – mostly owing to greatly increased numbers of tourists attracted by the opportunity for water sports – and the consequent loosening of controls on diving in the waters of the Mediterranean coast have forced the government to consider ways of accommodating divers without placing the archaeological heritage in danger. This is a difficult question for the policy makers of any country as dependent as Turkey on mass tourism and where archaeological sites are an essential part of its tourist attractions. As yet, no programme for establishing specific 'underwater archaeological parks' in Turkish waters has been established, but there are continuing discussions between the Ministry of Culture and tourist operators over this and related issues.

The establishment of archaeological diving parks is a relatively recent approach which takes into account the need to balance access to sites with their preservation. Some countries such as the USA (where the system is at its most developed), Israel and Italy have established archaeological diving parks and it appears to be a useful approach.[31] At Sebastos (Caesarea Maritima) in Israel is an example of an archaeological diving park based on an ancient underwater site where divers are guided around the site of the submerged city and harbourworks in much the same way as visitors to land sites.[32] These parks provide an effective means of diverting recreational divers with an interest in visiting sites of historical and archaeological interest from areas where there is a risk of archaeological sites being disturbed. Obviously, the determined commercial salvor will not be deterred by such moves but the diversion of recreational divers interested in archaeology to parks not only reduces pressures on sites but can also make policing protected areas easier.

To put such an approach into practice would require a radical rethinking of the criteria for the designation of archaeological sites, involving the introduction of different levels of archaeological or historical 'significance' and decisions as to the degree of protection to be given to a site based on such criteria. As the law stands at present, a designated site is totally restricted with no diving or even swimming allowed on the site or within the water column above it. A

---

29   On Sweden, see further ch. 10.
30   See note 22.
31   On the USA, see ch. 13; on Italy, see ch. 6.
32   A. Raban 'Archaeology Park for Divers at Sebastos and Other Submerged Remnants in Caesaraea Maritima, Israel' (1992) 21 *International Journal of Nautical Archaeology* 27; for information on underwater archaeological parks in Italy, see P.A. Gianfrotta 'Parchi Archeologici Subacquei (la situazione in Italia)', in G.Vedovato and L.Vlad Borelli *La Tutela del Patrimonio Archeologico Subacqueo*, Atti del Convegno Internazionale, Centro Universitario Europeo per i Beni Culturali, Ravello, 27-30 May 1993.

more flexible system is needed whereby there are different levels of protection relating to the archaeological importance of known sites, possibly falling into three levels and ranging from the absolute protection of designated sites to sites of lesser importance where access is simply restricted.[33] The development of a site within a 'conservation zone' on land is based on a tiered system of designation relating to the quality of the site and the density of the finds on it, with planning permission given to sites of least quality and density. Thus a system for tiered designation with established criteria is already practised on land. A system of graded designation would fit in well with the institution of 'archaeological parks' where sports divers could be encouraged to dive and which may be in areas which contain sites in the lowest category of protection. It should be possible for divers to visit these sites but only in controlled conditions under which there can be open access to some sites while others cannot be touched or disturbed in any way. Obviously, as with land sites which are now open to visitors, it would remain an offence to remove any objects or remains. There already exists in Turkey an infrastructure of coastal protection areas, of which nine include coastal waters, and coastal national parks, of which three include coastal waters.[34] Although these are not specifically designed to protect archaeological sites, they could serve as the legal and administrative basis for a system of archaeological parks were they to be established.

3.3 Construction projects and planning laws

The areas most affected by coastal development are also those where many ancient wrecks are located since ancient trading vessels tended to follow the coastline closely. The fact that much coastal development is related to the tourist industry which is often located at or near ancient sites on land exacerbates this. The protection of archaeological sites by the application of planning regulations to coastal waters and through the education of the public officials involved in the decision-making process is an important element in protection. The principle by which construction projects and other public or private works on land must take the archaeological heritage into consideration should be extended to the underwater environment as well. Currently, anyone wishing to develop or build on a designated site on land must first apply to one of fifteen Regional Councils in Turkey whose job it is to study such planning applications and to decide whether permission should be granted. A similar requirement could be applied to coastal zone development. Planning laws can also provide for certain measures to limit the extent of marine pollution by controlling the quantity and condition of sewage and industrial waste discharge into the sea. However, the problem of marine pollution is one shared by all the countries bordering a particular sea and Turkey should seek joint action with the other Black Sea and Mediterranean States on this matter. States such as Turkey with significant marine archaeological sites must bring pressure to bear for the inclusion of archaeological site protection into international and regional instruments such as the 1976 Convention for the Protection of the Mediterranean Sea Against Pollution (the Barcelona Convention)[35] since it is an issue which has to be dealt with on both a national and regional level.

On paper, the 1983 Law is a very strict one which prohibits interference with any sites or objects which could be regarded as of archaeological importance and prohibits the removal of artefacts from Turkey. However, a legislative system should always be judged by its effectiveness and enforceability. It is noteworthy that no legal action has yet been taken over interference with an ancient or historic wreck or artefacts looted from underwater sites under this legislation.

---

33   See further A. Firth and B. Ferrari 'Archaeology and Marine Protected Areas' (1992) 21 *International Journal of Nautical Archaeology* 67.
34   Law No. 3621 *Kıyı Kanunu* (Coastal Protection Law) in Turkish Ministry of Culture *Taşinmaz Kültür ve Tabiat Varliklari Mevzuati* (Ankara, 1990) 102; and *Milli Parklar Yönetmeliği* (Regulations for National Parks) *ibid.* at 218.
35   (1976) 15 *International Legal Materials* 290.

Furthermore, the evidence of large-scale antiquities smuggling clearly shows that the enforceability of the law is limited. It is therefore a matter of urgency that Turkey should reconsider its approach to the protection of the underwater archaeological heritage in the face of its increasing vulnerability.[36] Some specific proposals for amending the existing legislation and for developing new strategies towards protection within the current framework have been given above. The fundamental question remains, however, whether such proposals are sufficient, or whether a specific law dealing with the underwater archaeological heritage is needed to replace the current dual-purpose law with its clear limitations.

---

36   For example, *Türkiye Arkeolojik Kazı Politikasi [Archaeological Excavation Policy of Turkey]* (Ministry of Culture and Tourism, Ankara, 1989), a policy document for the Directorate-General of Antiquities, *inter alia*, signalled a shift away from excavation to identification and listing of sites. This is a particularly valuable approach in the case of underwater sites which are extremely vulnerable to accidental or deliberate disturbance since they are often undocumented.

Chapter 12

UNITED KINGDOM

Sarah Dromgoole[*]

1.   Introduction

The 6,500 miles or so of UK coastline are rich in shipwrecks of varying ages. Among them are wrecks dating back to at least as far as the Bronze Age, but more common are wrecks dating from the seventeenth century onwards. These include several Dutch East Indiamen and other merchantmen; military ships of both British and foreign flag, including a number of Spanish Armada galleons; and vessels with royal associations. As far as non-wreck remains are concerned, there is nothing so spectacular as the harbours at Caesarea Maritima in Israel or Alexandria in Egypt, but ancient wooden round-houses, fish-traps and other structures have been found and, of course, there are much more recent remains, such as amphibious vehicles and other remnants of the two World Wars. The fact that much of the Channel and the North Sea was once dry land populated during the Palaeolithic and Mesolithic periods means that there is also considerable archaeological potential. Without doubt, however, wrecks are the primary form of underwater cultural heritage.[1]

The UK coast is under significant pressure from human activities and these pose a considerable threat to the underwater heritage. Despite the chilliness of the waters, sport diving is a popular hobby[2] and the activities of amateur divers have the potential to cause great damage to wreck sites. Damage or destruction may also be caused by land reclamation work and the building of marinas; dredging to clear navigation channels or for aggregates; pipeline and cable laying; sailing and fishing. In recent years, commercial treasure-hunters have also become increasingly active. As is the case everywhere, natural forces such as sandbank movements and tidal changes may have a further, serious, impact.

While the term 'underwater cultural heritage' strictly speaking encompasses archaeological remains found in inland waters as well as in the marine zone, this essay focusses on remains found in coastal waters. UK law separates its treatment of remains in inland and coastal waters, those in inland waters being governed by the legal regime for land-based remains, to which this essay will refer only briefly.

2.   Historical Background

Significant interest in the wrecks lying in UK coastal waters began to be shown when scuba-diving equipment became generally available in the late 1960s. The consequent growth in underwater exploration brought about the discovery of numerous wrecks. Among these were

---

[*]   The author would like to thank the following for information provided: Martin Dean, Archaeological Diving Unit, Department for Culture, Media and Sport; Marion McQuaide, Ministry of Defence; Veronica Robbins, Receiver of Wreck, Maritime and Coastguard Agency; Steve Waring, Royal Commission on the Historical Monuments of England. The views expressed here are, of course, those of the author alone.

[1]   For an account of marine archaeological remains found in UK waters, see V. Fenwick 'United Kingdom' in J. Delgado (ed.) *British Museum Encylopaedia of Underwater and Maritime Archaeology* (London, 1997) p. 438.

[2]   In 1992 it seems that 70,000 divers undertook 1.5 million dives off the UK coast: Royal Commission on the Historical Monuments of England *The National Inventory of Maritime Archaeology for England* (1996).

several of considerable historical importance, including the *Mary*, a yacht belonging to Charles II which sank in 1675; the *Association* and the *Romney*, British warships lost in 1707; and three Dutch East Indiamen, the *Hollandia, de Leifde* and *Amsterdam*. At this time, underwater archaeology as an academic discipline was only at a nascent stage[3] and little if any compunction was shown by treasure seekers and souvenir hunters. Stories arose of:

> underwater fighting, of the sabotaging of rival groups' equipment, of the uncontrolled use of explosives to 'loosen up' wrecks and in one instance injuring a diver, of a shooting incident, of powered boats weaving about dangerously over a wreck as divers [were] surfacing, of the disappearance of silver coins and bronze cannons from wrecks, and of their being secretly brought ashore at secluded areas of coastline, and even of cannons being hidden in coffins.[4]

Until this time there had been little need in the UK for laws to protect historical shipwrecks from such activities. The only relevant legislation was the Merchant Shipping Act 1894, which contained provisions for dealing with material from wrecks once it was brought ashore. What was lacking was a legal mechanism to prevent or control interference with wrecks lying on the seabed and, as a result, chaos ensued.

The catalyst which focussed parliamentary attention on the matter and effected change was the plight of the wreck of HMS *Association*. When she and several of her companion vessels struck rocks off the Scilly Isles in 1707, they had been returning from a successful military campaign in the Mediterranean and were carrying large quantities of gold and silver coins. When the site of the *Association* was discovered in 1967, mishandling of the situation by the Ministry of Defence, which exercises rights of title over all Crown vessels,[5] led to competing teams of divers fighting over the wreck and the site being rendered almost unrecognisable by the use of explosives.[6]

The events in relation to the *Association,* and other wrecks of historical importance which were similarly treated, led to a Private Member's Bill[7] being laid before Parliament, which was intended to provide an interim measure of protection for historic wrecks while a comprehensive review of the 1894 Merchant Shipping legislation was taking place.[8] The Bill's sole aim in respect of historic wrecks[9] was to control salvage operations on certain sites of special importance and to secure the protection of these wrecks from unauthorised interference. The Bill had a smooth passage through Parliament and was enacted in 1973 as the Protection of Wrecks Act.[10]

---

3   See Fenwick, *op. cit.* note 1 at p. 439.

4   P. Marsden 'Archaeology at Sea' (1972) 46 *Antiquity* 198.

5   The MOD exercises on behalf of the Crown ownership rights over all Crown vessels, no matter how old, until such rights have been formally abandoned (which is unlikely to happen), or until the Crown transfers its rights to another. In the years since 1967, the MOD has occasionally transferred historic vessels by deed to a reputable archaeological group to hold on trust for the general public.

6   For further details, and references, see S. Dromgoole 'Protection of Historic Wreck: The UK Approach, Parts I and II' (1989) 4 *International Journal of Estuarine and Coastal Law* 26-51, 95-116 at p. 36. The site was so badly damaged that when legislation to control such activities was brought into force in 1973 (see below), the *Association* "was not considered worth protecting": P. Marsden 'The Origin of the Council for Nautical Archaeology' [1986] *International Journal of Nautical Archaeology* 179.

7   *Cf.* a Government Bill. The particular significance of the bill being a Private Member's Bill is that such bills may not make any significant charge on the public revenue.

8   For details of the outcome of this review, see Dromgoole, *op. cit.* note 6 pp. 95-96.

9   The Bill also included a provision prohibiting interference with certain dangerous wrecks, which was designed to deal with one particular wreck, the *Richard Montgomery*, an American cargo vessel which went aground in the Thames Estuary in 1944 and which held a large quantity of ammunition. In fact it appears that the only reason that the Bill was afforded parliamentary time was because it included this provision.

10   For the Parliamentary Debates on the Bill, see Hansard HL Vol. 342, Col. 914; HC Vol. 851 Col. 1848; HC Vol. 855, Co. 1656.

3. Current Legal Framework

Twenty-five years on, and UK statute law relating to the underwater cultural heritage is today little different from that which existed upon the enactment of the Protection of Wrecks Act in 1973. Merchant Shipping legislation has recently been consolidated in the Merchant Shipping Act 1995, but the provisions relating to wreck contained in this Act are little changed from those of the 1894 Merchant Shipping Act.[11] As far as the Protection of Wrecks Act 1973 is concerned, although it was designed simply as an interim measure, its substance has remained unamended since its original enactment.

There have been two significant statutory developments, however, which have the potential to be useful in protecting the underwater heritage. One was the enactment of the Protection of Military Remains Act 1986, the purpose of which is to protect the sanctity of military wrecks containing human remains. Secondly, there was the enactment of the Ancient Monuments and Archaeological Areas Act 1979 and, in particular, section 53 of that Act which is designed to afford protection to monuments in territorial waters.

3.1 Merchant Shipping Act 1995

Legislative provisions for the reporting, handling and disposal of wreck are to be found in Part IX of the Merchant Shipping Act 1995, which largely re-enacts Part IX of the 1894 Act of the same name. Dating from a time when casualties on the coast were numerous, these provisions were designed to deal with the safekeeping and disposal of property from vessels in distress or recently wrecked, and not from vessels which had been lying on the seabed for a period of many years. The provisions had a three-fold purpose: to reunite owners with their lost property, to provide a salvage reward for the finder, and to afford an extra source of revenue for the Exchequer. With the decline in shipping casualties brought about by improvements in technology, increasingly the provisions have been used for dealing with material brought ashore from wrecks which have been on the seabed for a considerable period of time, possibly for centuries.

The term "wreck" for the purposes of Part IX of the 1995 Act "includes jetsam, flotsam, lagan and derelict found in or on the shores of the sea or any tidal water."[12] The meaning of jetsam, flotsam and lagan was considered in the *Cargo ex Shiller*, where it was held that:

> flotsam, is when a ship is sunk or otherwise perished, and the goods float on the sea. Jetsam, is when the ship is in danger of being sunk, and to lighten the ship the goods are cast into the sea, and afterwards, notwithstanding, the ship perish. Lagan...is when the goods which are so cast into the sea, and afterwards the ship perishes, and such goods are so heavy that they sink to the bottom...[13]

The term "derelict" for the purposes of Part IX of the Act probably has the same meaning as it does in salvage law, in other words that the vessel has been physically abandoned by the master and crew without intention of returning, or hope of recovery.[14]

---

11   A few small-scale amendments were made to the 1894 provisions by the Merchant Shipping (Registration, etc.) Act 1993 and these have been incorporated into the 1995 Act. The 1995 Act has also been slightly amended in respect of wreck by the Merchant Shipping and Maritime Security Act 1997, see further below.

12   1995 Act s. 255. This definition is unchanged from that in s. 510 of the 1894 Act. It should be noted that aircraft and hovercraft are now also encompassed within the term "wreck": Aircraft (Wrecks and Salvage) Order (1938) Art. 2(b) (S. R. & O. 1938, No. 136); Hovercraft (Application of Enactments) Order 1972 (S.I. 1972, No. 971) Art. 8(1).

13   [1877] 2 P.D. 145, citing *Att. Gen. v. Sir Henry Constable* [1601] 5 Co. Rep. 106.

14   The fact that a vessel is a derelict does not necessarily mean that the owner has abandoned ownership rights. *Cf.* the meaning of 'dereliction' under civil law: see S. Dromgoole and N. Gaskell 'Interests in Wreck' (1997) 2 *Art Antiquity and Law* 103-136, 207-231 at p. 123 f.n. 185.

In the context of historical remains, the archaic and technical definition of wreck has the potential to cause difficulty. For example, in the case of an isolated find it may not be possible to establish whether the object was deliberately thrown overboard to lighten a ship, or was accidentally dropped overboard, or – in some cases – even whether it originated from a ship at all. The need to draw such fine distinctions in order to reach a conclusion about the disposal of marine finds clearly may cause unnecessary complications in deciding on the ultimate fate of, in some cases important, cultural artefacts.[15]

The 1995 Act provides for a receiver of wreck service to administer the provisions relating to wreck. Until 1993 there were over 100 receivers, mainly customs officers, located at various points around the coast. However, changes to the customs service brought about by the establishment of the European Single Market resulted in the centralisation of the receiver service in 1993[16] and the transfer of its administration to HM Coastguard, which in 1994 became the Coastguard Agency. There is now just one receiver, based in Southampton, whose department forms part of the Maritime and Coastguard Agency, which itself is an executive agency of the Department of the Environment, Transport and the Regions (DETR).[17]

Section 236(1) of the Act provides:

> If any person finds or takes possession of any wreck in United Kingdom waters[18] or finds or takes possession of any wreck outside United Kingdom waters and brings it within those waters he shall:
> (a) if he is the owner of it, give notice to the receiver stating that he has found or taken possession of it and describing the marks by which it may be recognised;
> (b) if he is not the owner of it, give notice to the receiver that he has found or taken possession of it and, as directed by the receiver, either hold it to the receiver's order or deliver it to the receiver.

The equivalent provision in the 1894 Act required, without an option, that wreck found by someone other than its owner be *delivered* to the receiver.[19] This requirement caused problems as the receiver service has never had specialised facilities for the storage of archaeological material. When such material first started to be brought ashore in quantity in the 1960s and 1970s it was taken into the receiver's custody, where in some cases it simply disintegrated.[20] The statutory change reflects the practice, which had gradually developed, of allowing finds to remain in the finder's possession while their ultimate disposal was being determined. This remains the practice, the finder being required to agree, *inter alia*, to take all reasonable care of the property, to indemnify the Maritime and Coastguard Agency for any loss or damage caused to the property while in his or her possession, and to surrender the property to the receiver of wreck when requested to do so.[21]

---

15 In practice it appears that a pragmatic view is taken and the origins of a find will not be investigated too closely. A similar approach is adopted in respect of material found in the inter-tidal zone, in reaching a conclusion as to whether the Merchant Shipping Act or the Treasure Act 1996 apply. The Treasure Act makes provision for finds of treasure on land in England, Wales and Northern Ireland, and abolishes the common law concept of treasure trove. It provides that "[a]n object is not treasure if it is wreck within the meaning of Part IX of the Merchant Shipping Act 1995": s. 3(7) of the Treasure Act 1996.

16 The Merchant Shipping (Registration, etc.) Act 1993 amended the 1894 Act to allow for this change to take place. See, now, the 1995 Act s. 248(2).

17 The Maritime and Coastguard Agency was created as a result of a merger in 1998 of the Maritime Safety Agency and the Coastguard Agency. For more information on the Agency, see its website: http://www.mcagency.org.uk.

18 I.e. territorial waters. The UK claims a twelve mile territorial limit: Territorial Sea Act 1987 s. 1(1)(a).

19 Merchant Shipping Act 1894 s. 518. This requirement was removed and the present text in para. (b) was inserted by the Merchant Shipping (Registration, etc.) Act 1993 Sch. 4, para. 22.

20 Hansard H.C. Vol. 851, Col. 1855.

21 These requirements are laid down in a form entitled 'Report of Wreck and Salvage' that finders of wreck are required to complete.

An interesting question of interpretation relates to the introductory wording of section 236(1):

> If any person *finds or takes possession of* any wreck in United Kingdom waters or finds or takes possession of any wreck outside United Kingdom waters and brings it within those waters ...[22]

Does finding include, for example, simply coming across a wreck site or artefacts on the seabed without *recovering* any material? From an archaeological point of view this interpretation would be useful since it would mean that more information could be gathered about the underwater heritage. However, the second part of the clause suggests that this is not the interpretation intended: "[i]f any person...finds or takes possession of any wreck outside United Kingdom waters *and brings it within those waters...*".[23] This suggests that mere discovery is not enough, and that recovery of the material is required. It therefore seems probable that the word "finds" was being used merely as an alternative to the more legal expression "takes possession of".[24] This is certainly the interpretation adopted by the receiver service, which continues to see its role as being to give legitimate owners the opportunity of recovering their property and to ensure that "law-abiding" salvors of wreck receive a reward.[25]

Where the receiver takes possession of any wreck,[26] within 48 hours he must make a record describing the wreck and identifying any distinguishing marks and keep the record available for inspection by any person "during reasonable hours without charge".[27] Where, in the opinion of the receiver the value of the wreck exceeds £5,000 he must also send a description to Lloyd's in London, where notice must be posted in some "conspicuous position".[28] These provisions are designed to provide potential claimants with the opportunity to come forward, but the provision for the making of a publicly accessible record of the find will also be of benefit to archaeologists.

Provision is made in section 240(1) that the receiver may "at any time" sell any wreck in his possession if, in his opinion: it is under the value of £5,000; it is so much damaged or of so perishable a nature that it cannot with advantage be kept; or it is not of sufficient value to pay for storage.[29] Where wreck is sold under this provision, the proceeds of sale less the expenses of sale, will be held by the receiver "for the same purposes and subject to the same claims, rights and liabilities" as if the wreck had not been sold.[30] The provision for immediate sale of wreck is discretionary in nature. It is not always used in the cases listed, but will be used where it seems the best course of action in the circumstances.

Each reported find is treated according to the individual circumstances of the case. A special procedure is in place for dealing with reports of *historic* material, which the receiver deems to be any material which appears to be over 100 years old. The receiver relies upon a network of

---

22   Emphasis added.
23   Emphasis added.
24   N. Gaskell, 'Merchant Shipping Act 1995' *1995 Current Law Annotated Statutes* 21/237.
25   Maritime and Coastguard Agency, *Notes on Wreck Law* (undated).
26   Presumably this includes the constructive possession which would be acquired through a finder's declaration that he or she was holding wreck on the receiver's behalf.
27   1995 Act s. 238(1) and (2). Section 520(1) of the 1894 Act required the receiver to post a notice describing the wreck in the customs house nearest to where the wreck was found. This was amended by the Merchant Shipping (Registration, etc.) Act 1993 Sch. 4, para. 23.
28   1995 Act s. 328(1) and (3). Such notice may be of benefit to insurers of recent casualties and also to successors in title to the insurers of vessels lost many years ago. On insurers' interests, see further Dromgoole and Gaskell, *op. cit.* note 14, p. 127 *et seq.*
29   This provision has been recently amended in order to provide the receiver with a power to sell wreck immediately where it appears unlikely that an owner will come forward to claim it: see further below.
30   Section 240(2). As to these purposes, and claims, rights and liabilities, see further below.

contacts in order to identify finds of historical or archaeological interest, often using a regional museum within the locality of the finder. Unless the finder asks for the report to be treated in confidence, reports of historic material are notified to the relevant Royal Commission on Historic Monuments in case they are of interest for the National Inventory of Maritime Archaeology which each Commission maintains.[31] If a find evidences a potential new site, then the Archaeological Diving Unit of the Department for Culture, Media and Sport will also be notified.[32] These procedures for the identification of historic wreck and the notification of historic finds to interested parties have been adopted by the current incumbent of the office of receiver of wreck. They are not enshrined in statute and have no formal basis.

Provided a claim to ownership of the wreck is established[33] within *one year* from the time when the wreck came into the receiver's possession, the owner shall – on paying salvage, fees[34] and expenses – be entitled to have the wreck delivered or to the proceeds of sale.[35] Under this provision the lawful successors of an original owner may claim their property centuries later and the hulls of several historic wrecks in UK waters have been claimed by foreign governments. Cargo and personal possessions on board a wreck may also be claimed, although in practice it may be more difficult to trace a line of succession to such property.[36] Having said that, in a remarkable and unprecedented ceremony the receiver of wreck recently returned seven marble sculptures dating from the second century to the Republic of Turkey, which was able to provide evidence of its ownership.[37] The marbles had been illegally shipped out of Turkey by a Dutch diplomat in the 1880s on board the SS *Castor*, which sank off Dungeness on route to Amsterdam. The Turkish authorities paid a salvage reward to the finders, and the receiver's expenses, as required by the 1995 Act.

It is interesting to note that section 240, which provides for the immediate sale of wreck in certain cases, has recently been amended by the Merchant Shipping and Maritime Security Act 1997, section 22, to provide the receiver with the power to sell wreck in his possession before the end of the one year ownership claim period where it is the receiver's opinion that it is unlikely that any owner will establish a claim to the wreck within that year.[38] In such cases, provision is made for the salvor to receive an "advance payment" out of the proceeds of sale, on account of any salvage that later becomes payable. This provision affords the receiver greater flexibility in dealing with wreck material. Where the requirements of the provision are met, the uncertainty created by

---

31   There are three Royal Commissions, for England, Scotland and Wales. They were established in the early part of the twentieth century for the purpose of making records of historic buildings and archaeological sites in order to provide information to a wide range of users. The records are open to the public. The National Inventory of Maritime Archaeology was established in 1992 after a pilot project and forms part of the National Archaeological Record, which itself forms part of the National Monuments Record. The National Inventory of Maritime Archaeology includes records of sites and isolated finds within territorial waters dating earlier than 1945. The Environment and Heritage Service of the Department of the Environment for Northern Ireland maintains a similar inventory covering the territorial waters of Northern Ireland.

32   In order that consideration can be given to whether or not the site should be designated under the Protection of Wrecks Act 1973: see further, section 3.2 below.

33   In the case of historic wreck, the practice seems to be that, provided a claim is made within the one year period, it does not need to be *established* within that period. Indeed, some claims are under investigation for several years before sufficient evidence is available to make a determination.

34   Although the Act provides for the payment of a fee to the receiver by whichever party is found to be entitled to wreck, it is now the practice to waive payment of this fee in the case of historic wreck.

35   1995 Act s. 239(1).

36   For a detailed discussion of ownership rights in relation to historic vessels, see Dromgoole and Gaskell, *op. cit.* note 14, p. 113 *et seq.*

37   See *The Times* 15 July 1998, *The Independent* 17 May 1995, 11 July 1998.

38   A further requirement that must be fulfilled is that no statement must have been given to the receiver under s. 242(1) of the Act by a person claiming to be entitled by royal grant to unclaimed wreck. On such claims, see further below.

the usual need to wait one year before knowing how a find is to be disposed of is avoided. From an archaeological point of view this is advantageous as it means that historical material can be sold or donated to a museum, which will then be prepared to invest in care and conservation measures.[39]

The Crown has title to all *unclaimed* wreck found in the UK or in UK waters except where the right has been granted to another person.[40] The Act makes provision for lords of the manor and other persons entitled by royal grant to unclaimed wreck, including successors in title, to provide the receiver with a statement containing details of their title and an address to which notices of finds may be sent.[41] Where unclaimed wreck is found at a place where such entitlement has been proved, the Act provides that – on payment of expenses and salvage – the wreck shall be delivered to the grantee.[42] While the granting of such rights usually occurred long ago, even recently there have been occasions when grantees have claimed entitlement to historically significant material. For example, in 1991 the Lord of the Manor of Ermington claimed entitlement to historical finds from two sites in the Erme Estuary in Devon, based on a grant of the right to unclaimed wreck made in 1271.[43] A provision in section 528 of the 1894 Merchant Shipping Act giving power for the Crown to purchase such rights was repealed in 1993.[44] Why the provision was repealed is unclear, but it was probably thought to be obsolete.

Where neither an owner, nor a grantee of the Crown's right to unclaimed wreck makes a claim, section 243 of the 1995 Act provides for the sale of the wreck and for the proceeds to be paid into the Exchequer after the payment of salvage to the finder and the receiver's expenses. However, in the case of unclaimed *historic* wreck in practice the Crown effectively forfeits its financial interest and efforts are made by the receiver to ensure that the material is deposited in a publicly accessible museum. Finders are encouraged to waive their right to salvage in order that finds can be donated to a museum, but where a finder is unwilling to give up the right to salvage, the receiver will offer the material for sale to a museum, at a price based on its current commercial valuation. In either case, the choice of the museum is made in consultation with the finder and relevant organisations, but one located near to the site of the find is considered preferable. Where the right to salvage is claimed, the finder will receive the net proceeds of sale after the payment of the receiver's expenses. Where a museum cannot be found which wishes to buy the wreck, the finder is usually offered the material in lieu of a salvage payment, although in such cases the finder must pay any expenses that have been incurred.

Prior to the centralisation of the receiver service, the number of reports of wreck had dropped to a handful each year and it was common knowledge that there was widespread flouting of the reporting provision. However, the current incumbent of the office of receiver has made considerable efforts to encourage the reporting of finds and to educate amateur divers in this respect and this has led to an increase in reports. In 1998 there were approximately 160 reports in total, of which approximately 25 percent were historic in nature.[45] The number of reports of

---

39   If the one year period has to expire before disposal can be determined, difficulties may arise in the case of fragile marine artefacts which require specialist conservation. The finder may not have appropriate facilities or expertise, and a museum may be unwilling to assist before it knows that it will acquire the find permanently.

40   1995 Act, s. 241. In *Pierce v. Bemis (The Lusitana)* [1986] Q.B. 384 it was held that the Crown had no right to unclaimed wreck found outside UK waters. For a criticism of this decision see Dromgoole and Gaskell, *op. cit.* note 14, pp. 210-211.

41   1995 Act s. 242(1).

42   1995 Act s. 243(2).

43   M. Williams 'A Legal History of Shipwreck in England' (1997) XV *Annuaire de Droit Maritime et Oceanique* p. 71 at p. 87. The fact that both these sites have now been designated under the Protection of Wrecks Act 1973 (see section 3.2 below) shows that the finds were of historical importance. The claim by the Lord of the Manor of Ermington is still under investigation by the receiver of wreck.

44   See Merchant Shipping (Registration, etc.) Act 1993 Sch. 4, para. 26.

45   These figures relate to new finders only, in other words they do not include individual reports from established wreck sites.

historic wreck therefore remains small and clearly not all finds are reported. However, the policy has been to achieve gradual compliance with the law through a process of education,[46] and a criminal prosecution would only be brought if an offence was committed blatantly and wilfully. While the Act provides for a number of offences in relation to wreck, prosecutions have rarely taken place and there have been none since 1993.

3.2 Protection of Wrecks Act 1973

As mentioned earlier, the Protection of Wrecks Act 1973 was enacted in response to the surge in diving activity that occurred in the late 1960s and early 1970s. Its purpose was to protect sites of special historical or archaeological importance from uncontrolled interference, looting and destruction.

The 1973 Act is short, comprising only three substantive sections, two of which are relevant here.[47] Section 1(1) provides:

> If the Secretary of State[48] is satisfied with respect to any site in United Kingdom waters[49] that:
> (a) it is, or may prove to be, the site of a vessel lying wrecked on or in the seabed;[50] and
> (b) on account of the historical, archaeological or artistic importance of the vessel, or of any objects contained or formerly contained in it...the site ought to be protected from unauthorised interference he may by order designate an area around the site as a restricted area.

The extent of the restricted area is whatever the Secretary of State thinks appropriate to ensure protection for the wreck and to facilitate enforcement.[51]

A person commits an offence if, within a restricted area, he does any of the following without the authority of a licence granted by the Secretary of State:

> (a) he tampers with, damages or removes any part of a vessel lying wrecked on or in the sea bed, or any object formerly contained in such a vessel; or
> (b) he carries out diving or salvage operations directed to the exploration of any wreck or to removing objects from it or from the sea bed, or uses equipment constructed or adapted for any purpose of diving or salvage operations; or
> (c) he deposits, so as to fall and lie abandoned on the sea bed, anything which, if it were to fall on the site of a wreck (whether it so falls or not), would wholly or partly obliterate the site or obstruct access to it, or damage any part of the wreck.[52]

---

46   Consideration is currently being given to the possibility of organising a wreck 'amnesty', whereby those in possession of unreported wreck would be able to come forward and declare it without fear of prosecution.

47   The third, s. 2 of the Act, provides for the creation of prohibited areas around dangerous wrecks: see further, note 9 above.

48   In England, this is the Secretary of State for Culture, Media and Sport. In Scotland, it is the Secretary of State for Scotland and in Wales the Secretary of State for Wales. In Northern Ireland, the Environment and Heritage Service (Department of the Environment, Northern Ireland) acts as agent in this respect for the Secretary of State for Culture, Media and Sport.

49   I.e. territorial waters: see s. 3(1).

50   Section 3(1) defines 'seabed' to include any area submerged at high-water of ordinary spring tides and therefore the provision includes wrecks, such as the *Amsterdam*, which lie on the foreshore.

51   Section 1(b). In practice the restricted areas vary in radius from 50 m to 300 m.

52   Section 1(3). A person also commits an offence if he "causes or permits" any of these things to be done without the authority of a licence. These offences are subject to the saving provisos in s. 3(3), which relate to action taken to deal with an emergency or in the exercise of statutory functions, or out of necessity due to "stress of weather or navigational hazards".

The Act provides that licences may be granted to persons who appear to the Secretary of State "to be competent, and properly equipped, to carry out salvage operations in a manner appropriate to the historical, archaeological or artistic importance" of the wreck in question.[53]

3.2.1 Administration of the Act

The Act applies in England, Scotland, Wales and Northern Ireland. In England, it is currently administered by the Department for Culture, Media and Sport (DCMS), in Scotland by Historic Scotland, in Wales by Cadw (the Welsh historic monuments executive agency) and in Northern Ireland by the Environment and Heritage Service of the Department of the Environment for Northern Ireland. An Advisory Committee on Historic Wreck Sites, appointed by DCMS in consultation with Historic Scotland, Cadw and the Environment and Heritage Service, gives expert advice on the selection of sites for designation and on the issuing of licences.[54] Since 1986 an Archaeological Diving Unit (ADU) has been employed to provide full-time archaeological advice and expertise.[55] Among other things, the ADU assesses sites that have been proposed for designation and visits licensed sites on a regular basis to monitor the work being undertaken.

3.2.2 Designation of sites

There are currently 46 designated wreck sites.[56] One of the first to be designated, in 1974, was that of King Henry VIII's flagship *Mary Rose*, undoubtedly the most famous vessel to be afforded designated status.[57] Other well-known wrecks with designated status are the *Amsterdam*, a Dutch East Indiaman, which ran aground on the foreshore near Hastings in 1749 and whose remains are well-preserved in the sand of the beach,[58] and the *Girona*, a Spanish Armada vessel wrecked off the Giant's Causeway in Northern Ireland in 1588.[59]

During the Parliamentary Debates on the Protection of Wrecks Bill, anxiety was expressed in both Houses of Parliament that designation orders be restricted to sites of *special* importance.[60]

---

53   Section 1(5).
54   The Committee is a non-statutory body. Its membership is designed to reflect the various interests involved in underwater archaeology: for details, see Advisory Committee on Historic Wreck Sites, *1997 Annual Report*.
55   Since 1986 the contract to provide these services has been held by the Institute of Maritime Studies at St. Andrew's University. The ADU has gradually grown in size and now employs three full-time diving archaeologists and two part-timers. For further information on the ADU, see its website: http://www.st-and.ac.uk/institutes/sims/deswreck.html.
56   Of these sites, 36 are off England, four off Scotland, five off Wales and one off Northern Ireland. There is provision in s. 3(2) of the Act for the variation or revocation of designation orders. Occasionally the co-ordinates of a restricted area as set out in an order have been varied to more accurately reflect the extent of the wreck site and two orders have been revoked because the sites had been excavated and the remains were no longer deemed worthy of designation.
57   As a result of overloading with ordnance, the *Mary Rose* sank, before the King's eyes, off Southsea on the south coast of England in 1545. The site of the wreck was located in 1970 and the remains of the hull were raised in 1982 and put on display in the Mary Rose Museum in Portsmouth. Parts of the wreck remain on the seabed and for this reason the site remains designated. For a very readable account of the loss, and subsequent finding and raising of the wreck, see A. McKee *How We Found The Mary Rose* (Souvenir Press, 1982).
58   The history of this vessel, from her loss to the present day, has been a remarkable story. For further details, see P. Marsden *The Wreck of the Amsterdam* (London, 1985). See also *The Observer* 7 March 1993, *The Guardian* 20 June 1995.
59   Finds from the site, which was discovered in 1967, are housed in the Ulster Museum in Belfast. For further details on the *Girona*, see Delgado, *op. cit.* note 1, p. 171. For an account of the *Girona*'s salvage, see R. Stenuit *Treasures of the Armada* (London, 1972).
60   See Hansard HC Vol. 851, Col. 1867; HL Vol. 342, Col. 923. Since a very rough estimate of the number of wrecks around British shores is between 15,000 and 20,000 (Dromgoole, *op. cit.* note 6, p. 40) such anxiety is not perhaps suprising.

The Act lays down two requirements for designated status. First of all, the Secretary of State must be satisfied that "[the site] is, *or may prove to be*, the site of a vessel..." and secondly, that the vessel, or any objects contained or formerly contained in it must be of "historical, archaeological or artistic importance".[61] The wording of the first requirement has allowed sites to be designated which consist of a collection of objects which might have been carried on board a vessel, with no remains of the vessel itself having yet been found. Indeed, in the case of the 'Smalls' designated site, the find-spot consists of a single item only, an Hiberno-Norse sword guard dating to about A.D. 1100, which was discovered in 1991.[62]

While the Act does not include detailed criteria for the identification of wrecks of "historical, archaeological or artistic importance", the Advisory Committee on Historic Wreck Sites has recently published some non-statutory criteria for use when assessing whether or not a site should be designated. The criteria, which relate to: period, rarity, documentation, group value, survival/condition, fragility/vulnerability, diversity, and potential, are not definitive but are to be seen as indicators "which contribute to a wider judgment based on the individual circumstances of each case".[63]

There is no specific age criterion in the 1973 Act for the selection of sites for designation. While the non-statutory criteria include a criterion relating to "period", this makes no reference to age nor gives any indication as to just how old a wreck must be to qualify as "historical" or "archaeological" for the purposes of the Act. While there are one or two designated sites which are estimated to date back to the Bronze Age,[64] the majority of designated sites date from the sixteenth to the eighteenth centuries. However, there are also two nineteenth century designated wrecks, the *Iona II*, a passenger ferry which sank in 1864,[65] and the *Resurgam*, the world's first mechanically propelled submarine, which was lost in 1880.[66] These sites were designated in 1990 and 1996 respectively. In 1998, a twentieth century wreck was also designated: HMS *A1*, the first British designed and built submarine used by the Royal Navy.[67] Arguably, the relatively recent designation of these more modern vessels is an indication of a relaxation of attitude on the part of the Advisory Committee regarding the age at which a vessel can qualify as being of historical or archaeological importance.

In the early years of operation of the 1973 Act, the Advisory Committee did not actively look for wreck sites to designate, but instead generally relied upon parties interested in undertaking an excavation to apply for a site to be designated.[68] In recent years, the Advisory Committee has taken a more proactive approach and it has become part of the brief of the ADU to bring to the attention of the Committee sites which might be worthy of designation.

Once an application for designation is made, which happens about once or twice a year, it is passed to the Advisory Committee for consideration. In compliance with the 1973 Act,[69] a number of bodies with maritime responsibilities and interests are consulted before a site is

---

61   1973 Act s. 1(1). Emphasis added.
62   For further details, see the ADU website, note 55 above. Note that, where the name of the wrecked vessel is not known, designated sites are known by the location of the site.
63   The non-statutory criteria will soon be published on the ADU website: note 55 above.
64   The 'Moor Sand' site consists of a scatter of Middle Bronze Age implements; the 'Langdon Bay' site has yielded more than 350 Middle Bronze Age objects, which are in the custody of the British Museum: see the ADU website, note 55 above. This website provides details of all the designated wreck sites.
65   The *Iona II* represents a one-off design for a fast passenger ferry for the River Clyde and was also employed an an early Federal blockade runner during the American Civil War.
66   For further details, see the ADU website, note 55 above. See also *The Times* 12 May 1997.
67   DCMS Press Release 301/98, 2 December 1998. See the government's press release website: http://www.nds.coi.gov.uk.
68   At the same time they would usually apply for a licence to survey or excavate the site.
69   Section 1(4): "Before making [a designation] order...the Secretary of State shall consult with such persons as he considers appropriate having regard to the purposes of the order...".

designated, including government departments and agencies responsible for fisheries, dumping and dredging, and Marine Nature Reserves; the Crown Estate Commissioners in relation to the Crown's ownership of the seabed;[70] and diving organisations. Generally, the sort of representations that are received from these bodies relate to the marking of sites and the extent of restricted areas, and there appear to have been no cases where a proposed designation order has been abandoned because of representations received.

The Act provides for emergency designation orders to be made in cases of immediate urgency,[71] such cases usually occurring at the height of the diving season in mid-summer, when the Advisory Committee is not due to meet for some time.[72] A full application for designation will be presented at the next Committee meeting and the usual consultees will then be given the opportunity to make representations.

3.2.3 Licences

As stated earlier, the 1973 Act provides that licences shall be granted only to persons who appear to the Secretary of State "to be competent, and properly equipped, to carry out salvage operations in a manner appropriate to the historical, archaeological or artistic importance" of the wreck in question.[73] This provision appears to have been interpreted quite liberally. Licences have in fact been granted at one time or another for the majority of designated sites and certainly in the past it appeared to have been the policy of the Advisory Committee to have a licensee 'working' each site, believing this to be the most effective way of enforcing designation orders. Frequently, licences have been granted to the finder of a site, or to a party who was undertaking recovery work on a site prior to its designation. Such persons may be amateur divers or commercial salvage operators. The reasoning behind this practice is that it is felt to be preferable that such persons work within the legal framework so that their activities can be monitored and archaeological guidance provided, rather than that they work surreptitiously and without supervision.

While the Act does not make provision for different types of licence, it does provide that licences may be granted subject to conditions or restrictions[74] and this has resulted in several types of licence coming into existence. Until 1997 there were two types of licence: a 'survey' licence and an 'excavation' licence. A survey licence allows non-intrusive site investigation. In the view of the Advisory Committee, the skills required for pre-disturbance archaeological fieldwork can be acquired by amateurs through training programmes and therefore, apart from in the case of the most vulnerable wreck sites, there is usually no requirement for the on-site presence of a qualified marine archaeologist. The requirements for an excavation licence are more rigorous and generally such licences will be granted only once the site has been fully surveyed to the satisfaction of the Committee. A qualified and experienced marine archaeologist, willing to take an active, on-site role in directing the excavation work, has to be nominated and approved by the Committee. Details must be submitted of the work programme, and of the resources and equipment available, including on-site and support conservation facilities, and the Committee needs to be convinced that these are satisfactory.

---

70 Virtually all of the seabed below mean low-water is owned by the Crown as far as the limit of territorial waters. The Crown Estate Commissioners act on behalf of the Crown in this respect.

71 Section 1(4). For an illustration of the speed with which emergency orders can be put into effect, see Dromgoole, *op. cit.* note 6, p. 43-44.

72 The Committee usually meets three times a year, in March, July and November: Advisory Committee on Historic Wreck Sites, *1997 Annual Report* p. 2.

73 Section 1(5). Licences may also be granted to persons who have a legitimate reason for requiring a licence, for example, to attend to submarine cables and pipelines: s. 1(5).

74 Section 1(5)(b).

In 1997 a review of the categories of licence was undertaken which concluded that two additional categories of licence should be created. The first is a 'visitors' licence. The restrictions imposed by the 1973 Act on designated sites have been interpreted as precluding *any* unauthorised diving activity in restricted areas, whether or not interference with the remains takes place.[75] This meant that it was not possible for designated sites to be visited by amateur divers and others interested merely in viewing a site, or the work being undertaken upon it. This restriction conflicted with the archaeological principle that public access should be encouraged wherever possible and the new visitors licence is designed to overcome this difficulty. The second new licence is a 'surface recovery' licence, which is limited to the recovery of material exposed on the seabed without disturbing the site itself.[76] Again, this is in accordance with established archaeological principles, in this case the principle that non-intrusive techniques should be encouraged.

Licences are granted to an individual, rather than to a team or organisation, in order that one person has overall responsibility, and licences are generally issued subject to the condition that diving is limited to named individuals.[77] Licences are issued annually and licensees are required, as a condition of the licence, to make an annual report to the Advisory Committee detailing their activities on the site. Duration of site spent at the site, methods of operation, equipment used, a site report and a log of finds complete with drawings and diagrams must all be included. The final section of the report will generally include an application for licence renewal, together with proposals and objectives for the coming year's work. The report must satisfy the Committee before a licence will be re-issued.[78] One of the responsibilities of the ADU is to visit designated sites at least once every three years in order to: assess the condition of the site; observe the standard of work of the licensees and compliance with licence conditions; and provide general advice and assistance.[79] The ADU's site reports will be used to assist the Committee in reaching decisions on whether or not licences should be re-issued.

Survey licences are the most common type of licence. In 1997, of the 45 sites then designated, 22 had a survey licence, and 14 an excavation licence, issued in respect of them. Three visitors licences had been issued, two in respect of sites for which a survey or excavation licence had also been issued, and one in respect of a site for which no other licence had been issued. The surface recovery licence had not yet been used.

3.2.4 *Enforcement*

During the Parliamentary Debates on the Protection of Wrecks Bill, concern was expressed in both Houses of Parliament about the question of enforcement of the restrictions imposed on designated sites, particularly since public finance cannot be committed under a Private Member's Bill. At that time it was recognised that the greatest aid to enforcement would be the licensees of sites, who would be anxious to protect their own interests, and this has in fact proved to be the

---

75   While s. 1(3)(a) makes it an offence to tamper with, damage or remove remains in a restricted area and therefore requires interference before an offence takes place, s. 1(3)(b) makes it an offence to carry out diving operations "directed to the exploration" of remains and also to use "equipment constructed or adapted for any purpose of diving". It is this last offence which means that divers need to have a licence simply to dive over a wreck site without touching it or entering any remains. The inclusion of s. 1(3)(a) suggests that it may not have been the intention of the drafters of the Act to preclude such activity, but this is certainly the effect of the provision taken as a whole.

76   Further details of the new licences are set out in the Advisory Committee's annual report for 1997, which is available from DCMS, and will also soon be available on the ADU website, note 55 above.

77   In relation to the new visitors licence, it is envisaged that the names of the divers planning to visit a site will be faxed in advance to DCMS or other responsible agency.

78   While the Act (s. 1(5)(b)) provides that licences may be varied or revoked by the Secretary of State at any time after giving not less than one week's notice to the licensee, it appears that this provision has been rarely if ever used.

79   Advisory Committee on Historic Wreck Sites, *1997 Annual Report*.

case. Some support has also been forthcoming from others engaged in coastal activities, such as customs officers, coastguards and harbour-masters, who have been prepared to report suspicious activities within restricted areas.[80]

By their very nature, however, designated wreck sites are highly vulnerable to unlicensed interference. Generally speaking, their co-ordinates are published in the designation order and the fact that they have been designated suggests that they may contain something worthy of investigation. While they may be worked on regularly during the diving season by their licensees, the season is short, lasting approximately four months only, and for the rest of the year the site may well be left unmanned for days or weeks. In such cases, unauthorised interference with a site may not be discovered for some considerable time, during which any evidence regarding the identity of the culprits is likely to have disappeared. While the Act has prevented large-scale looting and destruction of sites and conflict between rival salvage groups, small-scale pilfering by divers working alone or in pairs appears to be not uncommon.

There has been only one successful prosecution under the 1976 Act, in 1987, for unauthorised interference with a designated site. In this case the culprits were caught red-handed on the site by members of the ADU. Such clear evidence to bring a successful prosecution is rarely available however, and again, as with offences under the Merchant Shipping Act 1995, it appears that the policy is generally to use education as a means of persuading divers not to infringe the Act, rather than to use prosecutions as a deterrence.[81]

3.3   Protection of Military Remains Act 1986

In the early 1980s a number of incidents took place which gave rise to concern about the sanctity of UK military wrecks containing human remains. The first was the government-authorised salvage of gold from HMS *Edinburgh*[82] in 1982, when controversy was caused by newspaper reports suggesting that the divers had shown a lack of respect for the human remains on board.[83] The second was the Falklands campaign in 1982, which led to general public concern about the sanctity of the vessels and aircraft which became casualties. The third incident, "which really brought matters to a head and convinced [the Ministry of Defence (MOD)] of the need for legislation",[84] involved HMS *Hampshire*, which sank during World War I off the Orkney Islands, with the loss of many military personnel. Despite the MOD's refusal to grant permission, in 1983 a German consortium dived on the wreck and raised items including personal belongings. The inability of the MOD to enforce its unofficial war graves policy[85] made it realise that legislation was necessary to provide it with a mechanism to control such activities. The Protection of Military Remains Act came before Parliament as a Private Member's Bill, but appears to have been a Government Bill in all but name.

---

80 Responsibility for the bringing of prosecutions in relation to unlicensed diving on designated sites lies with the police and the Crown Prosecution Service. There is some evidence that local police forces may not always be sufficiently aware of their responsibilities in this regard.
81 It is interesting to note that in the foreword to the annual report of the Advisory Committee for 1997, the chairperson of the Committee stated that the Committee's role was to "encourage partnership" between the diving and archaeological communities. As part of this policy of education, DCMS has provided some funding support for an underwater archaeology training scheme for amateur divers.
82 The *Edinburgh* sank in the Arctic Circle in 1942 while carrying five tons of gold bullion to be used as part-payment by Russia for American weapons and supplies provided earlier in the War: B. Penrose, *Stalin's Gold* (1982) xi.
83 See, e.g., *The Sunday Times* 18 October 1981. It was later admitted that the allegations of disrespect made against the divers were unfounded and *The Sunday Times* newspaper made an out-of-court settlement in this respect.
84 Parliamentary Under-Secretary of State for Defence Procurement: Hansard H.C. Vol. 90, Col. 1232 (1985-86).
85 While the MOD had readily used the term 'war grave' in respect of ships sunk in wartime in order to deter diving, the term had no legal basis.

The Act applies to any aircraft which has, at any time, crashed while in military service, and may be applied to certain vessels which have sunk or stranded while on military service. Under the Act it is possible for the Secretary of State for Defence to designate a particular vessel, even if its location is unknown, and also to designate certain areas as controlled sites. The two types of designation, i.e. designation of a vessel and designation of a controlled site, may be applied in the UK, in the territorial waters of the UK, or in international waters.[86] However, they may not be used in the territorial waters of another State and therefore could not be used to protect a British military wreck such as HMS *Birkenhead,* which sank in South African waters in 1852 with great loss of life.[87] In international waters, offences under the Act may be committed only by someone on board a British-controlled ship, or by a British national.[88]

Vessels may be designated provided they sank or stranded on or after 4th August 1914, the outbreak of World War I.[89] As well as vessels which were on British military service, it is interesting that the Act also allows the designation of vessels which were in the military service of another State, where those remains are in UK waters. Under the Act those places which comprise the remains of all aircraft which have crashed while on military service, and the remains of designated vessels, qualify as "protected places".

Where the *location* of an aircraft or vessel is known, the Secretary of State for Defence may designate the area as a "controlled site". It must, however, appear that less than 200 years has elapsed since the loss of the aircraft or vessel. Where the remains are of a vessel or aircraft which was in British military service, the remains may be in the UK, UK waters, or international waters. Where the remains are of a vessel or aircraft which was in the military service of another State, the remains must be located in the UK, or in UK waters.

As is the case under the Protection of Wrecks Act 1973, the Secretary of State has power to grant licences authorising diving or salvage activities. However, such licences are likely to be granted only in exceptional cases, for example where the wreck poses a serious threat to navigation or to the environment.

There are various offences in relation to unauthorised interference with remains in "protected places" and "controlled sites".[90] While the offences in relation to controlled sites are based on strict liability, the offences in relation to protected places depend on whether the defendant believed, or had reasonable grounds for suspecting, that the place comprised "any remains of an aircraft or vessel which has crashed, sunk or been stranded while in military service".[91] In contrast to the 1973 Act, the 1986 Act gives authorised persons wide powers to stop and board vessels, and to seize equipment.[92]

Despite its primary purpose of protecting the sanctity of human remains, the 1986 Act indirectly could provide significant protection to military wrecks of historical value. Its protection may extend to military wrecks up to 200 years old. Interestingly, the 1986 Act does not state that it does *not* apply to wrecks already designated under the 1973 Act. Theoretically, therefore, it would be possible for a wreck to be designated under both Acts, although in practice this would

---

86   Section 1(6) and s. 1(2)(b).
87   However, the UK government acted to protect this wreck by reaching a bilateral agreement with the government of South Africa in relation to proposed salvage attempts: see further, ch. 8. See also Dromgoole and Gaskell, *op. cit.* note 14, pp. 116-117.
88   Section 3(1).
89   Section 1(3)(a).
90   Interestingly, none of the offences relate specifically to human remains, despite the fact that the primary reason for the enactment of the Act was to provide such remains with protection.
91   Section 2(1)(b). The location of protected places will usually be unknown and therefore, when divers come across remains on the seabed, they may not realise that they are military remains until some interference has already taken place.
92   1986 Act s. 6.

be unlikely to happen. The fact that licences under the 1986 Act would be granted only in exceptional circumstances means that the protection afforded to a wreck under this Act would arguably be greater than that under the 1973 Act, where licences to survey or excavate are regularly issued. In certain circumstances, the 1986 Act may also provide protection for wrecks of historical significance which *could not* receive protection under the 1973 Act. First of all, the 1986 Act extends protection to aircraft and therefore provides a mechanism for the protection of historic military aircraft which crashed at sea. Secondly, under the 1986 Act a wreck can be afforded protection *before* its location is detected, while under the 1973 Act not only must the location be known, but also the wreck's "historical, archaeological or artistic importance" must be assessed, before a designation order can be made. Thirdly, while the 1973 Act applies only to UK waters, the 1986 Act provides some measure of protection for the wrecks of British military vessels situated in international waters. During the two World Wars, most losses in action occurred in international waters and modern technology has now made accessible, and therefore vulnerable, wrecks found on the deep sea floor. The Act therefore offers the potential for quite considerable protection of military wrecks of historical significance.

So far, the facility in the 1986 Act to protect a vessel, either by designation or by the creation of a controlled site, has not been used. The Act therefore generally[93] applies only to aircraft. The reason that no vessels have been designated, or controlled sites created, appears to be that the MOD considers that the very existence of the Act, helped no doubt by the potent notion of the 'wargrave', is proving to be a sufficient deterrent in itself to interference with military wrecks without the need to activate these provisions.

3.4   Ancient Monuments and Archaeological Areas Act 1979

The Ancient Monuments and Archaeological Areas Act 1979[94] is the primary legislation in the UK safeguarding ancient monuments and archaeological remains on land.[95] As is the case with the Protection of Wrecks Act 1973, it aims to protect sites of special archaeological or historical importance from unauthorised interference. The Act makes provision for the compilation of a schedule listing the monuments to receive protection. The criterion for "scheduling" a monument is that it must appear to the Secretary of State "to be of *national* importance".[96] In practice, in England DCMS undertakes the selection, upon the advice of English Heritage. In Scotland and Wales, Historic Scotland and Cadw respectively have authority to undertake selection of sites for scheduling.

It is an offence for any person to demolish, destroy, alter or repair a scheduled monument without the consent of the Secretary of State,[97] who has a statutory duty to consult with the relevant heritage agency on applications for consent.[98] Generally speaking, scheduled monument consent is *not* issued in order for excavation of the site to take place, the policy being that scheduled monuments should be preserved *in situ* for the benefit of future generations. There is recognition that excavation is destructive and that future generations are likely to be able to elicit greater information from archaeological sites than is currently possible.

---

93   But see the discussion of s. 2(3)(c), a provision which may have surprisingly wide implications, in S. Dromgoole 'Military Remains on and around the Coast of the United Kingdom: Statutory Mechanisms of Protection' (1996) 11 *International Journal of Marine and Coastal Law* 23-45 at p. 31.

94   The Act applies in England, Wales and Scotland. The Historic Monuments and Archaeological Objects (Northern Ireland) Order 1995 makes similar provision for Northern Ireland.

95   The Act consolidates legislation dating back to the Ancient Monuments Protection Act 1882.

96   Section 1(3) (emphasis added). In England the relevant Secretary of State is the Secretary of State for Culture, Media and Sport, in Scotland it is the Secretary of State for Scotland, and in Wales the Secretary of State for Wales.

97   Section 2.

98   Schedule 1 to the Act.

The 1979 Act provides a range of measures for the enforcement of its provisions. For example, a person with a proprietary interest in an ancient monument[99] may, by deed, constitute the Secretary of State guardian of that monument,[100] or a management agreement may be made with the occupier of an ancient monument for the purposes of maintaining the monument.[101] Field monument wardens are empowered to inspect sites to ascertain the condition of a scheduled monument and to check for infringements of the legislation. The Act contains various provisions allowing for public expenditure to "defray or contribute towards" the cost of acquisition of any ancient monument;[102] the cost of the preservation, maintenance and management of any ancient monument;[103] the removal of an ancient monument for the purpose of preserving it;[104] and archaeological investigations.[105] There is also power for the compulsory acquisition of any ancient monument if necessary in order to secure its preservation.[106]

Provision is made for the scheduling of "monuments" and "monument" is defined widely to include:

(a) any building, structure or work, whether above or below the surface of the land, and any cave or excavation;
(b) any site comprising the remains of any such building, structure or work or of any cave or excavation; and
(c) any site comprising, or comprising the remains of, any vehicle, vessel, aircraft or other movable structure or part thereof which neither constitutes nor forms part of any work which is a monument within paragraph (a) above;[107]
and any machinery attached to a monument shall be regarded as part of the monument if it could not be detached without being dismantled.[108]

Despite inclusion of the word "ancient" in the title of the 1979 Act, a monument does not have to be ancient to be scheduled. There is no reference to age in the Act and monuments from as recent as the Cold War are now being considered for scheduling.

As well as sites on land, sites in inland waters may be scheduled, and so may sites in territorial waters.[109] Section 53(1) provides:

A monument situated in, on or under the sea bed within the seaward limits of United Kingdom territorial waters adjacent to the coast of Great Britain...may be included in the Schedule.[110]

The Parliamentary debates on the Ancient Monuments and Archaeological Areas Bill made it clear that one type of monument in territorial waters envisaged as a potential candidate for scheduling were the Solent forts[111] and some of these have since been scheduled. However, as yet, it appears

---

99   "Ancient monument" is defined in s. 61(2) to mean any scheduled monument and "any other monument which in the opinion of the Secretary of State is of public interest by reason of the historic, architectural, traditional, artistic or archaeological interest attaching to it".
100   Section 12.
101   Section 17.
102   Section 24(1).
103   Section 24(2).
104   Section 24(2).
105   Section 45(1).
106   Section 10.
107   This provision for the scheduling of movable structures was not available prior to the 1979 Act. It has been used primarily for the scheduling of boats found on land, for example the Roman boat at New Guy's House, Bermondsey, and the barges at the Waltham Abbey gunpowder works.
108   Section 61(7).
109   The provision for scheduling in territorial waters was first introduced in the 1979 Act.
110   However, a site designated under the Protection of Wrecks Act 1973 may not be scheduled: s. 61(8)(b).
111   Hansard H.C. Vol. 965, Col. 1363 (1978-79). These defensive fortifications were built at the time of the Napoleonic Wars.

that no *underwater* site in territorial waters has been scheduled. As far as England is concerned, it is the policy of English Heritage not to recommend subtidal monuments for scheduling, the reason for this being that the territorial remit of English Heritage does not currently extend to the territorial sea.[112]

In respect of shipwrecks in coastal waters, it is difficult to see how scheduling as a legal mechanism of protection would be preferable to designation under the 1973 Act. First and foremost, the protective devices afforded by the 1979 Act rely heavily on the occupation of land and are therefore largely inappropriate in the marine sphere. Secondly, the criterion for scheduling a monument under the 1979 Act is also inappropriate for dealing with historic wrecks. The international nature of maritime transport means that vessels of many different flags are wrecked in UK waters and the question of whether the wreck of a vessel with a non-British flag could qualify as of "national importance" would then arise. While it could perhaps be said that a vessel with a non-British flag is of national importance if it had some historical connection with the UK, it would certainly be difficult to argue that a non-British vessel which had simply been passing through UK waters in peacetime without an intention to call at a British port was of national importance.

Despite these drawbacks, the power to schedule marine sites could nonetheless prove useful. In particular, it would afford a means of protecting *non-shipwreck* remains in territorial waters, including fixed structures, aircraft and vehicles. There would also be other advantages to working within the framework of the 1979 Act. Legislation for the protection of ancient monuments dates from the late nineteenth century, when governments of the day felt able to make a substantial commitment to the protection of the heritage of the nation. The 1979 Act makes specific provision for public expenditure and the heritage agencies have significant budgets in this regard. The infrastructure which has been established to administer the legislation is extensive and includes considerable archaeological and conservation expertise. If a marine site was scheduled, all these facilities would become available, which would provide many benefits which are unavailable under the 1973 Act.

4.   Assessment of the Current Legal Framework

4.1   Treatment of artefacts

The provisions in the Merchant Shipping Act 1995 relating to wreck apply to all finds brought ashore in the UK, *including* material raised from sites designated under the Protection of Wrecks Act 1973. Considering the origins and purposes of these provisions, it is surprising that they apply to material recovered from the most important historic wreck sites known to exist in UK waters. In the past, incidents have arisen in relation to the operation of the provisions which have caused concern and, occasionally, outrage in the archaeological community.[113] However, any attempt to remove historical material from the remit of the Merchant Shipping legislation would face complex and controversial issues relating to, *inter alia*, ownership rights, salvage law and payment of rewards, and anyone arguing that this should be done faces an uphill battle persuading the government that it is necessary, or indeed, desirable.

---

112   The duties and powers of English Heritage, as set out in the National Heritage Act 1983 ss. 32-38, relate to "England", a term which is not defined for the purposes of the Act. However, caselaw suggests that, "except where the jurisdiction has been extended by an Act of Parliament, England...stop(s) at low-water mark...": *Harris v. Franconia (Owners)* (1877) 46 L.J.Q.B. 363 per Lord Coleridge C.J. at p. 363. This restriction on jurisdiction does not apply to Historic Scotland or to Cadw, which have jurisdiction over territorial waters in Scotland and Wales respectively. There are plans to extend the remit of English Heritage to territorial waters when the Parliamentary timetable permits: see further, section 4.3 below.

113   See Dromgoole, *op. cit.* note 6, p. 32 in respect of artefacts from the *Girona* and *ibid.* p. 50 in respect of material from the *Invincible*.

While the provisions of the Merchant Shipping Act are considered by many as fundamentally inappropriate for dealing with historic material, arguably they do have some redeeming features. The statutory duty to report finds is obviously useful from an archaeological point of view as it provides an opportunity for a public record to be made of finds. While it is true that the Act applies salvage law to the underwater cultural heritage and thereby encourages interference with sites and recovery of material, it can also be argued that the application of salvage law at least provides for the payment of a reward to the finder and so affords an inducement to the reporting of finds. In the current political climate in the UK, it is quite inconceivable that any government would countenance replacement of the current salvage reward, which is payable by the party ultimately found to be entitled to the property, with some kind of finder's reward payable by the State. Without the salvage regime, therefore, and in the absence of powerful enforcement measures to protect historic sites, it would be likely that interference and recovery would still take place, only clandestinely and with no record being made of material brought ashore.

As well as protecting the interests of finders, the Merchant Shipping Act also upholds the rights of owners and their successors in title. As far as pre-nineteenth century wrecks are concerned, an ownership interest is probably most likely to be claimed by States in respect of warships and other State vessels, since it will be relatively easy for them to prove their line of succession. In making such a claim, a State will usually be motivated by a desire to preserve the historical and cultural interest in a wreck and, for this reason, it may well prove to be an appropriate and satisfactory custodian. In the case of nineteenth and twentieth century wrecks, it is much more likely that a private owner or insurer, or a successor in title to the original owner or insurer, will assert a claim. While 100 years is often used in legislative instruments as the age that defines the scope of a special protective regime, those representing the interests of owners and insurers argue vociferously that even wrecks over 100 years of age may be of legitimate commercial interest. In reality, it is difficult to identify a cut-off date or age beyond which it can be said to be justifiable to deprive those with legitimate property interests of their rights.

The other main interest upheld by the Merchant Shipping provisions is the Crown's right to unclaimed wreck. This is undoubtedly anachronistic, but has proved useful from an archaeological point of view as it is now used to assert control over the disposal of historic artefacts. This means that it is possible to ensure that they are deposited as a collection with a public museum, whether this be by way of sale or donation. Indeed, the author argues that the Crown's right should be extended, so that it covers wreck found *outside* territorial waters and brought within those waters. Such wreck is currently returned to the finder if no owner comes forward to claim it.[114] Where this occurs, no control can be exercised over the ultimate disposal of the material, which may well end up being dispersed at auction. In fact, there is some anecdotal evidence that the current state of the law on this point is encouraging salvors to land material found outside UK waters in the UK, seeing it as a 'jurisdiction of convenience', and it would be regrettable if the UK gained a reputation in this respect.

Allied to the Crown's right to unclaimed wreck are the rights of royal grantees to unclaimed wreck. These rights are also anachronistic, but in no sense justifiable or useful. Clearly, the ultimate fate of historically significant material should not depend upon favours granted by medieval monarchs and therefore these rights should be abolished, or the power to purchase them reinstated.

In recent years those that administer the Merchant Shipping provisions have recognised historic wreck as a special category of wreck with special needs, and they have shown themselves willing to adapt the rules and administrative practice in order to ameliorate any adverse effects that the legislation may have. Further improvements could certainly still be made. Apart from the statutory amendments suggested above, further adjustments to the administrative practice are

---

114   See further, note 40 above.

necessary. In particular, there is a need to develop and formalise some of the current procedures, especially those relating to identification of material of historical interest, notification to interested parties of historic finds, and choice of museums to which finds will be offered for sale or donation. At present these procedures are somewhat *ad hoc* and require further consideration and refinement, in consultation with interested parties. Indeed, it may be that a non-statutory code of practice should be developed in this regard.

Ultimately, the provisions of the Merchant Shipping Act can be adapted only so far in the interests of historic wreck. Their purpose is now to protect the private interests of the finder and owner, and where these interests conflict with the public, historical, interest, the private interests undoubtedly prevail. While it is unlikely that the government would act to deprive finders, and – perhaps more especially – owners, of their existing rights, if pressure was brought to bear it might be willing to consider redressing the imbalance between public and private interests that currently exists.

4.2   Protection of underwater sites

The Protection of Wrecks Act 1973 adopts a site-specific mechanism of protection for historic sites, rather than some form of blanket protection. A mechanism based on the designation of certain sites of special importance has certain inherent defects. In particular, it provides no protection for sites as yet unknown but potentially of great historical and archaeological value. Such sites are at considerable risk from human activity: before they are discovered, they may be damaged or destroyed by accidental or careless dredging and other commercial operations; upon their discovery, they may be looted before they can be protected by designation. In the UK, some attention has already been addressed to the problem of commercial operators disturbing hitherto unknown sites. A non-statutory code of practice for seabed developers is now in operation, which has been endorsed by various organisations involved in commercial seabed operations and by bodies representing archaeologists.[115] It sets out procedures for consultation and co-operation between developers and archaeologists, and imposes reciprocal duties upon them in relation to seabed operations and archaeological rescue work. This is a welcome development, especially as it mirrors the co-operation between developers and archaeologists which takes place in respect of land sites. As far as the time-lag between discovery of a site and its designation is concerned, a relatively simple means of overcoming this would be amendment of the 1973 Act to allow for a temporary designation order to be made while the site's historical and archaeological importance is being assessed.

The 1973 Act is a short and simple piece of legislation, which provides a good basic framework for the protection of historic shipwreck sites, while affording a considerable degree of flexibility to its administrators to develop policy and practice as they see fit. Its most serious defect, which arose from its origins as a Private Member's Bill, is that it makes no provision for public expenditure. As a result, the scope of the legislation is limited, as are the resources available for its administration.

The limitations upon the scope of the legislation can be illustrated by the fact that, in contrast to the Ancient Monuments and Archaeological Areas Act 1979, no provision is made in the 1973 Act for public expenditure towards the cost of the preservation and maintenance of designated wrecks. The Act therefore provides no protection whatsoever against damage by

---

115   The Code was introduced in 1995 by the Joint Nautical Archaeology Policy Committee, which represents a wide variety of bodies with an interest in the underwater cultural heritage. Activities affecting the seabed are regulated by a wide range of consent procedures and it is therefore difficult to ensure that each procedure takes adequate account of the potential impact of the proposed activity on the underwater heritage.

natural causes, such as sandbank movements, tidal changes, erosion, etc. Designated wrecks may therefore face serious damage or even destruction from such causes, yet the government is powerless to take preventive or emergency action to safeguard them.[116] A further defect in the Act, which arises at least partly from the financial limitations, is the absence of any 'teeth' for its enforcement, such as powers to stop and search vessels, and to seize equipment, which could potentially cause problems where cases arise of blatant and wilful infringements. Fortunately, it appears that such infringements are, for now at least, rare.

The limitation upon the resources available for the administration of the Act meant that – from the outset – there has been a lack of full-time archaeological expertise to direct and manage the implementation of the statute.[117] This has had an impact on policy-making, which has failed to keep pace with developments in archaeological thought and practice. One result of this has been that scant attention has been paid to the fundamental archaeological principle that sites should be protected *in situ* wherever possible. Instead, it has been the policy to issue survey or excavation licences for the majority of designated sites. Consideration needs to be given to developing an overall management plan for what is, after all, a limited archaeological *resource*. The resource as a whole needs to be assessed and priorities set. Sites should be excavated either because there are good scientific reasons for excavation, or because a site is under some kind of threat. Other sites should be 'mothballed' for excavation when adequate resources are available, and others protected *in situ* for future generations. In line with the archaeological principle that public access to sites should be encouraged, the interests of amateur divers should continue to be taken into account and recognition afforded to the valuable contribution that they can make to basic survey and excavation work. Some sites are probably too valuable or fragile to allow interference by anyone other than qualified and experienced marine archaeologists, but others may be sufficiently robust that they can be surveyed or excavated by amateurs under appropriate supervision. Generally speaking, it should be possible for sites to be visited on a 'look but don't touch' basis.

An interesting point has recently arisen, which has the potential to seriously undermine the effectiveness of the 1973 Act. In 1997 the wreck of the *Hanover* was discovered. She was a postal packet vessel which sank in 1763 reputedly carrying gold bullion worth approximately £50 million in today's terms. The finder had spent ten years searching for the wreck and he proceeded to initiate salvage attempts. When his activities became known, a designation order was placed on the site, which meant that the finder was prohibited from continuing his operations. He therefore sought, and obtained, an injunction restraining the Secretary of State for Culture, Media and Sport from giving effect to the designation order.[118] The ground for the injunction appears to have been that there had been a failure to consult the finder, as salvor in possession[119] of the site, before the designation.[120] While the injunction arose through the application of domestic administrative law

---

116   The Dutch East Indiaman, *Amsterdam*, is one designated wreck which has suffered as a result of the lack of powers in this regard. The wreck lies buried in sand on the foreshore at Hastings and is believed to be one of the most complete surviving East Indiamen. However, it is now threatened by scouring action which is removing the protective layer of sand and exposing the wreck's timbers: *The Guardian*, 20 June 1995.

117   While the ADU was created in 1986 to provide archaeological expertise, its functions are limited and it is not responsible for policy formulation.

118   P. Fletcher-Tomenius and M. Williams 'The Protection of Wrecks Act 1973: A Breach of Human Rights?' (1998) 13 *International Journal of Marine and Coastal Law* 623-642 at p. 623.

119   For an explanation of the concept of 'salvor in possession', see Dromgoole and Gaskell, *op. cit.* note 14, pp. 217-221.

120   Fletcher-Tomenius and Williams, *op. cit.* note 118, p. 633. The 1973 Act does not provide expressly for such consultation to take place although it does provide for consultation with such persons as the Secretary of State considers appropriate: s. 1(4). In the case of the *Hanover*, it appears that the finder later agreed that the site could remain designated and he was granted a licence to excavate the site under the supervision of a qualified marine archaeologist. The finder is now claiming substantial damages for loss caused by the temporary suspension of his salvage attempts: *ibid.* at p. 633.

principles, the incident also alerted DCMS and the Advisory Committee on Historic Wreck Sites to the potential impact of the European Convention on Human Rights.[121] The First Protocol of the Convention, in article 1, provides that "no one shall be deprived of his possessions except in the public interest". The spectre is thus raised of the salvor in possession of a wreck site arguing that the placing of a designation order and, more particularly, the refusal to grant an excavation licence after designation, is an infringement of this provision. The protection that the Convention affords to such interests is qualified by the public interest and this may mean that the salvor's argument could be successfully challenged. However, until the precise effect of the article is explored, there is a danger that the Advisory Committee will be reticient, or perhaps even unwilling, to designate any site which has a salvor in possession without his or her consent, or will feel obliged to issue a licence to excavate to such a salvor. This would clearly have a significant impact on the effectiveness of the legislation.

4.3   Type of legislation and its administration

The UK is fortunate in having legislative provisions in the 1973 Act which are *specifically* designed for the protection of the underwater cultural heritage. General protective provisions which apply to both land and underwater heritage are unlikely to deal adequately with the special circumstances applying to underwater sites and, in particular, wrecks.[122] It is unfortunate, however, that the 1973 Act – in administrative and financial terms – is very much a poor relation to the legislation for protection of monuments on land.

A significant obstacle to satisfactory protection of the underwater heritage in UK waters is that responsibility for this heritage is divided between a number of different government departments and agencies. This situation is obviously far from ideal, especially as it is considered to be procedurally incorrect for one department or agency to be seen to meddle in the affairs of another. Therefore it might be difficult for, say, DCMS or one of the heritage agencies to be critical of the Merchant Shipping regime, since this falls within the remit of a different department. While there is now regular liaison between the responsible departments and agencies, the establishment of formal lines of communication would undoubtedly be beneficial. For example, it might be possible to form an inter-departmental/agency committee which met on a regular basis to discuss issues of mutual interest or concern.

The heritage agencies are undoubtedly the most appropriate bodies to administer the Protection of Wrecks Act, concerned as they are with administering the equivalent legislation on land. While an anomaly currently exists in this respect as far as England is concerned in that English Heritage is not responsible for administering the Protection of Wrecks Act, it is government policy to transfer responsibility for the 1973 Act to English Heritage as soon as the Parliamentary timetable permits the legislative amendment necessary to extend the remit of English Heritage to the territorial sea.[123] Once English Heritage takes over responsibility for the Act in England, where the vast majority of designated sites are located, it seems likely that a review of the Act will take

---

121   This point takes on special significance in the UK as the Human Rights Act 1998 will shortly be coming into force. This Act requires courts to have regard to the provisions of the European Convention on Human Rights in all cases before them. The date on which it will come into force has not yet been set, but is likely to be in 2000.

122   See further, Dromgoole, *op. cit.* note 6, pp. 113-114. See also L.V. Prott and P.J. O'Keefe *Law and the Cultural Heritage Vol. 1 Discovery and Excavation* (1984, Professional Books Ltd.)p. 112 *et seq.*

123   A window of opportunity for this will arise shortly because of the imminent merger between English Heritage and the Royal Commission on the Historic Monuments of England. Administratively, the merger will take place in April 1999, although legislation is required to formally undertake the merger and this is expected to be enacted in 2000. It may be that this opportunity could be used to extend the territorial remit of the merged body (which will be known as English Heritage).

place. This could potentially lead to amendment of the Act or, alternatively, to its repeal and replacement by specific provisions for protection of the underwater cultural heritage incorporated into the Ancient Monuments legislation. Either eventuality will provide an opportunity for the underwater heritage to be finally placed on an equal footing to land heritage,[124] administratively and financially. At this stage, it is also possible that some gentle inter-departmental pressure might be brought to bear for a reconsideration of the operation of the Merchant Shipping provisions in order that the public interest be given greater weight when decisions are made on the fate of historical material.

5.   Conclusions

Over the last ten years or so significant advances have been made in the protection of the underwater cultural heritage in UK coastal waters. In the main, these advances have been achieved not by legislative change, but by other means. Gradual but steady improvements have been made in the implementation of the legislation. In particular, the Merchant Shipping provisions are now administered with considerable sympathy to the cultural interest and the operation of the 1973 Act has been refined, and extended to cover a much larger number of sites.[125] The approach that has been developed is to do as much as possible through liaison with, and education of, the amateur diving community and this co-operative approach is a great strength of the system.

It is, however, twenty-five years since enactment of the Protection of Wrecks Act 1973. Over those twenty-five years a great deal has changed, not least the discipline of marine archaeology itself and attitudes towards it. The imminent take-over of responsibility for the Protection of Wrecks Act in England by English Heritage provides an opportunity for a comprehensive review to take place. It is to be hoped that this opportunity will be grasped and a thorough review undertaken, in liaison with all government departments and agencies with responsibilities in the field.

Before concluding, mention should be made of wrecks beyond the UK's twelve mile territorial limit. Technological advances have made accessible wrecks which lie in the deepest of waters and there is now an urgent need to afford such wrecks protection. Although an international initiative is currently under way in this field, it is likely to be a considerable period of time before any international agreement comes into force. During this time, States should be encouraged to take action: on a unilateral, bilateral or interstate basis. A number of States have already acted unilaterally by extending their territorial jurisdiction, for the purpose of protecting the underwater cultural heritage, beyond the generally accepted twelve mile limit. In view of the UK's trenchant opposition to anything hinting at creeping jurisdiction, it is inconceivable that it would take the same course of action. However, in other less controversial ways it might be persuaded to take measures to protect historically important wrecks in international waters. Indeed, it has already shown itself willing to act to protect the sanctity of maritime graves in such waters. As well as the extra-territorial scope of application of the Protection of Military Remains Act 1986 discussed earlier, a statutory provision was enacted in 1997 to provide a mechanism for giving effect to interstate agreements to prevent or control interference with non-military vessels in international waters.[126] The provision was designed specifically to enable the UK to implement agreements concerning

---

124   The government recognised that equal treatment should be afforded to the underwater cultural heritage as long ago as 1990: Department of the Environment White Paper *This Common Inheritance* September 1990 (Cmnd. 1200).

125   In August 1998 there were only 28 designated sites: Dromgoole, *op. cit.* note 6, p. 41. There are now 46.

126   Merchant Shipping and Maritime Security Act 1997 s. 24. The provision specifically excludes military vessels from the scope of its application, presumably because it was felt that the extra-territorial provisions of the Protection of Military Remains Act 1986 would be adequate in the case of such vessels.

the *Estonia*[127] and the *Titanic*.[128] Both the 1986 Act in so far as it extends to international waters, and the 1997 provision, create offences only in relation to UK nationals or those on board British-controlled vessels and therefore are in line with the nationality principle of State jurisdiction. While this means that their effect will be limited, they are nonetheless useful.

It is encouraging to see that the UK government has been prepared to extend some measure of protection to wrecks in international waters. While the measures taken so far were designed to protect the sanctity of human remains, these and similar measures could be used to protect cultural interests. In particular, the government should be encouraged to participate in, and even initiate, bilateral and interstate agreements for the purpose of protecting wreck sites of historical importance.[129]

It is to be hoped that the UK government will take a positive attitude towards the UNESCO initiative to produce a convention on the protection of the underwater cultural heritage. In this respect, a further encouraging development is that the UK has exercised a reservation under the International Salvage Convention 1989, which is now in force in the UK, in respect of "maritime cultural property" in order to allow for the exclusion of such property from the ordinary rules of salvage.[130] This reservation may be usefully employed in the future to enable the UK to sign up to an international convention providing for the exclusion of such property from the salvage law regime, or – indeed – to enable it to amend its domestic law relating to cultural property in territorial waters in order to exclude the application of salvage law. The fact that the reservation has been exercised suggests that such action on the part of the UK is not completely out of the question.

---

127   In 1995 an agreement was signed by the governments of Estonia, Finland and Sweden regarding the ferry *Estonia*, which sank in 1994 while travelling from Tallinn to Stockholm with the loss of almost 900 lives. The agreement states that the site of the wreck is to be regarded as a final resting place for the victims, that the *Estonia* cannot be raised and that legislation should be enacted to make it an offence to disturb the site. While the UK is not a contracting party to this agreement, s. 24 of the 1997 Act was designed specifically to enable the UK to implement it: see N. Gaskell, 'Merchant Shipping and Maritime Security Act 1997' *1997 Current Law Annotated Statutes* 28/24.

128   A draft agreement has been prepared by the US State Department regarding the wreck of the *Titanic* and it is envisaged that the US, UK, France and Canada will be signatories.

129   For a more detailed discussion of the measures that could be taken, see S. Dromgoole 'A Protective Legal Regime for the Underwater Cultural Heritage: The Problem of International Waters' (1997) XV *Annuaire de Droit Maritime et Oceanique* 119 at pp. 125-128.

130   See Art. 30(1)(d) of the 1989 Convention.

Chapter 13

UNITED STATES OF AMERICA

Ole Varmer and Caroline M. Blanco[*]

1.   Introduction

The sea and its bed have provided a natural barrier to salvage of the underwater cultural heritage (UCH), which has been accumulating since the dawn of humankind. While much of the UCH is stable and preserved by the marine environment, it remains vulnerable to its greatest risk, unregulated salvage. Until the advent of SCUBA technology in World War II, access to these irreplaceable resources was limited to those who could hold their breath long enough to dive and return with goods from the wreck. In the 1960s, a cottage industry of treasure hunting and salvage evolved in Florida, particularly in Key West, where salvage of recent marine casualties had previously been part of the local industry and custom. Armed with SCUBA, remote-sensing devices and equipment able to blow away vast amounts of the seabed habitat, treasure hunters began to salvage gold, silver and jewels that had been lost for generations.

Archaeologists, historians and others decried the loss and destruction of the UCH and have suggested that various governments protect the public's interest in these resources. The United States (US) and the underlying coastal State governments have been entrusted with the protection and preservation of the UCH. These entities are therefore faced with the awesome task of protecting and managing the UCH for use by present and future generations.

Protection of our UCH is becoming increasingly difficult due to advances in deep water exploration and exploitation technology. Submersible vehicles now provide access to the deepest parts of the ocean. Even the *Titanic,* which is under 12,500 feet of water, is subject to potential loss or destruction by salvors. There is no US program or statute providing *comprehensive* protection of the UCH. The location, ownership and control of the UCH primarily determine which national or state preservation laws apply. For the most part, the national government has delegated to the individual states responsibility for the protection and management of the UCH on state submerged lands. Outside three nautical miles, the UCH is protected if it is in a National Marine Sanctuary. In addition, any UCH that is likely to be affected by activities of the national government, including the issuing of permits, is subject to environmental and historic preservation law considerations. However, these US preservation laws are limited in scope, and leave much of the UCH vulnerable to loss or destruction from private activities, such as salvage.

2.   Overview of Issues Concerning Protection and Salvage of UCH

In order to create legal rights to their finds, treasure salvors file *in rem* actions against the vessels and their cargo (hereinafter 'shipwrecks') in US federal district admiralty courts. Generally, they assert that – under the law of finds – title to an abandoned shipwreck is vested in the person

---

*   The views expressed in this chapter are the personal opinions of the authors and do not represent the official positions of the US government, the National Oceanic and Atmospheric Administration (NOAA), or the Department of Justice.

who finds it and reduces it to his or her possession.[1] Alternatively, they argue that, because the shipwrecks are in 'marine peril', the public interest would be best served by salvaging the shipwreck and returning it into the stream of commerce.[2] If successful, they obtain a salvage award for services rendered, which often amounts to the vast majority of the recovered treasure.[3]

The national and underlying state governments have countered the salvors' claims with various arguments, including their own claims of ownership of the UCH. The US government's initial position was that it owned abandoned shipwrecks on its outer continental shelf. In the landmark case, *Treasure Salvors v. The Unidentified Wrecked and Abandoned Sailing Vessel ("the Atocha"),*[4] however, the court determined that, while the US had ample authority to exercise its sovereign prerogative to claim ownership of abandoned shipwrecks, it had not done so under the Outer Continental Shelf Lands Act, the Antiquities Act, or the Abandoned Property Act.[5] The court explained that US control over the outer continental shelf was limited to exploration and exploitation of natural resources. The US had not asserted its sovereign prerogative over historic resources on the outer continental shelf under the Outer Continental Shelf Lands Act, or otherwise.[6] In support of its opinion that the Outer Continental Shelf Lands Act was limited to natural resources and did not include the UCH the court noted that the 1945 Truman Proclamation and the 1958 Convention on the Continental Shelf were both limited to natural resources.[7] The fallout from the *Treasure Salvors* case is significant and has affected US legislation on the UCH, including the Abandoned Shipwreck Act and the Archaeological Resources Protection Act, which are discussed below.

3. US Statutes Protecting Certain Underwater Cultural Heritage

3.1 Abandoned Shipwreck Act of 1987

For decades, US state governments have asserted ownership rights to the UCH pursuant to the Submerged Lands Act and state historic preservation laws. In some cases, states have successfully argued that the Eleventh Amendment to the US Constitution, which recognizes states' sovereign immunity from suit, barred federal admiralty courts from determining the states' interests in shipwrecks on state submerged lands. In other cases, states waived their immunity and prevailed in convincing federal admiralty courts that they owned the shipwrecks in their sovereign state submerged lands. However, in a majority of the federal admiralty cases, salvors prevailed in getting ownership rights to the UCH under the law of finds.

---

1   *Treasure Salvors v. The Unidentified Wrecked and Abandoned Sailing Vessel (the 'Atocha'),* 569 F.2d 330, 337 (5th Cir. 1978): the court preferred law of finds over salvage as did the treasure hunter who got ownership of the shipwreck rather than an award of money or percentage of the salvaged objects.
2   The salvor obtains an award and a lien on the salvaged property for services rendered if three conditions are met: the shipwreck is in 'marine peril'; the salvor's services are voluntarily rendered; and the salvor achieves success in whole or in part in recovering shipwrecked property: *see The Sabine,* 101 U.S. [11 Otto] 384 (1879).
3   *See Columbus-America Discovery Group v. Atlantic Mut. Ins.,* 974 F.2d 450, 459 (4th Cir. 1992): the court preferred the law of salvage over finds; 90 percent of treasure was awarded to the salvors.
4   569 F.2d 330 (5th Cir. 1978).
5   Outer Continental Shelf Lands Act 43 U.S.C. s. 1331; Antiquities Act 16 U.S.C. s. 470; Abandoned Property Act 40 U.S.C. s. 310.
6   The rule in the US, largely established by this landmark case, is that the sovereign must expressly exercise its authority over the UCH.
7   *Treasure Salvors,* 569 F.2d at 338-40.

In response to the need to protect certain UCH and address this confusion over ownership, the role of admiralty law and other public interests, Congress passed the Abandoned Shipwreck Act (ASA).[8] Congressional findings support the view that the states already had the authority to manage the UCH pursuant to the Submerged Lands Act and that the ASA merely codified this minority view of admiralty cases.[9] However, confusion as to the scope of the ASA continues to cloud the governments' ability to protect and manage the UCH.

3.1.1 US asserting ownership over abandoned shipwrecks

In passing the ASA, the US Congress exercised its sovereign prerogative to protect certain UCH by asserting title to abandoned shipwrecks embedded in state submerged lands and to those located on state submerged lands and determined to be of historic significance.[10] Under section 6(c), title to these shipwrecks is then simultaneously transferred to the states.[11] Title to abandoned shipwrecks on certain federal public lands, such as national parks and Indian lands is reserved to the US from transfer to the states.[12] Many presumed that the ASA protected all historic shipwrecks in or on state submerged lands. However, subsequent litigation has shown the vulnerability of the ASA. In some cases, salvors shifted their strategy by arguing that the shipwrecks are not abandoned and, therefore, not covered by the ASA. In turn, they demanded liberal salvage awards or divided up the recovered goods pursuant to salvage contracts with owners/insurers. These cases revive the old dispute between salvors and sovereigns as to whether the law of salvage or historic preservation laws apply. The debate involves questions of what the states must demonstrate to prove that a shipwreck is 'abandoned' and, conversely, what a salvor must show to prove that the law of salvage applies. The results are mixed but clearly bring into question the scope of protection afforded by the ASA.

3.1.2 The issue of abandonment

The ASA protects "any abandoned shipwreck" that is "(1) embedded in submerged lands of a State; (2) embedded in coralline formations protected by a State on submerged lands of a State; or (3) on submerged lands of a State and is included in or determined eligible for inclusion in the National Register."[13] Unfortunately, the term "abandoned" is not expressly defined by the ASA.[14] This is because Congress relied on the *Treasure Salvors* case and its progeny where federal admiralty courts traditionally inferred the abandonment of long-lost shipwrecks by the passage of time and the absence of a claim therein.[15] Under admiralty law, the process for determining

---

8   43 U.S.C. ss. 2101-2106 (effective 28 April 1988).
9   43 U.S.C. s. 2101.
10   43 U.S.C. s. 2105 (a). The UCH is "historic" if it is eligible for listing on the National Register of Historic Places.
11   43 U.S.C. s. 2105(c).
12   43 U.S.C. ss. 2101, 2105. The ASA assertion of title and the transfer of that title to states with reservations for public lands is very similar to the transfer and reservations of title to submerged lands under the Submerged Lands Act.
13   43 U.S.C. s. 2105(a).
14   "Shipwreck" is defined to mean "a vessel or wreck, its cargo, and other contents": 43 U.S.C. s. 2102(d). It should be further noted that shipwrecks entitled to sovereign immunity, such as warships or other sovereign non-commercial vessels, are generally not considered to be abandoned by the flag nation, regardless of their location. US Navy vessels are not abandoned: ASA Guidelines Vol. 55 Fed. Reg. 50120 (4 Dec. 1990). See further, J. Ashley Roach "Sunken warships and military aircraft" (1996) 20 *Marine Policy* 351-354.
15   "The Committee notes that . . . abandonment . . . may be implied . . . by an owner never asserting any control over or otherwise indicating his claim of possession of the shipwreck." H.R. Rep. No. 100-514(I), at 2. See also *Moyer v. Wrecked & Abandoned Vessel, Known as the Andrea Doria*, 836 F. Supp. 1099, 1105 (D.N.J. 1993): an insurance company's failure to attempt salvage from 1956 to 1993 constituted abandonment.

abandonment is by express renunciation or by inference based on the totality of the circumstances.[16] With regard to long-lost historic shipwrecks, the inference of abandonment by the courts became tantamount to a presumption that such wrecks were abandoned by the mere passage of time.[17] However, by not codifying this meaning of "abandonment", Congress left the determination of its definition to the National Park Service, the entity charged with developing the ASA's implementing guidelines,[18] the individual states and ultimately federal admiralty courts. This has proved to be a perilous path as conflicting case law has subsequently developed which directly threatens the underlying historic preservation purpose of the ASA.

These shortcomings of the ASA came to a head in the Ninth Circuit case *Deep Sea Research (DSR), Inc. v. The Brother Jonathan and California.*[19] The *Brother Jonathan* is a double side-wheeled paddle steamer that sank off the coast of California in 1865. Shortly after it sank, five San Francisco insurance companies paid claims on approximately one-third of the cargo. The remaining two-thirds of the cargo and the vessel itself were uninsured.

The Ninth Circuit held that California did not prove by a preponderance of the evidence that "the vessel is abandoned and embedded in the subsurface or coralline formations of the territorial waters of the State" or, in the alternative, that the vessel "is abandoned" and "eligible for listing in the National Register". Even though there was no effort to salvage the vessel for well over 100 years, the court held that this long-lost historic shipwreck was not abandoned, was not subject to the ASA, and, therefore, could be salvaged under admiralty law. The court reasoned that technological advances and the payment of insurance on a third of the cargo made salvage possible. In effect, it presumed the law of salvage applied, instead of following the traditional admiralty cases where abandonment was presumed by the passage of time and absence of an ownership claim.

The Ninth Circuit's analysis of why it found that the *Brother Jonathan*[20] was not abandoned further reveals how other UCH is vulnerable. The court found no inference of abandonment from the fact that no action had been taken to recover the wreck or its cargo since 1865. The recent technological developments that enabled the discovery and recovery of the UCH negated the inference of abandonment that existed under traditional admiralty law. In other words, due to technological advances and corresponding interests in recovery by a salvor-subrogee of an insurer of part of the cargo, a shipwreck that was clearly abandoned and protected by the ASA in 1988 has subsequently been determined to be no longer abandoned and thus subject to the law of salvage. Citing the ASA guidelines, the court also stated that, if the full value of insurance is paid, the shipwreck should not be considered abandoned.

---

16   *Russell v. Forty Bales of Cotton*, 21 F. Cas. 42, 46 (S.D. Fla. 1872): abandonment was inferred by "the absence of a claimant or the neglect to claim"; *Commonwealth v. Maritime Underwater Surveys, Inc.*, 531 N.E.2d 549, 552 (Mass. 1988): "[S]ince the Wydah has rested undisturbed and undiscovered beneath the sea for nearly three centuries, it is proper to consider the wreck abandoned"; T. Schoenbaum, *Admiralty and Maritime Law* s. 16-7, at 240 (2nd ed. 1994): "In virtually all of the treasure salvage cases involving wrecks of great antiquity, the law of finds, not salvage is appropriate because '[d]isposition of a wrecked vessel whose very condition has been lost for centuries as though its owner were still in existence stretches the fiction to absurd lengths" (quoting *Treasure Salvors*, 569 F.2d 330, 332(5th Cir. 1978)).

17   *Ibid.*; *Martha's Vineyard Scuba Headquarters, Inc. v. Unidentified, Wrecked & Abandoned Steam Vessel*, 833 F.2d 1059, 1065 (1st Cir. 1983): long-lost shipwreck presumed abandoned.

18   The definition of abandoned shipwreck in the ASA Guidelines follows the admiralty cases that presume abandonment by the passage of time and the absence of a claim therein. In addition, the definition adds that a shipwreck may be considered abandoned if an owner fails to either mark and subsequently remove the wrecked vessel and its cargo or to provide legal notice of abandonment to the US Coast Guard and US Army Corps of Engineers. Rivers and Harbors Act (33 U.S.C. s. 409). Such shipwrecks ordinarily are treated as being abandoned after the expiration of 30 days from the sinking.

19   102 F.3d 379 (9th Cir. 1996).

20   102 F.3d 379 (9th Cir. 1996).

In determining whether the owners and insurers had abandoned the vessel that sank in 1865, the court considered recent statements of the insurers, in their assignment of title to DSR, which assured DSR that they had title to one-third of the cargo. The court acknowledged that the remaining two-thirds of cargo were uninsured and therefore abandoned. However, the court ruled that, for purposes of judicial economy, the ship and cargo should be treated as a unified *res* and, therefore, allowed salvage of the entire shipwreck, including the two-thirds that the court indicated were abandoned. It reasoned that the application of the ASA to the abandoned portion and salvage law to the non-abandoned portion of the shipwreck would lead to separate legal proceedings in state and federal courts. While the court said that it was unlikely that Congress intended such a confusing and inefficient approach in adopting the ASA, the Ninth Circuit ruled that the law of salvage should apply, instead of the ASA.

In practice, the Ninth Circuit followed the *Columbus-America Discovery Group v. Atlantic Mutual Insurance Company* case by relying on a new factor, technological advance, to reject the presumption of abandonment.[21] The court reasoned that the development of deep water technology made locating and recovering the shipwreck possible, and thus there should no longer be an inference of abandonment. In place of the inference of abandonment, the court held that there was a presumption that the law of salvage should apply. The Sixth Circuit has similarly departed from the traditional admiralty approach to determining abandonment and followed the *Brother Jonathan* and *Columbus-America* cases.[22] In contrast, the traditional admiralty analysis of abandonment is the one that was followed by most of the other circuits prior to 1988 and the one Congress relied on when it enacted the ASA. It is also the approach to abandonment followed by the Seventh and Third Circuits in analyzing whether a shipwreck is abandoned under the ASA.[23]

Perhaps because of this confusion in the circuit courts, the US Supreme Court granted *certiorari* in the *Brother Jonathan* case on all three issues in the *writ*: 1) whether the Eleventh Amendment bars a federal court from deciding *in rem* admiralty action where a state asserts title to the shipwreck under the ASA; 2) whether the lower court erred in ruling that the ASA pre-empts[24] state laws which regulate shipwrecks which are not abandoned; and 3) whether the lower court erred in finding that a long-lost historic shipwreck is not protected by the ASA because an insurance company may have paid a claim on a portion of the ship's cargo.

With regard to the issue of abandonment, the US, California and others took issue with the Ninth Circuit's holding and analysis before the US Supreme Court. The US argued that the Ninth Circuit erred in its approach to determine whether a shipwreck is abandoned within the meaning of the ASA. Consistent with traditional admiralty case law and other ASA cases, the US argued that the Ninth Circuit erred in rejecting the inference of abandonment when a long period of time had passed and the owner of the vessel had not attempted to salvage the vessel or establish a

---

21   974 F.2d 450 (4th Cir. 1992).
22   *Fairport Int'l Exploration Inc. v. The Shipwrecked Vessel Known as The Captain Lawrence*, 105 F.3d 1078, 1085 (6th Cir. 1997); see also 913 F.Supp. 552, 558 (W.D. Mich. 1995): Michigan showed that the previous owner was a salvor; he made no effort to recover the vessel; he declined US Coast Guard offers of salvage assistance; he stated the uninsured wreck was a total loss, the damage assessment was greater or equal to the value of the vessel $200; and finally, that technology was available to salvage the wreck at the time of the casualty.
23   *See Zych v. Unidentified, Wrecked and Abandoned Vessel (Seabird)*, 941 F.2d 525 (7th Cir. 1991); *Sunken Treasure, Inc. v. Unidentified, Wrecked & Abandoned Vessel*, 857 F.Supp. 1129 (D. St. Croix 1994). *See also Martha's Vineyard Scuba Headquarters, Inc. v. Unidentified, Wrecked & Abandoned Steam Vessel*, 833 F.2d 1059, 1065 (1st Cir. 1987) and *Treasure Salvors* (5th Cir. 1978).
24   California also argued that its historic preservation statute precluded the application of salvage law to California's UCH. The Ninth Circuit rejected the argument with little analysis holding that the California statute was pre-empted by the ASA to the extent it protected shipwrecks that were not abandoned within the meaning of the ASA.

claim therein. As the US noted, the primary flaw in the Ninth Circuit's rationale was that it did not infer abandonment because modern technology only recently enabled the shipwreck to be salvaged. This is not only a departure from traditional admiralty cases, but it effectively requires an express renunciation of title before the ASA may be applied. The US also questioned the treatment of the *Brother Jonathan* as a unified *res* and argued that the Ninth Circuit was clearly in error in ruling that the vessel and two-thirds of the cargo which the Ninth Circuit admitted were abandoned could nevertheless be subject to the law of salvage.

The US also explained how the Ninth Circuit erred in finding that the savings provision of the ASA (section 7) pre-empted California's historic preservation law. The US noted that the pre-emption issue need not be reached if, on remand, the lower court finds that the *Brother Jonathan* is abandoned and subject to the ASA.

The US argument before the Supreme Court was focussed primarily on the constitutional issue involving the Eleventh Amendment state sovereign immunity from federal court *in rem* actions under admiralty law. California argued that the Eleventh Amendment was a bar against such federal court actions and that the state's interest in the shipwreck should be determined in a state court. While concurring with California on the substantive issues of the ASA and the preservation of historic shipwrecks, the US disagreed with California on the issue of federal court jurisdiction. The US argued that the Eleventh Amendment was not a bar and that federal courts should determine whether the law of salvage or the ASA applied. The US then suggested that, if the lower court finds that all or some of the shipwreck is not abandoned, the case be remanded to the lower court to reconsider the issue of pre-emption.

Consistent with the suggestions of the US Solicitor General's Office, the Supreme Court vacated the Ninth Circuit ruling that the law of salvage applied to the *Brother Jonathan* and remanded the case for reconsideration of the issue of abandonment. The Court said that:

> the meaning of 'abandoned' under the ASA conforms with its meaning under admiralty law. The District Court's full consideration of the ASA's application on remand might negate the need to address the issue of whether the ASA pre-empts [the California historic preservation statute].

Under the Supreme Court's rationale, it could easily have affirmed the Ninth Circuit's ruling, which was based on admiralty law. Instead, the Supreme Court vacated the ruling and remanded the case as suggested in the US brief. The Supreme Court subsequently vacated the *Fairport (Captain Lawrence)* decision to the Sixth Circuit in the light of its decision in the *Brother Jonathan* case. By vacating the Ninth and Sixth Circuits' rulings on abandonment, the Supreme Court's decision also implicitly calls into question the new approach to the abandonment analysis taken in the Fourth Circuit in the *Columbus-America* admiralty law case.

Regardless, the *Brother Jonathan* case is now before the US District Court in California where there will be a new trial on whether the *Brother Jonathan* is an abandoned shipwreck subject to the ASA, or not abandoned and subject to the law of salvage. If the lower court also follows the suggestions in the briefs filed by the US, it should find the shipwreck is abandoned and that the ASA applies instead of the law of salvage.

3.1.3 *Law of finds and salvage does not apply: constitutional issues of admiralty court jurisdiction under Article III and sovereign immunity of states under the Eleventh Amendment*

In addition to asserting and transferring title to abandoned shipwrecks, Congress in the ASA expressly stated that the "law of salvage and finds shall not apply to abandoned shipwrecks...".[25] In enacting the ASA, Congress sought to end the management of the UCH by

---

25   43 U.S.C. s. 2106.

federal admiralty court, and instead rely on state and national agencies to protect and manage this important cultural heritage.[26] Salvors have attempted to elevate their activities above the province of Congress by arguing, albeit unsuccessfully, that this effort to prevent the application of the law of salvage to the UCH violates Article III[27] of the US Constitution because all cases of admiralty and maritime jurisdiction must be before federal admiralty courts, not state courts.

In *Zych v. Unidentified, Wrecked and Abandoned Vessel, Believed To Be The "Seabird"*,[28] the court held that Congress has the authority to define and even limit admiralty court jurisdiction. It specifically held that the ASA does not interfere with Article III's purpose of ensuring national control over navigation, as well as interstate and foreign commerce in federal admiralty courts. The court also noted that the result in this case was consistent with the result in maritime admiralty cases. "In fact, in a remarkable twist, this provision of the ASA [section 2106(a)] has no effect on the law of salvage because the law of salvage does not apply to abandoned shipwrecks."[29] Article III federal admiralty courts used to determine whether the maritime law of salvage or the common law of finds applied; now, at least in state waters, the Article III federal admiralty courts will determine whether the law of salvage or the ASA applies. The ASA codified the exception to the law of finds whereby the sovereign has constructive possession of abandoned property embedded in its submerged lands. So the abandoned shipwreck is the property of the state and not of the finder.

The *Zych* court held that, since the wreck was abandoned and owned by the state under the ASA, the Eleventh Amendment precluded a federal admiralty court from hearing litigation concerning a state-owned shipwreck.[30] The court acknowledged that the intent of the ASA is to have states, not admiralty courts, protect and manage abandoned shipwrecks, and rejected the salvors' arguments that admiralty courts should determine whether the ASA applies.

Since 1982, it was generally accepted that, because of the state's sovereign immunity under the Eleventh Amendment[31] of the US Constitution, a federal "court did not have the power . . . to adjudicate the State's interest in the property without the State's consent."[32] However, the Supreme Court has subsequently ruled in the *Brother Jonathan* case that the Eleventh Amendment does not bar federal courts from deciding whether the law of salvage or the ASA applies, unless the state is in "actual possession" of the shipwreck.[33] Citing decisions from the 1800s, the Court noted that the US and foreign sovereigns are not immune from an *in rem* admiralty case unless the sovereign is in "actual possession" of the vessel.[34] It then reasoned that the sovereign immunity of the several states under the Eleventh Amendment should be the same as the standard for US and foreign sovereigns.[35] As a result, Justice Stevens admitted that he had made an error in his

---

26 "The purpose of [the ASA] is to give states title to certain abandoned shipwrecks that are buried in state lands or have historical significance and are on state lands, and to clarify the regulatory and management authority of states for these abandoned shipwrecks": HR Rpt 98-887, 98th Cong. 2d Sess., page 2 (7/6/84).

27 "[T]he judicial Power shall extend . . . to all Cases of admiralty and maritime Jurisdiction": U.S. Const. art. III, @ 2, cl. 1.

28 746 F.Supp. 1334 (N.D. I'll. 1990), rev'd, 941 F.2d 525 (7th Cir. 1991), on remand, 811 F.Supp. 1300 (N.D. Ill. 1992) aff'd, 19 F.3d 1136 (7th Cir. 1994) cert. denied 513 U.S. 961 (1994).

29 *Ibid.* at 1141 citing *Chance v. Certain Artifacts Found and Salvaged*, 606 F.Supp. 801, 804 (S.D. Ga. 1984)(pre-ASA case) and *Columbus-America Discovery Group* (post-ASA case).

30 *Zych v. Seabird*, 19 F.3d at 1136 (7th Cir. 1994); see also *Zych v. Unidentified, Wrecked & Abandoned Vessel ("Lady Elgin")*, 755 F. Supp. 213 (N.D. Ill. 1991), rev'd, 960 F.2d 665 (7th Cir. 1992); both citing *Florida Department of State v. Treasure Salvors, Inc.*, 458 U.S. 670 (1982).

31 The Eleventh Amendment bars suits in federal court against states. States argue that disputes over their interests should be heard in the sovereign state courts and not in federal court.

32 *Florida Department of State v. Treasure Salvors, Inc.*, 458 U.S. 670, 682 (1982).

33 *California v. Deep Sea Research, Inc. (the 'Brother Jonathan')*, 118 S.Ct. 1464 (1998).

34 118 S.Ct. at 1470-1473.

35 118 S.Ct. at 1470-1473.

plurality decision in the 1982 Supreme Court *Treasure Salvors* case and agreed that California may be bound by a federal court's *in rem* adjudication of rights to the *Brother Jonathan* and its cargo.[36]

The meaning of "actual possession" in the context of shipwrecks in and on state submerged lands is likely to be litigated in the years to come. To trigger the Eleventh Amendment, states may now have to make a reasonable showing that they have control or custody of the shipwreck, or that they immediately occupy the shipwreck site. States are likely to argue that they are in "actual possession" of shipwrecks embedded in their state submerged lands which are controlled by state statutes and regulations concerning state natural and cultural resources. To the extent that such laws and management programs exercise control sufficient to exclude the unauthorized use of the UCH sites by others, such arguments may be successful.

Alternatively, states will need to provide reasonable evidence that the ASA applies. This would involve the state presenting circumstantial evidence that the shipwreck is abandoned and embedded in state lands. The sovereigns will argue that historic shipwrecks should be presumed to be abandoned if the owner did not attempt to salvage, or otherwise claim the shipwreck for a specified period of time, i.e., 60 years or more. If a state can show that the shipwreck is embedded in state submerged lands, the federal admiralty court should find that the shipwreck is abandoned and that the ASA applies. The state should also provide evidence of the historical significance of the shipwreck. If the shipwreck is not embedded, the state will need to show that the shipwreck has been determined eligible for inclusion in the National Register.

The ASA is alive and well. However, by not defining abandonment the *Brother Jonathan* Supreme Court decision ensures that historic shipwrecks will continue to be subject to challenge by the salvage industry in federal admiralty court. The ASA should ultimately prevail in protecting shipwrecks embedded in state submerged lands and perhaps other historic shipwrecks, but it may take years of litigation before this is fully realized. In the interim, the Supreme Court's decision also raises questions over the protection and management of historic shipwrecks by the sovereigns.

3.1.4 Protection and management of abandoned shipwrecks

The ASA directs states to protect abandoned shipwrecks and defers to the states the determination of how they should be managed consistent with some broad provisions. States are to offer recreational and educational opportunities to interested groups, including divers and researchers.[37] Unlike US land-based cultural heritage statutes, the ASA establishes a multiple use management regime for the protection of shipwrecks that also incorporates the protection of natural resources.[38] These provisions are consistent with integrated coastal management[39] and the multiple use management approach under the National Marine Sanctuaries Act which is discussed below. The ASA also encourages states to develop underwater parks to provide additional protection to the UCH and to apply for grants made available for such purposes.[40] To assist states and national managers of submerged lands, the ASA directs the National Park Service to develop guidelines for implementation of the ASA.[41]

---

36   118 S.Ct. at 1474.
37   43 U.S.C. s. 2103.
38   43 U.S.C. s. 2103.
39   The ASA guidelines urge states to integrate their UCH management into their state Coastal Zone Management Act (CZMA) plans to allow the use of section 307(c) consistency to protect historic wrecks and the use of CZMA grant money to fund research and management: 16 U.S.C. ss. 1451, 1456(c). (Section 307(c) requires that national government actions be "consistent" with approved CZMA programs). Thus, the CZMA presents another national procedural protection for national actions to comply with state UCH management programs.
40   43 U.S.C. s. 2103(b).
41   43 U.S.C. s. 2104.

The ASA guidelines[42] encourage states to assign their authority over abandoned shipwrecks to an appropriate and adequately staffed state agency. It is advised that states utilize advisory boards to consider the recommendations and advice of those who use or have an interest in the UCH. The long term management of the UCH should reflect the broad, diverse and often conflicting interests in the UCH. Consistent with the ASA, provisions are made for the recovery of shipwrecks for the public by the private sector, subject to the control of the appropriate state UCH management program. However, it is also advised that the unscientific use of treasure hunter technology should be banned because it destroys natural resources as well as valuable archaeological information.[43] Of particular import is the suggestion that states create and manage underwater parks or preserves to provide additional protection to historic shipwrecks.

The ASA guidelines have similar provisions for federal agency managers. These guidelines supplement the other US cultural heritage laws comprising the Federal Archaeological Program (FAP). The FAP and particularly the ASA guidelines have been instrumental in the development of the National Marine Sanctuary UCH management program as discussed below.

3.2 National Marine Sanctuaries Act

The National Marine Sanctuaries Act (NMSA)[44] authorizes the Secretary of Commerce, through the National Oceanic and Atmospheric Administration (NOAA), to set aside discrete marine areas of special national – and sometimes international – significance.[45] NOAA protects and manages these "areas of the marine environment possess[ing] conservation, recreational, ecological, *historical*, research, education, or aesthetic qualities which give them special national significance."[46]

The NMSA shows much promise in protecting historical sanctuary resources[47] because it is a far-reaching statute. Sanctuaries may be established out to 200 nautical miles offshore, the outer limits of the exclusive economic zone. To date, there are twelve national marine sanctuaries protecting significant natural resources and the UCH.[48] Most sanctuaries are in coastal waters where some of the most significant natural features are located and where most human uses occur. It is because of this human use that most of the UCH is located in coastal waters, including shipwrecks and submerged sites of early humans.[49] However, the only national marine sanctuary designated solely to protect an historic shipwreck is located some sixteen miles off the coast of North Carolina. Thus, in 1975, the ironclad Civil War vessel, *USS Monitor*, became the first national marine sanctuary and the cornerstone for the national marine sanctuary UCH management program.[50]

---

42   The guidelines are advisory and therefore non-binding upon the states and federal agencies: 55 Fed. Reg. 50116 (1990).

43   55 Fed. Reg. 50132 (1990).

44   Also known as Title III of the Marine, Protection, Research and Sanctuaries Act of 1972, 16 U.S.C. s. 1431, *et seq.*

45   16 U.S.C. s. 1433 sets out the standards and factors to consider in the designation process set out in s. 1434.

46   16 U.S.C. s. 1431(a)(2) (emphasis added).

47   "Historical" means a resource possessing historical, cultural, archaeological, or paleontological significance, including sites, structures, districts, and objects significantly associated with or representative of earlier people, cultures, and human activities and events": 15 C.F.R. s. 922.2(c).

48   15 C.F.R. Pt. 922 sets forth each sanctuary's regulations.

49   B. Terrell, *Fathoming Our Past: Historical Contexts Of The National Marine Sanctuaries* (NOAA Publication 1994).

50   The Sanctuary Program was established in 1972 to protect natural resources. After the *Monitor* was found in 1973, it was designated as a sanctuary in 1975 as part of a strategy to prevent its salvage. The NMSA was subsequently amended in 1984 to expressly include the existence of the UCH as a factor for sanctuary designation: 16 U.S.C. s. 1433.

3.2.1 Protection and multiple use management

The *Monitor* was designated as a national marine sanctuary to protect this nationally significant resource from looting and salvage. For over fifteen years it was managed as an archaeological site; direct physical access was permitted only as part of proposed archaeological research on the *Monitor*. In the 1990s, NOAA denied requests for permission to dive in the sanctuary and photograph the *Monitor*. While NOAA's decisions withstood legal challenge,[51] the underlying policy restricting public access at this site came under the scrutiny of Congress and others. The restrictive access policy continues to be roundly criticized by the diving community which fears that there will be restrictions on diving in other sanctuaries.

Moreover, recent evidence has revealed that the *Monitor* was deteriorating much more rapidly than indicated by prior research.[52] As a result, NOAA began issuing 'special use' permits for non-intrusive diving in the sanctuary without requiring that scientific research be conducted on the *Monitor*. This permit practice reflects the change in the public's interest in how the *Monitor* should be managed, particularly in regards to public access. The current permit practice is consistent with the ASA requirement that divers and others be permitted access to our UCH. It also further facilitates the multiple use mandate of sanctuaries under the NMSA.

Generally, sanctuary management is required:

> to facilitate to the extent compatible[53] with the primary objective of resource protection, all public and private uses of the resources of these marine areas not prohibited pursuant to other authorities.[54]

In every sanctuary, the public is allowed to dive and enjoy viewing the UCH: no permit is required.[55] While such non-intrusive public access is clearly a compatible use of the sanctuary, any unauthorized removal of, or injury to, the UCH has been determined to be incompatible with the primary objective: resource protection.[56]

NOAA has very broad and comprehensive enforcement authority to protect and manage sanctuary resources[57] and uses under the NMSA. Injunctive relief is available to prevent the destruction of sanctuary resources.[58] For example, in *US* v. *Fisher*, treasure salvors were enjoined from using propeller wash deflection devices in the Florida Keys National Marine Sanctuary.[59]

---

51   *Gentile v. NOAA*, 6 O.R.W. a, 1990 NOAA LEXIS 50 (4 January 1990): research required for permit; facilitating multiple use does not entitle public to physical access; *Hess v. NOAA*, 6 O.R.W. 720a, 1992 NOAA LEXIS 53 (26 March 1992): denial of permit held reasonable because the application for "research" was inadequate and does not propose elements of the scientific approach and methodology to be used.

52   Congress directed NOAA to develop a plan for its stabilization, preservation and recovery of artifacts and materials from the *Monitor*.

53   For an analysis of uses of natural sanctuary resources see O. Varmer and A. Santin, *Ocean Management under the Marine Protection, Research and Sanctuaries Act: Sanctuaries, Dumping and Development* (Coastal Zone 1993 published papers): compatible uses include: research, education, recreation, and commercial fishing. Oil, gas, and mineral development, as well as ocean dumping, are generally considered to be incompatible uses.

54   16 U.S.C. s. 1431(b)(5).

55   With the exception of the aforementioned permits required to dive in the *Monitor* NMS.

56   The two regulations protecting the UCH are discussed in the text associated with the *Craft* case and footnotes 74-77.

57   Sanctuary resources are defined to mean "any living or non-living resource of a national marine sanctuary that contributes to the conservation, recreational, ecological, *historical*, research, educational, or aesthetic value of the sanctuary": 16 U.S.C. s. 1432(8)(emphasis added). The 1972 Act did not define sanctuary resource; it was added in 1988 along with the liability provision for injury of sanctuary resources.

58   16 U.S.C. s. 1437(i).

59   Prop-wash deflectors (or 'mailboxes') can punch a hole in the seabed 30 feet across and several feet deep in hard packed sediment in fifteen seconds. In this case, the salvors uncovered and removed around 200 artifacts from the nearly 600 holes they made.

The preliminary injunction was primarily based on the irreparable harm caused by treasure hunting devices to natural sanctuary resources, particularly seagrass beds.[60] The court initially deferred making a decision on whether the salvage of historic sanctuary resources would continue under admiralty law. However, the court subsequently issued a permanent injunction against any salvage or removal of the UCH, unless expressly authorized by NOAA pursuant to a sanctuary permit.[61]

Within national marine sanctuaries, it is expressly prohibited to engage in any activity that destroys, causes the loss of, or injures sanctuary resources, including the UCH.[62] Under section 312,[63] those responsible for such injury[64] are held strictly liable for any response costs[65] and damages.[66] As litigation in these matters can continue for years, the NMSA also provides for the recovery of the accrued interest on the amount of damages and response costs.[67] In *US v. Salvors Inc.*, the court awarded $351,648 based on NOAA's estimate for its seagrass restoration project, $211,130 in damage assessment and response costs, and $26,533 in interest accrued on NOAA's assessment and response costs for a total of $590,311.[68] Because there is no requirement under the NMSA to show any negligence, intent or culpability of defendants, NOAA needed only to show that the defendants caused the destruction, loss of, or injury to, sanctuary resources, in order to establish that the defendants were strictly liable for all of the resulting damages, including response costs.[69] The NMSA does, however, provide defenses for such claims.

A person is not liable under section 312 if it can be shown that the injury to sanctuary resources: (1) was caused solely by an act of God, an act of war, or a third party, and the person acted with due care; (2) was caused by an activity authorized by federal or state law; or (3) was negligible.[70] In *US v. Fisher*, the salvors argued that they were not liable for any damages because, they claimed, their exploration and salvage activities were authorized by federal admiralty law and any injury caused was negligible. These arguments were rejected. The court held that neither general admiralty law nor particular admiralty court orders provide a defense for liability because they are not "federal law" within the meaning of the NMSA.[71] Rather, "federal law" was interpreted narrowly so as only to include licenses, permits, and other authorizations pursuant to federal statutes, and does not include authorizations developed under federal common law and its corresponding cases. The court further stated that the NMSA precludes the application of the laws of finds and salvage in the Florida Keys National Marine Sanctuary.[72]

---

60   22 F.3d 262 (11th Cir. 1994): US evidence that salvors used prop-wash deflectors to make 100 craters in the sanctuary seabed held to show a substantial likelihood of success on the merits sufficient for issuance of a preliminary injunction.

61   The court found that allowing the Fishers to continue to use mailboxes and remove artifacts was likely to cause further, irreparable, harm to the UCH. The court noted that this activity is now regulated by NOAA through the issuance of permits and, accordingly, the defendants were permanently enjoined from removing sanctuary resources or using prop-wash deflectors without a NOAA sanctuary permit: *US v. Salvors Inc.*, 977 F.Supp. 1193 (S.D. Fla. 1997).

62   16 U.S.C. s. 1436 (NMSA section 306).

63   16 U.S.C. s. 1443.

64   "Injure" means to change adversely, . . . [and] includes . . . to cause the loss of or destroy: 15 C.F.R. 922.3.

65   "Response costs" means the costs of actions taken by the US to minimize further loss, destruction or injury: s. 1432(7).

66   "Damages" includes: compensation for the cost of replacing, restoring, or acquiring the equivalent of a sanctuary resource, or the assessed value of the resource; and the cost for assessing the damage and monitoring the injured, restored or replaced resources: 16 U.S.C. s. 1432(6).

67   16 U.S.C 1443(a): liability and interest.

68   NOAA sought damages for the injury to the UCH including the loss of contextual information and a proposed UCH restoration project. The court held that the loss of contextual information was negligible since the defendants recorded the location of the artifacts it removed. NOAA did not challenge the defendants' conservation methods which appeared to meet FAP standards.

69   *US v. Salvors Inc.*, 977 F.Supp. 1193 (S.D. Fla. 1997).

70   16 U.S.C. s. 1443(a)(3).

71   *US v. Fisher*, 22 F.3d at 270; *US v. Salvors Inc.*, 977 F.Supp. 1193 (S. D. Fla. 1997).

72   *US v. Salvors Inc.*, No. 92-10027 (S.D. Fla. 30 April 1997) p. 10 f.n. 4.

Another argument made by the salvors and rejected by the *Fisher* court was that their rights to explore and salvage were authorized under admiralty law and the *MDM Salvage*[73] case, which preceded sanctuary designation and, therefore, could not be terminated by the NMSA. In support of their assertion, they cited section 304(c), which provides that any rights of access or subsistence use may not be terminated by sanctuary designation, but may be regulated.[74] The *Fisher* court's rejection of their argument is consistent with the holding of a Ninth Circuit sanctuary case in which harm to, and loss of, the UCH was at stake.

In *Craft v. US*, the National Park Service became aware of routine looting of the UCH by scuba divers and set up a 'sting' operation in the Channel Islands National Park and adjacent National Marine Sanctuary. They caught the divers excavating the sanctuary seabed and removing the UCH and seized their hammers, chisels and other excavation tools.[75] The *Craft* court ruled against the plaintiffs' argument that admiralty law provided a right to recover historic shipwrecks from "marine peril" under section 304(c) or otherwise. In particular the court held that:

> even if defendants have a right under the statute [NMSA section 304(c)], the Secretary acted within its authority to regulate that right. . . . [A]nyone holding a pre-existing right [must] apply for a permit to ensure that recovery is done in an environmentally and archaeologically sound manner. . ..[76]

NOAA's authority under the NMSA to protect historic sanctuary resources from unwanted salvage has withstood every legal challenge to date. The courts have consistently ruled that admiralty law provides no legal haven for the removal of, or injury to, the historic sanctuary resources and, accordingly, have uniformly ordered salvors to strictly adhere to sanctuary regulations and NOAA's permitting regime.

There are two regulations implemented in all sanctuaries that provide broad protection of the UCH by prohibiting: 1) the removal of,[77] or injury to, historic sanctuary resources and 2) any alteration of the seabed. Both of these regulations were applied in the administrative enforcement proceedings against the divers caught excavating the seabed and looting historic sanctuary resources in the *Craft* case. An Administrative Law Judge assessed civil penalties in the amount of $132,000 for violating these two regulations. The Judge assessed the maximum fine, $50,000 per regulatory violation for a total $100,000, against the dive master for establishing a system to warn divers of any approaching enforcement patrols.[78] The penalty was challenged as being unreasonably high. The district court found that the dive master's announcements about sanctuary rules against taking the UCH were made in a "mocking derision" of the law. In addition, the use of a bell to warn of the presence of enforcement patrols was found particularly egregious. The Ninth Circuit agreed, stating that "there can be no doubt that appellants were aware that their activities were prohibited . . . appellants' claims that they lacked fair warning that their actions were prohibited ring hollow." The court ruled that the fine was reasonably based on the heinous acts of the dive master.

---

73   *MDM Salvage*, 631 F. Supp. 308, 314 (S.D. Fla. 1988).

74   16 U.S.C. s. 1434(c).

75   6 O.R.W. 150 (NOAA 1990), 1990 NOAA LEXIS 29.

76   *Craft*, No. 92-1769 (C.D. Cal. 1992); 22 October 1992, Order of Judge Stephen Wilson, p 4.

77   Removal of any UCH in a national marine sanctuary requires a research and recovery permit which complies with professional archaeological standards and requirements as set forth in the FPA.

78   To date, this is the highest US assessment of civil penalties for the removal of any heritage resources, UCH or terrestrial. The cap on civil penalties has been raised from $50,000 per violation to $110,000 for each violation. Another important aspect of the NMSA's enforcement mechanisms is the authority under s. 307 to seek the forfeiture of vessels: s. 1437(d). Forfeiture is a rare occurrence; bonds are usually posted for vessels to ensure the recovery of civil penalties or damages. However, in some circumstances, particularly when the operator abandons the vessels, the authority is a potentially helpful management tool.

In *Craft*, the appellants also challenged the application of the regulation prohibiting alteration of the seabed to their removal of the UCH. Craft argued that the seabed regulation was intended to control oil, gas and mineral exploration and development, not the recovery of the UCH. As such, there was no notice to the public that this regulation would apply to the salvaging of the UCH from the seabed. Therefore, Craft argued that enforcement of this seabed regulation against salvaging the UCH was a violation of their rights to due process under the US Constitution. The court held that the language contained in the seabed regulation was sufficiently clear, especially as applied to the plaintiffs' activities.[79] The court read the prohibition broadly to include the defendants' excavation of the UCH and rejected the argument that the alteration of the seabed was *de minimus*. The court stated that, unless the activity falls within the two exceptions set forth in the regulation: anchoring and bottom trawling, any alteration of the seabed would clearly be prohibited. As a result, the regulation could technically be applied to activities such as handfanning without a permit. The sanctuary regulation of UCH was upheld and found to be consistent with the NMSA purposes to protect and preserve sanctuary resources as well as to promote research, education, recreation, and the aesthetic value of the area.

The court decisions in *US v. Salvors Inc.* and *Craft v. US* provide a very strong legal basis for the protection of the UCH in national marine sanctuaries. Consistent with article 303 of the United Nations Convention on the Law of the Sea 1982, these decisions should apply to the enforcement of sanctuary regulations against foreign salvage operations conducted in sanctuaries within 24 miles from the baseline used for measuring the territorial sea. Beyond that 24 miles, the enforcement of regulations prohibiting the removal of sanctuary UCH against foreign flagged treasure salvors may be deemed by some to be suspect. However, enforcement of the regulation protecting the seabed and other natural resources against foreign flagged vessels appears consistent with international law, including the 1982 Convention. Since treasure salvage operations generally involve disturbance of the marine environment, marine environmental regulations may provide indirect protection of the UCH from unwanted treasure salvage.

As mentioned earlier, and illustrated through the discussion of the sanctuary cases, it is unlawful to conduct an activity prohibited[80] by sanctuary regulations, unless it is conducted pursuant to a permit or other written authorization issued by NOAA under the sanctuary regulations. In all sanctuaries, activities that are intrusive to the UCH are permitted only if conducted pursuant to an archaeological research permit. In the first twenty years of the program, private recovery of the UCH was rare and permitted only when the UCH was threatened and could no longer be preserved *in situ*. The UCH would be removed pursuant to professional archaeological research and recovery requirements, and then be conserved and curated in an institution of public access, presumably in perpetuity.

---

79   On appeal, plaintiffs only argued the constitutionality of the regulation. The Ninth Circuit ruled that the regulation of the alteration of the seabed was neither overbroad nor unconstitutionally vague as applied to the appellants' conduct, and upheld the district court. The court noted that the degree of vagueness tolerated by the Constitution is greater for a statute providing for civil sanctions than for one involving criminal penalties, because the consequences of imprecision are less severe. Additionally, the court noted that a scienter requirement may mitigate vagueness. Finally, the court found that the most important factor to consider is whether the law threatens to inhibit the exercise of constitutionally protected rights, in which case a more stringent vagueness test applies: *Craft*, 34 F.3d 918, 922 (1994).

80   If an activity falls within a narrowly construed exception, it is not prohibited. Rather, it is an activity that is allowed to be conducted in the sanctuary without a permit from NOAA.

On 1st July 1997, the Florida Keys National Marine Sanctuary regulations became effective, including the permitting regime allowing the privatization of certain public resources.[81] At a minimum, all recovery must be supervised by a professional archaeologist and meet the other rigid FAP standards and requirements as to methodology and conservation. No UCH is permitted to be removed until it is determined to be in the public's interest: *in situ* preservation is preferred. Any UCH that is permitted to be recovered must be kept together in a collection and be made available for future research and other public access. Only after the archaeological research and recovery is completed and the UCH has been properly conserved and curated, permittees apply for a 'special use' permit to transfer certain objects to their custody. Such transfer will be granted if NOAA and Florida archaeologists determine that the objects are no longer of archaeological significance.[82] This permit system is the result of a compromise reached with Florida on how the UCH should be managed in the Florida Keys National Marine Sanctuary. NOAA has determined it is consistent with the NMSA and is primarily based upon the ASA directive for the inclusion of private recovery of shipwrecks as a multiple use for such UCH. NOAA, Florida[83] and the Advisory Council for Historic Preservation entered into a Programmatic Agreement pursuant to section 106 of the National Historic Preservation Act, which demonstrates that the Florida Keys National Marine Sanctuary permit system is in compliance with national historic preservation law and policies. It is very important, however, that the permittees conducting such activities strictly adhere to the permit conditions, regulations and Programmatic Agreement in order to protect and conserve the UCH for present and future generations. Time and experience will tell whether this compromise permit program furthers the public's interest in the UCH.

4. US Land Based Cultural Heritage Statutes Applicable to Certain Underwater Cultural Heritage Sites

There are three historic preservation statutes that were primarily developed for the protection of terrestrial sites but which also apply to the protection of the UCH in certain circumstances. They are the Antiquities Act, the Archaeological Resources Protection Act, and the National Historic Preservation Act.

4.1 Antiquities Act

The Antiquities Act of 1906[84] has two main components: (1) a criminal enforcement component, which provides for the prosecution of persons who appropriate, excavate, injure or destroy any historic or prehistoric ruin or monument, or any object of antiquity situated on lands owned or controlled by the US; and (2) a component that authorizes examination of ruins, the

---

81   It should be noted that the NMSA does not assert ownership over the UCH or other sanctuary resources. NOAA is a trustee of sanctuary resources. NOAA is a co-trustee with Florida for the UCH located on state lands within the sanctuary. Florida owns the abandoned shipwrecks and other UCH pursuant to the ASA, the Submerged Lands Act and state historic preservation laws. Sixty-five percent of the Florida Keys National Marine Sanctuary is located within state lands and waters.

82   16 U.S.C. § 1441. Such special use permits are also referred to as "deaccession/transfer permits". Objects eligible for transfer under this permit include duplicative gold and silver bullion, unworked precious stones, and coins.

83   Most of the sanctuary is within Florida submerged lands and waters. Under the ASA, Florida owns the abandoned shipwrecks in the state submerged lands. Under the NMSA, NOAA is a trustee for the public's interest in sanctuary resources. There is no assertion of ownership of sanctuary resources in the NMSA. NOAA is a co-trustee with Florida for the UCH in and on Florida submerged lands.

84   16 U.S.C. s. 431, *et seq.*

excavation of archaeological sites and the gathering of objects of antiquity on lands owned or controlled by the US through the granting of a permit.

The Antiquities Act was unsuccessfully asserted to apply to the outer continental shelf in the matter of *Treasure Salvors*[85] but was subsequently determined to apply in a national seashore. The *Lathrop*[86] case turned on the Act's permitting provision, and did not concern the ownership of the UCH or seabed. The court ruled against the salvors who argued that requiring permits for dredging the seabed and salvaging the UCH within the boundaries of the national seashore interfered with Lathrop's rights under the admiralty law of salvage and the common law of finds. The court stated that:

> Congressional enactments restricting the *manner* in which a potential salvor excavates property located on federally owned or managed lands does not offend these sound constitutional limitations [to maritime law and admiralty jurisdiction].[87]

The Antiquities Act permitting provision can, therefore, be used as a protection tool in waters over which the US has ownership or control, such as marine protected areas.

The Antiquities Act is still in effect, and its permitting provision remains a potentially useful tool for protecting the UCH. However, its enforcement was subject to a constitutional attack in two cases. In *US v. Diaz*,[88] the Ninth Circuit held that the Antiquities Act definitions of "object" could also include objects made recently and, as a result, provided insufficient notice to the public of the applicability of the Act's penalty provisions. The court held that the Act was unconstitutionally vague and therefore a violation of due process. However, the Tenth Circuit subsequently upheld the constitutionality of the Antiquities Act in *US v. Smyer*.[89] The court distinguished the *Diaz* case which involved face masks made only a few years before, from the objects appropriated in the *Smyer* case which involved artefacts that were 800-900 years old and taken from ancient sites. The court found that, as it applied to the case before it, the Act suffered "no constitutional infirmity" and must be considered "in the light of the conduct with which the defendant is charged."[90] These challenges to the Antiquities Act ultimately resulted in the enactment of the Archaeological Resources Protection Act in 1979.[91]

4.2 Archaeological Resources Protection Act

The Archaeological Resources Protection Act[92] also applies to "archaeological resources" of at least 100 years of age located in national parks, national wildlife refuges and other specific areas on national public lands. The Act requires a permit for any excavation, removal, or alteration of archaeological resources. The enforcement provision provides for the imposition of both civil and criminal penalties against violators of the Act. The criminal enforcement provision was successfully used in *US v. Hampton*.[93] In that case, a salvor was prosecuted for salvaging the UCH in Florida's Key Biscayne National Park. The matter resulted in a plea bargain. The

---

85   *Treasure Salvors*, 569 F.2d 330 (5th Cir. 1978) ruled that the US did not own or control the outer continental shelf for purposes of protecting the UCH. This ruling not only precluded the application of the Antiquities Act to the *Atocha*, but it also influenced subsequent legislation of the Archaeological Resources Protection Act and the ASA restricting their application beyond three miles from the shoreline.

86   *Lathrop v. The Unidentified, Wrecked & Abandoned Vessel*, 817 F. Supp. 953 (M.D. Fla. 1993).

87   *Lathrop*, 817 F. Supp. at 962 (emphasis in original).

88   499 F.2d 113 (9th Cir. 1974).

89   596 F.2d 939 (10th Cir. 1979).

90   *Ibid.*

91   It should be noted, however, that these cases addressed enforcement of the Antiquities Act, and not the permitting provision, which has never been subject to such a constitutional attack.

92   16 U.S.C. § 470ee *et seq.*

93   CRIM DOC. Nos. P169925, P169927, and P169928 (S.D. Fla. 1986).

Archaeological Resources Protection Act does not typically apply in the marine environment unless the US owns the seabed of the marine protected area. However, as the Act's prohibition against trafficking archaeological resources has been applied to such resources taken from private land, it may also be used to prohibit the trafficking of the UCH.[94]

4.3 National Historic Preservation Act

The National Historic Preservation Act of 1966 was enacted to recognize that the nation is "founded upon and reflected in its historic heritage."[95]

> [T]he preservation of this irreplaceable heritage is in the public interest so that its vital legacy of cultural, educational, aesthetic, inspirational, economic, and energy benefits will be maintained and enriched for future generations. . . .[96]

The Act requires that national government agencies survey, inventory and assess the historical significance of heritage resources including the UCH, prior to undertaking any action, such as issuing permits, expending funds, developing projects, and taking other government actions.[97]

Section 106 of the National Historic Preservation Act requires that national government agencies take into account the effect of any proposed federal, federally assisted, or federally licensed "undertaking" on any historic property[98] that is included in, or eligible for inclusion in, the National Register of Historic Places.[99] In addition, such agencies must afford the Advisory Council on Historic Preservation and the State Historic Preservation Office a reasonable opportunity to comment on the proposed undertaking.[100] The agency must complete the section 106 process prior to issuing any license or permit, or going forward with any other undertaking.[101] Section 106 does not prevent the undertaking from occurring, but it does require that the adverse effects to heritage resources be minimized. To fulfil the section 106 requirements for a class of undertakings that would require numerous individual requests for comments, the national agency may enter into a Programmatic Agreement with the Advisory Council and the state.[102] As long as the activities are conducted in accordance with the Programmatic Agreement, no further consultations are required for compliance with section 106. The purpose of the section 106 process is to identify potential conflicts between historic preservation concerns and the needs for federal undertakings in the public interest.[103]

The other main provision of the National Historic Preservation Act is section 110(a)(2) which requires national government agencies to manage heritage resources under their jurisdiction

---

94   See *US v. Gerber* 999 F.2d 1112 (7th Cir. 1993).
95   16 U.S.C. ss. 470 *et seq.*, 470(b)(1).
96   16 U.S.C. s. 470(b)(4).
97   Another statute that requires national agencies to consider the effects of their activities on the environment, including heritage resources, is the National Environmental Policy Act: 42 U.S.C. s. 4321 *et seq.* Like the National Historic Preservation Act, the National Environmental Policy Act is procedural in nature and does not contain any enforcement mechanism to prevent harm to heritage resources committed by third parties.
98   "Historic property" means any prehistoric or historic district, site building, structure, remains or object eligible for inclusion on the National Register, i.e., meets the National Register listing criteria: 36 C.F.R. s. 800.2 (e).97 "Historic property" means any prehistoric or historic district, site building, structure, remains or object eligible for inclusion on the National Register, i.e., meets the National Register listing criteria: 36 C.F.R. s. 800.3 (c).
99   16 U.S.C. s. 470f.
100   36 C.F.R. s. 800.1(a).
101   36 C.F.R. s. 800.3(c).
102   36 C.F.R. s. 800.13(a).
103   36 C.F.R. s. 800.1(b).

and control. Such management includes the obligation to survey, inventory, and determine the eligibility of historic properties for nomination to the National Register.[104] Section 110(a)(2) also requires that each agency exercise caution to assure that properties that may be eligible for inclusion are not "inadvertently" transferred or sold.[105]

5.   Conclusions

As discussed throughout this chapter, the US has certain statutes that offer some protection to the UCH located within US waters, albeit they are limited in scope. For example, the ASA, while protective of certain categories of UCH, has proven to be vulnerable to legal attacks by treasure salvors. The NMSA, in contrast, has proven to be a strong legal tool, however, it only protects the UCH within national marine sanctuaries. Likewise, the application of the Antiquities Act is, arguably, limited to marine protected areas, such as national seashores, where the US has either ownership of, or expressly asserted control over, the UCH. The Archaeological Resources Protection Act is even more limited in scope. It only protects the UCH that is located in or on submerged lands owned by the US, and expressly exempts the outer continental shelf.

Furthermore, the reach of one of the most important pieces of federal historic preservation legislation, the National Historic Preservation Act, is also limited in its protection of the UCH. It merely requires national agencies to comply with the procedural requirements of that statute to ensure that federal agencies preserve and protect the UCH under their jurisdiction and consider the effects of their federal undertakings on the UCH. Accordingly, the UCH located in the vast majority of US waters is left unprotected and vulnerable to unregulated salvage.

Comprehensive legislation to protect the UCH is greatly needed. Such legislation should protect the UCH located in waters from the shoreline out to the 200 mile exclusive economic zone, and should include several important components: (1) a US assertion of its historic preservation interest in all UCH under its jurisdiction or control (including sunken US flagged vessels regardless of their location), without terminating any property rights of others including those of foreign sovereigns;[106] (2) a permitting regime to regulate research and recovery of the UCH in an environmentally and archaeologically sound manner; (3) a US assertion of title to abandoned[107] UCH located in the twelve mile territorial sea and a contiguous zone out to 24 miles consistent with international law; (4) an enforcement provision to prohibit unauthorized activities affecting the UCH and/or the marine environment; and (5) a provision stating that the maritime law of salvage and common law of finds shall be inapplicable to all UCH.

---

104   16 U.S.C. s. 470h-2(a)(2).
105   National agency compliance with the s. 106 process prior to any property transfer or sale would meet this requirement.
106   Another component could also include a provision authorizing the US Department of Justice to enter federal courts to represent foreign sovereign nations, at their request, in protecting UCH in which they have an interest located in US waters. One additional aspect of this proposed legislation is that it would favor a national policy of *in situ* preservation.
107   UCH which has been left on the seabed for over 50 years should be presumed abandoned.

Chapter 14

INTERNATIONAL WATERS

Patrick J. O'Keefe

International waters are those beyond the territorial seas of States. The currently accepted breadth of the territorial sea is twelve nautical miles. This means that there is a vast area of sea beyond that limit with a wealth of cultural heritage – almost exclusively in the form of shipwrecks – lying beneath it. No attempt can be made to calculate just how many wrecks there are. No records exist for the great majority and the search for them has really only just commenced. What has been found to date is usually as a result of systematic search based on historical records or chance finds in accessible waters on the continental shelf. But the deep seabed is now attainable by those with the funding and expertise. Ballard, finder of RMS *Titanic* at approximately 13,200 feet beneath the Atlantic, was reported in 1997 to have found Roman and Islamic wrecks in the Mediterranean using technology capable of reaching 20,000 feet, enough to reach 98 per cent of all ocean floors.[1]

There are suggestions that wrecks in deep water will be better preserved than those where it is shallower.[2] First, wrecks in shallow water in many cases sank as a result of collision with rocks, reefs and land with the result that they are severely damaged. Those in deeper waters were usually overwhelmed by the sea in storm and more often sank relatively intact. Secondly, in deep and cold water there is less organic activity which means that wooden and similar structures have a greater chance of survival.

1.   Regulation

Some States exercise jurisdiction over part of the area being discussed here. For example, Australia and Ireland have legislation applying to historic wrecks on their adjacent continental shelves,[3] while that of Spain applies to cultural heritage on its continental shelf.[4] The USA has created a reserve on its continental shelf to protect the wreck site of the USS *Monitor* under its Marine Protection, Research and Sanctuaries Act of 1972.[5] Other States compel persons – such as those engaged in oil exploration, dredging, cable-laying – working on their continental shelves, to disclose any discovery of cultural heritage that they may encounter on the seabed. Morocco controls all archaeological explorations within its exclusive economic zone. These cases, while they can be regarded as indicative of emerging international law, will not be discussed in this chapter but rather left to the individual entries for the relevant jurisdictions.

---

1   *The Times* 1 August 1997 p. 1.
2   W. Bascom *Deep Water, Ancient Ships: The Treasure Vault of the Mediterranean* (1979).
3   See further, chs. 1 and 5 respectively.
4   See further, ch. 9.
5   See further, ch. 13. See also E.M. Miller 'The *Monitor* National Marine Sanctuary' (1985) 28 *Oceanus* 66.

1.1   The 1958 Conventions

Traditionally, there has been no international control over underwater cultural heritage beyond the territorial sea. In 1958 four international conventions were adopted to codify certain parts of the international law of the sea. None of these applied to cultural heritage. In fact, the International Law Commission in its explanatory comments on the draft Convention on the Continental Shelf, stated:

> It is clearly understood that the rights in question do not cover objects such as wrecked ships and their cargoes (including bullion) lying on the seabed or covered by the sand of the subsoil.[6]

During negotiations for the Convention at Geneva in 1958 the matter was raised in the Fourth Committee under the proposal to include "mineral and other non-living resources". The question was posed whether this included shipwrecks and their cargoes. The answer was that these were not resources: the phrase was meant to include only shells and similar objects. There was no further debate on the issue. The next development came with the United Nations Convention on the Law of the Sea 1982.

1.2   United Nations Convention on the Law of the Sea 1982

Cultural heritage had a low priority during the negotiations for the Convention. Greece and Turkey were the main proponents of provisions dealing with this and the USA led the opposition.[7] Unfortunately, the outcome was unhelpful for protection of the underwater cultural heritage.
Article 149 states:

> All objects of an archaeological and historical nature found in the Area shall be preserved or disposed of for the benefit of mankind as a whole, particular regard being paid to the preferential rights of the State or country of origin, or the State of cultural origin, or the State of historical and archaeological origin.

This provision is replete with problems: what exactly are the objects concerned; what is meant by 'preserved *or* disposed of' (italics added); is there any ranking among the States that are supposed to have preferential rights? More importantly, article 149 refers to objects found in the 'Area'. This means the "sea-bed and ocean floor and subsoil thereof, beyond the limits of national jurisdiction", i.e. the deep seabed. No case is known where article 149 has been applied.
The other provision of the Convention dealing with cultural heritage is article 303 of which paragraph 2 is relevant here:

> In order to control traffic in such objects [those of an archaeological and historical nature], the coastal State may, in applying article 33, presume that their removal from the sea-bed in the zone referred to in that article without its approval would result in an infringement within its territory or territorial sea of the laws and regulations referred to in that article.

This is a fiction designed to fudge the issue of jurisdiction. The zone referred to is the 'contiguous zone' in which a State can exercise control to "prevent infringement of its customs, fiscal, immigration or sanitary laws and regulations within its territory or territorial sea". Removal of

---

6   (1956) *Yearbook of the International Law Commission* Vol. II, 298.
7   For details of the various negotiations, see A. Strati *The Protection of the Underwater Cultural Heritage: An Emerging Objective of the Contemporary Law of the Sea* (1995).

objects of an archaeological and historical nature from the seabed in the contiguous zone has little to do with these laws other than that usually a crime is involved and goods may be liable to forfeiture. The provision purports to give States some control over what happens to underwater cultural heritage beyond 12, but within 24 nautical miles, of their coastline. However, article 303(2) has never been implemented in the form envisaged.

There is a general duty in article 303(1) which requires States "to protect objects of an archaeological and historical nature found at sea" and to "co-operate for this purpose". This applies also to the deep seabed. Strati reads into the provision certain specific duties on the part of States, such as the "obligation to report the accidental discovery of marine archaeological sites" and "the need for the *in situ* protection of archaeological objects".[8] However, there is no indication that States, apart from those mentioned in section 1 above, currently adopt such an interpretation and they do not seem to have relied on article 303(1) in exercising jurisdiction over their adjacent continental shelves.

There may have been a belief during the drafting of the Convention that some provision for underwater cultural heritage within the 12-24 mile zone was all that was necessary. The Vice-Chairman of the delegation of the USA has stated: "... the vast seaward reaches of the economic zone and continental shelf were really not relevant to the problem. The main issue was the policing of the area immediately beyond the territorial sea."[9] Even if that belief was correct at the time, and there is much evidence against it, it is certainly not true today.

1.3   Inter-state agreements

There is currently one agreement dealing with cultural heritage beyond the territorial sea. The Agreement Between Australia and The Netherlands Concerning Old Dutch Shipwrecks[10] applies to wrecked vessels of the Vereenigde Oostindische Compagnie (VOC: Dutch East India Company) "lying on or off the coast of Western Australia". This Agreement is implemented in Australia by the Historic Shipwrecks Act 1976.[11] Neither the Agreement nor the Act specify what is meant by "lying on or off the coast", but the general tenor of both documents indicates that Dutch wrecks on the continental shelf off Western Australia would be covered, and Australian legislation on historic shipwrecks specifically applies to the continental shelf.

Canada, the UK and the USA are working on an agreement to protect the remains of RMS *Titanic*, sunk on the continental margin some 95 miles south of the Grand Banks of Newfoundland.[12] Only the nationals of a small number of States have the technology to operate at this depth and, if all were to agree on a plan of protection, it would probably be effective for the present. Another example of an inter-state agreement is that concerning the M/S *Estonia*. This could hardly be said to be a significant wreck in terms of cultural heritage but the Agreement Between the Republic of Estonia, the Republic of Finland and the Kingdom of Sweden Regarding M/S *Estonia* is a useful example of a regional arrangement for wreck protection. Under this, the three States undertake:

---

8   *Ibid.* at p. 333.
9   B. Oxman, 'The Third United Nations Conference on the Law of the Sea: The Ninth Session (1980)' (1981) 75 *American Journal of International Law* 240.
10   1972 Australian Treaty Series No. 18.
11   On this Act, and on the Agreement, see further ch. 1.
12   It has been reported that a British company is planning to take tourists to view the *Titanic* at £19,500 per head. The director of the company states that there will be no contact with the wreck: *Guardian Weekly* 8 March 1998 p. 10.

... to institute legislation, in accordance with their national procedures, aiming at the criminalization of any activities disturbing the peace of the final place of rest, in particular any diving or other activities with the purpose of recovering victims or property from the wreck or the sea-bed.[13]

In view of the location of the wreck site and the fact that those most likely to be interested in it would have the nationality of one of the three States Parties, this agreement has force behind it. But what would be the situation if German divers started working on the site from a vessel flying the Liberian flag? This raises the more general issue of controls over persons working on sites of importance to the cultural heritage beneath international waters.

1.4   National legislation

The only relevant national legislation is the UK's Protection of Military Remains Act 1986 which provides that certain acts affecting military remains committed in international waters by British nationals or those aboard British controlled vessels may be offences.[14]

2.   Ownership

Article 303(3) of the United Nations Convention on the Law of the Sea states that "Nothing in this article affects the rights of identifiable owners ...". Apart from limiting the scope of the Convention, this statement immediately raises the question of who is an "identifiable owner"?

When a ship sinks, an owner's property rights are not normally immediately lost. States continue to recognise those rights until the owner abandons them, whether expressly or by implication.[15] This applies to wrecks beyond, as well as within, territorial seas. The wrecks of the VOC are a good example of this principle in operation. Under Dutch law, the Netherlands, by virtue of article 247 of the 1798 Constitution of the Batavian Republic, is the present legal successor of the VOC. When the Dutch wrecks were discovered off Western Australia, the Dutch government claimed rights as owner in succession. The Australian government viewed the wrecks as having been abandoned since no effort had been made to locate them for 300 years. As a compromise, the Netherlands transferred "all its right, title and interest in and to the wrecked vessels" to Australia, while Australia recognised that the Netherlands had a continuing interest "particularly for historical and other cultural purposes" in articles recovered from the wrecks. The Agreement[16] does not state that the Netherlands had title to the wrecks and thus does not constitute an acknowledgement of this claim by the Australian government. Rather, whatever title the Netherlands did in fact have under its law and/or any other system of law, was transferred to Australia.

A recent case which vividly illustrates the difficulties of establishing ownership rights is *Columbus-America Discovery Group v. Atlantic Mutual Insurance Co. (The Central America).*[17] The SS *Central America* sank some 140 years ago with the loss of 425 lives and a large amount of gold. In 1988 she was found by the Columbus-America Discovery Group 160 miles off the South Carolina coast at a depth of about one and a half miles. The bulk of the gold (US$1,219,189

---

13   The full text is reprinted in (1996) 20 *Marine Policy* 355.
14   See further, ch. 12. See also S. Dromgoole 'Military Remains on and around the Coast of the United Kingdom: Statutory Mechanisms of Protection' (1996) 11 *International Journal of Marine and Coastal Law* 23-45.
15   See further, S. Dromgoole and N. Gaskell 'Interests in Wreck' in N. Palmer and E. McKendrick, eds., *Interests in Goods* (2nd edn., 1998) ch. 7, pp. 141-204.
16   The Agreement Between Australia and The Netherlands Concerning Old Dutch Shipwrecks, see section 1.3 above. See also ch. 1.
17   (1990) 742 F. Supp. 1327, (1992) 974 F.2d 450.

in 1857 values) comprised commercial shipments from Californian merchants, bankers and express companies to New York banks. These shipments were insured: approximately one-third by New York insurers and the remainder by the London market. Contemporary newspapers record the insurers as saying that they would pay for losses on presentation of proper proof and, later, that claims were paid. In 1991, the Columbus-America Discovery Group moved in the US District Court for Virginia to have itself declared the owner of the gold raised both then and in the future. Opposing Columbus-America were a number of insurers who claimed to have paid out on the lost gold. The District Court found that they were not able to produce any "substantial documents or proof of their claims".[18] Since such documents must have existed for any claims to have been paid, the court drew the inference that they had been deliberately destroyed. This, coupled with no effort to locate or recover the gold for over 100 years, amounted to abandonment. The Court of Appeals for the Fourth Circuit took a different view.[19] They considered it more likely than not that the documents were lost or unintentionally destroyed. They also placed some reliance on the conduct of would-be finders in approaching a couple of the insurance companies from the late 1970s onwards seeking information and contracts. The case thus illustrates the difficulty of establishing when even a relatively recently wrecked vessel has been abandoned.

3.   Salvage

Salvage is the voluntary rendering of assistance to vessels in real danger. As compensation for that assistance, a salvage reward is paid based on the value of what has been saved. There are serious questions as to whether this concept has any relevance to those wrecks which constitute part of the cultural heritage.

First of all, in most situations it is difficult to conceive of these wrecks as being in real danger. This was certainly the view taken by Lissaman J. in *Her Majesty v. Mar-Dive*[20] concerning the *Atlantic* which sank in 1852 in about 162 feet of water in Lake Erie. She is buried at least thirteen feet, up to her natural water line, in the mud at the bottom of the lake. In the course of his judgment arising from a claim to salvage rights, Lissaman said:

> … danger of loss or damage to the subject matter of the service is the very foundation of a claim to salvage and the degree of danger has been said to be the most important element to consider in awarding salvage. … the *Atlantic* has been resting undisturbed on the lakebed of Lake Erie since she sank in 1852. Therefore, I conclude that the salvage proposed by Mar-Dive will not save the *Atlantic* from any danger.[21]

The point is that when a ship sinks it comes to achieve equilibrium with its environment. Any disturbance of this will bring about changes in the chemical processes at work which will start to cause more rapid deterioration.

Some courts in the USA have gone to great lengths to find an element of danger in order to justify a grant of salvage rights over a wreck. This line of argument began with the decision of the Court of Appeals, Fifth Circuit, in *Treasure Salvors, Inc. v. Unidentified Wrecked and Abandoned Sailing Vessel,* where it was said: "There is no dispute that the *Atocha* was lost. Even after the discovery of the vessel's location it is still in peril of being lost through the actions of the

---

18   (1990) 742 F. Supp. 1327.
19   (1992) 974 F.2d 450. For an analysis of the appeal decision, see P.J. O'Keefe 'Gold, Abandonment and Salvage: *The Central America*' [1994] *Lloyd's Maritime and Commercial Law Quarterly* 7-12.
20   [1997] *American Maritime Cases* 1000.
21   [1997] *American Maritime Cases* 1000 at 1062-63.

elements."[22] This peculiar argument was reiterated by the same circuit court in *Platoro Ltd., Inc. v. Unidentified Remains, Etc.*[23] The Florida District Court in *Cobb Coin Co., Inc. v. Unidentified, Wrecked, Etc.* added the possibility of being lost through the action of pirates![24] Other courts have emphasised the property aspect:

> Because property is far less certain of being recovered once it has sunk, especially when it has sunk in deep water, we perceive that its sinking sharply increases the degree of danger to its continued existence and utility as property.[25]

This has strayed very far from the original concept of salvage relating to a real and immediate danger.

Salvage is a commercial operation. Much archaeological excavation involves material of no commercial value. Excavating to archaeological standards in most cases will mean that there is no profit even if all the material remains were to be sold. Consequently, there is a temptation for profit seekers to extract commercially valuable material as fast as possible to the detriment of everything else. A classic illustration of this occurred in respect of the *Geldermalsen*, a Dutch East Indiaman wrecked in 1752 in the South China seas. It was said to have been found within the Indonesian exclusive economic zone in 1985 by Michael Hatcher who raised its cargo of ceramics. The following, taken from a laudatory book written just after the sale of the cargo in 1986, for £10 million, describes Hatcher's method of work:

> Hatch has to recover as much as possible as quickly as possible, preferably in one season, before rivals infringe on the site, and costs escalate out of control of even very wealthy individuals and into the realms of red-tape-bound institutions and governments. He cannot spend time marking down the location of every single object on a wreck, in three dimensions. On the "G" he did a rough archaeological survey, and John Bremmer's pictures provided useful data. But photographs also played into the hands of Hatch's critics. One shot shows a diver prising open a chest, while a plank disappears into the deep. On the plank are Chinese characters. Historians would dearly like to know the exact text of that inscription.[26]

To counter this type of situation, some courts in the USA have included among criteria used in assessing a salvage reward whether the work was done according to archaeological standards. In *Columbus-America Discovery Group v. Atlantic Mutual Insurance Company,* the Court of Appeals for the Fourth Circuit said of the six criteria that the Supreme Court has listed for fixing a salvage award:

> We thoroughly agree with all six and, in cases such as this, would add another: the degree to which the salvors have worked to protect the historical and archaeological value of the wreck and items salved.[27]

This has grave problems. Do courts understand the principles of archaeological excavation? The emphasis in judgments seems to be on measurement, conservation and popular publications:

> The district court noted further that Columbus-America had published a book and promoted a television account of its endeavours, and had provided educational materials to schools

---

22   (1978) 569 F.2d 330 at 337.
23   (1963) 695 F.2d 883 at 901.
24   (1982) 549 F.Supp. 540 at 557.
25   *Columbus-America Discovery Group v. Atlantic Mutual Insurance Co.* [1995] *American Maritime Cases* 1985 at 2007.
26   M. Hatcher (with A. Thorncroft) *The Nanking Cargo* (1987) p. 162.
27   (1992) 974 F.2d 450 at 468.

interested in teaching their students about the *Central America* and its history. The court found that "the efforts to preserve the site and its artifacts have not been equaled in any other case...". [28]

But the unreported judgment of the District Court shows that the experts were only aboard the search vessel 'from time to time' rather than continuously supervising operations. Moreover, archaeologists allege that not a single archaeological report or publication has come out of the project.

> No overall site photographs, a site map, or any other archaeological information has been released.... Archaeological study and documentation of 'Central America' would be particularly significant because no detailed record of a Panama Route steamship of the period exists. More importantly, the apparent high degree of preservation of passenger baggage, which is very similar to that observed at the Titanic wreck site, would offer a detailed opportunity to assess the material culture of the period, and its use and transportation on a vessel travelling from the 'frontier' of Gold Rush California, and could be compared with collections of the same period from the wrecks of 'Bertrand' and 'Arabia'. [29]

In most cases the court will have to proceed on the salvor's evidence of how the excavation was conducted: logically, the salvor would be unlikely to produce evidence against his interest. Moreover, a site cannot be put back together after an excavation. Is the court going to refuse to award any salvage for an excavation which does not conform to archaeological standards?

Finally, if the salvor is awarded the material raised, it is usual that this will be sold off and dispersed. Consider the following description of salvage and dispersal:

> A few miles north of Margate, where the Thames estuary runs into the North Sea, two East Indiamen lay on the seabed, the *Albion* grounded in 1765 and the *Hindustan* in 1803.
> Both ships, outward bound on their last voyage, had been laden with bullion to buy spices, silks and porcelain from the East. The bullion was recovered soon after sinking: but the ships themselves, with their fittings and less valuable contents, were left undisturbed in the water. Then a few years ago, salvage men came – sea-borne scrap merchants armed with mechanical grabs for fast, efficient retrieval of scrap from the seabed. Up came ribs and decks, torn from the wreckage, the planks broken in the jaws of the grab. Up came iron guns, ship's barometers, surgical instruments, delftware drug jars with original ointment and hundreds of other items. Everything was dumped in a Custom's warehouse at Ramsgate. There it lay for a year while, by direction of the *Merchant Shipping Act*, an owner was sought. None was found; and the wreckage, returned to the salvage men, was put up for auction. The finds were dispersed into the antiques trade. [30]

Dispersal goes against the notion that it is particularly important to maintain collections from wreck sites as entities. For example, there is an Arrangement attached to the Agreement Between Australia and The Netherlands Concerning Old Dutch Shipwrecks [31] providing for the disposition of material from the wrecks. This recognises that historic, educational, scientific and international considerations require representative collections in Australian and Dutch museums. Nevertheless, in making the distribution, "the first principle to be observed is that the total assemblage should be capable of reassembly to allow further statistical and scholarly analysis."

Many of the cases referred to above concerned wrecks within 24 miles of the coast. However, it is highly likely that courts, particularly those in the USA, will attempt to apply the

---

28   [1995] *American Maritime Cases* 1985 at 2008.
29   J. P. Delgado (ed.), *Encyclopaedia of Underwater and Maritime Archaeology* (1997) pp. 93-94.
30   Anon 'All at Sea and Undefended' (1994) (September) *British Archaeological News* 6.
31   See further section 1.3 above.

same principles to wrecks beneath international waters as they did in *Columbus-America Discovery Group v. Atlantic Mutual Insurance Company*. Courts in the USA have taken jurisdiction over the remains of RMS *Titanic* and RMS *Lusitania* – 300 miles off the coast of Canada and just within twelve miles of the coast of Ireland respectively – to deal with issues of salvage. Courts and governments in other States may well reject such claims.[32] In Ireland, there are court proceedings under way to determine ownership rights to the cargo of the *Lusitania*,[33] the view being taken that the claimant in the Virginia courts would have to establish his ownership rights in Ireland independently of what the former awarded. It is significant that, in January 1995, the Irish Commissioners of Public Works made an Underwater Heritage Order in respect of the *Lusitania* which means that in Irish law it is prohibited to carry out diving or salvage operations on the wreck.[34]

4.   International Co-ordination

In light of the above situation, efforts have been made over the past twenty years to co-ordinate international action to protect underwater cultural heritage beyond the territorial sea.

4.1   Council of Europe

In 1978 the Parliamentary Assembly of the Council of Europe adopted Recommendation 848 (1978) on the underwater cultural heritage. This recommended that a European Convention on the topic be prepared and it listed in an Annex minimum legal requirements for such a Convention including extension of national jurisdiction over underwater cultural heritage to 200 miles and exclusion of wreck and salvage law. In 1979, the Council of Ministers set up an Ad Hoc Committee of Experts to prepare the Convention. In 1985, following six meetings, the Committee produced a draft[35] which was not adopted as Turkey objected to its territorial scope of application.[36]

The matter came up again during negotiations for the European Convention on the Protection of the Archaeological Heritage (Revised) 1992. This defines "elements of the archaeological heritage" to be "all remains and objects and any other traces of mankind from past epochs" which, *inter alia*, "are located in any area within the jurisdiction of the Parties".[37] The Explanatory Report to the Convention states:

> Among the members of the Council of Europe some States restrict their jurisdiction over shipwrecks, for example, to the territorial sea, while others extend it to their continental shelf. The Revised Convention recognizes these differences without indicating a preference for one or the other.[38]

Here is implied recognition of the right of States to extend their jurisdiction if they consider it necessary for effective protection of the underwater cultural heritage.

---

32   As did Lissaman J. in *Her Majesty v. Mar-Dive* where a Californian court purported to exercise jurisdiction over a wreck in Canadian internal waters.

33   See *The Sunday Tribune* (Dublin) 14 June 1998 p. 5. For further details, follow 'The Lusitania Investigations' by J. Maas in *The Sunday Press* (Dublin) 22 January 1995 pp. 1 and 5, 29 January 1995 p. 7, 5 February 1995 p. 11, 12 February 1995 p. 3, 19 February 1995 p. 1, 26 February 1995, p. 1.

34   See further, ch. 5.

35   The final version is not a public document but has been summarised and reproduced in part in Strati, *op.cit.* note 7.

36   D.J. Attard 'The International Regime for the Protection of Archaeological and Historical Objects Found at Sea' paper delivered at the Forum for the debate on the Mediterranean Maritime Heritage, 12-14 November 1997.

37   Article 1.

38   Doc. MPC(91) 8 p. 4.

4.2   International Law Association

In 1988 the International Law Association (ILA), founded in 1873 as a private non-governmental organisation of persons interested in international law, formed a Committee on Cultural Heritage Law. This is one of many committees through which the Association conducts its academic activities. Members of the Committee came from Algeria, Australia, Canada, China, Denmark, Ecuador, France, Germany, Greece, Hungary, India, Italy, Japan, Netherlands, Mexico, the UK and the USA. Members were government officials, academics, consultants, judges and private legal practitioners. Several were legal advisers to governments on heritage matters. Many had a special interest in the underwater cultural heritage and had worked closely with underwater archaeologists over a long period of time.

The Committee took as its first task the preparation of a convention on protection of the underwater cultural heritage beyond the territorial sea. In its work it consulted with the International Council on Monuments and Sites (ICOMOS), the Comité Maritime International, the International Maritime Organisation and the United Nations Division of Ocean Affairs and Law of the Sea (DOALOS) although the last two organisations at the time were not interested.

The Draft Convention adopted by the Sixty-Sixth Conference of the Association at Buenos Aires in 1994 contained a number of innovative proposals.[39] States might, if they wished, establish a cultural heritage zone in the area beyond the territorial sea up to the outer limit of the continental shelf. In this area they would have jurisdiction over activities affecting the underwater cultural heritage. In addition, States would be required to prohibit their nationals and ships flying their flag from activities affecting underwater cultural heritage in respect of any area not within the territorial sea or cultural heritage zone of another State Party. States would also be required to prohibit the use of their territory for support of such activities. These prohibitions would not apply if the activities were in accordance with a "Charter for the Protection and Management of the Underwater Cultural Heritage" prepared by ICOMOS.[40] Provision was made for seizure of underwater cultural heritage excavated contrary to the principles contained in the Charter. Salvage law was expressly excluded from applying to underwater cultural heritage. The ILA Draft was stated not to apply to warships, military aircraft and their contents.

Acting under Resolution of the Sixty-Sixth Conference, the Secretary-General of the ILA forwarded the Draft Convention and the Committee's three Reports to UNESCO for consideration.

4.3   UNESCO

The UNESCO Secretariat prepared a feasibility study referring to the ILA draft. The Executive Board of UNESCO considered the feasibility study at its meeting in May 1995 and decided that States needed to further examine the jurisdictional aspects. The views of States were sought and later that year put before the General Conference of UNESCO which reacted favourably but decided further discussion was needed. In accordance with its wishes, a meeting of experts representing expertise in archaeology, salvage and jurisdictional regimes was held in Paris in May 1996. The views of this meeting were sent to all Member States of UNESCO and to those with observer status: the UK and the USA. On 12 November 1997, the UNESCO General Conference adopted Resolution 29C/6.3 to the effect that "the protection of the underwater cultural heritage should be regulated at the international level and that the method adopted should be an international convention". The Director-General was invited to prepare a draft convention, circulate

---

39   For the text of the Draft, see (1996) 20 *Marine Policy* 305-307, (1997) 6 *International Journal of Cultural Property* 121-127.

40   On the ICOMOS Charter, see further, section 5.2 below.

this to States for comment and observations and then convene a group of governmental experts "representing all regions together with representatives of the competent international organisations in order to consider this draft convention for submission to the General Conference at its thirtieth session" in 1999. A document[41] containing the Draft Convention on the Protection of the Underwater Cultural Heritage was circulated to Member States of UNESCO and others in April 1998, and a meeting of governmental experts to consider the draft was scheduled for the end of June 1998.

5. Aspects of the UNESCO Draft Convention

It is important to note that the Draft is not the view of the UNESCO Secretariat alone. The document states that the text has been proposed by both UNESCO and the United Nations DOALOS with the advice of the International Maritime Organisation.

5.1 Jurisdiction

It is obvious that some States – most notably the UK and the USA – are against the concept of a 'cultural protection zone'. They regard it as an example of 'creeping jurisdiction' whereby States try to whittle down the freedoms of the high seas. On the other hand, some of the States which object to the creation of a new zone, do not object to States exercising jurisdiction over activities affecting underwater cultural heritage on the continental shelf. That is, they object to the creation of a new zone but not to a redefinition of State rights *per se*. In an attempt to accommodate these positions, the UNESCO Draft provides for the compulsory reporting of any finds of underwater cultural heritage in the exclusive economic zone or on the continental shelf of a State Party. As noted above, a number of States already have this requirement in licence arrangements for such activities as oil exploration, dredging, cable-laying, etc. In an attempt to give content to article 303(1), the UNESCO Draft permits States Party "to regulate and authorise all activities affecting underwater cultural heritage in the exclusive economic zone and on the continental shelf". The notion of a cultural heritage zone has thus been abandoned. This is a redefinition of States' rights in these areas but, as with the ILA Draft, the implementation of those rights is left at the option of the State Party.

The other forms of jurisdiction – nationality, port State and flag State – utilised in the ILA Draft attracted no criticism from governments or experts. They have been incorporated into the UNESCO Draft to give States the basis for indirectly controlling activities on the deep seabed and on the continental shelf where the adjacent State has not implemented its rights under the Convention.

5.2 The Charter

The ICOMOS Charter[42] is intended to provide a standard against which activities are to be measured. Some of its provisions have attracted criticism from those States with a treasure seeking lobby. For example, the Charter emphasises preservation *in situ* and states further that "funding must not require the sale of underwater cultural heritage", both of which would limit commercial operations. However, commercial incentives are banned by the Draft itself and thus that argument

---

41   UNESCO Doc. CLT-96/CONF.202/5.
42   Officially known as the 'ICOMOS International Charter on the Protection and Management of Underwater Cultural Heritage' ratified by the Eleventh General Assembly of ICOMOS, Sofia, Bulgaria, October 1996. For the text of the Charter, see (1997) 6 *International Journal of Cultural Property* 128-133. The Charter is also available, in both English and French, from ICOMOS.

loses its validity. Some adverse comment was directed at the Introduction to the Charter and so the Draft incorporates only its operative provisions.

States have also been concerned about the method to be used for incorporating the Charter into the Convention. The ILA Draft had it as an Annex to the Convention with ICOMOS being given the power to make amendments subject to States notifying their non-acceptance of any such amendment to the Director-General of UNESCO. Some States want the substantive provisions of the Charter incorporated in the Convention itself. More important is the view that an outside body should not have the power to make amendments binding on sovereign States, even though they may have the right to opt out. The UNESCO Draft ensures that States will be notified of amendments and thus that their sovereign will to accept or not accept the amendments is better assured.

5.3   Salvage

Article 303(3) of the United Nations Convention on the Law of the Sea states that: "Nothing in this article affects … the law of salvage". Some contend that this prevents any interference with the law of salvage. That argument cannot be supported. The paragraph itself says that it is only relevant to article 303. Moreover, article 303(4) states:

> This article is *without prejudice* to other international agreements and rules of international law regarding the protection of objects of an archaeological and historical nature [italics added].

In addition to these internal qualifications, there is the reservation allowed to States in the International Convention on Salvage 1989: namely, that they reserve the right not to apply the Convention to maritime cultural property of prehistoric, archaeological or historic interest situated on the seabed. By allowing such a reservation the Salvage Convention specifically recognises that the United Nations Convention on the Law of the Sea does not prevent exclusion of salvage law.

Exclusion of salvage law from applying to underwater cultural heritage could raise a number of practical problems. For example, what is the situation of a State which has become party to the Salvage Convention without making the reservation? The Convention states that a reservation must be made at the time a State becomes party. Does this mean that the State in question could not then become party to the UNESCO Convention if it had not excluded the application of salvage law? But the UNESCO Draft, following that of the ILA, only applies to abandoned shipwrecks. Are these outside the scope of the Salvage Convention and/or salvage law in general?

Moreover, the treatment of underwater cultural heritage would in any case be subject to the criteria set out in whatever document is attached to the Convention. Only by complying with this can material be brought ashore without seizure in a Member State.

In light of these complexities and the attitude of some States as already indicated, a bald exclusion of salvage law might not be the best approach. The UNESCO Draft requires that States Party "shall provide for the non-application of any internal law or regulation having the effect of providing commercial incentives for the excavation and removal of underwater cultural heritage". Excavation on land is not normally allowed for commercial purposes and it has been strongly urged by States that it not be allowed in respect of the underwater cultural heritage. Consequently, the UNESCO Draft provides that States modify their laws to exclude such incentives but it will be for each State Party to decide which of its laws have this effect.

5.4   Warships

The ILA Draft specifically excluded warships and military aircraft from its coverage. This accords with the attitude of a number of States. Mention has already been made of the UK's Protection of Military Remains Act 1986 which specifically applies to such remains beyond the territorial sea of the UK. The official position of the USA is that:

> ... salvors should not presume that sunken U.S. warships have been abandoned by the United States. Permission must be granted by the United States to salvage sunken U.S. warships, and as a matter of policy, the U.S. Government does not grant such permission with respect to ships that contain the remains of deceased servicemen.[43]

The first wreck protected under the Australian Historic Shipwrecks Act 1976 was a Japanese submarine sunk in action off Bathurst Island to the north of the Australian mainland.

In spite of this wish of States, one must ask two questions. First, should warships be excluded? Take, for example, the remains of the British vessels HMS *Repulse* and HMS *Prince of Wales* which lie approximately 88 km east of the Malaysian coast. What would be the position if a salvage company from another country were to start stripping these wrecks? In theory, Britain could exercise her rights as owner to forbid salvage operations[44] although this would require legal proceedings, possibly in a number of different jurisdictions. The use of force is problematic on legal no less than practical grounds. Perhaps bringing warships under the umbrella of an international regime would provide more extensive protection, particularly if the existing means of protection were left untouched.

The second question to be considered is, if warships were left outside the Convention, should this apply to all such vessels? Since the Hague Peace Conference of 1907, the concept of warship has become relatively fixed. But vessels such as privateers used in earlier times are not so easy to classify and the further back one goes the more difficult it becomes. Perhaps only vessels sunk after a certain date, e.g. 1850, should be excluded.

The UNESCO Draft has followed that of the ILA and excluded warships from its application.

5.5   Definitions

Defining the underwater cultural heritage is a complex task. The United Nations Convention on the Law of the Sea used the phrase "objects of an archaeological and historical nature", although article 303 is headed "Archaeological and Historical Objects" which may have a different connotation. Hayashi takes both as meaning "all kinds of wrecks and related objects of archaeological and/or historical importance found at sea".[45] On the other hand, it seems that, during negotiations for the Convention, there was considerable uncertainty as to what exactly would be covered by describing objects as 'historical' or 'archaeological' – some viewing it as comprising nothing later than Byzantine in Europe or pre-Colombian in the Americas.[46]

The ILA Draft attempted to avoid these problems by referring to "all underwater traces of human existence"[47] provided that these have been lost or abandoned and have been underwater for at least 100 years. Certain aspects of the heritage were singled out for special mention so as to draw the attention of the law-maker and administrator. Wrecks and their cargoes were

---

43   Letter from Department of State to Maritime Administration, 30 December 1980, reprinted in US Department of State (1980) 8 *Digest of United States Practice in International Law* 1004.
44   Dromgoole and Gaskell, *op. cit.* note 15 p. 160.
45   M. Hayashi 'Archaeological and Historical Objects Under the United Nations Convention on the Law of the Sea' (1996) 20 *Marine Policy* 291.
46   Oxman, *op.cit.* note 9 at p. 241.
47   A phrase taken from the European Convention on the Protection of the Archaeological Heritage (Revised) 1992.

particularly emphasised. The archaeological and natural contexts of these traces were stressed for it is here that the major archaeological interests lie.

In view of the problems sometimes found in establishing abandonment, a definition was incorporated in the text. The underlying notion is that abandonment takes place when the technology for reaching the wreck has existed for 25 years but the owner has not utilised it in recovery operations. In cases where the technology does not yet exist, the owner has to make assertions of interest every 50 years in order to keep the claim afloat.

There was considerable discussion of the definition contained in the ILA Draft at the Paris meeting of experts in 1996. In particular the 100 year cut-off was criticised as not reflecting any archaeological criteria. However, this is a common administrative device in national legislation and does not seem to have caused problems in practice.

The UNESCO Draft has incorporated the definition of underwater cultural heritage and abandonment contained in the ILA Draft without substantial change.

6.   Conclusion

The legal regime applying to the underwater cultural heritage in international waters is at a turning point. That currently existing is fragmented and unsatisfactory for effective protection of the heritage. States now have it within their power to introduce a new scheme, overcoming these defects. Certain vested interests will be opposed to any change. But States must act to preserve for humanity these traces of the past. In the case of the underwater cultural heritage, they often come to us as a result of calamity. It is our duty to ensure that those who suffered can tell us something of themselves rather than disappearing entirely.

SELECTED BIBLIOGRAPHY

Alexander, B., 'Treasure Salvage beyond the Territorial Sea' (1989) 20 *Journal of Maritime Law and Commerce* 1-19

Allen, B., 'Coastal State Control over Historic Wrecks Situated on the Continental Shelf as Defined in Article 76 of the Law of the Sea Convention 1982' *Special Publication of the Institute of Marine Law*, University of Cape Town, No. 14 (1991)

Amess, J., 'Operation of the Commonwealth Historic Shipwrecks Act' in W. Jeffery, J. Amess (eds.), *Proceedings of the Second Southern Hemisphere Conference on Maritime Archaeology* (1983) pp. 47-56

Arend, A., 'Archaeological and Historical Objects: The International Legal Implications of UNCLOS III' (1982) 22 *Virginia Journal of International Law* 777-803

Bach, J.P.S., 'A Brief History of the Australian-Netherlands Committee on Old Dutch Shipwrecks (ANCODS)' in W. Jeffery, J. Amess (eds.), *Proceedings of the Second Southern Hemisphere Conference on Maritime Archaeology* (1983) pp. 57-64

Blake, J., 'The Protection of Turkey's Underwater Archaeological Heritage – Legislative Measures and Other Approaches' (1994) *International Journal of Cultural Property* 273-293

Blake, J., 'The Protection of the Underwater Cultural Heritage' (1996) 45 *International and Comparative Law Quarterly* 819-843

Braekhus, S., 'Salvage of Wrecks and Wreckage: Legal Issues Arising from the Runde Find' [1976] *Scandinavian Studies in Law* 39-68

Brice, G., 'Salvage and the Underwater Cultural Heritage' (1996) 20 *Marine Policy* 337-342

Caflisch, L., 'Submarine Antiquities and the International Law of the Sea' (1982) XIII *Netherlands Yearbook of International Law* 3-32

Cassidy, W., 'Historic Shipwrecks and Blanket Declaration' (1991) Vol. 15, No. 2 *Bulletin of the Australian Institute for Maritime Archaeology* 2-3

Ciciriello M.C., 'International Protection of the Underwater Cultural Heritage' University of Rome II (Tor Vergata) Department of Public Law, *Yearbook 1990-91*, Vol. III (1994) 417-434

Crawford, I.M., 'Maritime Archaeology Legislation in Western Australia' (1977) *Papers from the First Southern Hemisphere Conference on Maritime Archaeology* pp. 30-33

Delgado, J. (ed.), *British Museum Encyclopaedia of Underwater and Maritime Archaeology* (British Museum Press, 1997)

Dromgoole, S., 'Military Remains on and around the Coast of the United Kingdom: Statutory Mechanisms of Protection' (1996) 11 *International Journal of Marine and Coastal Law* 23-45

Dromgoole, S., Gaskell, N., 'Draft UNESCO Convention on the Protection of the Underwater Cultural Heritage 1998' (1999) 14 *International Journal of Marine and Coastal Law* 171-192.

Dromgoole, S., Gaskell, N., 'Interests in Wreck' in N. Palmer, E. McKendrick (eds.), *Interests in Goods* (2nd edn., 1998), Chapter 7 (republished in (1997) 2 *Art Antiquity and Law* 103-136, 207-231)

Edmonds, L., Kenderdine, S., Nayton, G., Staniforth, M., *Historic Shipwrecks National Research Plan* (1995) (Australia)

Fletcher-Tolmenius, P., Williams, M., 'The Protection of Wrecks Act 1973: A Breach of Human Rights?' (1998) 13 *International Journal of Marine and Coastal Law* 623-642

Giesecke, A., 'Shipwrecks: The Past in the Present' (1987) 15 *Coastal Management* 176-195

Green, J., 'The Management of Maritime Archaeology under Australian Legislation' (1995) Vol. 19 No. 2 *Bulletin of the Australian Institute for Maritime Archaeology* 33-44

Hayashi, M., 'Archaeological and Historical Objects under the United Nations Convention on the Law of the Sea' (1996) 20 *Marine Policy* 291-296

Henderson, G. (ed.), *Guidelines for the Management of Australia's Shipwrecks* (1994)

Hoagland, P., 'Managing the Underwater Cultural Resources of the China Seas: A Comparison of Public Policies in Mainland China and Taiwan' (1997) 12 *International Journal of Marine and Coastal Law* 265-283

Hutt, S., Zander M., Varmer, O., *Heritage Resources Law: Protecting the Archeological and Cultural Environment* (John Wiley & Sons, Inc., 1999)

Kaoru, Y., Hoagland, P., 'The Value of Historic Shipwrecks: Conflicts and Management' (1994) 22 *Coastal Management* 195-213

Kariotis, Th. (ed.), *Greece and the Law of the Sea* (Martinus Nijhoff, 1997)

Kendall, F.J., *An Assessment of the Effectiveness of Existing Legislative Arrangements for Protecting and Preserving Australia's Underwater Cultural Heritage* (1990)

Korthals Altes, A., 'Submarine Antiquities: A Legal Labyrinth' (1976) 4 *Syracuse Journal of International Law and Commerce* 77-96

Matysik, S., 'Legal Problems of Recovery of Historical Treasures from the Sea-bed' in M. Frankowska (ed.), *Scientific and Technological Revolution and the Laws of the Sea* (Poland, 1972) 141-153

O'Keefe, P., 'Protecting the Underwater Cultural Heritage: The International Law Association Draft Convention' (1996) 20 *Marine Policy* 297-307

O'Keefe, P., Nafziger, J.A.R., 'Report on the Draft Convention on the Protection of the Underwater Cultural Heritage' (1994) 25 *Ocean Development and International Law* 391-418

Owen, D., 'The Abandoned Shipwreck Act of 1987: Good-Bye to Salvage in the Territorial Sea' (1988) 19 *Journal of Maritime Law and Commerce* 499-516

Owen, D., 'Some Legal Troubles with Treasure' (1985) 16 *Journal of Maritime Law and Commerce* 139-179

Prott., L.V., O'Keefe, P.J., 'Final Report on Legal Protection of the Underwater Cultural Heritage', Appendix II to Council of Europe, Parliamentary Assembly, *The Underwater Cultural Heritage*, Report of the Committee on Culture and Education (Rapporteur: J. Roper), Doc. 4200-E, Strasbourg, 1978

Prott, L.V., O'Keefe, P.J., *Law and the Cultural Heritage, Vol. 1: Discovery and Excavation* (1984)

Prott., L.V., O'Keefe, P.J., 'Law and the Underwater Heritage' in UNESCO, *Protection of the Underwater Heritage*, Technical Handbooks for Museums and Monuments, 4 (1981)

Roach, J.A., 'Sunken Warships and Military Aircraft' (1996) 20 *Marine Policy* 351-354

Ryan, P., 'Legislation on Historic Wreck' (1977) *Papers from the First Southern Hemisphere Conference on Maritime Archaeology* pp. 23-27

Strati, A., 'Deep Seabed Cultural Property and the Common Heritage of Mankind' (1991) 40 *International and Comparative Law Quarterly* 859-894

Strati, A., *The Protection of the Underwater Cultural Heritage: An Emerging Objective of the Contemporary Law of the Sea* (Martinus Nijhoff, 1995)

Strati, A., 'The Protection of the Underwater Cultural Heritage in International Legal Perspective' in *Archaeological Heritage: Current Trends in its Legal Protection*, International Conference held in Athens, 26-27 November 1992 (P. Sakkoulous Bros., 1995) pp. 143-167

Van Meurs, L., 'Legal Aspects of Marine Archaeological Research', *Special Publication of the Institute of Marine Law*, University of Cape Town, No. 1 (1985)

Varmer, O., 'The Case Against the "Salvage" of the Cultural Heritage' (1999) 30 *Journal of Maritime Law and Commerce* (forthcoming) (See also the other papers published herewith, which arise from a symposium entitled 'Sunken Treasure: Law, Technology and Ethics' held in 1998.)

Williams, M., 'A Legal History of Shipwrecks in England' (1997) XV *Annuaire de Droit Maritime et Océanique* (Nantes) 71-92

Zander, C. M., 'The Antiquities Act – Regulating Salvage of Historic Shipwrecks' (1996) 19 *Cultural Resources Management* 28

Zander, C.M., Varmer, O., 'Closing the Gaps in Domestic and International Laws: Achieving Comprehensive Protection of Submerged Cultural Resources' (1996) 1 *Common Ground* 60-70

Zhao, H., 'Recent Developments in the Legal Protection of Historic Shipwrecks in China' (1992) 23 *Ocean Development and International Law* 305-333